Strictly Business Body Language

Using Nonverbal Communication for Power and Success

Jan Latiolais-Hargrave

KENDALL/HUNT PUBLISHING COMPANY
4050 Westmark Drive   Dubuque, Iowa 52002

CONTENTS

Introduction

The more times that I am asked by leading newspapers, magazines or television shows to comment on a person's body language, the more committed I become in my belief of the endless amount of information that can be gathered from watching a person and reading his nonverbal communication.

The story that remains in my mind of the accuracy with which we can read the behavior of another person through his body language happened several years ago. The *New York Post* had been known to contact me from time to time for my opinion of people and their behavior at current events around the globe. During Bill Clinton's televised testimony, it wasn't unusual for them to contact me several times a week for my take on Mr. Clinton's body language. They asked questions such as, "Is he lying?" "Is he being truthful?" "What does his nonverbal communication reveal about his inner most thoughts?" "What does it mean when he bites his lower lip?" "What about when he crooks his eyebrow?"

On one particular Friday afternoon, a reporter from the *New York Post* called and asked if I would take a look at three pictures and give comments on each. She was writing a story on body language and was inquiring specifically about the placement of people's fingers and hands while they are seated. Of course I agreed, and told the reporter to fax me the pictures immediately. I told her to call back in fifteen minutes for my analogy. She indicated to me that I would not be able to see the individual's faces or feet in the pictures, nor could she tell me if all three people were in the same room or not.

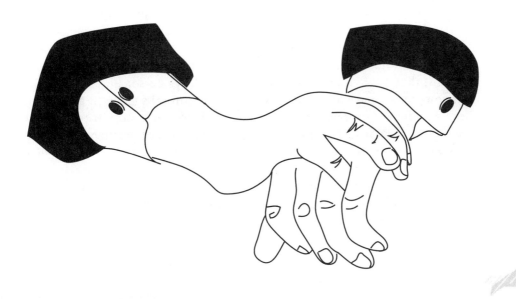

I imagined that these were people who had interviewed for jobs at the *New York Post* and that she wanted me to tell her which of the three was the most reliable, most honest and most suited for the job.

The first picture was that a man's hands. His hands were resting on his lap and were cupped together with his thumbs and little fingers twisted and intertwined. After studying the placement of his fingers, I carefully examined the photo for more information. I noticed that the man in the picture wore a suit and a shirt that required cufflinks. I made a note of the cufflinks because I thought they gave me insight into the individual's personality. A man who interviews for a job wearing a shirt that requires cufflinks gives off a different impression from a man who interviews for a job and wears a shirt that simply needs a button. This type of clue can reveal the level of position a person is applying for or it can give indications to the degree of vanity in the man himself.

The woman's hands in the second picture were comfortably placed on her lap. Her fingers were spread wide apart and her right hand was over her left hand. I noticed that she wore a pinkie ring on her right little finger and was dressed in a suit. Her flat lap indicated to me that her legs were not crossed.

The third picture arrived quickly thereafter. It contained a woman's hands clasped together and held tightly in front of her, over her crossed knees. She was wearing a dark colored dress.

I made my notes then received the call from the Post reporter. She asked, "Do you have your analysis ready?" I said, "I certainly do!" She asked, "Well, what do you think about the guy?"

"Whoever this guy is, I wouldn't trust him as far as I could throw him." I said. "I think that he has lied to you in the past and I feel that he will lie to you in the future." "In fact," I said, "I think that he's afraid of getting caught over something that he did." "He's nervous, uptight and holding back information." She said, "Wow, wait until I tell you who that is."

She then asked about the second person, the woman with her hands crossed on her lap. I told her, "She's the most honest of the three." "She's prim, proper, socially skilled and knows what she's talking about." "If I had to hire one of the three, you bet it would be this lady!" She said, "Wait until you find out who that is."

"What do you read from the third person's body language," she asked. "She's seated in a courtship gesture," I answered. "A lady tends to cross her legs toward a man who interests her and away from a man who does not." "She will then clasp her fingers together and hold on to her upper crossed leg, as she begins to feel more and more insecure." It is a gesture indicative of a lady

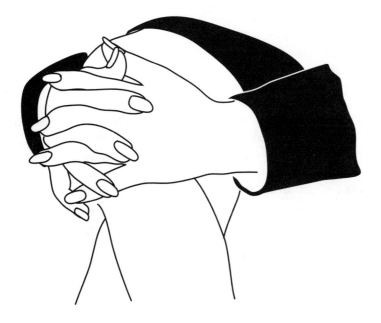

desiring to hold on to the man she is with, but instead clutches herself in an effort to look 'prim and proper.' I continued by saying, "She's very pensive and seems to be holding back information."

The reporter cut me off and excitedly said, "Stop, I must tell you who these people are." "You have hit the nail on the head." I said, "Who are these people?" She replied, "The first person is Marv Albert (the sports announcer), the first lady is Barbara Walters and the second female is currently dating Marv Albert."

In this book *you* will learn the language of the body and understand that every time you talk to someone your body supplements what you say with dozens of small gestures, eye movements, changes in posture and facial expression.

In the last twenty years, and increasingly in the last ten, a great deal of research has been carried out in nonverbal communication. In writing this book, I have summarized many of the studies by the leading behavioral scientists and have combined them with similar research done by people in other disciplines—sociology, linguistics, anthropology, education, psychiatry, family counseling, professional negotiating and selling. The book also includes many features developed from the countless reels of videotape and film that I have reviewed, plus some of my experiences and encounters with the thousands of people who I have interviewed, recruited, trained, managed and sold to over the past fifteen years.

To make it immediately useful as possible, I have extracted twenty-five basic rules for successful silent speech. These are explained in relevant chapters and also collected in the final chapter. If you are mainly interested in enhancing your silent speech sales skills as rapidly as possible, without concerning yourself on *how* and *why* each rule was formulated, then I suggest you turn directly to chapter eleven.

Silent speech is important to you. It significantly affects your chances of succeeding or failing in any encounter, whether personal or professional. Research suggests that only some 7 percent of the meaning in any conversation is contained in the words spoken. The majority of information is communicated by means of a complicated mixture of appearance, posture, gesture, gaze and expression. This offers a potent instrument of persuasion to those able to use it effectively and is especially important in situations where you suspect attempts to conceal stress, disguise deceptions or hide hostility.

The Table of Contents describes for you the topics that you can expect to encounter later in the book. Hopefully, this will help to convince you that it will be worth your while to persevere with your reading of the book and perhaps to participate in some of the practical exercises and experiments that are suggested in each chapter. My main wish, though, is that by the time you reach the end of the book, you will have a clearer idea of what is meant by the term 'body language,' what kinds of behavior it includes and also, from their omission, what kinds of behavior it is not meant to include.

The entire book considers the role of body language in personal development, with discussion to its role in the area of sales and interactive skills. It examines how effective use of body language can contribute to personal growth and better performance during sales negotiations. In addition, the role of body language in the development of synergic relations is explored, together with its role in establishing rapport, empathy and a sense of togetherness.

This book was originally intended as a working manual for salespeople, sales managers and executives, but any person, regardless of his vocation or position, can use it to obtain a better understanding of life's most complex event—a face-to-face encounter with another person.

Mastering the Nonverbal Art of Selling: A Framework for Understanding

During the average 30-minute sales call, buyer and seller exchange approximately 800 different nonverbal messages, yet most salespeople focus only on the verbal part of the sale. Some listen to the tone of the voice—how the words are said, and some take literally each spoken word. Salespeople who pay attention to body language focus almost exclusively on facial expressions. Obviously, these are all necessary areas of interest. Words, the way they are spoken, and the speaker's face all give the seller information about how the sales call is doing. Voice and face, though, are only part of the picture. The body, the communication channel over which we have the least control, and understand the least, has the most impact.

Body Language Is Not New

Understanding the power of nonverbal communication will put you in excellent company. Man has used gestures since he appeared on earth. The Greeks were quite familiar with interpreting a man's character by watching how he carried himself and expressed his ideas with his body.

As far as the technical study of nonverbal communication goes, perhaps the most influential pre-twentieth-century work was that of Charles Darwin in 1872. His research spawned the modern studies of facial expressions and body language. Modern researchers around the globe have since validated Darwin's findings and observations. Dr. Albert Mehrabian, a noted researcher in the field of nonverbal communication, found that the total impact of a message is about 7 percent verbal (words only), 38 percent vocal (including tone of voice, inflection and other sounds) and a massive 55 percent through nonverbal expressions. Professor Ray Birdwhistell made some similar conclusions as to the amount of nonverbal communication that takes place among humans. He estimated that the average person actually speaks words for a total of ten or eleven minutes a day and that the standard sentence takes only about 2.5 seconds. Like Mehrabian, he found that the verbal component of a face-to-face conversation is less than 35 percent and that over 65 percent of communication is done nonverbally.

Researchers in the field of body language generally agree that the verbal channel is used primarily for conveying information, while the nonverbal channel is used for negotiating interpersonal attitudes, and in some cases is used as a substitute for verbal messages. Regardless of culture, words and movements occur together with such predictability, that Birdwhistell concluded that a well-trained person should be able to tell what movement a man is making by simply listening to his voice.

Charlie Chaplin and many other silent movie actors, pioneers of nonverbal communication skills, used this means to entertain and amuse many of us on the screen. Each actor was classified as good or bad as to the extent to which he could use gestures and other body signals to connect effectively.

Julius Fast published a summary of all nonverbal communication research done by behavioral scientists in a book in 1970. It was at that time that the public first became interested and aware of the existence and importance of body language.

Understanding nonverbal communication is not only necessary for individual success, it is also a vital part of a successful sales process. Since making selling easier and more rewarding is the goal for business, recently the sales industry has also decided on the value of understanding nonverbal communication selling power for increasing sales results, overcoming buyer resistance and boosting overall sales profits. History provides a dramatic example of how self-enhancing gestures and postures can lead to victory:

> After the legendary televised debate between the presidential candidates Richard Nixon and John F. Kennedy, the majority of the TV audience, based on positive body language, found Kennedy far superior to Nixon. The majority of the radio audience, however, judged Richard Nixon the winner of the debate.

In selling, some salespeople are still at the level of the candidate who had to learn about nonverbal communication through the school of hard knocks. Although most sales people know how to say the right things, they often lose the sale because of self-defeating nonverbal expressions.

Let that no longer be. Details to learning how to read another person's nonverbal gestures, from head to toe, are contained herein.

Three Stages to Increased Nonverbal Selling Power

Reading a prospect's body language is not the only goal in mastering nonverbal communication. Expertise in this area is usually gained, in phases, with time and practice. Three stages of awareness and skill are necessary before one becomes an expert in nonverbal selling power.

Awareness of the Buyer: This stage involves learning the five major nonverbal communication channels and interpreting the buyer's nonverbal signals. It is a shorthand system of scanning the buyer for clusters of gestures. Instead of looking for specific movements or postures that 'mean' the client is bored, defensive or angry, a group of gestures from the five channels needs to be analyzed. These groups of gestures can indicate whether your buyer is open and receptive to your presentation, whether there are obstacles to your strategy that warn you to exercise caution, or they can alert you to stop and redirect your sales approach entirely.

Awareness of Self: Your own nonverbal expressions can make or break a sale. Ask yourself: "How can I communicate in order to enhance the impact of my verbal selling skills?" "How am I perceived by the buyer?" "How can I avoid communicating self-defeating nonverbal signals during the call?" This stage requires roll playing and practice. Constructive criticism from peers and videotaping yourself in mock sales situations will show you how you look and act when your mind is concentrating on what you are saying. Once you understand your own nonverbal behavior, and how you use it to interact with clients, you are more aware of your impact on others.

Management of Self and Buyer: To reach this stage, you need to develop the ability to consistently apply your new nonverbal communication techniques together with your existing professional selling skills. Awareness and observation of the buyer and yourself will give you the ability to:

- spot negative nonverbal signals early in the sale;
- respond faster and more accurately to the buyer's nonverbal signals;
- increase your 'fluency' in managing your own nonverbal expressions;
- intensify your ability to combine verbal and nonverbal skills.

Body language reflects people's true feelings when they are unaware of their gestures. Your clients are visually telling you when they are uncertain, need more information, want a chance to ask questions or have strong objections—it's all in plain sight. And, so are your responses. You may mirror their emotions by making similar gestures, or take on a defensive posture in response to an objection. If they ask a question and you feel uncertain about how to answer, your body will be the messenger of your uncertainty.

Once you are totally aware of the buyer's movements and your gestures, you can put nonverbal selling power to work for you by managing your own and your client's body language.

How can you do this? By responding, instead of reacting, to your client's messages. It entails being friendly and positive, reassuring and understanding, both verbally and nonverbally. Exercise all 100 percent of your communications impact by using 55 percent of the message you send without opening your mouth.

Inborn, Genetic, Learned

Much research and debate has been done to discover whether nonverbal signals are inborn, learned, genetically transferred or acquired in some other way. Evidence collected from observation of blind and/or deaf people who could not have learned nonverbal signals through the auditory or visual channels and from observing the gestures and behavior of many different cultures around the world has aided in the findings.

The conclusions of this research indicate that some gestures fall into each category. For example, most children are born with the immediate ability to suck, indicating that this is either inborn or genetic. The smiling gestures of children born deaf and blind occur independently of learning or copying, which means that these must also be inborn gestures. When facial expressions of people from five widely different cultures were studied, it was found that each culture used the same basic facial gestures to show emotion. This led researchers to conclude that these gestures also must be inborn.

Speaking of inborn gestures, when you cross your arms on your chest, do you cross left over right or right over left? Most people cannot confidently describe which way they do this until they try it. Where one way feels comfortable, the other feels completely wrong. Evidence suggests that this may be a genetic gesture that cannot be changed.

It can be concluded that much of our basic nonverbal behavior is learned and the meaning of many movements and gestures is culturally determined. Most basic communication gestures are the same all over the world. When people are happy they smile; when they are sad or angry, they frown or grimace. Nodding the head is almost universally used to indicate 'yes' or affirmation. It appears to be a form of head lowering and is probably an inborn gesture, as deaf and blind people also use it. Shaking the head from side to side to indicate 'no' is also universal and may well be a gesture that is learned in infancy. When a baby has had enough milk, he turns his head from side to side to reject his mother's breast. The young child who has had enough to eat, shakes his head from side to side to stop his parent's attempt to spoon feed him and in this way, quickly learns to use the side-to-side head shaking gesture to show disagreement or a negative attitude.

Gesture Clusters and Congruence

One of the most serious mistakes a novice in body language can make is to interpret a solitary gesture in isolation from other gestures or other circumstances. Similar to any other language, body language consists of words, sentences and punctuation. Each gesture is like a single word and a word may have several different meanings. It is only when you put the word into a sentence with other words that you can fully understand its significance. Gestures come in sentences and invariably tell the truth about a person's feelings or attitudes. The 'perceptive' person is one who can read the nonverbal sentences and accurately match them against the person's verbal sentences.

Incongruence of gestures occurs as we observe a speaker standing behind a lectern with his arms tightly folded across his chest (defensive) and chin down (critical and hostile), while telling his audience how receptive and open he is to their ideas. Or, he may attempt to convince the audience of his warm, humane approach all the while giving short, sharp karate chops to the lectern. Sigmund Freud once noted that while a patient was verbally expressing happiness with her marriage, she was unconsciously slipping her wedding ring on and off her finger. Freud was aware of the significance of this subconscious gesture and was not surprised when marriage problems began to surface.

Observations of gesture clusters and congruence of the verbal and nonverbal channels are the keys to accurate interpretation of body language. In addition to looking for gesture clusters and congruence of speech and body movements, all gestures should be considered in the context in which they occur. If, for example, someone is sitting at a bus terminal with his arms and his legs tightly crossed with his chin down and it is a chilly winter's day, it would most likely mean that he is cold, not defensive. If, however, a person used these same gestures while you were sitting across a negotiation table from him trying to sell him an idea, product or service, the gestures could be correctly interpreted as meaning that the person is negative or defensive about the situation.

Faking Body Language

A commonly asked question is, "Is it possible to fake your own body language?" The general answer to this question is "no" because of the lack of congruence that is likely to occur in the use of the main gestures, the body's micro signals and the spoken words. For example, open palms are associated with honesty, but when the faker holds his palms out and smiles at you as he tells a lie, his micro gestures give him away. His pupils may contract, one eyebrow may lift or the corner of his mouth may twitch. These micro signals contradict the open palm gesture and the sincere smile resulting in the receiver tending not to believe what he is hearing. Thankfully, the human mind seems to possess a fail-safe mechanism that registers *tilt* when it receives a series of incongruent nonverbal messages.

The face is used more often than any other part of the body to cover up lies. We use smiles, nods and winks in an attempt to cover up, but unfortunately for us, the body signals tell the truth. It is difficult to fake body language for a long period of time. The complexity with lying is that our subconscious mind acts automatically and independently of our verbal lie, so our body language gives us away. This is why people who rarely tell lies are easily caught, regardless of how convincing they may sound. The moment he begins to lie, his body sends out contradictory signals. It is these signals that give us our feeling that the person is not telling the truth. During the lie, the subconscious mind sends out nervous energy that appears as a gesture that can contradict what the person has just said. People whose jobs involve lying, such as actors and television announcers, have refined their body gestures to the point where it is difficult to see the lie, and onlookers fall for their stories, hook, line and sinker.

To deter us from spotting their lies, actors refine their gestures in one of two ways. First, they practice what 'feels' like the right gestures when they tell the lie. This is only successful when they have practiced telling numerous lies over long periods of time. Second, as difficult as it is to do, they eliminate most gestures while they are relaying the lie.

Try this simple test when an occasion presents itself. Tell a deliberate lie to an acquaintance and make a conscious effort to suppress all nonverbal gestures while your body is in full view of the other person. Even when your major body gestures are consciously suppressed, numerous micro gestures will still be transmitted. These micro gestures include facial muscular twitching, expansion and contraction of pupils, sweating at the brow, flushing of the cheeks, increased rate of eye blinking and numerous other microscopic gestures that signal deceit. Research using slow motion cameras shows that these micro gestures can occur within a split second. Usually only trained professional interviewers, salespeople and those whom we call highly perceptive who can consciously detect them during a conversation or negotiation. Results show that the most successful interviewers and salespeople are those who have developed the automatic ability to read the micro gestures during their face-to-face encounters with other people.

It is obvious, then, that to be able to lie successfully, you must have your body hidden or out of sight. Police interrogation involves placing the suspect on a chair in the open or placing him under lights with his body in full view of the interrogators; his lies are much easier to see under those circumstances. Naturally, telling lies is easier if you are sitting behind a desk where your body is partially hidden, or while peering around a closed door. The best way to lie is over the telephone!

How to Learn Body Language

Set aside at least fifteen minutes a day to study and read the gestures of other people, as well as acquire a conscious awareness of your own gestures. A good reading ground is anywhere that people meet and interact. An airport is a particularly good place for observing the entire spectrum of human gestures, as people openly express eagerness, anger, sorrow, happiness, impatience and many other emotions. Television also offers an excellent way of learning nonverbal communication. Turn down the sound and try to understand what is happening by first watching the picture. By turning the sound up every five minutes, you will be able to check how accurate your nonverbal readings are and before long it will be possible to watch an entire program without any sound and understand what is happening.

During the first few days of your awareness program in nonverbal communication, you may feel self-conscious and uncomfortable. You will be surprised to notice how many gestures you make, the way you sit, and how often you

fiddle with objects or mask your facial expressions in response to a variety of situations. Relax. Enjoy your new knowledge and appreciate the competitive edge you will have once you move on to the management of these signals.

You may be asking yourself, "How will I ever be able to concentrate on what I'm saying and what my client is saying if I have to think about all of these other things?"

First, recognize that your subconscious mind is already an expert at body language. You are only training yourself to look for more nonverbal messages. Trust your intuition to make your impressions more accurate. A thorough understanding of body language allows you to be able to modify your own reactions and thus improve your sales calls.

Secondly, know that most people can hear at a rate of 400–500 words per minute, yet speak at a rate of 125–180 words per minute, about three times slower. Instead of becoming distracted during that extra listening time, use it constructively. Scan client signals; decide what messages they are sending out, and then plan your response.

Close Encounters: Territories, Zones and Awareness of the Five Major Channels of Communication

Moving closer to a client so that you can scan him for nonverbal signals can be overdone. If you violate the buyer's 'intimate space,' usually a distance of up to 1½ feet, you are likely to get only negative readings.

Close Encounters

The amount of space a client needs to feel comfortable varies according to an assortment of factors. Cultural differences, age, sex, personality and the type of relationship you have with him all come into play. Generally speaking, Eastern Europeans, the French and Arabs prefer a much closer distance than British people do. Peers will tolerate a closer range of contact than people with a wide gap in age. Conversations between females will occur at closer range than male-female talks, and male-to-male encounters show the most distance. People who are outgoing by nature will want to be in a closer, friendlier position than those who are shy or aloof. Once you have worked with a client over a number of years, your speaking distance will be less than it would be if you were calling on a client for the first or second time.

Because of these differences, estimates for the amount of space a person will need in a given situation vary.

Intimate Space: Up to 1½ feet. Back off. This is too close for business situations.

Personal Space: 1–2 feet. Use for longtime clients, and only if *they* are comfortable.

Social Space: 4–7 feet. This distance allows room for stretching and gesturing without invading your client's territory.

Public Space: 10 feet or more. This is a good distance for delivering a speech or making small presentations.

Every country is a territory staked out by clearly defined boundaries and sometimes protected by armed guards. Within each country are usually smaller territories in the form of states and counties. Within these are even smaller territories called cities, within which are suburbs, containing many streets that, in themselves, represent a closed territory to those who live there. The inhabitants of each territory share an intangible allegiance to it and have been known to turn to savagery and killing in order to protect it.

A territory is also an area or space that a person claims as his own, as if it were an extension of his body. A person's own personal territory includes the area that exists around his possessions, such as his home which may be bounded by fences, the inside of his motor vehicle, his own bedroom or even his personal chair.

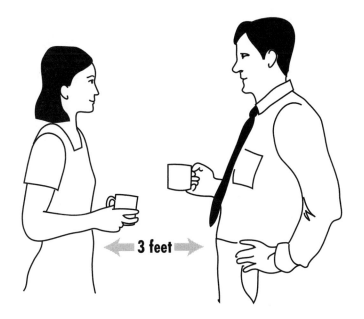

3 feet

Along with his personal territory, man has his own private portable 'air bubble' that he carries around with him and its size is dependent on the density of the population where he grew up. This personal zone distance, which is culturally determined, tells others whether the person is accustomed to crowding or likes 'wide open spaces' and prefers to keep his distance from others.

PRACTICAL APPLICATIONS OF ZONE DISTANCES

While we will tolerate strangers moving within our personal and social zones, the intrusion of a stranger into our intimate zone causes physiological changes to take place within our bodies. The heart pumps faster, adrenaline pours into the bloodstream, blood is pumped to the brain and the muscles begin preparation for a possible fight or flight situation.

In other words, putting your arm in a friendly way on or around someone you have just met may result in that person's feeling negative toward you, even though he may smile and appear to enjoy it so as not to offend you. If you want people to feel comfortable in your company, the golden rule is 'keep your distance'.

Crowding at concerts, movies, in elevators, trains or busses results in unavoidable intrusion into other people's intimate zones. Reactions to this invasion of personal space are interesting to observe. In Western cultures, people follow a list of silly, unwritten rules when faced with a crowded situation such as a packed elevator or bus. The rules include:

1. You are not permitted to speak to anyone, including a person you know.
2. You must avoid eye contact with others at all times.
3. You are to maintain a 'poker face'—no emotion is permitted to be displayed.
4. If you have a book or newspaper, you must appear to be deeply engrossed in it.
5. The bigger the crowd, the less body movement you are permitted to make.
6. In elevators, you are compelled to watch the floor numbers above your head.

Words such as 'miserable', 'unhappy' and 'despondent' have been used to describe people who travel to work in rush hour on the bus. These labels result because of the blank, expressionless look on the faces of the travelers, but they are misjudgments on the part of the observer. What the observer sees, in fact, is a group of people adhering to the unwritten rules that apply to the unavoidable invasion of their intimate zones in a crowded public place.

An angry mob or group of protesters fighting for a mutual purpose does not react in the same way as people do when their territory is invaded; in fact, something quite different occurs. As the density of the crowd increases, each individual has less personal space and takes a hostile stance. The size of the mob grows, each person becomes angrier and uglier and fighting usually takes place. Police, who try to break up the crowd so that each person can regain his own personal space and become calmer, use this information.

Only in recent years have governments and town planners given any credence to the effect that high-density housing projects play in depriving individuals of their personal territory. The consequences of high-density living and overcrowding are never ending. Overactive adrenal glands, resulting from the stress caused by the deprivation of each individual's personal territory as the population increases causes negative effects to the body's defenses.

In view of this, it is easy to see why areas that have the highest density of human population also have the highest crime and violence rates.

Police interrogators, to break down the resistance of criminals being questioned, use territorial invasion techniques. They seat the criminal on an armless, fixed chair in an open area of the room and encroach into his intimate and close intimate zones when asking questions. It takes only a short while for this territorial harassment to break down the criminal's resistance.

Management people can use this same approach to extract information from subordinates who may be withholding details, but a salesperson would be foolish to use this type of approach when dealing with customers.

Cultural, Country and City Factors Affecting Zone Distances

Americans who meet and converse stand at an acceptable 2 to 4 feet from each other and remain standing in the same place while talking. A Japanese person feels comfortable conversing with another person in a smaller 10-inch intimate zone. When an American and a Japanese person begin a conversation, it is as though they are slowly moving around the room. The American begins to move backwards away from the Japanese person and the Japanese person gradually moves towards the American. In their attempt to adjust to a culturally comfortable distance from each other, they give the impression that both are dancing around the conference room with the Japanese person leading. It is therefore obvious why, when negotiating business, Asians and Americans look upon each other with some suspicion. Sometimes Americans refer to Asians as 'pushy' and 'familiar' and Asians refer to Americans as 'cold', 'stand-offish' and 'cool'. The lack of awareness of the distance variation of the intimate zones for different countries can easily lead to misconceptions and inaccurate assumptions about one culture by another.

As previously mentioned, the amount of personal space required by an individual is related to the population density of the area in which he was brought up. Those who are brought up in sparsely populated rural areas require more personal space than those raised in densely populated capital cities. Watching how far a person extends his arm to shake hands can give a clue to

whether he is from a major city or from a remote countryside. City dwellers have a primate 18-inch 'bubble', the measured distance between wrist and torso when they reach to shake hands. People brought up in a country town, where the population is far less dense, may have a territorial 'bubble' of up to 4 feet or more.

Country people have a tendency to stand with their feet firmly planted on the ground and to lean forward as far as they can to meet your handshake, whereas a city dweller will step forward to greet you. People raised in remote or sparsely populated areas usually have a large personal space requirement, which may be as wide as 30 feet. Often, these people prefer not to shake hands, but to stand at a distance and wave.

City salespeople find this sort of information particularly useful for calling on farmers in sparse rural areas to sell farming equipment. Considering that the farmer may have a 'bubble' of 3 to 6 feet or more, a handshake could be a territorial intrusion, causing the farmer to react negatively and be on the defensive. Successful countryside salespeople unanimously insist that the best negotiating conditions exist when they greet the rural dweller with an extended handshake.

Like personal air space, property owned by a person or a place regularly used by him constitutes his private territory and he will fight to protect it. Such things as a person's home, office and car represent a territory because each has clearly marked boundaries in the form of walls, gates, fences and doors.

If the head of the house asks a visiting salesperson to be seated and the salesperson quite innocently sits in 'his' chair, the prospective buyer can become inadvertently agitated about this invasion of his territory and thus be put on the defensive. A simple question by the salesperson such as, "Which chair is yours?" can avoid the negative results of making such a territorial error.

Concerning zone knowledge, it is important to remember that others will invite or reject you, depending on the respect that you have for their personal space. This is why some secretly dislike the happy-go-lucky person who slaps everyone he meets on the back or continually touches people during a conversation. As a number of factors can affect the spatial distance a person takes in relation to others, it is wise to consider every criterion before making a judgment about why a person is keeping a certain distance.

Exploring the Five Channels

Since you are now aware of the important part spatial distances and nonverbal communication plays in a sales situation, monitoring your client's body language may not be as complicated as it seems. There are only five major nonverbal communication channels: body angle, face, arms, hands and legs that need to be explored fully.

A quick scan of these five channels takes only seconds—quite a small amount of time to invest in improving your sales career.

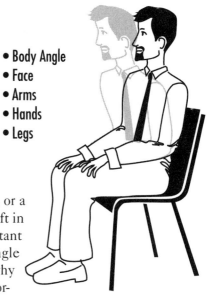

- **Body Angle**
- **Face**
- **Arms**
- **Hands**
- **Legs**

Since a client's body language is most reliable when it changes from one gesture or stance to another, movement and intensity of these changes will be emphasized in detail and the role each plays in a sales situation. Eyes that stare, unblinking and undirected, say something different than eyes that move from you to your brochures during the business meeting. Legs that are crossed casually and remain still may not be a cause for concern until they are more tightly crossed, or a foot starts to swing, or the crossing is coupled with a shift in the client's body away from you. In any case, it is important to look for a cluster of gestures in any channel. A single gesture in one channel doesn't mean anything. That is why it is important to scan all five channels and use that information in a sales situation to increase your selling power. Although all five channels will be introduced here, they will be explained and examined in detail in the following chapters.

Channel One—Body Angle

An upright posture or a body movement directed toward you is an important clue signaling that the sale is headed in the right direction. Just as a client will sit closer to you if he feels comfortable and friendly, he will lean his body toward you if he is intent on listening to your presentation.

When a customer leans back or away from you, he is sending a negative message. By using the other channels you will be able to decide whether he is bored, angry, apprehensive or demonstrating superiority.

Show interest and a cooperative attitude toward your client by directing your body angle toward him. Back and forth motions indicate drive and a positive attitude. Avoid side-to-side movements because they suggest insecurity and doubt. Too much motion or complete stillness is likely to project nervousness or tension, so concentrate on using naturally flowing movements. And, if you get into a rhythm that matches your client's speech patterns, he will really feel that you are in step with what he is saying.

Channel Two—Face

There is more to a face than a smile. Although a client may hide his disinterest or disagreement behind a grin, his real feelings may be revealed in other ways.

Eye Contact—a customer will avoid eye contact if he is trying to cover up his true emotions, and gaze past you or around the room if he is bored. Increased eye contact signals honesty and interest.

Skin Color—a sudden flush or slowly deepening redness of your client's face sends out a vivid warning that something is wrong. Anger and embarrassment glow like a shiny red apple on some people.

Skin Tautness—tenseness and anger can be detected by looking for signs of tightness around the cheeks, jaw line and in the neck area. To understand this, try holding your breath and feel the increased stiffness in these areas on yourself. If you can consciously relax your facial and neck muscles when you begin to feel tense in a sales situation, you will feel more relaxed and make a better presentation.

Smiles—smiles that are genuine involve the whole face. If the rest of your client's body language tells you that he is open and interested, and that his smile is genuine, you can be sure that your presentation is hitting the mark.

Channel Three—Arms

Where your client puts his arms, how he moves them and the extent of his movements, will give you further information about his underlying attitude. In studying the arms channel, intensity is a key factor.

If the client has his upper arms and elbows as far back on his chair as they will go, and raises his hands into a 'stop' gesture, prepare for a defensive movement. The client who hangs one arm over the back of the chair will tend to also lean farther away from you, a negative reaction, or go to a hands-behind-the-head position of dominance. In either case, you do not have his full attention or acceptance. When the client has his arms well onto the desk as part of his overall body language—he is leaning forward and exhibiting interest in your proposal.

Arms are used to provide support for hand movements. Because of this connection, their position can give you advance warning of the hand signals that are likely to follow.

A client will use more arm movement when he is very involved in conveying an opinion. The broader and more vigorous the gestures, the more emphatic is the client's point. These can be positive, open gestures or angry threats.

Channel Four—Hands

There are thousands of hand gestures. How can you decide what your client's hands are revealing? By dividing these gestures into three main groups, you will get a general idea of whether the customer is reacting in a positive, cautious or negative way to your sales call.

1. Open and relaxed hands, especially when the palms are facing you, are a positive selling signal.
2. Self-touching gestures, such as hands on chin, ear, nose, arm or clothing, indicate tension. Probing for difficulties, or simply relaxing the pace of your presentation, may calm the client.
3. Hand gestures that contradict a facial expression indicate the client's true feelings. Watch for tightly clasped hands or fists.

It is very important for you to avoid self-touching and involuntary hand gestures during the sales call. No matter how calm or positive your words are, if the client senses tension or a negative reaction on your part, he will be on his guard and much less receptive to your presentation.

Channel Five—Legs

Most people believe that leg crossing is done for comfort. Did you ever stop to think about why people are comfortable in that position? Usually it's because their bodies are reflecting how they feel inside. A study of 2,000 people by Nierenberg and Calero in, *How to Read a Person Like a Book*, found that no sales were made while the participants had their legs crossed. Even if all other channels appear to be open and positive, the customer who keeps his legs crossed may have some minor reservations that will prevent you from completing the sale if these uncertainties are not uncovered and unanswered.

A client who keeps his feet on his desk, is displaying an attitude of ownership and dominance. It says, "Go ahead and try to sell me." Crossed legs or crossed ankles signal that there is something preventing a completely open mind. The client is probably feeling defensive or reserved and tends to be uncooperative. On the other hand, uncrossed legs send a message of cooperation, confidence and friendly interest in the other person.

When the client's legs are crossed away from you, his body is usually also shifted away from you and the sales call is not going well. Although it is best not to cross your legs at all, a leg crossed towards the client is acceptable in the early phase of a sale. If the client mirrors the legs crossed towards position, he is feeling that the two of you are alike and tuned in to each other.

Clustering and Consistency

A single gesture is like a word standing alone. Without a sentence to give it a context, you can't be sure of its meaning. Clusters of gestures are the sentences and paragraphs of body language. A puzzled facial expression shows you only part of what your client is thinking. Does he need more information? Is there something you said that contradict something he's heard from another company? Paying attention to his other nonverbal communication channels will give you a clearer indication of his feelings. If he is puzzled and positive, you'll want to act one way. If he is puzzled and negative, your approach will go in another direction.

Increasing Your Nonverbal Selling Power

Your goal in increasing your nonverbal selling power lies in:

- Selecting the appropriate distance—allowing enough space for the buyer to feel comfortable.
- Scanning the buyer's five nonverbal communication channels—body angle, face, arms, hands, legs—so that you can easily decide on the most effective verbal and nonverbal response strategy.

The worst thing a seller can do is mimic a buyer's negative signals or react to the client with anything but positive, helpful nonverbal messages. Making the most of this new knowledge allows you to proceed with confidence from the opening of the sale to the successful close.

The body language of failure—no eye contact, fidgeting, nervousness, defensiveness, confrontation and poor posture—are interpreted as the nonverbal messages of fear, weakness or discontent.

The body language of success—good eye contact, a comfortable, erect body posture, and open gestures that move toward the buyer—are signals that give the impression of power, confidence and satisfaction.

The Hidden Power of Your Handshake: Palm Gestures

Throughout history, the open palm has been associated with truth, honesty, allegiance and submission. Many oaths are taken with the palm of the hand over the heart. The palm is held in the air when someone is giving evidence in a court of law; the Bible is placed in the left hand and the right palm is proudly held up for the members of the court to view.

Palms touch together during handshakes. By using the handshake correctly during the first moment of physical contact with another person, you can, in less than five seconds, confirm an already favorable impression or do much to correct an initially unfavorable one. The handshake provides us with direct and immediate information about another person.

During the course of a handshake, information is conveyed in six ways:

1. The appearance of the hand: the length, shape and cleanliness of the palm, fingers and nails.
2. The texture of the grip: whether the hand is soft and delicate or hard and rough.
3. The degree of dryness or dampness.
4. The amount of pressure used: ranging from overly strong to insufficiently firm.
5. The time spent in contact with the other person: by increasing or decreasing the time spent shaking hands from the average five seconds, the meaning of the handshake is significantly changed.
6. The style of grip: the dominant style, the submissive style and the double-hand grip each convey a different message.

Openness and Honesty

In sales encounters, people use two basic palm positions. The first has the palm facing upwards. The second has the palm facing down as if it is restraining something. Upwards-facing palms signify acceptance, while downwards-facing palms signify control.

One of the most valuable ways of discovering whether a client is being open and honest or distrustful is to look for palm displays. For example, when someone wishes to be totally open or honest, he will hold one or both palms out to the other person and say something such as, "Let me be completely open with you." When someone begins to open up or be truthful, he will expose all or part of his palms to another person. Like most body language, this is a completely subconscious gesture, one that gives you a feeling or hunch that the other person is telling the truth. When a child is lying or concealing an object, his palms are hidden behind his back. Similarly, a person who wants to conceal his whereabouts after a night out with friends will often hide his palms in his pockets or in an arm-fold position when he tries to explain where he was. Thus, the hidden palms give the impression that someone is holding back the truth.

During a sales negotiation, it is wise to look for the customer's open palms when he gives reason why he cannot buy the product, because only valid reasons are given with exposed palms.

It is possible to make yourself appear more credible by practicing open palm gestures when communicating with others; conversely, as the open palm gestures become habitual, the tendency to tell untruths lessens. Interestingly, most people find it difficult to lie with their palms exposed. The use of palm signals can, in fact, help to suppress some of the false information others may give and it also encourages them to be open with you. Briefly placing your right hand over your heart as you speak signals honesty.

Palm Power

The human hand gives one of the least noticed, but most powerful nonverbal signals. When used correctly, palm power invests its user with a degree of authority and the power of silent command over others. To understand handshake styles, let's first explore palm command gestures.

There are three main palm command gestures: the palm-up position, the palm-down position and the palm-closed-finger-pointed position. The differences of the three positions can perhaps be shown in this example: suppose that you ask someone to pick up a box and carry it to another location in the same room. Assume that you use the same tone of voice, the same words and facial expressions and change only the position of your palm as you request the box to be moved.

The palm facing up is used as a submissive, non-threatening gesture, reminiscent of the pleading hand of a street beggar. The person being asked to move the box will not feel that the request is given with pressure and, in a normal superior/subordinate situation, will not feel threatened by the command.

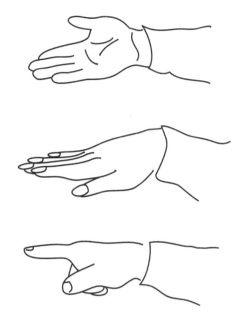

When the palm is turned to face downwards, you will have immediate authority. The person to whom you have directed the request feels that he has been given an order to remove the box and may feel antagonistic towards you, depending on your relationship with him. For example, if the person to whom you gave the request was a co-worker of equal status, he could reject your palm-down request and would be more likely to carry out your wish if you had used the palm-up position. If the person to whom you give the request is your subordinate, the palm-down gesture is acceptable, as you have the authority to use it.

Once the palm is closed into a fist with the pointer finger extended, the pointed finger becomes a symbolic club with which the speaker figuratively beats his listener into submission. The pointed finger is one of the most irritating gestures that a person can use while speaking, particularly when it beats time to the speaker's words. If you are a habitual finger-pointer, try practicing the simple palm-up or palm-down position and you will find that you create a more relaxed attitude and have a more positive effect on other people.

Shaking hands is a relic of the caveman era. Whenever cavemen met, they would hold their arms in the air with their palms exposed to show that no weapons were being held or concealed. This palms-in-air gesture became modified over the centuries and such gestures as the palm raised in the air, the palm over the heart and numerous other variations developed. The modern form of this ancient greeting ritual is the interlocking and shaking of the palms, which in most English-speaking countries, is performed both on initial greeting and on departure. The hands are normally pumped three to seven times during the hand-shaking ritual.

Dominant and Submissive Handshakes versus Vertical Handshakes

Assume that you have just met a client for the first time and you greet each other with a customary handshake. One of three basic attitudes is transmitted through the handshake. There is dominance: 'I can dominate this person. He will do as I wish', submission: 'This person is trying to dominate me. I'd better be cautious', and equality: 'I like this person. We will get along well together'.

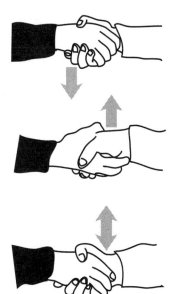

These attitudes are transmitted subconsciously and, with practice and conscientious application, proper handshake techniques can have an immediate effect on the outcome of a sales encounter.

Turning your hand so that your palm faces down in the handshake transmits dominance. Your palm need not be facing the floor directly, but should be facing downwards in relation to the other person's palm. This tells him that you wish to take control in the encounter that follows. Studies of fifty-four successful senior management people have revealed that not only did forty-four initiate the handshake, but they also used dominant handshake control.

Just as the dog shows submission by rolling on its back and exposing its throat to the aggressor, so the human uses the palm-up gesture to show submission to others. The reverse of the dominant handshake is to offer you hand with your palm facing upwards. This is particularly effective when you want to give the client control or allow him to feel that he is in command of the sales meeting.

When two dominant people shake hands, a symbolic struggle takes place as each person tries to turn the other's palm into the submissive position. The result is a vice-like handshake with both palms remaining in the vertical position as each person transmits a feeling of respect and rapport to the other.

When you receive a dominant handshake from another person, it is not only difficult to force his palm back over into the submissive position, but it becomes very obvious when you do it. There is a simple technique for disarming the dominant handshake that, in addition to giving you back the control, can enable you to intimidate the other person by invading his personal space. To perfect this disarmament technique, you need to practice stepping forward with your left foot as you reach to shake hands. Next, bring your right leg forward, moving in front of the person and into his personal space in order to complete the maneuver, and then shake the person's hand. This tactic allows you to straighten the handshake position or to turn the other person's hand into the submissive position. It also allows you to take control by invading the other person's intimate zone.

Analyze your own approach to shaking hands to determine whether you step forward on your left or right foot when you extend your arm to shake hands. Most people are right footed and therefore, at a great disadvantage when they receive a dominant handshake, as they have little flexibility or room to move within the confines of the handshake and it allows the other person to take control. Practice stepping into a handshake with your left foot and you will find that it is quite simple to neutralize a dominant handshake and take control.

Another simple maneuver to counter the palm-down thrust is to grasp the person's hand on top and then shake it. With this approach, you become the dominant party, as you not only have control of the other person's hand, but your hand is in the superior position, on top of his with your palm facing down. As this can be embarrassing to the aggressor, it should be used with caution and discretion.

Hands placed and left in a vertical position during a handshake signal 'equal opportunity' negotiations for both parties involved.

Handshake Styles

The glove handshake is sometimes called the politician's handshake. The initiator tries to give the receiver the impression that he is trustworthy and honest, but when this technique is used on a person he has just met, it has the reverse effect. The receiver feels suspicious and cautious about the initiator's intentions. The glove should only be used with people to whom the initiator is well known.

Few greeting gestures are as uninviting as the dead fish handshake, particularly when the hand is cold or clammy. The soft, placid feel of the dead fish makes it universally unpopular and most people relate it to weak character, mainly because of the ease with which the palm can be turned up. Surprisingly, many people who use the dead fish are unaware that they do so, therefore it is wise to ask your friends to comment on your own handshake delivery.

The knuckle grinder is the trademark of the aggressive 'tough guy' type. It is too abrasive to use during a sales call and unfortunately, there is no effective way to counter it, apart from a verbal comment about it.

Like the palm-down thrust, the stiff-arm thrust tends to be used by aggressive types. Its main purpose is to keep you at a distance and out of the initiator's intimate zone. People brought up in rural areas who have a larger intimate zone to protect their personal territory also use it. With rural dwellers, however, there is a tendency to lean forward or even balance on one foot when delivering the stiff-arm thrust.

The fingertip grab is like the stiff-arm thrust that has missed the mark; the user mistakenly grabs the other person's fingers. Even though the initiator may appear to have a keen and enthusiastic attitude toward the receiver, in fact he lacks confidence in himself. Like the stiff-arm thrust, the main aim of the fingertip grab is to keep the receiver at a comfortable spatial distance.

Pulling the receiver into the initiator's territory can mean one of two things; first, the initiator is an insecure type who feels safe only within his own personal space or second, the initiator is from a culture that has a small intimate zone and he is behaving normally.

The intention of the double-handed handshake is to show sincerity, trust or depth of feeling towards the receiver. Two significant elements should be noticed. First, the left hand is used to communicate the extra feeling that the initiator wishes to transmit and its extent is related to the distance that the initiator's left hand is moved up the receiver's right arm. The elbow grasp transmits more feeling than the wrist hold, and the shoulder hold transmits more sentiment than the upper-arm grip. Second, the initiator's left hand represents an invasion into the receiver's intimate and close intimate zones. In general, the wrist hold and the elbow grasp are acceptable only between close friends or relatives and in these cases; the initiator's left hand penetrates only the receiver's intimate zone. The shoulder hold and the upper-arm grip enter the receiver's close intimate zone and may involve actual body contact. They should be used only between people who experience a close emotional bond at the time of the handshake. Unless the extra feeling is mutual or the initiator has a good reason for using a double-handed handshake, the receiver will become suspicious and mistrust the initiator's intentions. It is quite common to see politicians greeting voters and salespeople meeting their new customers with a double-handed handshake without realizing that this can be social suicide, putting the receiver off.

Who Reaches First?

Although it is a generally accepted custom to shake hands when meeting a person for the first time, there are some circumstances in which it may be unwise for you to initiate the handshake. Considering that a handshake is a sign of welcome, it is important to ask yourself several questions before you initiate one:

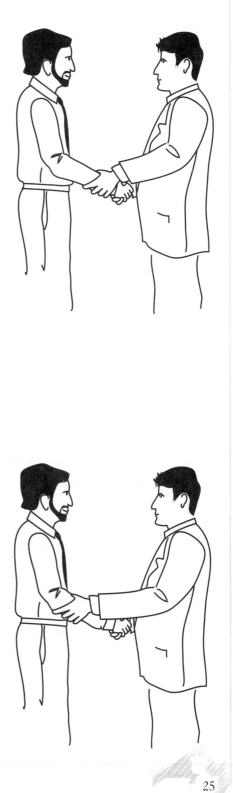

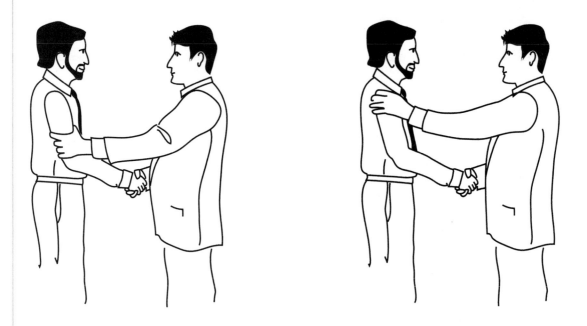

"Am I welcome?" "Is this person glad to meet me?" Sales trainees are cautioned that, if they initiate the handshake with a buyer on whom they call unannounced and uninvited, it can produce a negative result as the buyer may not want to welcome them and is forced to do something that he may not want to do. It is important to note that people with arthritis and those whose hands are their profession may become defensive if they are forced to shake hands. Under these circumstances, someone in sales would be wise to wait for the other person to initiate the handshake and, if not forthcoming, to nod as a sign of greeting.

Use the following guidelines to achieve a friendly handshake and access to your client's attitudes and emotions early in your opening.

1. Keep your hand in a vertical (straight up and down) position—palm down communicates a dominant attitude; palm up communicates a submissive demeanor.
2. Apply moderate pressure—overly forceful handshakes (bone-crushers) convey aggression and a lack of consideration; limp handshakes (dead fish) convey insecurity, or lack of interest.
3. Move your arm at a moderate pace—quick, jerky, overly enthusiastic hand pumping sends all but the most familiar clients into retreat; no movement at all shows a lack of energy and cooperativeness.
4. Pay attention to how your client returns your handshake—all of these interpretations apply to clients too!

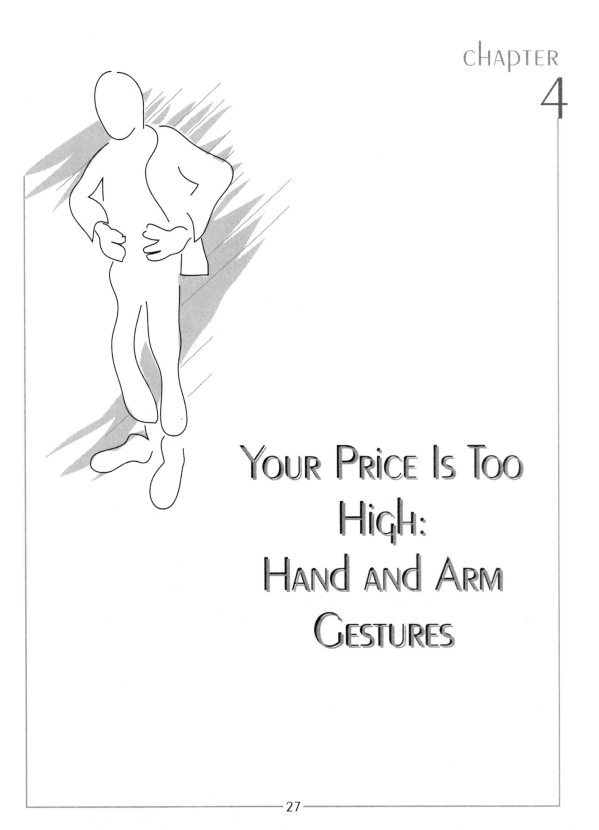

Your Price Is Too High: Hand and Arm Gestures

What does *your* body communicate when your prospect says: "Your price is too high?" Think of your last sales call and try to remember specifics—your body angle, facial expressions, the position of your arms, hands and legs. Most salespeople show negative changes in their body posture when hearing objections.

When a client sees signals such as crossed arms and legs, head scratching, swaying from side to side, nose rubbing and fingers under the collar, your problems are intensified. The prospect may think: "Ah, now I've come to the weak spot!" Even though your verbal reply is flawless, your nonverbal expressions may communicate: "I'm uncomfortable about this," or "I don't know if I will be able to convince you about buying from me."

Salespeople who communicate negative nonverbal signals after hearing the prospect's objections fail to recognize that 99 percent of all customer objections are preceded by negative body language gestures. For these reasons, it can be easily understood why positive gestures on the part of the salesperson are absolutely necessary the moment he notices a customer's objections. It is far better to deal with problems early. As soon as the salesperson notices the first disapproving nonverbal signal, it should be managed and responded with open, concerned gestures in efforts to salvage the situation.

Rubbing the Palms Together

Rubbing the palms together is a way in which people nonverbally communicate positive expectation. The dice thrower rubs the dice between his palms as a sign that he expects to win, the master of ceremonies rubs his palms together and says to his audience, "We have long looked forward to hearing our next speaker," and the excited salesperson struts into the sales manager's office, rubs his palms together and says excitedly, "We've just received a huge order, boss!" However, the waiter who comes to your table at the end of the evening quickly rubbing his palms together and asking, "Anything else, sir?" is nonverbally telling you that he is expecting a tip.

The speed at which a person rubs his palms together signals what he's thinking and feeling. For example, you want to buy a home and you go to see a real estate agent. After describing the property you are seeking, the agent rubs his palms together quickly and says, "I've got just the right place for you!" The agent has signaled that he expects the results to be to *your* benefit. But how would you feel if he rubbed his palms together very slowly as he told you that he had the ideal property? He would then appear to be cunning or devious and would give you the feeling that the expected results would be to *his* advantage rather than yours. Salespeople are taught that if they use the palm-rub gesture when describing products or services to prospective buyers, they should be certain to use a fast hand action to avoid putting the buyer on the defensive. When the buyer rubs his palms together and says to the salesperson, "Let's see what you have to offer!" it is a signal that the buyer is expecting to be shown something good and is likely to make a purchase.

A word of warning: a person who is standing at a bus terminal in freezing winter conditions and who rubs his palms together briskly may not necessarily be doing this because he is expecting a bus. He does it because his hands are cold!

Thumb and Finger Rub

Rubbing the thumb against the fingertips or against the index finger is commonly used as a money expectancy gesture. Some salespeople use it while saying to their customers, "I can save you 40 percent." It is also customary to rub the index finger and thumb together and say to a friend, "Lend me ten dollars." It is not a suitable gesture during negotiations and is obviously a sign that should be avoided at all times by professional people when dealing with clients.

Hands Clenched Together

At first this seems to be a confidence gesture as people who use it are often smiling and sound happy. Research on the hands-clenched position concludes that it is a frustration gesture, signaling that the person doing it is holding back a negative attitude and is somewhat frightened. The gesture has three main positions; hands clenched in front of the face, hands resting on a desk or on the lap when seated and thirdly, hands placed in front of the crotch when standing.

There also appears to be a correlation between the height at which the hands are held and the strength of the person's negative mood; that is, the higher the hands are held, the more difficult the person would be to handle. Like all negative gestures, some action needs to be taken to unlock the person's fingers to expose his palms and the front of his body, or the hostile attitude will remain. In these cases, it would be wise for the salesperson to hand something to the client; a book or a pam-

phlet, causing the client's clenched hands to drop as he picks up the object and thus becomes more open in his body language.

Hands Steepled Together

Fingertips' that touch describe the steeple position, and it is one gesture that can be understood and interpreted in isolation from other gestures. People who are confident, superior types or who use minimal, restricted body gestures often use this signal, and, by doing so, they convey their self-assured attitude.

This fascinating gesture is frequently used in superior/subordinate interactions to indicate an assertive or 'know-it-all' attitude. Managers will use this position while giving instructions or advise to subordinates.

The gesture has two versions, the raised steeple, the position usu-

ally taken when the steepler is giving his opinions or ideas and is doing the talking. The lowered-steeple gesture is normally used when the steepler is listening rather than speaking. When the raised-steeple position is taken with the head tilted back, the person tends to assume an air of smugness or arrogance.

Although the steeple gesture is a positive signal, it can be used in either positive or negative circumstances and may be misunderstood. For example, a salesman presenting his product to a potential buyer may have observed several positive gestures (open palms, head up, body leaning forward) given by the buyer during the interview, then notice the steeple position. If the steeple follows a series of other positive gestures, appearing when the salesperson shows the buyer the solution to his problem, the salesman has been given a cue to close the sale and should ask for the order and expect to get it.

On the other hand, if the steeple gesture follows a series of negative gestures (arm folding, leg crossing, looking away and numerous hand-to-face gestures), and is done towards the close of the sales presentation, the buyer is signaling that he is confident he will not buy or that he can easily get rid of the salesman. In both these cases the steeple gesture means confidence, but one has positive results and the other negative consequences for the salesperson. The movements preceding the steeple gesture are the key to the outcome.

Gripping Hands, Arms and Wrists

Prominent male members of the British Royal Family are noted for their habit of walking with their heads up and chin out while gripping one palm with the other palm behind the back. This gesture is also used by the policeman patrolling his beat, the principal of the local school when he leisurely walks through the schoolyard, senior military personnel and others in positions of authority.

It is a superiority/confidence gesture position that allows the person doing it to express his vulnerable stomach, heart and throat regions to others in a subconscious act of fearlessness. It has been proven that if you take this position when you are nervous and in a high-stress situation, such as being interviewed by newspaper reporters or simply waiting outside a dentist's office, you can begin to feel relaxed, confident and even authoritative.

The palm-in-palm gesture should not be confused with the hand-gripping-wrist gesture which is a signal of frustration and an attempt at self-control. In this case, one hand tightly grips the other wrist or arm as if it is an attempt by one arm to prevent the other from striking out.

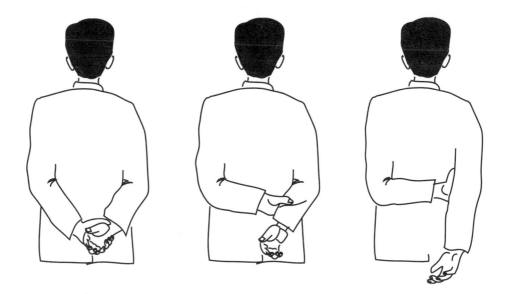

Interestingly, the further the hand is moved up the back, the angrier the person is becoming. It is this type of gesture that has given rise to the expression, "Get a good grip on yourself." Salespeople calling on a potential buyer who have been asked to wait in the buyer's reception area often use this gesture. It is a poor attempt by the salesman to disguise his nervousness and anger. If this self-control gesture is changed to the palm-in-palm position, a calming and confident feeling can result.

Thumb Displays

In palmistry, the thumbs denote strength of character and ego. The nonverbal use of thumbs agrees with this. Exposed thumbs grasping jacket lapels are used to express dominance, superiority or even aggression. Thumb displays are positive signals and are used in the typical pose of the 'cool' manager in the presence of his subordinates. People who wear high-status or prestige clothing and those who wear new and attractive outfits have a tendency to use the thumb display.

Hand Parade

There are thousands of hand gestures. How can you decide what your client's hands are revealing? Divide hand gestures into three main groups and you will get a general idea of whether the customer is reacting in a positive, cautious or negative way to your sales call.

1. Open and relaxed hands, especially when the palms are facing you, are a positive selling signal.
2. Self-touching gestures, such as hands on chin, ear, nose, arm or clothing, indicate tension. Probing for difficulties, or simply relaxing the pace of your presentation may calm the client.
3. Involuntary hand gestures, especially if they contradict a facial expression, indicate the client's true feelings. Watch for tightly clasped hands or fists.

Remember to avoid self-touching and involuntary hand gestures during your sales call. No matter how calm or positive your words are, if the client senses tension or a negative reaction, he will be on his guard and much less receptive to your presentation.

Hear, Speak and See No Evil: Hand-to-Face Gestures

How can you tell when someone is lying? Recognition of the nonverbal deceit gestures can be the most important sales observation skills you can acquire. There are two methods of lying: to *conceal* and to *falsify*. In concealing, the liar withholds some information without actually saying anything untrue. In falsifying, an additional step is taken; not only does the liar withhold true information, but he also presents false information as if it were true.

When there is a choice about *how* to lie, liars usually prefer concealing to falsifying. There are many advantages. For one thing, concealing usually is easier than falsifying. Nothing has to be made up and there is no chance of getting caught without having the whole story worked out in advance.

Concealment lies are easier to cover afterward if discovered. The liar does not go as far out on a limb and has many available excuses—ignorance, the intent to reveal later, memory failure and so on. The person who says, "to the best of my recollection" provides an out if later faced with something he has concealed. If the truth later comes out, the liar can always claim not to have lied about it, that it was just a memory problem.

Deceit, Doubt, Lying

One of the most commonly used symbols to defy deceit is that of the three wise monkeys who hear, speak and see no evil. Their hand-to-face actions depicted form the basis of the human deceit gestures. In other words, when we see, speak and hear untruths or deceit, we often attempt to cover our mouth, eyes or ears with our hands. Children use these obvious deceit gestures quite openly. If a young child tells a lie, he will often cover his mouth with his hands in an attempt to stop the deceitful words from coming out. If he does not wish to listen to a reprimanding parent, he simply covers his ears with his hands. When he sees something he doesn't wish to look at, he covers his eyes with his hands or arms. As we grow older, our hand-to-face gestures become more refined and less obvious but they still occur when we're covering up, witnessing doubt or exaggerating the truth.

Hand-to-face gestures should not be interpreted in isolation of other gestures. Someone using a hand-to-face gesture doesn't always guarantee that he is lying to you. It can, however, indicate that the person is uncomfortable about deceiving you or what he is saying and further observation of his other gesture clusters can confirm your suspicions.

In most instances, the hand-to-face gestures associated with deceit are done with the left hand. It is not to indicate that a left-handed individual would lie more than a right-handed person. Reasoning for this lies in the fact that the left hand is operated by the right, creative side of the brain and since a person's right brain activity is more so associated with ingenuity and imagination, words and thoughts stored there are easier to be brought out, or 'come to life,' when the speaker uses his left hand. It is further substantiated by the fact that throughout our lives we are taught to associate the left hand with bad or negative movements and connect the right hand with good or positive gestures. History has shown that in some countries, the left hand is so associated with negativity that it cannot be placed on the dining table; it is strictly used for wiping purposes.

The Mouth Guard

The mouth guard is one of the few adult gestures that is as obvious as if a child were doing it. The hand covers the mouth and the thumb is pressed against the cheek as the brain subconsciously instructs it to try to suppress the deceitful words that are being said. Sometimes this gesture may only be several fingers over the mouth or even a closed fist over the mouth, but its meaning remains the same.

People try to disguise the mouth-guard gesture by giving a fake cough. When playing the role of criminal, Humphrey Bogart often used this gesture when discussing criminal activities with other gangsters or when being interrogated by the police to show nonverbally that he was being dishonest.

If the person speaking repeatedly uses this gesture, it indicates that he is uncomfortable about the information coming from his mouth and is usually telling a lie. If, however, he covers his mouth while you are speaking, it is a sign that he feels *you* are lying! An unsettling sight for a public speaker to see is his audience all using this gesture while he's speaking. In a small audience or a one-to-one sales situation, it is wise to stop the presentation or delivery and ask, "Would you care to comment on what I've just said?" This allows the other person's objections to be brought out into the open, giving you the opportunity to qualify or clarify your statements and to answer questions.

Nose Touching

In essence, the nose-touch gesture is a sophisticated, disguised version of the mouth-guard gesture. It may consist of several light rubs below or on the side of the nose, or it may be one quick, almost undetectable touch. Women perform this gesture with small discreet strokes to avoid smudging their make-up.

One explanation of the origin of the nose-touch gesture is that, as the negative thought enters the mind, the subconscious instructs the hand to cover the mouth, but, at the last moment, in an attempt to appear less obvious, the hand pulls away from the mouth and a quick nose-touch gesture is the result. Another explanation is that nervousness from lying causes the delicate nerve endings in the nose to tingle, and the rubbing action takes place to satisfy this feeling. "But what if the person only has an itchy nose?" is frequently asked. A very deliberate rubbing or scratching action, as opposed to the light strokes of the nose-touch gesture, normally satisfies the itch in a person's nose. Like the mouth-guard gesture, it can be used both by the speaker to disguise his own deceit and by the listener who doubts the speaker's words.

The Eye Rub

'See no evil' reveals the wise monkey. The eye rub is the brain's attempt to block out the deceit, doubt or lie that it sees or to avoid having to look at the face of the person to whom he is telling the lie. Men, when lying, rub their eyes vigorously and if the lie is a big one, they will often look away towards the floor. Women use a small, gentle rubbing motion just below the eye, either because they have been brought up to avoid making robust gestures, or to avoid smudging their make-up. Untruthful women tend to avoid a listener's gaze by looking up at the ceiling.

'Lying through your teeth' is a common phrase referring to a gesture cluster of clenched teeth and a false smile, combined with an eye-rub and an averted gaze. Movie actors use this gesture to portray insincerity and hypocrisy.

The Ear Rub

This gesture is an attempt by the listener to 'hear no evil' as he tries to block the words by placing his hands around or over his ears. It is a sophisticated adult version of the hands-over-both-ears gesture used by the young child who wants to block out his parent's reprimands. Variations of the ear-rub gesture include rubbing the back of the ear, the finger drill (where the fingertip is screwed back and forth inside the ear), pulling at the earlobe or bending the entire ear forward to cover the ear hole. This last gesture is a signal that the person has heard enough and now wants to speak.

The Neck Scratch

In the neck scratch, the index finger of the writing hand scratches below the earlobe, or may even scratch the side of the neck. The person most often scratches five times. Rarely is the number of scratches less than five and seldom more than five. This gesture is a signal of doubt or uncertainty and is a nonverbal message meaning, "I'm not sure I agree." It is very noticeable when the verbal language contradicts it. For example, when the person says something such as, "I can understand how you feel," yet scratches his neck, one can be certain he is not in agreement with the speaker.

The Collar Pull

Desmond Morris noted that research into the gestures of those who tell lies revealed that the telling of a lie caused a tingling sensation in the delicate facial and neck tissues and a rub or scratch was required to satisfy it. This seems to be a reasonable explanation of why some people use the collar-pull gesture when they tell a lie and suspect that they have been caught. It's as if the lie causes a slight trickle of sweat to form on the neck of the deceiver when he feels that you believe he is lying. A person who is angry or frustrated often feels a need to pull his collar away from his neck in an attempt to let the cool air circulate around it. When talking with someone who is obsessively using this gesture, questions such as, "Would you repeat that, please?" or "Could you clarify that point, please?" could cause the would-be deceiver to give himself away.

Fingers in the Mouth

Usually fingers are placed in the mouth when a person is under pressure. It is a subconscious attempt by the person to revert to the security of his childhood as he sucked a bottle or his mother's breast. After a few years, the young child substitutes his thumb for the breast and as an adult he substitutes his fingers. Not only are fingers placed in the mouth but insecure adults also insert such things as pencils, pins, paper clips, pipes and the like into it. Whereas most hand-to-mouth gestures involve lying or deception, the fingers-in-mouth gesture is an outward manifestation of an inner need for reassurance. Giving guarantees and assurances is the appropriate response if you notice this gesture in another person.

Interpreting and Misinterpreting

The ability to accurately interpret hand-to-face gestures in a given set of circumstances takes considerable time and conscious observation to acquire. We can confidently assume that, when a person uses one of the hand-to-face gestures just described, a negative thought has entered his mind. The question is, "What is negative?" It could be doubt, deceit, uncertainty, exaggeration, apprehension or outright lying. The real skill of interpretation is the ability to pick which of the negatives mentioned is the correct one. This can best be done by an analysis of the gestures that precede the hand-to-face gesture and then interpreting it in context.

A friend of mine whom I play blackjack with often rubs his ear or touches his nose during the game, but only when he is unsure of his next move. I have discovered that when I signal the dealer my intention for another card, my friend immediately uses gesture clusters that signal what he thinks about my proposed hand. If he sits back in his chair and uses a steepling gesture (confidence), I can assume that he has anticipated my move and may already have thought of a counter move. If, as I touch my card, he covers his mouth or rubs his nose or ear, it means that he is uncertain about my move, his next move or both. The more I stall and the more confident I act after he has reacted with negative hand-to-face gestures, the greater are my chances of winning.

During a videotaped role-play of an interview scene at a management seminar, the interviewee suddenly covered his mouth and rubbed his nose after he had been asked a question by the interviewer. Up to that point in the role-play, the job applicant had kept an open posture with open coat, palms visible and leaned forward when answering questions, so at first it was thought that it was an isolated set of gestures. The mouth-guard gesture was displayed for several seconds before he gave his answer, then he returned to his open pose. When he was questioned about the hand-to-mouth gesture at the end of the role-play, he said that when he was asked a particular question, he could have responded in two ways; one negative, one positive. As he thought about the negative answer and of how the interviewer might react to it, the mouth-guard gesture occurred. When he thought of the positive answer, however, his hand dropped away from his mouth and he resumed his open posture. His uncertainty about the interviewer's possible reaction to the negative reply had caused the sudden mouth-guard gesture to occur.

This illustrates how easy it can be to misinterpret a hand-to-face gesture and to jump to wrong conclusions. Only by constant study and observation of these gestures and by having regard to the context in which they occur, can one eventually learn to reach an accurate assessment of someone else's thoughts.

Cheek and Chin Gestures

A good speaker is said to be one who instinctively knows when his audience is interested in what he says and when his listeners have had enough. Likewise, a good salesperson senses when he is hitting his client's hot buttons, and knows the empty feeling that results when he is giving a sales presentation to a potential buyer who says very little and just sits there watching. Fortunately, understanding and recognizing a number of hand-to-cheek and hand-to-chin gestures can tell the salesperson how well he is doing and how to proceed.

Boredom

When the listener begins to use his hand to support his head, it is a signal that boredom has set in and his supporting hand is an attempt to hold his head up to stop himself from falling asleep. The degree of the listener's boredom is related to the extent to which his arm and hand are supporting his head. Extreme boredom and lack of interest are shown when the head is fully supported by the hand and the ultimate boredom signal occurs when the head is on the desk or table and the person is snoring.

Professional speakers and salespeople often misinterpret drumming the fingers on the table and continual tapping of the feet on the floor by audience members as boredom signals, but in fact, they signal impatience. When you notice these signals, a strategic move must be made to get the finger drummer or foot tapper involved in your presentation, thus avoiding his negative effect on the other members who are listening. Audience members who display boredom and impatience signals together are signaling to the speaker that it is time for him to end the speech. It is worth noting that the speed of the finger tap or foot tap is related to the extent of the person's impatience—the faster the taps, the more impatient the listener is becoming.

Evaluation

A closed hand resting on the cheek, often with the index finger pointing upwards depicts evaluation. Should the person begin to lose interest but wish to appear interested, for courtesy's sake, the position will alter slightly so that the heel of the palm supports the head. Genuine interest in shown when the hand is placed on the cheek, not used as a head support.

When the index finger points vertically up the cheek and the thumb supports the chin, it means that the listener is having negative or critical thoughts about the speaker or his subject. Often the index finger rubs or pulls at the eye as the listener's negative thoughts continue. Because a gesture position affects a person's attitude, the longer a person holds the gesture, the longer the critical attitude will remain. This gesture is a signal that the listener requires immediate action, either involve him in what is being said or end the talk. A simple move, such as handing something to the listener to alter his pose, can cause a change in his attitude. This gesture is often mistaken as a signal of interest, but the supporting thumb tells the truth about the critical attitude.

Chin-Stroking

The next time you have the opportunity to present an idea to a group of people, watch them carefully as you express your idea and you will notice something fascinating. Most, if not all the members of your audience, will bring one hand up to their face and begin to use evaluation gestures. As you come to the conclusion of your presentation and ask for the group to give opinions or suggestions about the idea, the evaluation gestures will cease. One hand will move to the chin and begin a chin-stroking gesture.

The chin-stroking gesture is the signal that the listener is making a decision. When you have asked the listeners for a decision and their gestures have changed from evaluation to decision-making, the following movements will indicate whether their decision is negative or positive. If, for example, crossed arms and legs follow the chin-stroking gesture and the buyer sits back in his chair, the salesperson has been nonverbally told, 'No.' He would be wise to review the positive main points of the presentation immediately before the buyer verbalizes his negative answer and loses the entire sale.

If the chin-stroking gesture is followed by a leaning forward readiness gesture and open palms, the salesperson only needs to ask how the buyer would prefer to pay for the product and the buyer will proceed and make his purchase.

A salesperson would be foolish to interrupt or to speak when a buyer begins the chin-stroking gesture after he has been asked for a decision to purchase. His best strategy is to carefully observe the buyer's next gestures, those will indicate the decision he has reached and then the salesperson should proceed with the close.

Variations of Decision-Making Gestures

A person who wears glasses follows evaluation clusters by removing his glasses and placing one arm of the frame in his mouth instead of using the chin-stroking gesture when making a decision. A pipe-smoker will put his pipe in his mouth. When a person places an object such as a pen or a finger in his mouth after having been asked for a decision, it is a signal that he is unsure. Reassurance is needed. The object in his mouth allows him to stall before making an immediate decision. As it is bad manners to speak with your mouth full, the buyer feels justified in not giving a quick answer.

Gestures with Glasses

Like pipe smoking, the glasses-in-mouth gesture can be used to stall or delay a decision. In negotiating, it has been found that this gesture appears most frequently at the close of the discussion when a choice has to be made. The act of continually taking the glasses off and cleaning the lenses is another method used by people who wear glasses to stall for time. When this gesture is seen immediately after a decision has been asked for, silence is the best tactic.

The gestures that follow this stall gesture signal the person's intention and allow an alert negotiator to respond accordingly. For example, if the person puts the glasses back on, this often means that he wants to 'see' the facts again, whereas folding the glasses and putting them away signals his intention to terminate the conversation.

Actors in motion pictures made during the 1920s and 1930s used the peering-over-glasses gesture to portray a person with a critical or judgmental personality. Often the person is wearing reading glasses and finds it more convenient to look over the tops, rather than removing them to look at the other person. Whoever is on the receiving line of this look may feel as though he is being judged or scrutinized. Looking over the glasses is a very costly mistake, as the listener inevitably responds to this look with folded arms, crossed legs and a correspondingly negative attitude. People who wear reading glasses should remove them when speaking and put them back on to listen. This not only relaxes the other person but also allows the wearer to have control of the conversation. The listener quickly learns that when the glasses are off, he must not interrupt the speaker, and when they are put back on, he had better start talking.

Smoking Gestures

Smoking is an outward manifestation of an inner turmoil or conflict. It is one of the displacement activities that people in today's high-pressure society use to release the tensions that build up from social and business encounters.

Smoking gestures play an important part in assessing a person's attitude, as they are usually performed in a predictable, ritualistic manner. The cigarette ritual involving tapping, twisting, flicking, waving and other mini-gestures indicates that the person is experiencing more tension than may be normal.

The direction in which the smoke is exhaled, up or down, indicates whether the person has a positive or negative attitude towards his circumstances. A person who is feeling positive, superior or confident will blow the smoke in an upward direction most of the time. Conversely, a person in a negative, secretive or suspicious frame of mind will exhale cigarette smoke in a downward motion. Blowing cigarette smoke down and from the corner of the mouth indicates an even more negative or secretive attitude. There also appears to be a relationship between how positive or negative the person feels and the speed at which he or she exhales the smoke. The faster the smoke is blown upwards, the more superior or confident the person feels; the faster it is blown down, the more negative he feels.

Observation of smoking gestures during a sales encounter, shows that when a smoker is asked to buy, those who have reached a positive decision blow their cigarette smoke upwards, whereas those who have decided not to buy blow it downwards. To allow the customer time to reconsider his decision, the alert salesperson, seeing the smoke being blown downwards during the close of a sale should quickly resell the customer on all the benefits he would receive by purchasing the product. Blowing smoke out through the nostrils is a sign of a superior, confident individual who may be irritated and trying to look ferocious, like an angry bull.

Pipe smokers perform a cleaning, lighting, tapping, filling, packing and puffing ritual with their pipes as a very useful way for them to relieve tension when they are under pressure. Sales research has shown that pipe smokers usually take longer to make a decision to buy than do cigarette smokers or non-smokers. The pipe ritual is usually performed during the tense moments of the sales presentation. Pipe smokers, it seems, are people who like to stall decision-making and do so in an unobtrusive and socially acceptable way.

Cigars have always been used as a means of displaying superiority because of their cost and size. Cigars are used to celebrate a victory or achievement such as the birth of a baby or clinching a business deal; therefore, it is not surprising that most of the smoke exhaled by cigar smokers is upwards.

The continual tapping of a cigar or cigarette end on an ashtray shows that the smoker is experiencing an inner conflict and that you may need to reassure him. Another interesting smoking phenomenon is that most smokers smoke their cigarette down to a certain length before extinguishing it in the ashtray. If the smoker lights a cigarette and suddenly extinguishes it earlier than he normally would, he has signaled his decision to terminate the conversation. Watching for this termination signal can allow you to take control and close the conversation, making it appear that it was your idea to end it.

Head-Rubbing and Head-Slapping Gestures

An exaggerated version of the collar-pull gesture is the palm rubbing the back of the neck in what is labeled as the 'pain-in-the-neck' gesture. It is a gesture often associated with frustration or anger and, when this is the case, the angry person slaps the back of his neck first and then begins to rub his neck. Let us assume, for example, that you asked a subordinate to complete a certain task for you and that the subordinate had forgotten to do it within the time required. When you ask him for the results, he nonverbally signals his forgetfulness by slapping his head, either on the forehead or the back of the neck, as if he were symbolically hitting himself. Although slapping of the head communicates forgetfulness, the person signals how he feels about you or the situation by the position where he slaps his hand on his head, either his forehead or his neck. If he slaps his forehead, he signals that he is not intimidated by your having mentioned his forgetfulness, but when he slaps the back of his neck, he is nonverbally telling you that you are literally a 'pain-in-the-neck' for pointing out his error. Those who habitually rub the backs of their necks have a tendency to be negative or critical of others, whereas those who routinely rub their foreheads to nonverbalize an error tend to be open, easy-going and critical of themselves.

Nervous, Negative or Defensive: Arm Barriers

Hiding behind a barrier is a normal human response that is learned at an early age as a means of protection. As children, we hid behind solid objects such as tables, chairs, furniture and our mother's skirts whenever we found ourselves in a threatening situation. This hiding behavior becomes more sophisticated as we grow up, and by the age of six, when it is unacceptable to hide behind solid objects, we learn to fold our arms tightly across our chests whenever a threatening situation arises. During our teens, we learn to make this crossed-arms gesture a little less obvious by relaxing our arms and combining the gesture with crossed legs.

Folded-Arms Gestures

If you go into a client's office, and her arms are already crossed, notice the room temperature. She might just be cold! Or she may have just gotten off the phone from an unpleasant conversation. Maybe she's thinking about the argument she had with her spouse the previous night. The point is this: you can't attribute her gesture to your being there until she does something in reaction to something you do or say. Once you've started your presentation and she suddenly crosses her arms, then you can be fairly certain that you caused this reaction. Now is the time to stop what you're doing and find out why the client is reacting that way towards you.

By folding one or both arms across the chest, a barrier is formed that is, in essence, an attempt to block out the impending threat or undesirable circumstances. One thing is certain; when a person has a nervous, negative or defensive attitude, he will fold his arms firmly on his chest, a strong signal that he feels threatened.

Research conducted about the folded-arms position in body language has shown some interesting results. When a listener folds his arms, not only has he negative thoughts about the speaker, but he is also paying less attention to what is being said. Because of this fact, it would be wise if training centers had chairs with arms to allow the attendees to leave their arms uncrossed and become more receptive to the seminar.

People claim that they habitually take the arms-folded position because it is comfortable. Any gesture will feel comfortable when you have the corresponding attitude; that is, if you have a negative, defensive or nervous attitude, the folded-arms position will feel good.

It is imperative to remember that in nonverbal communication, the meaning of the message is also in the receiver, not only the sender. You may feel 'comfortable' with your arms crossed or your back and neck stiffened, but studies have shown that the reception of these gestures is negative.

Standard Arm-Cross Gesture

In the standard arm-cross position, both arms are folded together across the chest as an attempt to 'hide' from an unfavorable situation. This universal gesture signifies the same defensive or negative attitude almost everywhere. It is commonly seen when a person is among strangers in public meetings, lines, cafeterias, elevators or anywhere that he feels uncertain or insecure. Experienced speakers know that this gesture demonstrates the necessity of a good 'ice breaker' to move an unreceptive audience into a more open posture that will alter their attitudes.

When you see the arm-cross gesture occur during a face-to-face encounter, it is reasonable to assume that you have said something with which the other person disagrees, so it is pointless to continue your line of argument even though the other person may be verbally agreeing with you. The nonverbal medium does not lie—the mouth lies. Your objective should be to try to discover the cause of the arms-folded gesture and to move the person into a more receptive position. Remember: as long as the arms-folded gesture remains, the negative attitude will remain. The attitude causes the gestures to occur and prolonging the gesture forces the attitude to remain.

A simple, but effective, method of breaking the folded-arms position is to hand the person a pen, a book or something that forces him to unfold his arms to reach forward. This moves him into a more open posture and accepting attitude. Asking the person to lean forward to look at a visual presentation can also be an effective means of opening the folded-arms position. Another useful method is to lean forward with your palms facing up and say, "I can see you have a question, what would you like to know?" or, "What do you think?" and then sit back to indicate that it is the other person's turn to speak or ask questions. By leaving your palms visible, you nonverbally tell the other person that you would like an open, honest answer. A salesperson should never proceed with the presentation of a product until he has uncovered the prospective buyer's reason for suddenly folding his arms.

Reinforced Arm-Cross

If as well as the bold arm-cross gesture the person has clenched fists, he is indicating to you that he has a hostile and defensive attitude. This cluster is often combined with clenched teeth and a red face, in which case a verbal or physical attack may be imminent. A submissive palms-up approach is needed to discover what caused the hostile gestures if the reason is not already apparent. The person using this gesture cluster has an attacking attitude, as opposed to the person using the standard arm-cross and is only taking on a defending position.

Arm-Gripping Gesture

Hands tightly gripping the upper arms to reinforce the position and to stop any attempt to unfold the arms and expose the body, characterize this arm-cross gesture. The arms can often be gripped so tightly that the fingers and knuckles turn white as the blood circulation is cut off. This arm-fold style is common to people sitting in a doctor or dentist's waiting room, or first time air travelers who are waiting for the plane to take off. It depicts a negative, restrained attitude.

Status can influence arm-folding gestures. A superior type can make his superiority felt in the presence of persons he has just met by the manner in which he holds or unfolds his arms. For example, at a company social function, the general manager is introduced to several new employees whom he has not met. Having greeted them with a dominant handshake, he stands at the social distance from the new employees with his hands by his sides, behind his back in the superior palm-in-palm position, or with one hand in his pocket. He rarely folds his arms to show the slightest hint of nervousness. Conversely, after shaking hands with the boss, the new employees take full or partial arm-fold gestures because of their apprehension about being in the presence of the company's top man. Both the general manager and the new employees feel comfortable with their respective gestures as each is signaling his status relative to the other. But what happens when the general manager meets a young, up-and-coming executive who is also a superior type and who may even feel that he is as important as the general manager? The likely outcome is that after the two have exchanged a dominant handshake, the young executive will make an arm-fold gesture across his body then leave both of his thumbs pointing vertically upwards. The thumbs-up gesture is a person's way of showing that he has a self-confident attitude and the folded arms give him a feeling of protection.

A salesperson, seeing the thumbs-up, needs to analyze why a buyer may have made this gesture to know whether his approach is effective. If the thumbs-up gesture has come towards the end of the sales presentation and is combined with many other positive gestures, the salesperson can move comfortably into closing the sale and should ask for the order. If, on the other hand, at the close of the sale, the buyer moves into the fists-clenched arm-cross position and has a poker face, the salesperson can be inviting disastrous consequences by attempting to ask for the order. Instead, he should quickly go back to his sales presentation and ask more questions to try to discover the buyer's objection. In selling, once the buyer verbalizes, "No," it can become difficult to change his decision. The ability to read and accurately interpret body language allows you to see the negative decision before it is verbalized and gives you time to take an alternative course of action.

Partial Arm-Cross Barriers

The full arm-cross gesture is sometimes too obvious to use around others because it tells them that we are negative or fearful. Occasionally, we substitute a subtler version—the partial arm-cross, in which one arm swings across the body to hold or touch the other arm to form the barrier.

The partial arm barrier is often seen at meetings where one person is a stranger to the group or is lacking in self-confidence. Another popular version of a partial arm barrier is when a person holds hands with his own self, a gesture commonly used by a person who must stand before a crowd to receive an award or give a speech. Desmond Morris found that this gesture allowed a person to relive the emotional security he experienced as a child when his parent held his hand under fearful circumstances.

Disguised Arm-Cross Gestures

Disguised arm-cross gestures are highly sophisticated gestures used by people who are continually exposed to others. This group includes politicians, salespeople, television personalities and the like who do not want their audience to detect that they are unsure of themselves or nervous. Like all arm-cross gestures, one arm swings across in front of the body to grasp the other arm but instead of the arms folding, one hand touches a handbag, bracelet, watch, shirt cuff or other object on or near the other arm. Once again the barrier is formed and the secure feeling is achieved. When cufflinks were popular, men constantly adjusted them as they crossed a room or dance floor where they were in full view of others. A man may simply adjust the band on his watch, check the contents of his wallet, clasp or rub his hands together, play with a button on his cuff or use any other gesture that allows his arms to cross in front of his body in an effort to help him feel secure. To the trained observer, however, these gestures are a dead giveaway because they achieve no real purpose except as an attempt to disguise nervousness.

Women are less obvious than men in their use of disguised arm-barrier gestures. They can grasp such things as handbags or books when they become unsure of themselves and no one thinks much of it. One common version of this is when a woman holds a glass of wine or soft drink with both hands. Did it ever occur to you that you need only one hand to hold a glass of wine? The use of two hands to hold the drink allows the nervous person to form an almost undetectable arm barrier.

Reassuring the Nervous Customer

Your relaxed and open postures will do wonders in reducing your prospect's initial apprehension. Some clients are harder to 'open up' than others. They may feel insecure or frustrated or they may be bored or overworked in their jobs. These complicated feelings show up as disinterest, hostility or simply nervousness. Some helpful hints for relaxing this type of client can be gained from one profession that must constantly sell 'unwanted' services—dentistry.

Dentists and their staffs are aware of the anxiety their services produce. They also realize that those who say they're not nervous may be the jitteriest patrons, so they look for 'displacement gestures.' Tapping fingers, flipping through magazines aimlessly, fiddling with objects and chain-smoking all indicate nervous energy. To calm their patients, dentists know that they need to reassure them through pleasant music, calm conversation and light humor. They know that their main goal is to assure the patient, through their own actions, that everything is fine.

In selling, you may notice similar displacement gestures. To help calm such a prospect, remember to:

1. Avoid 'mirroring' the client's negative nonverbal gestures or movements. Resist the subtle, subconscious urge to respond to these gestures by scratching your head, fiddling with a pen, jiggling coins in your pocket or by shifting your posture too often.
2. Lead the client to imitate your own expressions of confidence and reassurance. Communicate relaxed gestures and postures. Maintain a comfortable distance between yourself and your client and consciously lower your shoulders (raised shoulders indicate tension) and slightly tilt your head (shows interest).

Sales Hype
OR
Selling Strategy:
Leg Barriers

Most people believe that leg crossing is done for comfort. Did you ever stop to think *why* people are comfortable in that position? Usually it's because their bodies are reflecting how they feel inside. A study of 2,000 people found that *no* sales were made while participants had their legs crossed. Even if all other channels appear to be open and positive, the customer who crosses his legs may have some minor reservations that will prevent you from completing the sale if they are not uncovered and answered.

During a sales call much of the time is spent sitting down. That's why it is worth your time to develop and practice a comfortable, positive sitting position.

Study yourself when you walk into a room and sit down, what do you automatically do with your body? Scan your five nonverbal channels to check for signals that are detrimental in a sales situation. Do you lean back in your chair? Are your hands folded tightly, tucked under your arms in fists or grasping the arms of the chair? Do you cross your legs, tuck them under the chair, stick them way out in front of you or cross them at the ankles?

Experiment until you find an open, relaxed position that you can use *all the time*. Next, constantly be aware of how you sit, every time you sit. Shift into your new comfortable position whenever you fall back into your old habits. With practice, your new position will become your automatic one.

Crossed-Leg Gestures

Like arm-barrier gestures, crossed legs signal that a negative or defensive attitude exists. The purpose of crossing the arms on the chest was originally to defend the heart and upper body region. Crossing the legs is an attempt to shield and protect the genital area. Crossed arms indicate a more negative attitude than crossed legs do, and the crossed-arms gesture is more obvious than the crossed-legs gesture. Care should be taken when interpreting crossed-leg gestures on women as many are taught that this is how to 'sit like a lady.' Unfortunately for them, however, the gesture can make women appear defensive.

Two basic male crossed-leg sitting positions exist, the standard leg cross and the leg lock in the shape of the number four cross.

The European Leg-Cross Position

One leg is crossed neatly over the other, usually the right over the left. This is the normal male crossed-leg position seen in European cultures and typically displays a nervous, reserved or defensive attitude. However, this position is frequently a supportive gesture that occurs with other negative gestures and should not be interpreted in isolation or out of context. For example, people often sit this way during lectures or if they are in uncomfortable chairs for long periods. It is also common to see this gesture in cold weather. When the crossed-legs gesture is combined with crossed arms, the person has withdrawn from the conversation. A salesperson would be very foolish even to attempt to ask for a decision from a buyer if the buyer has taken this pose. A wise salesperson would ask probing questions to uncover the buyer's objection. The crossed-arms, crossed-legs pose is also popular among women who want to show their displeasure with a mate.

The Leg-Lock Position

The leg lock in the shape of the number four sitting position indicates that an argumentative or competitive attitude exists. It is the pose used by many American males who are locked into their own ideas.

In a selling situation, it would be unwise to attempt to close the sale and ask for the order when the buyer takes this position. The salesperson would need to use an open appeal, lean forward with his palms up and say, "I can see you have some ideas on this. I'd be interested in your opinion," and then sit back to signify that it is the buyer's turn to speak. This gives the buyer an opportunity to tell you his opinion. Women wearing trousers or jeans are often observed sitting in this leg-lock position when they are opposed to another person's ideas.

Leg Clamp and the Leg Lock

The person who has a hard and fast attitude in an argument or debate will often lock the leg into place with one or both hands, using them as a clamp. This is a sign of the tough minded, stubborn individual who may need a special approach to break through his resistance.

Standing Leg-Cross Gestures

The next time you attend a meeting or function, you will notice small groups of people all standing with their arms and legs crossed. Further observation will reveal that they are standing at a greater distance from each other than is customary, and that, if they are wearing coats or jackets, they are usually buttoned. If you were to question these people, you would find that one or all of them are strangers to the others in the group. Most people stand this way when they are among people whom they do not know well.

Now you notice another small group in which the people are standing with their arms unfolded, palms exposed, coats unbuttoned, leaning on one foot with their other foot pointing towards the other members of the group and moving in and out of each other's intimate zones. Close investigation reveals that these people are friends or personally know each other. Interestingly, the people using the closed arms and legs stance may have relaxed facial expressions and conversation that sounds free and easy, but the folded arms and legs tell you that they are not relaxed or confident.

The next time you join a group of people who are standing in the open friendly stance but among whom you know no one, stand with your arms and legs tightly crossed. One by one the group members will cross their arms and legs and remain in that position until you leave them. Then walk away and watch how, one by one, the members of the group assume their original open pose once again!

The 'Opening-Up' Procedure

As people begin to feel comfortable in a group and get to know others in it, they move through an unwritten code of movements taking them from the defensive crossed arms and legs position to a relaxed open position.

Step 1: Defensive position, arms and legs are crossed.

Step 2: Legs are uncrossed and feet are placed together in a neutral position.

Step 3: The arm folded on top in the arm-cross comes out and the palm is flashed while the person is speaking. It is not tucked back into the arm-cross position; instead the speaker uses it to hold the outside of his other arm.

Step 4: Arms unfold. The speaker gesticulates with one arm then places it on his hip or in his pocket.

Step 5: As interest develops, a person leans back on one leg and pushes his other leg forward to point at the person he finds the most appealing.

Defensive or Cold?

Many people claim that they are not defensive but cross their arms or legs because they feel cold. This is a cover-up. Note the difference between a defensive stance and the way a person stands when he or she feels cold. First of all, when someone wants to warm his hands he normally thrusts them under his armpits rather than tucking them under his elbows, as is the case with a defensive arm-cross. Secondly, when a person feels cold he will fold his arms in a type of body hug. His crossed legs are usually straight, stiff and pressed hard against each other, as opposed to the more relaxed leg posture of the defensive stance or position.

People who habitually take a crossed arms or legs position prefer to say that they are cold or comfortable rather than to admit that they could be nervous, shy or defensive.

The Ankle-Lock Gesture

Just as the crossed or folded arms or legs suggest a negative or defensive attitude, it is also the case with the ankle-lock gesture. The male version of the ankle lock is often combined with clenched fists resting on the knees or with the hands tightly gripping the arms of the chair. The female version varies slightly; the knees are held together, the feet are to one side and the hands relax side by side or one on top of the other on the upper legs.

During interviews or sales presentations, it is noted that the interviewee who locks his ankles is mentally 'biting his lip.' The locked-ankle gesture represents someone who is holding back a negative attitude, emotion, nervousness or fear. If the interviewer tries walking around to the job applicant's side of the desk and sits beside him, removing the desk barrier, the job applicant's ankles usually unlock and the conversation takes on an open, more personal atmosphere.

Leaders in the field of negotiating techniques find that whenever one party locks his ankles during a negotiation it means that he is holding back a valuable concession. They found that, by using proper questioning techniques and positive nonverbal communication, they could often encourage the other party to unlock his ankles and reveal his hidden fears.

There are always people who claim that they habitually sit in the ankle-lock position, or for that matter, any of the negative arm and leg clusters, because they feel comfortable. If you are one of these people, remember that any arm or leg position will feel comfortable when you have a defensive, negative or reserved attitude. Considering that a negative gesture can increase or prolong a negative attitude, and that other people interpret you as being defensive or negative, you would be well advised to practice using positive and open gestures to improve your self-confidence and relationships with others.

When analyzing leg crosses, take female fashion trends into consideration. Particularly notice how a woman's clothing might affect her leg positions, before jumping to conclusions.

The Foot Lock

Women who are shy or timid commonly use this gesture. The top of one foot locks around the other leg to reinforce a defensive attitude. When this gesture appears, you can be sure that the woman has become a mental recluse or has retreated like a tortoise into her shell. A warm, friendly, low-key approach is needed if you eventually hope to open this clam.

Other Typical Leg Positions

Feet on desk: this position indicates an attitude of ownership, superiority and dominance. It is not a posture that will elicit cooperation from the client. Instead, it says "Go ahead and try to sell me."

Legs crossed away from: this nonverbal gesture tells you that the sales call is not going well. When legs are in this position, the body is also shifted away from the other person. Cross your legs toward your client, if you must cross them at all.

Uncrossed: this is the ideal position for both you and your client. It sends a message of cooperation, confidence and friendly interest in the other person. Use it as much as possible!

Legs crossed toward: to encourage your client to assume an open posture, this position is acceptable in the early phase of a sale. Mirroring your client's position in this situation may make him feel that the two of you are alike and tuned in to each other.

Anatomy of an Encounter: Eye Signals and Other Popular Gestures and Actions

At the point of entering a crowded room you pause for a moment by the door and search for someone with a familiar face. You see a casual acquaintance, catch his eye and walk towards him. Greetings are exchanged; you shake hands, chat for a while, and then move away to talk with somebody else.

During every encounter, however brief, hundreds of nonverbal messages are exchanged. It's these cues, usually more than any words spoken, that influence the impression you form on one another.

Eye Signals

Body language specialists have been preoccupied with the eye and its effect on human behavior. We've all used such phrases as "He has shifty eyes," "She gave me the evil eye," or "He had that gleam in his eye." When we use these phrases, we unwittingly refer to the size of the person's pupils and to his or her gaze behavior. Eyes may well be the most revealing and accurate of all human communication signals because they are a focal point on the body and work independently of all other body parts.

In given light conditions, a person's pupils will dilate or contract as his attitude and mood changes from positive to negative and vice versa. When someone becomes excited, his pupils can dilate up to four times their normal size. Conversely, an angry or negative mood causes an individual's pupils to contract. This narrowing of a person's pupils is commonly referred to as 'beady eyes' or 'snake eyes.'

Once eye contact is made with another person, each individual scans the other's face for further information about attitudes and intentions based on silent speech signals.

Tests conducted with expert card players show that fewer games were won by the experts when their opponents wore dark glasses. If an opponent were dealt four aces in a game of poker and his eyes were visible, the expert would unconsciously detect his rapid pupil dilation. Knowing this, the expert would definitely not raise his bet.

The ancient Chinese gem traders watched the pupil dilation of their buyers when negotiating prices. The late Aristotle Onassis was noted for wearing dark glasses when discussing business deals so that his eyes would not reveal his thoughts.

The old cliché says, "Look a person in the eye when you talk to him." While communicating or negotiating with others, practice 'looking them in the pupil' and you'll get insight into their true feelings.

Gaze Behavior

A genuine basis for communication is established when you can see 'eye to eye' with another person. While some people can make us feel quite comfortable when they converse with us, others can make us feel ill at ease. This has to do primarily with the length of time they look at us or hold our gaze as they speak to us. When a person is being dishonest or holding back information, his eyes meet ours less than one-third of the time. When a person's gaze meets yours for more than two-thirds of the time, it can mean one of two things; first, he or she finds you very interesting or appealing, in which case, the gaze will be associated with dilated pupils; secondly, he or she is hostile towards you and may be issuing a nonverbal challenge; in this case, the pupils constrict. In studying eye gaze, it has been reported that when person A likes person B, he will look at him a lot. This causes B to think that A likes him, so B will like A in return. In other words, to build a good rapport with another person, your gaze should meet his about 60 to 70 percent of the time. This will also make him begin to like you. It is not surprising, therefore, that the nervous, timid person who meets your gaze less than one-third of the time is rarely trusted. Dark tinted glasses should be avoided during negotiations because proper eye contact cannot be established. The dark glasses make others feel that you are staring at them or that you have something to hide.

The length of time that one person gazes at another is culturally determined. Southern Europeans have such a high frequency of gaze that it is sometimes offensive to others and the Japanese gaze at the neck rather than at the face when conversing. Always be sure to consider cultural circumstances before jumping to conclusions.

Not only is the length of your gaze significant, just as important is the geographical area of the person's face and body at which you direct your gaze, as this also affects the outcome of a negotiation. These gaze signals are transmitted and received nonverbally and are accurately interpreted by the receiver.

The Business Gaze

During discussions on a business level, imagine that there is a triangle on the other person's forehead. By keeping your gaze directed at this area, between the other person's eyes and up to his forehead, you create a serious atmosphere and the other person senses that you mean business. Provided that your gaze does not drop below the level of the other person's eyes, you are usually able to maintain control of the interaction.

The Social Gaze

When your gaze drops below the other person's eye level, a social atmosphere develops. During social encounters, the gazer's eyes also look in a triangular area on the other person's face, in this case, between the eyes and the mouth.

The Intimate Gaze

This gaze goes across the eyes and below the chin to other parts of the person's body. In close encounters it is the triangular area between the eyes and the chest or breasts. Men and women use this gaze to show interest in each other.

Sideways Glance

The sideways glance is used to communicate either interest or hostility. When it is combined with slightly raised eyebrows or a smile, it communicates interest and is frequently used as a courtship signal. If it is combined with down-turned eyebrows, furrowed brow or the corners of the mouth down-turned, it signals a suspicious, hostile or critical attitude.

Eye-Block Gesture

Some of the most irritating people with whom we deal are those who use the eye-block gesture as they speak. This gesture occurs unconsciously and is an attempt by the person to block you from his sight because he has become bored or uninterested in you and feels that he is superior to you. Compared to the normal rate of six to eight blinks per minute during a conversation, during the eye-block gesture the eyelids close and remain closed for a second or longer as the person momentarily wipes you from his mind. The ultimate blockout is to leave the eyes closed and to fall asleep; hopefully this rarely happens during one-to-one encounters.

If a person feels superior to you, he uses the eye-block gesture and tilts his head backwards to give you a long look. It is commonly known as 'looking down one's nose' at someone else. When you see an eye-block gesture during a conversation, it is a signal that the approach you are using may be causing a negative reaction and that a new tack is needed if effective communication is to take place.

CONTROLLING A PERSON'S GAZE

When you are giving another person a visual presentation using books, charts or graphs, it is wise to gain control of his visual gaze. Research shows that of the information relayed to a person's brain, 55 percent comes via the eyes, 38 percent via the ears and 7 percent via the other senses. To maintain maximum control of another person's gaze, use a pen or pointer to point to the visual aid, while at the same time, verbalize what he sees. Next, lift the pen from the visual aid and hold it between his eyes and your own eyes. This movement has the magnetic effect of making him lift his head so that he is now looking at your eyes and sees and hears more clearly what you are saying. He is achieving maximum absorption of your message. Be sure that the palm of your other hand (open gesture) is visible when you are speaking.

Head Gestures

The two most widely used head movements are the head nod and the head shake. The head nod is a positive gesture used in most cultures to signify 'yes,' or affirmation. Research conducted with people who have been deaf and blind from birth shows that they also use this gesture to signify affirmation, which has given rise to the theory that this is an inborn gesture. The head shake, usually meaning 'no,' is also claimed to be an inborn action. It is, in fact, the first gesture a human being learns. When the newborn baby has had enough milk, he shakes his head from side to side to reject his bottle or his mother's breast. Similarly, the young child who has had enough to eat uses the head shake to reject his parent's attempt to spoon feed him.

The easiest way to uncover a disguised objection when dealing with others is to watch if the person uses the head shake gesture while verbalizing his agreement with you. Take, for example, the person who verbalizes, "Yes, I can see your point of view," while shaking his head from side to side. Even though his words may sound convincing, his head shake gesture signals that a negative attitude exists and you would be well advised to reject what he has said and to question him further.

Basic Head Positions

There are three basic head positions. The first is the head up position and is taken by someone who has a neutral attitude about what he is hearing. The head remains still and may occasionally give small nods. Hand-to-cheek evaluation gestures are often used with this position.

When the head tilts to one side, it shows that interest has developed. Charles Darwin was the first to note that humans, as well as animals, tilt their heads to one side when they become interested in something. If you are giving a sales presentation or delivering a speech, always make a point of looking for this gesture in your audience. When you notice them tilt their heads and lean forward using hand-to-chin evaluation gestures, you are getting your point across. When someone is speaking to you, use the head-tilted position and head nods to make him understand that you are listening to him.

When the head is down, it signals that the attitude is negative and even judgmental or critical. Unless you can get the person's head up or tilted, you may have a communication problem. Professional speakers and trainers usually do something that involves audience participation before they begin to address a group. This is intended to get the audience's heads up and to get their attention.

Both Hands Behind Head

This gesture is typical of a professional who is feeling confident, dominant or superior. It is as if he is saying, "I have all the answers," or "Everything's under control." It is a gesture used by the 'know-it-all' individual and most people find it irritating when someone does it to them. It is often used as a territorial sign to show that a person has staked a claim to a particular area.

There are several ways to handle this gesture, depending on the circumstances in which it occurs. If you want to discover the reason for the person's superior attitude, lean forward with palms up and say, "I can see that you know about this. Would you care to comment?" Then sit back, palms still visible, and wait for an answer. Another method is to force the person to change his position, which will in turn change his attitude. This can be accomplished by placing something just out of his reach and asking, "Have you seen this?" It forces the other person to release his hand clasp and lean forward. Copying the gesture is another good way to handle it.

On the other hand, if the person using the hands-behind-head gesture is reprimanding you, you will nonverbally intimidate him by copying his gesture. For example, two lawyers will use this gesture in each other's presence to show equality and agreement, but the mischievous schoolboy would infuriate the school principal if he used it in the principal's office.

The origin of this gesture is uncertain, but it is likely that the hands are used as an imaginary armchair in which the person lies back and relaxes.

Straddling a Chair

Centuries ago, men used shields to protect themselves from the spears and clubs of the enemy, and today, civilized man uses whatever he has at his disposal to symbolize this same protective behavior when he is under physical or verbal attack. This includes standing behind a gate, doorway, desk, the open door of his motor vehicle and straddling a chair. The back of the chair provides a shield to protect his body and transforms him into an aggressive, dominant warrior. Most chair straddlers slip into the straddle position unnoticed. They are discreet and overbearing individuals who will try to take control of other people or groups when they become bored with the conversation. The back of the chair serves as good protection from any 'attack' by other members of the group.

The easiest way to disarm the straddler is to stand or sit behind him, making him feel vulnerable to attack and forcing him to change his position, becoming less aggressive. With his back exposed, it makes him feel uncomfortable and unprotected.

How do you handle a one-to-one confrontation with a straddler on a swivel chair? It is pointless to try to reason with him, particularly when he is on a swiveling merry-go-round, so the best defense is a nonverbal attack. Conduct your conversation standing above and looking down upon him. Try moving within his personal territory. This invasion is very disconcerting to him and he may even fall backwards off his chair in an attempt to avoid being forced to change position.

If you have a straddler coming to visit you and his aggressive attitude annoys you, be sure to seat him on a fixed chair with arms to stop him from taking his favorite position.

Picking Imaginary Lint

When a person disapproves of the opinions or attitudes of others but feels inhibited in giving his point of view, he performs displacement nonverbal gestures. Picking imaginary pieces of lint from his own clothing is one such gesture. The lint-picker usually looks away from the other people or towards the floor while performing this minor, irrelevant action. He is signaling disapproval. When the listener continually picks imaginary pieces of lint off his clothing it is a good indication that he does not like what is being said, even though he may be verbally agreeing with everything.

Open your palms and say, "Well, what do you think?" or, "I can see that you have some thoughts on this. Would you mind telling me what they are?" Sit back, arms apart, palms visible and wait for an answer. If the person says he is in agreement with you but continues to pick the imaginary lint, you may need to take an even more direct approach to discover his hidden objection.

Aggressive and Readiness Gestures

The most common gesture used by man to communicate an uncompromising attitude is the hands-on-hips pose. It is a readiness gesture that carries with it an aggressive meaning. It is called the achiever stance, describing the goal-directed individual who uses this position when he is ready to tackle his objectives. People use this gesture to show an argumentative, dominant attitude and to let others know that they're ready for action.

Birds fluff their feathers to make themselves appear bigger when they are fighting or courting; humans use the hands-on-hips gesture for the same purpose, that is, to make themselves appear larger and more threatening. Males will commonly use it as a nonverbal challenge to other males who enter their territory.

It is important to consider the circumstances and gestures immediately preceding the hands-on-hips pose to make a correct assessment of the person's attitude. Several other gestures can further support your conclusions. For example, is the coat open and pushed back on to the hips, or is it buttoned when this aggressive pose is taken? Closed-coat readiness shows aggressive frustration, whereas, when the coat is open and pushed back, it is a directly aggressive pose. The person is openly exposing his heart and throat in a nonverbal display of fearlessness. This position is further reinforced when the individual places his feet evenly apart on the ground or clenches his fists. Women use the aggressive-readiness hands-on-hips cluster gestures to display critical evaluation and an impatient attitude.

Seated Readiness

One of the most valuable gestures that a negotiator can learn to recognize is seated readiness, that is, when the buyer leans casually forward. In the selling situation, if the potential buyer were to take this gesture at the end of the sales presentation and the meeting had progressed successfully up to that point, the salesperson could ask for the order and expect to get it. Video replays of insurance salespeople interviewing potential buyers revealed that, whenever the seated-readiness gesture followed the chin-stroking gesture, the client bought the policy. In contrast to this, if, during the close of the sale, the client took the arms-crossed position immediately following the chin-stroking gesture, the sale was usually unsuccessful. Unfortunately, most sales courses teach salespeople always to ask for the order with little regard for the client's body position and gestures. Learning to recognize such gestures as openness and readiness not only helps make more sales but helps to keep many more people in the selling profession.

The Starter's Position

When a person leans forward in his chair and places both of his hands on both of his knees, or leans forward with both hands gripping his chair, he is signaling a desire to end a conversation or encounter. Should either of these occur in the middle of a conversation it would be wise for you to take the lead and terminate it. This allows you to maintain a psychological advantage in the negotiation and to keep the control.

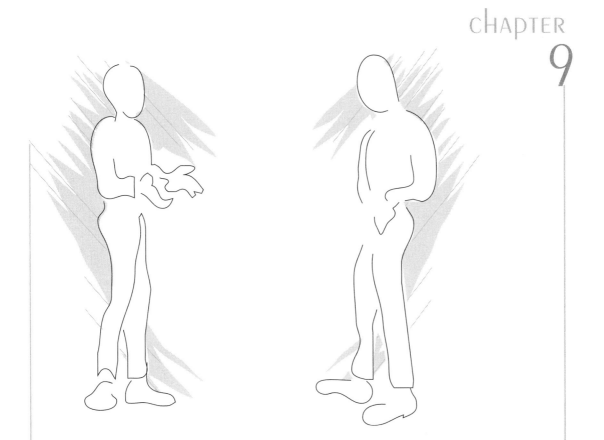

People Like People Who Are Like Themselves: Mirroring, Matching and Pointing

The next time you attend a social function or go to a place where people meet and interact, take note of the number of people who have adopted the identical gestures and posture of the person with whom they are talking. This 'mirroring' is a means by which one person tells the other that he is in agreement with his ideas and attitudes. In mirroring, you are nonverbally telling another person, "As you can see, I think the same as you, therefore I will copy your posture and gestures."

This copying of gestures occurs among people at the same status level or between good friends. It is common to see married couples walk, stand, sit and move in identical ways. Mirroring is one of the most important nonverbal lessons we can learn, for this is one way that others tell us that they agree with us or like us. It is also a way for us to tell others that we like them, by simply copying their gestures.

If an employer wishes to develop an immediate rapport and create a relaxed atmosphere with an employee, he need only copy the employee's posture to achieve this end. Similarly, an up-and-coming employee is often seen copying his boss's gestures in an attempt to show agreement. It is possible to influence a face-to-face encounter by copying the positive gestures and postures of the other person. It puts the other person in a receptive and relaxed frame of mind, as he can 'see' that you understand his point of view.

When meeting a 'cold' prospective customer, it is wise to deliberately copy the customer's positive movements until you feel that you have established a

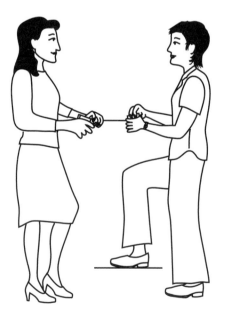

strong enough rapport to allow the presentation to proceed. Invariably, if the prospect begins to copy your gestures, a sale will typically result.

Research shows that when the leader of a group uses certain gestures and positions, subordinates copy them. Leaders tend to be the first of a group to walk through a doorway and typically prefer to sit on the end of a couch or bench rather than in the center of it. In the boardroom, the boss usually sits at the head of the table, often farthest from the door, and if he sits back in his chair and locks his hands behind his head, his subordinates will usually copy his position.

People who sell to married couples in their homes are well advised to watch the couple's gestures, to see who initiates the gestures and who follows.

For example, if the husband is doing all the talking and the wife sits there saying nothing, but you notice that the husband copies his wife's gestures, you will inevitably find that she makes the decisions and writes the check, so it is a good idea to direct your presentation to her.

Match Your Prospect's Language

You can get clues about the type of information your clients want to hear by listening to their own choice of words. Most people lean toward one of three major modes when communicating.

1. Visual-oriented language.
2. Auditory-oriented language.
3. Action-oriented language.

The clues they give you in their questions actually tell you how to phrase your statements and questions to get their attention.

VISUAL: Prospects who prefer visual information will use phrases such as, "That's *clear*," "I *see* what you mean," "Can you *show* that to me?" or "Can you *look* into that?" Charts, brochures and actually seeing the product will gain the interest of these clients. During your needs analysis and presentation, begin using phrases similar to the ones that your client uses. Also, make a mental note of the areas of your talk that you can stress to make the most of the client's visual preference.

AUDITORY: Customers who prefer auditory information use sound words such as "That *rings* a bell." "That doesn't *sound* quite right," "I don't think we're in *harmony* on this issue," or "They'll sure get a *bang* out of that." Anything that makes noise will interest this client—the pleasant click of a new machine, the soft chirping of modern telephone equipment, the quiet hum of a new computer. Also, these clients will be more attuned to your tone of voice, so concentrate on moderating your volume and using a good range of pitch. Make sure to include 'sound' words in your own vocabulary.

ACTION: Clients who desire action information use physical phrases such as "We'll have to *kick* that idea around," "I don't *grasp* what you are saying," "That doesn't *feel* right to me," or "We could use a *shot* in the arm." These are the people who love demonstrations where they can try out a product—they want to touch it, do it and hold onto it. Emphasize action words in your speech and zero in on anything in your presentation that moves.

Pointing

Have you ever had the feeling that someone to whom you are talking would rather be somewhere else than with you, even though he or she seems to be enjoying your company? A still photograph of that scene would probably reveal the following:

1. The person's head is turned *towards* you and facial signals such as smiling and nodding are evident.
2. The person's body and feet are pointing *away* from you, either towards another person or towards an exit.

The direction in which a person points his or her torso or feet is a signal of where he or she would prefer to be going.

During negotiations, when one person has decided to terminate the negotiation or wants to leave, he will turn his body or swing his feet to point towards the nearest exit. If you see these signals during a face-to-face encounter, you should do something to get the person involved and interested or else terminate the conversation on your terms, which allows you to maintain control in the situation.

Angles and Triangles: Open Formation

The angle at which people orient their bodies gives nonverbal clues to their attitudes and relationships with others. People in most English-speaking countries stand with their bodies oriented to form an angle of 90 degrees during ordinary social meetings. This serves as a nonverbal invitation for a third person to join in the conversation. The formation of the triangle invites a third

person of similar status to join the conversation. When a fourth person is accepted into the group, a square will be formed and for a fifth person, either a circle is formed or two triangles are formed.

Angles and Triangles: Closed Formation

When intimacy or privacy is required by two people, the angle formed by their torsos decreases from 90 degrees down to 0 degrees. A man wishing to attract a female partner uses this ploy, as well as other courtship gestures, when he makes his play for her. Not only does he point his body towards her, but he also closes the distance between them as he moves into her intimate zone. To accept his approach, she need only orient her torso angle to 0 degrees and allow him to enter her territory. The distance between two people standing in the closed formation is usually less than that of people standing in the open formation.

Inclusion and Exclusion Techniques

Both the open triangular position and the closed position are used to include or exclude another person from the conversation.

When a third person wishes to join two others who are standing in a closed formation, he may be invited to join the conversation only when the other two orient their torsos towards a mutual third point to form a triangle. If the third person is not accepted, the others will hold the closed formation position and turn only their heads towards him as a sign of recognition of the third person's presence, but the direction of their torsos shows that he is not invited to remain.

Sometimes a conversation among three people begins in the open triangular formation, but eventually two take the closed formation to exclude the third person and give a clear signal to the third person that he should leave the group to avoid embarrassment.

Interviewing Two People

Let's assume that you, person C, are going to interview or talk to persons A and B, and let us say that by either choice or circumstance you are sitting in a triangular position at a round table. Let us also assume that person A is very talkative and asks many questions and that person B remains silent throughout. When A asks you a question, how can you answer him and carry on a conversation without making B feel excluded? Use this simple but highly effective inclusion technique: when A asks a question, look at him as you begin to answer, then turn your head towards B, then back to A, then to B again until you make your final statement, looking at A (who asked the question) again as you finish your sentence. This technique lets B feel involved in the conversation and is particularly useful if you need to have B on your side.

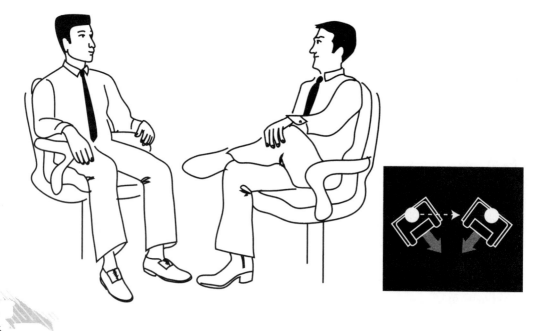

Foot Pointing

Not only does a person's feet serve as pointers, indicating the direction in which he would like to go, but they are also used to point at people whom he finds interesting or attractive. Imagine that you are at a social function and you notice a group of three men and one attractive woman congregated together. The conversation seems to be dominated by the men and the woman is just listening. Then you notice something interesting—the men all have one foot pointing towards the woman. With this simple nonverbal clue, the men are all telling the woman that they are interested in her. Subconsciously, the woman sees the foot gestures and is likely to remain with the group for as long as she is receiving this attention. She may eventually point one of her feet toward the man whom she finds the most appealing or intriguing.

Seated-Body Formations

If you are in a supervisory capacity and must counsel a subordinate whose work performance has been unsatisfactory and erratic, use the following body formations to nonverbally convey your message.

1. The fact that the counseling session is in your office and that you are the boss allows you to move from behind your desk to the employee's side (a cooperative position) and still maintain unspoken control.

2. The subordinate should be seated on a chair with fixed legs and no arms; one that forces him to use body gestures and postures, thus giving you a better understanding of his underlying attitude.
3. Sit on a swivel chair that has arms on it. This gives you more control and lets you eliminate or hides some of your own giveaway nervous gestures.

There are three main angle seated formations that can be used. Like the standing triangular position, the open triangular formation lends itself toward an informal, relaxed meeting and is a good position in which to open a counseling session. You can show nonverbal agreement with the subordinate from this position by copying his positive movements and gestures. As they do in the standing position, both torsos in the seated formation point to a third mutual point to form a triangle to show shared agreement.

By turning your chair to point your body directly at your subordinate, you are nonverbally telling him that you want direct answers to your questions. Combine this position with the business gaze and reduced body and facial gestures and your subject will feel tremendous nonverbal pressure. If, for example, after you have asked him a question, he rubs his eye and mouth and looks away when he answers, swing your chair to point directly at him and say, "Are you sure about that?" This simple movement exerts nonverbal pressure on him and can force him to tell the truth.

When you position your body at a right angle away from your subject, you take the pressure off the interview. It is an excellent position from which to

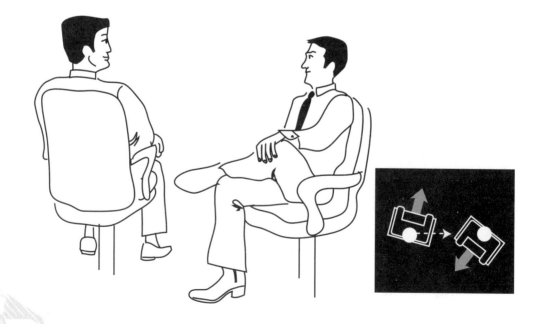

ask delicate or embarrassing questions, encouraging more answers without any pressure coming from you. If the person you are trying to crack is a difficult one, you may need to revert to the direct body point technique to get to the facts.

SUMMARY

If you want a person to have rapport with you, use the triangular position and, when you need to exert nonverbal pressure, use the direct body point. The right angle position allows the other person to think and act independently, without nonverbal pressure from you.

These techniques take much practice to master but they can become 'natural' movements before long. If you deal with others for a living, mastery of body point and swivel chair techniques are useful skills to acquire. In your day-to-day encounters with others, proper use of foot pointing, body pointing and positive gesture clusters such as open arms, visible palms, leaning forward, head tilting and smiling can make it easy for others not only to enjoy your company, but also to be influenced by your point of view.

Power Plays: Strategic Office Layout—Desks, Chairs, and Seating Arrangements

S trategic positioning in relation to other people is an effective way to obtain cooperation from them. Aspects of their attitude toward you can be revealed in the position they take in relation to you.

Although there is a general formula for interpretation of seating positions, the environment may have an effect on the position chosen. The following examples relate primarily for seating arrangements in an office environment with a standard rectangular desk.

Person B can take four basic seating positions in relation to person A.

B1: The corner position.
B2: The cooperative position.
B3: The competitive/defensive position.
B4: The independent position.

The Corner Position (B1)

People who are engaged in friendly, casual conversation normally use this position. The position allows for unlimited eye contact, the opportunity to use numerous gestures and to observe the gestures of the other person. Should one person begin to feel threatened, the corner of the desk can serve as a partial barrier. The corner position avoids a territorial division on the top of the table and is the most successful strategic position from which a salesperson can deliver a presentation to a new customer assuming A is the buyer.

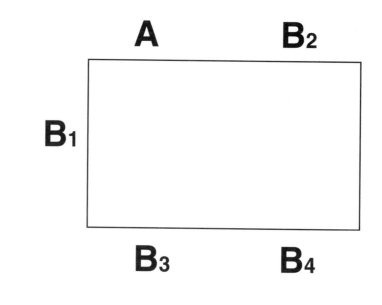

The Cooperative Position (B2)

This seating arrangement occurs when two people are mutually oriented, that is, they both think alike or are working on a task together. It is the most strategic position for presenting a case and having it accepted. The trick is, however, for B to be able to take this position without A feeling as though his territory has been invaded. It is also a highly successful position to take when B, the salesperson, introduces a third party into the negotiation. If a salesperson needed to have a second interview with a prospective client and had to introduce a technical expert to the client, the following strategy would be the most suitable.

The technical expert should sit at position B3 opposite customer A. The salesperson can sit either at position B2 (cooperative) or B1 (corner). This seating arrangement allows the salesperson to be 'on the client's side' and to question the technician on behalf of the client. It is known in business as 'siding with the opposition.'

The Competitive/Defensive Position (B3)

Sitting across the table from a person during a negotiation creates a defensive, competitive atmosphere and can lead to each party taking a firm stand on his own point of view. The table becomes a solid barrier between both parties and allows for a distinct division of ideas. This seating arrangement is taken by people who are either competing with each other or if one is reprimanding the other. It can also establish that a superior/subordinate role exists when it is used in A's office.

Research conducted in a doctor's office showed that the presence or absence of a desk had a significant effect on whether a patient was at ease or not. Only 10 percent of the patients were perceived to be at ease when the doctor's desk was present and the doctor sat behind it. This figure increased to 55 percent when the desk was absent and the doctor and patient sat side by side.

If B is seeking to persuade A, the competitive/defensive position reduces the chance of a successful negotiation unless B is deliberately sitting opposite as part of a pre-planned strategy. For example, if A is a manager who must severely reprimand employee B, the competitive position can strengthen the reprimand. On the other hand, if B needs to make A feel superior, B can deliberately sit directly opposite A.

If your business involves dealing with people, you are in the influencing business and your objective should always be to see the other person's point of view, to put him at ease and make him feel right about dealing with you. The competitive position does not lead towards this end. More cooperation will be gained from the corner and cooperative position than will ever be achieved from the competitive position. Conversations are shorter and more specific in this position than from any other.

Two people sitting directly opposite each other across a table unconsciously divide it into two equal territories. Each claims half as his own territory and will reject the other's encroaching upon it. Similarly, two people seated competitively at a restaurant table will mark their territorial boundaries with the salt, pepper, sugar bowl and napkins.

There will be occasions on which it may be difficult or inappropriate to take the corner position to present your case. Suppose you have a visual presentation; a book or sample to present to another person who is sitting behind a rectangular desk. First, place the article on the table. The other person will either lean forward and look at it, take it into his territory or push it back into your territory.

If he leans forward to look at it, you must deliver your presentation from where you sit as his action nonverbally tells you that he does not want you on his side of the desk. If he takes it into his territory, this gives you the opportunity to ask permission to enter his territory and take either the corner or cooperative position. If, however, he pushes it back, you're in trouble! The golden rule is never to encroach on the other person's territory unless you have been given verbal or nonverbal permission to do so.

The Independent Position (B4)

This is the position taken by people when they do not wish to interact with each other; it occurs in such places as a library, cafeteria or restaurant. It signifies a lack of interest and can even be interpreted as hostile by the other person if the territorial boundaries are invaded. This position should be avoided where open discussion between A and B is required.

Square Table (Formal)

Square tables create a competitive or defensive relationship between people of equal status. Square tables are ideal for having short, to-the-point conversations or to create a superior/subordinate relationship. The most cooperation usually comes from the person seated beside you and the one on the right tends to be more cooperative than the one on the left. The most resistance, though, usually comes from the person seated directly opposite you.

Round Table (Informal)

King Arthur used the Round Table as an attempt to give each of his knights an equal amount of authority and status. A round table creates an atmosphere of relaxed informality and is ideal for promoting discussion among people who are of equal rank as each person can claim the same amount of table territory. Removing the table and sitting in a circle also promotes the same result. Unfortunately, King Arthur was unaware that if the status of one person is higher than the others in the group it alters the power and authority of each other individual. The king held the most power at the Round Table and this meant that the knights seated on either side of him were nonverbally granted the next highest amount of power, the one on his right having a little more power than the one on the left. The amount of power diminished relative to the distance that each knight was seated away from the king.

Consequently, the knight seated directly across the table from King Arthur was, in effect, in the competitive/defensive position and was likely to be the one who gave the most trouble. Many of today's business executives use both square and round tables. The square desk, which is usually the work desk, is used for business activity, brief conversations, reprimands and the like. The round table, sometimes a coffee table with wrap-around seating, is used to create an informal relaxed atmosphere or to persuade.

Rectangular Tables

In a meeting of people of equal status the person sitting at position A at a rectangular table has the most influence, assuming that he does not have his back to the door. If A's back is facing the door, the person seated at B would be the most influential and would be strong competition for A. Assuming that A is in the best power position, person B has the next most authority, then C, then D. This information makes it possible to structure power plays at meetings by placing name badges at the seats where you want each person to sit so that you may have the maximum influence over them.

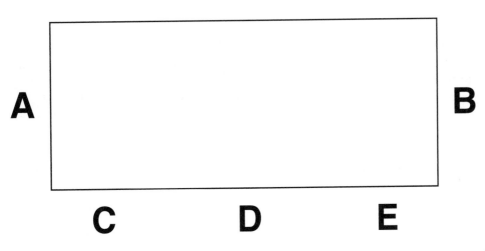

Getting a Decision over Dinner

Bearing in mind what has already been said about human territories and the use of square, rectangular and round tables, let us now look at the dynamics of taking a person to dinner where the objective is to obtain a favorable response to a proposition. To do this we must examine the factors that can build a positive atmosphere, discuss their potential and investigate the background of man's feeding behavior.

Anthropologists tell us that man's origin was that of a tree-dweller who was strictly vegetarian, his diet consisting of roots, leaves, berries, fruit and the like. About a million years ago, he came out of the trees onto the plains to become a hunter of prey. Prior to his becoming a land dweller, man's eating habits involved continual nibbling throughout the day. Each individual was entirely responsible for his own survival and for obtaining his own food. As a hunter, however, he needed the cooperation of other individuals to capture sizeable prey, so large cooperative hunting groups were formed. Each group would leave at sunrise to hunt throughout the day and return at dusk with the day's spoils. The food was then divided equally among the hunters, who would eat inside a communal cave.

At the entrance of the cave a fire was lit to ward off dangerous animals and to provide warmth. Each caveman sat with his back against the wall of the cave to avoid the possibility of being attacked from behind while he was engrossed in eating his meal. The only sounds that were heard were the gnashing and gnawing of teeth and the crackle of the fire. This ancient process of food sharing at dusk around an open fire was the beginning of a social event that modern man reenacts in the form of barbecues, cookouts and dinner parties. He also tends to react and behave in a similar fashion at these events the same way he did over a million years ago.

At a restaurant or dinner party, a positive decision in your favor is easier to obtain when your prospect is relaxed, free of tension and his defensive barriers have been lowered. To achieve this end, and keeping in mind what has already been said about our ancestors, a few simple rules need to be followed.

First, whether you are dining at your home or at a restaurant, have your prospect seated with his back to a solid wall or screen. Research shows that respiration, heart rate, brain wave frequencies and blood pressure rapidly increase when a person sits with his back to an open space, particularly where others are moving about. Tension is further increased if the person's back is towards an open door or a window at ground level. Many top restaurants have an open fireplace or facsimile near the entrance of the restaurant to recreate the fire that burned at the ancient cave feasts. It is best to use a round table and have your prospect's view of other people obscured by a screen or large green plant if you are to have a captive audience.

It is far easier to obtain a favorable decision under these circumstances than it will ever be in restaurants that have bright lighting, tables and chairs placed in open areas and the banging of plates, knives and forks. Fancy restaurants use these types of relaxation techniques to extract large amounts of money from their customers' wallets for ordinary food, and men use them when they need to create a romantic atmosphere to propose to women.

Power Plays with Chairs

The height of the back of a chair raises or lowers a person's status. The higher the back of the chair, the greater the power and status of the person sitting in it. Some kings, queens and popes have the back of their throne or official chair as high as 8 feet to show their status relative to their subjects. The senior executive usually sits in a high-backed leather chair while his visitor's chair has a low back.

Swivel chairs have more power and status than fixed chairs. They also allow the user freedom of movement when he is placed under pressure and can help hide some of his nervous gestures. Chairs with arm rests, chairs that lean back and chairs that have wheels are better than chairs that have none.

Chair Height

Status is gained if your chair is adjusted higher off the floor than that of your competitor. Some executives sit on high-backed chairs that are adjusted for maximum height while their visitors sit opposite, in the competitive position, on a sofa or chair that is so low that their eyes are level with the executive's desk. Another common power play is to place the visitor's low chair as far away as possible from the executive's desk into the social or public territory zone, to even further reduce his status.

Territorial and Ownership Gestures

People lean against other people or objects to show a territorial claim to that object or person. Leaning can also be used as a method of dominance or intimidation when the object that is being leaned on belongs to someone else. For example, if you are going to take a photograph of a friend and his new car or boat, you will inevitably find that he leans against his newly acquired property, putting his foot or hand on it. When he touches the property, it becomes an extension of his body and in this way he shows others that it belongs to him. Similarly, the business executive puts his feet up on his desk or desk drawers or leans against his office doorway to show his claim to his office and its furnishings.

However, an easy way to intimidate someone else is to lean against, sit upon or use his possessions without his permission. In addition to the obvious abuses of staking another person's territory or possessions such as sitting at his desk or borrowing his car without asking, there are other subtle pressure techniques. One is to lean against the doorway of another person's office or to inadvertently sit in his chair.

A salesperson calling on a customer at his home is well advised to ask him, "Which seat is yours?" before he sits down, as sitting in the wrong chair intimidates the customer and puts him off. Pressure techniques have a detrimental effect on the chance of a successful sale.

Some people are habitual doorway leaners and go through life intimidating most people from the first introduction. They are well advised to practice an erect stance with palms visible to make a favorable impression on others. People form 90 percent of their opinion about you in the first ninety seconds of meeting you, and remember, you never get a second chance to make a good first impression!

Ownership Gestures

A leg-over-chair gesture reflects an easy-going, relaxed and carefree attitude, but also signifies the man's ownership of that particular chair or space. It is common to see two close friends seated this way, laughing and joking with each other, but consider the impact and meaning of this gesture in different circumstances. Suppose an employee has a personal problem and goes into the boss's office to ask his advice on a possible solution. As the employee explains his problem, he leans forward in his chair, places his hands on his knees, puts his face down and looks dejected. The boss listens intently, sitting motionless, then suddenly leans back in his chair and puts one leg over the arm of his chair. In this circumstance the boss's attitude seems to immediately change to a lack of concern or indifference. In other words, he is showing little empathy for the employee or his problem and may even feel that his time is being wasted with the 'same old story.'

If the boss's chair has no arms (which is unlikely; this is usually the visitor's chair), his ownership gesture may be to put one or both of his feet on his desk. If his superior enters his office, it is unlikely that the boss would use such an obvious territorial/ownership gesture, but would resort to more subtle versions, perhaps putting his foot on the bottom drawer of his desk, or placing his foot hard against the leg of the desk to stake his claim to it.

These gestures can be quite annoying if they occur during negotiation. It is vital that the person change to a different position. The longer a person stays in the leg-over-chair or feet-on-desk position, the longer he will have an indifferent or hostile attitude. An easy way to break someone from this gesture is to hand him something that he cannot reach and ask him to lean across and look at it. Or, if you and he have a similar sense of humor, tell him he has a split in his trousers.

STRATEGIC OFFICE LAYOUT

Your office furniture should be arranged in such a way that you can have as much power, status or control over others as you wish. Just sitting behind a desk conveys a sense of power and positioning it so that all who enter must look across it to you suggests control. On the other hand, to create an accessible, open door image, situate your desk so that your back is to the door and that you must turn around to greet your visitors. This way there is nothing standing between the two of you. The texture of furniture can also set up status; a wooden desk gives off an entirely different impression than a metal desk does.

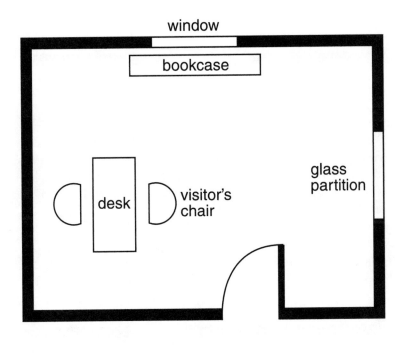

Certain objects strategically placed around the office can be used to increase the status and power of the occupant. Some examples include:

1. Low sofas for visitors to sit on.
2. A wall covered with photos, awards or qualifications that the occupant has received.
3. A slim briefcase. Those who do all the work carry large, bulky briefcases.
4. An expensive ashtray placed out of the reach of the visitor causing him inconvenience when ashing his cigarette.
5. Some red folders placed on the desk marked 'Strictly Confidential.'

If a supervisor keeps an employee waiting a long time (more than 15 minutes), devotes only a short time to the meeting when a longer conference is appropriate and meets only occasionally with the employee, then the supervisor is communicating a negative, disrespectful attitude toward that employee.

During a sales call, massive desks not only provide the client with a physical barrier, they serve as a visual barrier as well. If you can't see him from the chest down, how do you know if the buyer's legs are crossed, if he's tapping his foot or cleaning his nails.

It is best, therefore, to choose a chair that is beside the buyer's desk rather than one across from it. In order to see you better, the buyer will turn towards you forcing him to move away from his desk and thus expose all of his non-verbal communication channels to you.

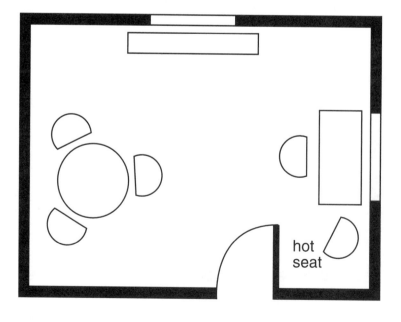

Personal Selling Power:
Basis for a Successful Close

Preparing for a sales call is not limited to thinking about the coming meeting while you're waiting in the client's office. Just as you can practice your presentation well before the call, you need to consider the type of visual impression you will make on your client as well.

A client needs to decide, in a short amount of time, whether you are reliable, truthful and professional. Even before you verbally greet the client, you should analyze your clothing, your posture and your neatness, because they all indicate to others how you feel about your job. Here are a few tips for creating a positive first impression that can make what you say—with your words, your tone of voice and your body language—much more effective.

1. Dress conservatively: Each area of sales has a uniform, from Wall Street pin stripe to Record Store Khakis and sports coat. Outlandish fashions may catch the client's attention, but they'll leave a *negative* impression.
2. Colors create an image: Solid suits of gray, beige and navy blue for men, and two-piece dresses with jackets or a suit in similar colors for women are basics. Avoid aggressive colors like orange or turquoise, and any color that doesn't suit your hair, eye and skin color.
3. Neatness counts: Attention to the details of your clothing, such as a well-pressed shirt and polished shoes, tell the customer that you're conscientious. A disheveled appearance gives the impression of disorganization and carelessness.
4. Quality is the key: No matter what the price of your suit or dress, get a good tailoring job. Watch accessories; ties, jewelry and attaché cases that are tacky can ruin your overall image.
5. Stand tall: Good posture and a confident stride indicate that you are happy and capable. Slouching or a shuffling gait can convey an 'I don't care about what I'm doing' attitude, and will make a well-tailored outfit hang poorly.

When you realize that the deciding factor for a sale could rest on your client's visual impression of you, doesn't it make sense to project the very best image possible?

USE AN EFFECTIVE WAITING POSTURE

Before you see your client, you will probably have to wait in a lobby, a reception room or an assistant's office. Take care to monitor your nonverbal behavior while you're deep in thought because office insiders are sure to notice you while you're in their territory. An efficient, observant secretary will be aware of your waiting posture and make a mental note of it—either positive or negative.

Sit in a comfortable, encouraging and composed posture. Then take a quick five-channel scan of yourself. Make sure that you aren't reinforcing your feelings of tension by using negative body language. Then:

1. Relax.
2. Use creative imagery, think positive thoughts.
3. Check over your appearance.
4. Resist visualizing your client as 'just like you.' Be prepared to bridge the differences between you and your potential customer.
5. Remind yourself that maximum flexibility will translate into maximum potential.
6. SMILE!

Your Basic Listening Posture

You are more likely to use a good listening posture if you have one ready to put into action. Showing your client that you are paying attention while he is answering your questions is very important. It encourages him to continue talking, thus giving you additional information. Keep in mind the following gestures that help to convey your interest and use the ones that you feel most comfortable with.

1. Tilt your head slightly.
2. Nod as major points are mentioned or in rhythm with the client's speech pattern.
3. Lean a bit back in your chair with your head raised slightly—make sure to keep your arms and hands open and move them in a positive manner as you stress your points.
4. Maintain good eye contact; a slight squint shows that you are considering what is being said.
5. Avoid self-touching gestures—although clients may use chin rubbing, lip pulling and cheek tapping when they are evaluating your statements, these gestures can also express uncertainty.
6. Prevent yourself from frowning.
7. Take notes—unless you have an excellent memory for details, you should jot down the client's needs, motivations and concerns.

Closing

Closing requires confidence and the conviction that your product or service is worth more than the price you're asking the prospect to pay. Top salespeople consistently show two behavior characteristics that get them the sale: the capacity to be friendly (empathy opens the sale) and the ability to be firm (ego drive closes the sale).

Although these attitudes may be present in every salesperson, they need to be applied in equal measure. Salespeople who are too friendly will get along fine with the customer, and will easily get a whole series of positive signals, but may lack the inner strength to ask for the order. Salespeople who are too firm, on the other hand, may bulldoze through a sale, annoy the prospect and cause unnecessary changes from positive to negative signals.

The ability to be friendly and to create positive signals is only a means to an end—the sale, the satisfied need, the happy customer and your satisfied ego. To turn positive signals into dollars, you need to balance this friendliness with firmness to close the sale.

1. Use a first trial close as soon as you notice several positive signals.
2. Never try to close when the customer signals uncertainty gestures.
3. Express 'buy from me' signals during the close.
4. Move closer to your customer by leaning forward, increase your eye contact with him and use head nods to seal the deal.

Visual, Auditory and Action Closes

By the time you have reached the closing phase of your sales call, you will know the type of language and information a client prefers to use and hear. If you have been matching your vocabulary to your customer's, a close stressing this preference will seem natural.

VISUAL CLOSES: These are the 'show and tell' type of closes. Using pen and paper, you demonstrate in black and white how your prospect will benefit from purchasing your product. When the customer signals that he is ready and after he has listened to several benefit statements, look at the client, pick up a pen and pad and say, "I'd like us to take a moment to review what we've discussed," then list the benefits that the new product would provide for his operation.

Another way to appeal to the visual buyer involves a written summary of the pros and cons of his buying decision. Draw a solid vertical line to divide a paper into two parts and say, "Here on the left side, we'll list the benefits that we've already discussed such as higher productivity (look at the customer, nod your head), lower downtime (look at the customer and smile), and the fact that you'll save approximately 14 percent on operating costs (make eye contact, then pause). Which one of these benefits would be the most important one for you?"

AUDITORY CLOSES: Prospects who prefer an auditory vocabulary and information are most likely to buy from you when your close involves decision-making statements or asking questions to which the only reasonable answer is 'Yes.' Examples are: "Do you like the quality of this storage building?" "Do you like the colors you selected earlier?"

This repeated 'Yes' mode has a powerful psychological impact on the auditory customer. Each additional 'Yes' increases his subconscious desire to repeat the positive internal experience of the 'Yes' sound. Top sales producers know the benefit from this phenomenon and obtain several 'Yes' responses before they ask for the order.

The extra incentive close for the auditory buyer involves you making your offer sound irresistible by verbalizing it with excitement in your voice. Saying: "We have only two units left (right hand-to-chest gesture) and we're providing a special two-hour training course for your personnel with the purchase of this new system (smile)," with enthusiasm in your voice, perks his attention.

The alternate-choice close is another method of close that appeals to the auditory buyer. To lead your customer from a thinking mode to a decision mode, ask a question about the details of your proposal. Asking, "Does this lease plan sound good to you or would you like to hear about owning this equipment?" forces him to make a judgment decision.

ACTION CLOSES: Action-oriented prospects show a number of 'I am ready to buy' signals early in the sales presentation. Signals such as:

- Nodding their head up and down.
- Making physical contact with you (i.e., placing a hand on your shoulder).
- Rubbing their hands together.
- Grabbing a pen for writing.
- Walking around your product, stroking parts of it (feeling the paint, adjusting the seat, opening the trunk, etc.).

Action-oriented buyers love to give you a hand; therefore, ask them to do things to help you with the demonstration. Since they like motion, prospects who use action-oriented language respond well to your leadership. If you've made a product presentation outside and realize that the prospect is still undecided, you could say: "Mrs. Phillips, let's take a moment and walk over to the office (start moving, continue talking as you walk)." "I'd like you to take a look at two large photographs of similar designs which I think will really suit your specific needs."

Sometimes your customer may be ready for the purchase, but needs a gentle push to make the decision. You, on the other hand, know that too much assertiveness may be counterproductive.

When this happens, begin packing up your sales literature, order forms and samples, leading the customer to believe that you are on your way out the door. Soon you'll see your prospect's defenses being lowered. As you notice these signals, turn to the customer and refocus on the dominant buying motive. Save a good product feature, a special finance offer, an extra incentive or a new creative solution to the client's problem for the pack-up-and-leave close. Your moving closer to the customer's door lowers his resistance to a successful comeback and final close.

Basics for a Successful Close

When you have used 100 percent of your communication abilities during a sales call, your close should follow automatically. Getting to the close means that you have managed your own and your client's body language effectively. To conclude your meeting successfully you should:

- Avoid beginning a close unless you have positive buying signals from your client.
- Continue to use your own open, encouraging signals and maintain good eye contact.
- Select a close that suits your client based on his preference for visual, auditory or action words and information.
- Immediately redirect your approach if the client signals doubt during your close—ask open questions, restate benefits and continue to respond with positive, supportive signals.
- Smile and thank the client for the order.
- Reassure the buyer that the order is only the beginning of a long-term relationship.
- Schedule a follow-up call to check on how his purchase has improved his business operation or personal situation.

The Rules of Nonverbal Selling Power
FIRST MEETINGS

Rule 1: Manage every second of a first meeting. Do not delude yourself that a bad impression can be easily corrected. Putting things right is a lot harder than getting them right the first time.

Rule 2: Always initiate the eyebrow flash (shows friendliness, approval or agreement) whenever possible. Be certain to respond to another's eyebrow flash unless your calculated intention is to signal hostility.

Rule 3: Break eye contact downward, unless it is your deliberate intention to convey a lack of interest in the other person or to throw them temporarily off balance by a disconcerting upward eye break.

Rule 4:   Never hold a gaze for more than three seconds when first meeting someone. Look, then break eye contact briefly. Even though the person receiving the message is unable to explain the reason for his feelings, any violation of this rule can generate a negative impression. The only exception to this rule is during a power play when it is your deliberate intention to distress your opponent.

Rule 5:   Use the smile most suitable to the situation. Smiling inappropriately can create as negative an impression as not smiling at all.

USING SPACE—WHILE STANDING

Rule 6:   Never invade another person's intimate zone unintentionally. If you do so deliberately, as a power-play strategy, be aware that you will provoke a powerful increase in arousal.

Rule 7:   Be certain that you are working at the correct spatial distance to achieve the results you require. Take into account individual and cultural differences, as well as the nature of the relationship. Learn to work at a variety of distances without feeling alienated or uneasy. The more flexible you can be in manipulating another person's various zones, the greater control you will be able to exert over the encounter.

Rule 8:   Never stand directly opposite an unknown male or adjacent to an unfamiliar female. With a man, start at a more side-on position and gradually work your way around to a more frontal one. With a woman, adopt the opposite approach by starting the encounter in a frontal position and then moving slowly to a more adjacent one.

Rule 9:   Never stand when someone else is sitting, unless it is your intention to dominate or intimidate the other person. Height is a powerful authority signal.

Rule 10: Avoid, if possible, deep arm chairs that compel you to sit far back. Sitting in this type of chair limits your ability to send out a number of important posture signals.

Rule 11: When chairs can be moved, the rules for personal distance apply. You can get away with sitting closer to another person than you could if standing, because the chair increases your sense of security and its arms provide a physical barrier between you and the other person.

WHILE SHAKING HANDS

Rule 12: Keep your hands dry and apply a moderate amount of pressure when shaking hands. Limit the handshake to three pumps and hold the handshake for approximately six seconds—under most circumstances.

Rule 13: To communicate dominance, use the palm-down handshake. To convey friendship and a desire for cooperation, use the vertical handshake. To convey submission, employ the palm-up handshake.

Rule 14: To avoid looking dishonest, stay away from wearing tinted, dark or reflecting glasses.

Rule 15: To increase the warmth and impact of your presence when first meeting someone, use a head tilt, direct eye contact until you remember their eye color and a warm smile. Use the same gesture whenever you are asking for help or cooperation.

Rule 16: When speaking to a group, ensure that your gaze includes them all. Avoid reading from a script; either memorize what you wish to say or use brief notes.

POWER PLAYS

Rule 17: A successful power play depends on your ability to control the other person's time and space.

Rule 18: Walk slowly, walk deliberately and walk tall. Take the time to review your surroundings. Adopt the manner of a proprietor, not the cautious air of someone who doesn't really belong there. Imagine that you own the place and move accordingly. Never allow yourself to be hurried.

Rule 19: Whenever possible, choose where and how you sit. Select a chair that is easy to get in and out of. Avoid the trap of a deep and confining punishment chair.

Rule 20: Your ability to dominate others can be enhanced by a deliberate invasion of their personal space.

Rule 21: To dominate another person, first take control of his time. The longer you compel them to wait—up to a point—the greater the dominance you demonstrate. Use the fifteen-minute test. If he is still patiently waiting for the meeting after that time, you will have dominated him to the point where his perceived status is significantly undermined.

Rule 22: Stick to the fifteen-minute rule for being kept waiting. At the end of this period, unless there is an obviously valid and genuine reason for the delay, abort the meeting.

READING OTHERS

Rule 23: Detect anxiety in another person by looking at his feet and his hands rather than his face. Watch for his body language 'leakage' gestures, as his small subconscious, controlled movements relieve his inner tensions.

Rule 24: No matter what you are trying to sell, silent speech buying signs tell you if the other person wants to make a deal. Key signs to watch for are: a sudden release of tension (sigh), intensified eye contact, greater proximity and increased chin touching.

Rule 25: Liars betray themselves in several ways. Watch for increased self-touching that involves rubbing or stroking the ears, nose or eyes. Aggressive, forced movements of the feet, hands or mouth can detect deceptions involving hostility.

Conclusion

Sales success is a combination of three factors: knowledge, skills and motivation. To translate knowledge into action skills, you need to practice, make mistakes, learn from them and grow. New action skills will increase your confidence tremendously and boost your motivation to an all-time high.

Study each picture sequence that follows and see what body language gestures you can interpret from what you have read in this book. You will be amazed to find how much your perceptiveness has improved.

1. Can you spot the liar?
2. Which man is holding back his opinion?
3. Which of the three shows the most disapproval and disinterest?
4. Who is the most defensive of the three? What gestures show this?
5. What lack-of-concern gesture do you see in this picture?

1. What four open and honest gestures can you identify from the man on the left?
2. What two defensive gestures are being used by the woman?
3. Can you spot the confident or superior gesture in the picture?
4. Who is using the critical evaluation gesture?
5. Who is the most argumentative and why?

If you haven't started your program of nonverbal selling power yet, here are some pointers to use as a guideline for improving your sales techniques.

- Watch what people do with their bodies every day for a week. You may want to use the five nonverbal communication channels as a starter—concentrate on Body Angle on Monday, Faces on Tuesday, Arms on Wednesday, Hands on Thursday and Leg Postures on Friday.
- Improve your nonverbal observation skills by watching TV interviews with the sound off. Note the guest's initial seating position (usually legs crossed away from the host), and the hand gestures (the confident guest uses frequent, open gestures). Also note the 'mirroring' effect when both people are on the same wavelength (positive or negative).
- Imitate gestures you've seen in a client's office, after the call, in order to 'feel and understand' what your customer has expressed nonverbally.

- Work on your listening posture, your opening seating position and your ability to express positive signals no matter what objections you hear.
- Ask your colleagues to role-play in small groups with you. Form triads (3 people per group), one plays the role of the buyer, one plays the seller and the third acts as observer. Learn to apply new techniques in a safe, controlled situation before you use them on a real customer.
- Develop a 'nonverbal call report' diary to use after your sales call. Write down what type of nonverbal signals you used on calls where you got the order and what signals you used when you lost a sale. Your own observations may be a bit too self-critical, but soon you'll see a pattern of success in your approach. Follow it. Your goal is to identify the characteristics of your own best performance and repeat them often.
- Finally, learn how to use verbal and nonverbal selling power simultaneously. Start by persuasive eye contact as you translate product features into customer benefits. Apply one new skill each day. Practice, practice, practice.

You have been reacting to nonverbal communication signals and sending out your body language messages all your life. Responding to these signals in a positive manner, instead of reacting to them in a negative way, will provide you with an enormous competitive edge. You've just added 93 percent to your communication potential. Putting *Strictly Business Body Language* to work will turn that potential into profit.

The Psychosocial Aspects of

DEATH AND DYING

DATE DUE

New York   St.
Mad...   ;bon   London
                                    uan

Singapore   Sydney   Tokyo   Toronto

McGraw-Hill

*A Division of The **McGraw·Hill** Companies*

9 0   DOC/DOC   0 9 8 7 6 5

ISBN: 0-8385-8098-X

Notice

Medicine is an ever-changing science. As new research and clinical experience broaden our knowledge, changes in treatment and drug therapy are required. The authors and the publisher of this work have checked with sources believed to be reliable in their efforts to provide information that is complete and generally in accord with the standards accepted at the time of publication. However, in view of the possibility of human error or changes in medical sciences, neither the authors nor the publisher nor any other party who has been involved in the preparation or publication of this work warrants that the information contained herein is in every respect accurate or complete, and they disclaim all responsibility for any errors or omissions or for the results obtained from use of the information contained in this work. Readers are encouraged to confirm the information contained herein with other sources. For example and in particular, readers are advised to check the product information sheet included in the package of each drug they plan to administer to be certain that the information contained in this work is accurate and that changes have not been made in the recommended dose or in the contraindications for administration. This recommendation is of particular importance in connection with new or infrequently used drugs.

Library of Congress Cataloging-in-Publication Data

Canine, John, 1948–
   The psychological aspects of death and dying / John Canine.
     p.   cm.
   ISBN 0–8385–8098–X (pbk. : alk. paper)
   1. Death—Social aspects—United States.   2. Death—United States—
Psychological aspects.   3. Bereavement—United States.   4. Funeral
rites and ceremonies—United States.   5. Undertakers and
undertaking—United States.   I. Title.
HQ1073.C35   1996
306.88—dc20
                                  96–3168

Acquisitions Editor: Tracy S. Roth
Production Service: Editorial Services of New England
Designer: Mary Skudlarek

DEDICATION

This book is dedicated to all funeral directors who care
enough about people to make bereavement aftercare a part of
their overall funeral service.

CONTRIBUTORS

Shirley Brogan, MA, LPC
Counselor
Maximum Living Consultants, Inc.

John D. Canine, EdD, PhD
College of Pharmacy and Allied Health Professions
Department of Mortuary Science
Wayne State University
Detroit, Michigan

Samuel L. Canine, PhD
Chairman
Pastoral Department
Dallas Theological Seminary
Dallas, Texas

Polly K. Nielson, PhD
President
Aerodometics, Inc.
Consultant
Maximum Living Consultants, Inc.

Cindy Skalsky, MA
Consultant
Maximum Living Consultants, Inc.

CONTENTS

FOREWORD

Psychosocial Aspects of Death and Dying, which has been three years in the making, is a unique text. Written specifically for university-level students studying funeral service, it presents in one volume materials from a variety of sources. Dr. John Canine has successfully compiled this material into a logical sequence to enable the reader to better understand death from its psychological and sociological perspectives and, with this knowledge, to become better prepared to confront the issues in his or her own life. This text presents the funeral service practitioner with a compact brief on these issues, and as a result offers a ready reference tool.

Dr. John Canine teaches at Wayne State University of Detroit, Michigan, and operates his own clinical counseling facility, Maximum Living Consultants, Inc. When meeting Dr. Canine, one is struck by the fact that he is an extraordinary listener who exudes an empathy that inspires immediate confidence. He also has the professional and academic background necessary to write such a text. With two master's degrees and two doctorate degrees in related fields, Dr. Canine has published and lectured on grief for many years, in addition to conducting his own clinical practice. In discussing his plans for this book, Dr. Canine expressed concern that nowhere in funeral service literature was there a single volume that could serve as a fundamental text on the psychological impact of death. It was his contention that such a book would be a valuable asset to instructors in funeral service education, as well as to their students. Dr. Canine's initial motivation for authoring this text was to provide a better teaching device for use specifically with funeral service students, and he has accomplished his goal well.

The American Board of Funeral Service Education (ABFSE) was approached by Dr. Canine, through the director of the Mortuary Science Department at Wayne State University, Dr. Mary Lou Williams, herself a distinguished anatomist and funeral service instructor. The ABFSE invited Dr. Canine to submit a précis of his ideas, which was reviewed by the ABFSE's Curriculum Committee. The committee found the advance material and ideas to be of significant potential value to funeral service education and, as a result, endorsed the book for future use. Appleton & Lange, the publisher of the ABFSE's first text, *Embalming: History, Theory and Practice,* by Robert Mayer, undertook an editorial review of the advance material and, after submitting sample chapters to several experts for review, offered to bring the book to fruition. With a publishing contract in hand, the ABFSE began to identify additional funding that would be needed beyond its own resources and applied to the National Funeral Directors Association (NFDA) for a publication grant. The NFDA has served as a valuable resource to the ABFSE for many years and has provided financial assistance for other special projects, including the *Embalming* text, when the final result was perceived to be of significant benefit to the funeral service profession. Without its support, this book might never have become a reality.

Today's student preparing for a career in funeral service is immersed in courses in three broad areas: the traditional technical focus, including embalming, restorative art and related sciences; a business management focus to begin preparation for ownership and management; and a social science focus in which grief psychology and bereavement counseling form a major component. This book will provide one of the basic foundations for this academic area.

Psychosocial Aspects of Death and Dying is the second in a series of text–reference books to be endorsed by the American Board of Funeral Service Education, and we are pleased to offer it to the student and practitioner in funeral service.

Gordon Bigelow, PhD
Executive Director
American Board of Funeral Service Education
Brunswick, Maine
August 1995

ACKNOWLEDGMENTS

I gratefully acknowledge the many individuals who assisted me in the writing of this book. A project of this magnitude demands help, and I had some wonderful people come to my assistance. First of all, before the book was written Dr. Mary Lou Williams, Dr. Gordon Bigelow, Ms. Laurie Burda-Mastrogianis, and Ms. Therese McNeil all contributed ideas to the author.

In Section I, Ms. Therese McNeil spent an enormous amount of time researching Chapters 2, 5, and 6.

In Section II, Dr. Polly Nielson assisted with Chapters 8 and 9. Ms. Jeri Williams did the research and some editing on Chapter 10. And, of course, I never could have written Chapters 14, 16, and 17 without the literature searches that Ms. Tana Zimmer and Mr. Daniel J. Canine (my son) did at Michigan State University library.

Most of Section III was written by contributing authors. I am grateful that my colleagues took an interest in this section. Thank you to Ms. Cindy Skalsky for Chapter 18, to my brother Dr. Samuel Canine for Chapter 19, to Dr. Polly Nielson for Chapters 20 and 21, and to Ms. Shirley Brogan for her excellent Chapter 15.

A big thank you goes to Ms. Susan Anderson and Cindy Skalsky for their tireless editing and rewriting of my original manuscript and to Bryan Durren for his artwork.

Last but not least, to all my friends at Marina Pointe (Pulte Homes, Inc.) who got my house up quickly so I would have a place to write. The view of the lake was fantastic—thanks to Howard, Jeff, Wendy, and Dennis.

The Psychosocial Aspects of

DEATH
AND
DYING

Section I

THE PSYCHOLOGY OF DEATH AND DYING

1

DEATH: AWARENESS AND ANXIETY

John D. Canine

Despite death's universal claim on each of us, the discussion of death is frequently uncomfortable and even distressing to many Americans. Our culture is uniquely anxious on this subject, demonstrating degrees of denial and avoidance that other societies, which regard death as a "natural part of life," might very well find amusing, not to mention futile. It is important for death care professionals to increase their own personal death awareness and to grasp the issues and concerns that underlie our society's attitudes and behaviors around death and dying. The quality of care, reassurance, and comfort they are able to offer will be greatly influenced by their own beliefs and personal ease with death.

This chapter offers a brief historical perspective on death in America and goes on to describe the current social, scientific, and cultural forces that contribute to death awareness and anxiety. It concludes with a review of death anxiety measurement instruments and some ideas for caregivers that might enable them to normalize or reduce excessive fear of death among the populations they serve.

DEATH: BRINGING IT OUT OF THE SHADOWS

Americans have lost their intimacy with death. For a variety of reasons that will be discussed later in this chapter, death has been removed from the common American experience. In our future-oriented society, with its high value on individual achievement, death is almost unthinkable because it eliminates both of those possibilities. There is no life, liberty, or pursuit of happiness when one dies. It is the destruction of the American dream and, as such, is repudiated, shunned, and replaced with silence, hostility, and fear.

This was not always the case. What might it have been like to experience dying and death 150 years ago in rural America? First, when someone was dying, everyone in the community knew it. A dying person was not in a hospital but was nursed and remained in the home. He or she was attended by family members, and visitors—including children—were welcomed. Family and friends were expected to speak "last words" to the individual and frequently witnessed the cessation of breathing, relaxation of the body, and loss of skin color.

With the assistance of the local "undertaker," the family would prepare the corpse for last rites and burial. On the day of the funeral, all work would stop and virtually everyone would attend the service. The community would see the body, carry it to the grave, and bury it. While the balance of community life at that moment was upset, the funeral, by virtue of its participative nature, was the first step in establishing the new balance that would be created in the aftermath of that individual's removal from the community. Death awareness and intimacy were deeply woven into the social fabric.

Today the situation is quite different, and several significant factors have contributed to the propensity toward avoidance and denial of death. First is the secularization of American society. Almost all religions view death as a "door" to a better life. In the Christian religion Jesus said, "I go to prepare a place for you, that where I am there you may be also" (John 14:2, 3). Saint Paul said, "To be absent in the body, is to be present with the Lord" (1 Corinthians 5:8). Even with the portent of judgment, death is seen as a transcendent experience, offering the possibilities of atonement and salvation. In our modern world, however, many people are uncertain about (or even reject) the traditional values and rites that accompany this transcendent view.

This leads to the second factor that has diluted Americans' intimacy with death: the deritualization of grief (Rando 1984). Every society has developed accepted rituals and behaviors to follow the death of one of its members, such as the Jewish custom of sitting shivah. In America's fast-paced, pluralistic, and sometimes cynical society, grievers and those who would support them often feel "without guidelines"—at a loss for appropriate actions and words. This might be compounded by criticism and resentment of funeral practices as being overly expensive, exploitative of a family's grief, or possibly even irrelevant.

Further undercutting our intimacy with death is the growth of impersonal technology around dying people. As our high-tech society increasingly promotes computer diagnosis of disease, institutional treatment with technically researched chemicals, and updated pathology printouts, the sick or dying person becomes literally and figuratively "detached" from loved ones, removed from the home, and possibly connected only to machines. This phenomenon does not lend itself to the patient's and/or the family's need for personal care: it might become difficult for a relative to even hold the patient's hand or kiss a cheek, and it builds an even greater sense of mystery and fear around death.

Parenthetically, it is ironic that, while children's direct exposure to dying and death has dramatically decreased due to medical advances and institutionalized health care, there has been a simultaneous increase in our culture's unrealistic attention and focus on death. Cartoons (Figure 1–1), horror and "slasher" films, books, magazines, and even some "legitimate" news broadcasts use death as a titillation and a vehicle to shock audiences, thus reducing it to a commodity. Hence, death care professionals (e.g., physicians, clergy, therapists, funeral directors) must be prepared to be called upon to interpret or make death "real" to the people they serve. In order to be effective and successful in this aspect of their work, it is vital that such professionals come to terms with and work through their personal death anxieties.

Take a moment to think about your own intimacy with death. Answer the following questions yes or no:

1. Have you ever seen a body fully prepared for a funeral?
2. Have you ever seen a body that was not embalmed?
3. Have you been with a person when he or she died?
4. Have you been in a situation in which you thought you might die?
5. Is anyone in your family, or a close friend, dying now?

Figure 1–1. Cartoons sometimes focus on death for its shock value. (Bryan Durren)

Now take some additional time to answer the following questions from the Death Anxiety Scale (Templer 1970), which examine the thoughts and attitudes you hold around your own death:

1. How often do you think about the possibility of your own death?
2. Would you want to know the exact time of death?
3. Would you want to know the exact mode of death?
4. What do you fear about death?
5. Do you have a will?
6. Do you have life insurance?
7. Are you willing to have an autopsy?

8. Are you willing to donate your organs?
9. How do you want to have your body disposed?
10. What kind of rites do you desire?
11. Would you sign a living will?
12. List the three most significant losses you have experienced.
13. In which of these losses do you feel you have basically completed your grief and moved toward creative living in the absence of the individual?
14. When you were a child, did your family talk about death?
15. Briefly describe how you would like to die.

The ability to come to terms with the reality of one's own death, to address the personal issues associated with it, and to understand the roots of any fears and anxieties (and, if needed, "remake" them) is a required task for any death care professional or death educator who hopes to bring death "out of the shadows" and create a climate of support, respect, tolerance, and caring for bereaved individuals.

DEATH AWARENESS: ONE OUT OF ONE DIES

Intellectually, everyone knows the statistics. But emotionally, everyone plans on a single exception: themselves. Our society's lack of intimacy with death has led to widespread denial of death, which, although manifested in a variety of ways, can be grouped into three primary styles of denial.

One style of denial is to simply ignore death. People make plans, save money, daydream, and wax poetic about "someday," as if the future were a never-ending ocean of time and possibility. Some people have never attended, or flatly refuse to attend, a funeral, believing that if they are not around to witness or experience the reality of death, they will somehow be immune to it—or better yet, that death must not exist at all! (See Figure 1–2.) The life insurance industry is skilled in using verbiage that plays into people's conviction of their own immortality. The sting of death is quite different when the policy salesperson asks, "How would your family be taken care of if you had died yesterday?" as opposed to "How will your family be taken care of if you die tomorrow?"

A second style of denial involves efforts to lessen the harshness of death. This most commonly takes the form of euphemistic language to hide or couch the painful reality grievers are confronting. Friends or associates might make vague references to the loved one "going on to a better place," or might deny death with expressions such as "departed," "expire," "pass away," and "just passed." The funeral industry has surfaced with marketing efforts targeted at "pre-need memorial planning," or other such phrasing that avoids the words "die," "death," or "dead." Further, it has become an expected function of the funeral director to lessen the harshness of death through beautification of the corpse—perhaps even trying to create the illusion of life or, at least, sleep. Family and friends visit the funeral home hoping to be able to comment "truthfully" that the deceased looks

Figure 1–2. Sometimes death awareness is an afterthought. (Wolff, *The Family of Women,* p. 161)

"natural," "lifelike," or "at peace." Certainly this final, visual impression of a dead loved one is important, but it should never be used to escape or deny the reality of the death and the necessary grieving that must take place.

The third style of denial that will be discussed here is far more subtle, and indeed morbid, than the other two. It consists of a distorted preoccupation with death that, to some degree, mimics pornography in its danger of dehumanizing genuine human feelings and emotions. According to anthropologist Geoffrey Gorer, the word "pornographic" relates to that which is obscene or offensive to one's taste (Gorer 1967). It is usually employed in a sexual context, referring to writing, photography, or works of art that are created specifically to excite people sexually and promote fantasies allowing them to "control" situations around which they feel anxious or out of control. A necessary component of sexual pornography is the objectification of people, body parts, and sexual activity. Robert Neal, in his book *The Art of Dying,* states, "It is a way of fulfilling a sexual need without being involved with another person. It occurs when a society is prudish. When society says that sex is disgusting or immoral and not to be talked about, sexual need is not destroyed but only forced into inhuman paths" (Neal 1973).

The pornography of death follows a similar pattern. Our society has prudish notions about death, seeing it as offensive, an unfit topic for conversation, perhaps even immoral or disgusting. Therefore, it should not be surprising that many people seek to objectify and thereby "control" death by perverting and distorting it.

It is difficult to delineate the degrees of desensitization that take place as our society is exposed to the increasingly detached manner in which death is presented by the news media, the frequency with which fictional bad guys are "blown away" on television while the "good guy" flirts with death, the special-effects thrills of film and cartoon "superheroes" dispatching their opponents, and the rumored traffic in "snuff" films, in which real people are purportedly murdered for entertainment purposes. There can be no doubt that death is everywhere. The real issue is not finding appropriate means of denial but instead finding avenues and activities that allow us to be authentic about it—that shed light on our deepest and highest feelings around it.

A person who becomes morbidly preoccupied with death or indulges in bizarre fantasies involving death closes himself or herself off from the genuine emotions and opportunities for self-growth and self-discovery that a realistic, mature look at the subject can provide. Grief reactions might be stifled and grow complicated; healing might be prolonged and/or require professional intervention. Denial of death is rampant in American society, and any death professional should be alert to its various styles and manners of expression. In addition, he or she might wish to make a personal as well as a professional commitment to inject a calm, rational, authentic approach to any discussion of death or dying and the feelings that might be attached to it.

FEAR OF DEATH

Some readers might be familiar with the tale of the Baghdad merchant who sent his servant out to buy provisions. The servant came back pale with fear, saying, "Master, just now in the bazaar I was jostled by a man in the crowd. I turned about, and I saw Death. He stared at me and made a threatening gesture. Therefore, lend me your horse and I will ride to Samarra, where Death cannot find me." The good merchant lent the horse, and the servant mounted it and rode off as fast as the horse could gallop. The merchant himself then went down to the bazaar, and as he strolled around, he too saw Death standing in the throng. He approached him, asking, "Why did you make a threatening gesture to my servant when you saw him earlier this day?" Death replied: "That was not a threatening gesture—merely a start of surprise. You see, I was astonished to find your servant in Baghdad, for tonight I have an appointment with him in Samarra" (Neal 1973).

The fear of death has many real components and is shaped by an individual's age, intellect, health, family history, psychological state, and religious background. Even current events—such as recent mass murders, natural disasters resulting in death, or deaths of well-known, prominent people—can influence a person's degree of fear. There are, however, three primary categories of fear associated with death that should be examined, and that might stimulate a more personal and accepting awareness of death among readers.

FEAR OF THE PROCESS OF DYING

Because the timing and nature of one's death are unknown, human beings recognize that, unless they die suddenly, they run the risk of dying over some greater or lesser amount of time. They are able to project and imagine the conflict between "dying with dignity" and "fighting for life." This intrapsychic struggle creates tension and fear around the process of dying. More will be said about the various processes of dying in Chapter 4, but for now let's continue to look at specific fears connected with the process of dying.

Fear One: The Process of Dying as Painful

Historically, the Christian faith has taught that, in the "end," the forces of good and evil fight to claim the immortal soul, and such separation of the soul from the body involves pain. The more contemporary view is that disease disrupts the natural biological processes, and people fear the agonizing pain they know might accompany conditions such as cancer or emphysema. Even with available pain medications, the possibility or reality of severe pain is a contributing factor to the increased interest in physician-assisted suicide (see Chapter 7).

Fear Two: The Process of Dying as Undignified

It is possible that our high-tech, scientific mind-set toward health care treatment, coupled with our prudishness about death, has dehumanized the process of dying to such an extent that some people might be ashamed or even embarrassed to die. On the other hand, there are genuine dignity issues for many people who might not readily accept hospital gowns, tubes, catheters, needles, and machines, as well as the pushing, probing, and prying nurses, interns, residents, and physicians. Men and woman alike fear the "humiliation" of urinating in a bedpan, bedsores causing unpleasant odors, and the severe weight and/or hair loss that might accompany illness, terminal or otherwise.

Fear Three: The Process of Dying as a Burden to Others

Statistically, few people die by accidental means, and with medical science prolonging life or (depending on how you look at it) prolonging the process of dying, it is not unrealistic to fear becoming a burden to others. Dying gives rise to a wide range of emotions among family members. Depending on the nature of the relationship, a dying person might evoke feelings of sympathy, love, tenderness, pity, hate, disgust, or guilt among individuals in his or her immediate circle. Some of the feelings might be linked to the financial or time constraints that the dying person's illness places on others. This fear of being a burden to others is likely to be particularly acute in societies like ours that place a high value on independence and self-sufficiency.

Fear of the Loss of Life

Death is the loss of life as we know it and can trigger feelings of enormous vulnerability. Loss of life means loss of control—over self, perhaps others, and life experiences. Death seems passive, not active. It flies in the face of a participative, masterful, alternative-filled existence. Individuals might fear the power of death to which they must ultimately submit.

Another facet of fearing the loss of life is the sense of incompleteness or failure. Death has no respect for unmet goals or ambitions, or unfinished tasks. People with a well-developed sense of responsibility—or sense of adventure—might become depressed or angry at the prospect of no more opportunity, creativity, new experiences, or fulfillment of a life's dream.

Finally, death as loss of life is feared because it means separation from people, places, and things that are loved and treasured. This fear is often accompanied by feelings of sadness, grief, and worry over the future of survivors.

Fear of What Happens after Death

This final category of fear encompasses physical, moral, and mystical components. Death means the destruction of the body whether through decay, fire, or disassembly for educational or humanitarian purposes. Few people can be expected to find these prospects pleasant, or even imaginable. The "fate" of the body can be of extreme concern to individuals who have spent years of effort trying to preserve it through proper nutrition, exercise, and rest. The funeral industry responds to this fear with embalming, sturdy caskets, and graves lined with metal. While a funeral director might be of help to clients in visualizing the services and rites that will be performed, there remains difficulty in associating oneself with the concept of a corpse.

Another fear associated with what happens after death involves fear of judgment. Although this thought is traditionally linked to certain religious teachings, it also can surface among nonreligious people. Stated simply, people wonder if there is a God, and wonder what God thinks about them—whether God likes them. Like a child who is fearful of an angry father, some people are afraid that eventually they will confront a hostile, punishing God who will make them suffer for mistakes they have made on earth.

Ultimately, fear of what happens after death is largely related to fear of the unknown. How can people prepare for a "post-death" experience when no one knows for certain if there is such a thing? As in life, when there is no information, and no control, anxiety increases.

DEATH ANXIETY: LITERATURE AND MEASUREMENT

Caring professionals both inside and outside the field of thanatology, most notably psychologists, are taking both a theoretical and an empirical interest in the subject of death anxiety. The topic is covered in an increasing variety of scientific and

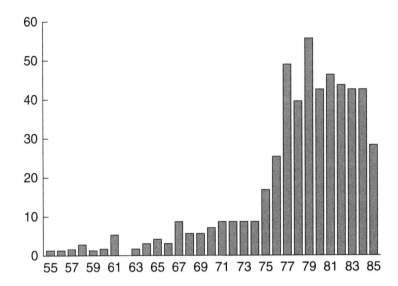

Figure 1–3. Number of articles published on death anxiety by year, 1955–85. (Wass, Felix, and Neimeyer 1988, p. 98)

professional journals, if not mass-market publications. To date, more than five hundred articles on death anxiety and closely related constructs have been published, providing the largest single body of material in the overall thanatological arena, and the field continues to attract new researchers (see Figure 1–3) (Wass, Berardo, and Neimeyer 1988). This diffusion of interested professionals, their various focuses of study, and wider publication outlets might bode well for a future that brings a better understanding of death and grief among a greater segment of the population.

Much of the literature is based on or makes reference to a small group of assessment instruments that have become widely accepted for their theoretical and empirical soundness. While many surveys and questionnaires about death anxiety have been developed, readers should be familiar with the four most well known measurement instruments.

The Death Anxiety Scale

Developed by Templer in 1970, the Death Anxiety Scale (DAS) involves fifteen short statements and questions to which participants respond. It is considered to have high reliability and has been used in more than 60 percent of studies published in the past ten years. Empirically, it is multidimensional and measures the following factors:

- General death anxiety
- Thoughts and talk of death

- Subjective proximity of death
- Fear of pain and suffering
- Fear of unknown

The DAS appeared earlier in this chapter as an exercise for readers.

The Threat Index

Developed by Krieger, Epting, and Leitner in 1974, the Threat Index (TI) is conducted in an interview format. Used in 23 percent of the studies published in the past ten years, it is considered to have a high degree of reliability while offering more "interpretability" than the DAS (Krieger, Epting, and Leitner 1974).

The Collett–Lester Fear of Death Scale

The Collett–Lester Fear of Death Scale (CL) assesses thirty-six items connected to four dimensions of death anxiety:

1. Death of self
2. Dying of self
3. Death of others
4. Dying of others

Although Collett and Lester developed the scale in 1969, it has been used in only 18 percent of the studies published in the past ten years, and its reliability is not considered to be especially high (Collett and Lester 1972).

The Hoelter Multidimensional Fear of Death Scale

Used in only 4 percent of the studies published since its development by Hoelter in 1977, the Hoelter Multidimensional Fear of Death Scale (MFODS) features eight independent subscales, each containing six items on which respondents indicate the extent of their agreement. No reliability tests have been performed (Hoelter 1979).

LESSENING THE FEAR OF DEATH

If death is to come out of the shadows and our culture is to become more educated, mature, and realistic in its attitudes and approach to dying, death, and grief, a great deal of the responsibility lies with death care professionals them-selves—their personal death awareness, their tolerance and acceptance of death anxiety, and their ability to communicate with informed concern and understanding. This chapter has attempted to be a starting point for that process. Death care professionals also might wish to review and consider the following six additional goals:

Goals for Death Care Professionals

1. Tactfully avoid euphemisms in speaking and writing so as to remove the "taboo" aspects of death language.
2. Promote and demonstrate comfortable and intelligent interaction (be socially and emotionally present!) with dying patients, who are living until they are dead.
3. Encourage death education for children so they can grow up with a minimum of death-related anxieties.
4. Perceive health care workers and other caregivers as professionals and human beings, neither omnipotent nor omniscient, but worthy of respect for their competency and connection to the dying person and his or her family.
5. Stay educated on changes and trends in the funeral industry.
6. Encourage, communicate, or participate in meaningful research in the field of death studies, grief, and bereavement.

SUMMARY

For a variety of reasons, Americans have lost their intimacy with death. Today several significant factors have contributed to the propensity toward avoidance and denial of death. First is the secularization of American society. The second factor is the deritualization of grief. Third, the growth of impersonal technology around dying people has further undercut our intimacy with death. As our high-tech society promotes computer diagnosis of disease, the sick or dying person becomes "detached" from loved ones, removed from the home and possibly connected only to machines. In addition, cartoons, films, books, magazines, and even news broadcasts have used death to titillate and shock audiences, thus reducing death to a commodity. The ability to come to terms with the reality of death, to address the personal issues associated with it, and to understand individuals' fears and anxieties is a required task for the death care professional.

The lack of intimacy with death has led to denial of death. Three styles of denial are (1) to simply ignore death, (2) to lessen the harshness of death, and (3) to distort death in such a way that it mimics pornography in dehumanizing genuine human feelings and emotions.

The fear of death is an issue in every culture. In America the fear of death has many real components and is shaped by an individual's age, intellect, health, family history, psychological state, and religious background. There are three categories of fear associated with death: the process of dying as painful, as undignified, and as a burden to others.

Death care professionals are taking a theoretical and empirical interest in the fear of death, or what is referred to as death anxiety. The topic is covered in an increasing variety of scientific and professional journals. Much of the literature is based on or makes reference to a small group of assessment instruments that have become widely accepted and are used for studies of death anxiety. The objective is to lessen the fear of death through close examination of anxiety issues. This chapter provides goals for death care professionals who want to make a contribution to bringing death out of the shadows in our culture.

REFERENCES

Collett, L. J., and D. Lester. 1972. The fear of death and the fear of dying. *Journal of Psychology* 72, 179–81.

Gorer, Geoffrey. 1967. The pornography of death. *Death, grief and mourning*. New York: Doubleday, 192–99.

Hoelter, J. W. 1979. Multidimensional treatment of fear of death. *Journal of Consulting and Clinical Psychology* 47, 996–99.

Krieger, S. R., F. R. Epting, and L. M. Leitner. 1974. Personal constructs, threat and attitudes toward death. *OMEGA* 5, 299–310.

Neal, Robert. 1973. *The art of dying*. New York: Harper and Row.

Rando, Therese. 1984. *Grief, dying, and death*. Champaign, Ill.: Research Press.

Templer, D. I. 1970. The construction and validation of a death anxiety scale. *Journal of General Psychology* 82, 165–77.

Wass, Hannelore, Felix Berardo, and Robert Neimeyer, eds., 1988. *Dying: Facing the facts.* 2d ed. New York: Hemisphere Publishing.

Wolff, Bernard Pierre. *The family of women*. West Germany.

2

CULTURAL ATTITUDES TOWARD DEATH

John D. Canine

Every human being on the planet eats. Every human sleeps, laughs, cries, bleeds, and, of those who wear pants, probably each puts them on one leg at a time. Death is another human experience that crosses all national, racial, religious, and ethnic boundaries. But within such social and cultural parameters lies a wide range of beliefs and behaviors, approaches and actions that different cultures bring to death rituals and to a family experiencing the loss of one of its members. In this chapter we briefly explore the dominant philosophical attitudes and ideas regarding death that give unique shape and character to a society's death and funeral customs. Then we examine the diversity, as well as effects of assimilation, among various significant groups within the United States as it affects their funeral traditions and influences current practices. The chapter concludes with information and examples for funeral professionals regarding education and outcomes when cultural differences are respected, accommodated, and embraced as a necessary part of the grief process.

PATTERNS OF RESPONSE TO DEATH

In general, a society's response to death is a function of how death fits into its teleological view of life, that is, the design or purpose of death, especially as it pertains to nature. Across all societies there seem to be three general patterns of response to death: death acceptance, death defiance, and death denial (Rando 1984).

Death Acceptance

A society that accepts death views death as a natural part of the life cycle. Shakespeare expressed a powerful death-accepting philosophy in *Henry V* when he wrote, "We owe God a death." Death-accepting societies are well represented throughout history, as illustrated by the story "Kisa Gotami" from Buddhist literature:

> Kisa Gotami lost her only infant, and she went in search of a remedy for her dead son. Carrying the corpse, she approached the Buddha and asked for a remedy.
> "Well, sister, can you bring some mustard seed?"
> "Certainly, Lord!"
> "But sister," said the Buddha, "it should be from a house where no one has died."
> Mustard seeds she found, but not a place where death had not visited. She understood the nature of life. (Narada 1973, p. 657)

In the present day there are cultures that not only naturally accept death but even celebrate it. In Mexico, *Dio de las Muerios,* or "Day of the Dead," is observed on November 2, the Catholic Church's traditional All Souls' Day. This is a time for celebration at the cemetery with friends and family. Food, song, and dance are shared at the graves of loved ones. Cakes are baked in the shape of skulls, and candies are passed out in the form of cadavers. During this Day of the Dead party atmosphere, death does everything the living do. There are displays of death dancing, death playing music, and cutout designs of death decorating the town. It is evident that life and death are celebrated together.

Death Defiance

In death-defying societies, the belief is that in death nothing need be lost—you *can* take it with you. A historical example of such a society was discovered in the 1960s on an archaeological dig near Moscow. Skeletons of two boys who died approximately twenty-three thousand years ago were found. Their elaborate grave suggested they were laid to rest amid solemn ritual, perhaps with a view of the afterlife. Both had been dressed from head to toe in clothing decorated with ivory beads carved from mammoth tusks, and both wore bracelets and rings of the same material. Both were further equipped with an assortment of ivory lances, spears, and daggers.

An example of a present-day death-defying culture is the Hmong, an ethnic minority found throughout southern China, Vietnam, Laos, Thailand, and Burma. One funeral ritual practice by the Hmong is reciting from the "TusQuabke," or guide for the deceased to the spirit world. If the proper verses are not recited, the person will not know he or she has died. The ritual is believed to help start the deceased's soul on its first major trip to the spirit world, and explains to the deceased how to make the trip.

Death Denial

The most profound example of a death-denying culture is found in the United States. This philosophy suggests that death is unnatural. American society's denial is exemplified by the following:

1. Through language—using terms such as "passed on" or "expired"
2. By the detachment of families from the funeral process—leaving all details to the funeral professional
3. By relegating family members to nursing homes or hospitals to die, removing them from familiar and comfortable surroundings
4. By avoiding conversation about the deceased for fear of loved ones' becoming upset

It would seem that Americans accept the notion that if they avoid talking about death, it will not happen. When a death actually occurs, the ability to successfully cope with that death can be difficult not only for the immediate family but also for the friends and other extended family members who want to help.

CULTURAL DIVERSITY AND FUNERAL PRACTICES IN THE UNITED STATES

In general, people who live in the United States deny death. But the maintenance of certain cultural influences can be a great source of comfort to family members. Table 2–1 shows a small sample of ethnic, cultural, and religious groups in the United States that provide traditions that can be beneficial to members in the grief process. It is important to be aware that within broad cultural groups there can be considerable differences. For example, in Table 2–1 the Asian category includes Chinese, Japanese, and Filipino, each of which has specific customs.

How does awareness of cultural differences help the funeral director?

TABLE 2–1. **SAMPLE OF ETHNIC, CULTURAL, AND RELIGIOUS GROUPS IN THE UNITED STATES**

Type of Group	Number of U.S. Groups (1,000s)
Total U.S. population	258,000
Religious preference:	
Jewish*	5,944
Christian**	136,407
Ancestry groups in U.S.:	
Native American	1,959
African-American	199,686
Asian	7,373
Hispanic	22,354

* Estimates of the Jewish community include those identified with Orthodox, Conservative, and Reformed synagogues.

** Estimates include Catholic, Protestant, Church of Latter-Day Saints, and Jehovah's Witnesses communities.

Source: U.S. Bureau of the Census, 1990 Current Population Reports.

Ultimately, sensitivity to cultural variances offers the funeral professional an opportunity to provide the best service possible. For example, in the Mexican-American culture, the emotional response to death is typically more open and demonstrative than in other groups. People stay longer at the graveside, walk about the cemetery, look at other graves, and reminisce. Funeral directors who are aware of these cultural nuances can anticipate and plan accordingly.

The following general overviews of four important cultural or religious groups in the United States provide an introduction to their traditions and rituals.

Jewish Religion and Culture

In the Jewish religion there are different denominational affiliations with certain constants among the mourning rituals, but each has its variants. There are two overriding values at the heart of the Jewish tradition in regard to death. One is *kavod hamet,* the requirement to "honor the dead"; the second is *nichum avelim,* the obligation to comfort the mourners. This concept speaks to the sanctity of the deceased, while simultaneously helping to bring comfort to those who are grieving.

The readying of the body for burial traditionally is done by a *cheura kadisha,* or holy society. This service was usually performed by laypeople but now has become more professionalized. After the preparation of the body, called *tahara,* the body is draped with a *tachrikin,* or simple linen garment.

Cremation is rare in the Jewish family. Most Jews rely on burial to conform to scripture: "From dust we came, to dust we return" (Genesis 3:19). Cremation also is associated with the Holocaust and therefore is repugnant to many Jews. Among traditional Jews there is a yearning to be buried in Israel. If this is not possible, earth or dirt from Israel is brought to be placed in the casket or mixed with the dirt that covers it. Also, there is the concept of "official mourner." The tradition designates seven relationships to be official mourners—father, mother, brother, sister, spouse, son, or daughter.

Usually the funeral service is held at a funeral home or synagogue, depending on local custom. The actual service begins with the cutting of a garment or black ribbon, symbolizing the individual being "cut away" from loved ones. Then there is the reading of Psalms, followed by the eulogy. After the eulogy, the family goes to the cemetery, where family members participate personally in placing earth (dirt) on the casket. As a final act, the family recites the homecoming prayer. The service begins the actual period of mourning, called shivah, Hebrew for seven. There is a break from the usual daily routine during this time. The shivah period (lasting seven days) enables the mourners to fully experience their grief. Families can share stories and memories of the deceased. The shivah ends when the family members say final prayers and go for a walk outdoors. This act signals the return to their responsibilities in this world.

Additional customs are observed after the burial. Family members might choose to change some regular activities to remind them that their lives were altered by a death. The time after the death is sometimes used for reflection and study as well. On the first anniversary of the death (*Yahrzeif*), the family gathers at the synagogue to remember the individual who died. It is a time to reflect on the life and gifts of their loved one. Also, it is customary to dedicate the headstone on this one-year anniversary. This is done with prayers and remarks about the deceased. As a final custom at the *Yahrzeif,* a donation is made in the name of the deceased to those in need.

African-American Culture

While it is impossible to make definitive statements about how blacks die and mourn because of the diversity that exists across such a wide and varied community, J. L. White, in *The Psychology of Blacks: An Afro-American Perspective,* writes:

> Death in the black community is perceived as a celebration of life, a testament to the fact that a life has been lived, that the earthly journey is completed. Those who serve as witness in the presence of death, extended family, friends and church members, all affirm the essence of the person's existence, are ready to testify to the fact that the deceased has fought the battle, borne the burden, and finished the course. They are ready to understand and say well done. (1984, p. 46)

No matter how particular customs have changed or evolved over time (either through the influence of other cultures or through increased urbanization), mourning customs among blacks are seen as a means of strengthening the community. A number of traditional customs continue to be part of African-American funerals:

- Church "sisters" come and prepare meals.
- "Flower girls," the female counterpart of pallbearers, give special attention to the closest family members.
- "Nurses," dressed in white, care for those who are overcome with emotion.
- Vocal music, such as solos and choir renditions, is a prominent part of the service.
- Flowers give visual comfort, a necessity for grievers.
- Church members say "their words" about the dead.
- Reception lines at the service are set up according to age, oldest to youngest.

These mourning practices exemplify some of the most organized efforts to aid mourners that funeral professionals are likely to encounter. These rituals provide direction not only to the immediate survivors but to the entire church community to which the deceased belonged.

Uniquely African-American art forms provide some distinctive expressions of grief. Music with "black" or gospel roots makes manifest the moods and essences of how grievers feel and how they express their feelings when faced with the death of a friend, a loved one, or a family member (Irish, Lindquist, and Nelson 1993). The musical customs of present-day African-American funeral rituals trace back to African origins, which are based on oral tradition. In his study connecting these traditions to the celebration of death in the black church, Craggett (1980) gave examples of dirges and laments, which are mournful musical compositions. The link between African-Americans and the continent of Africa remains strong and is reflected among the cultures of African people as well. Alassane Sow, a native of Senegal who spent ten years in the United States, observes that there is a striking similarity to the fact that, as in the United States, Senegalese funeral customs are a combination of tradition, acculturation, and urbanization with multiple influences from the Senegalese culture, other Islamic African nations, and Islam itself.

In Senegal, as in the United States, there is a "reinterpretation" of various customs to meet the changing needs of the population. For example, Islam dictates that there can be no weeping on cemetery grounds. Sow infers that women had never been allowed to go to the cemetery because they were more susceptible to crying. Today, more women attend cemetery services in Senegal because it has become more culturally acceptable for both men and women to cry.

Another similarity Sow identifies in both African culture and that of the United States is the celebration aspect. In Senegal, after the funeral service but before socializing between family and friends begins, a large pan of water is set out; it is used by those who attend the social to wash their hands as a spiritual symbol of detaching from the dead and giving life. It is said that those who do not wash wish to join the deceased. Clearly, there is an evolution of African-American funeral custom and ritual, but there remain distinct links of symbolism and attitude that assist in understanding or accepting death.

Native American Culture

Native American traditions are better defined by culture than by race. Identity focuses on the tribe or nation rather than on simply having Native American ancestry. For example, the Apache regard a dead person's body as an empty shell, while the Dakota speak to the body, visit it, and consider it sacred. The Navajo do not believe in an afterlife, while most other Native American tribes or nations do.

As expected, there have been varying degrees of influence by the dominant culture. The Dakota (Sioux) customs can serve as an example. This tribe, or nation, is the second largest in the United States and the largest in the upper Midwest. Among the Dakota, death is understood to be a natural counterpart of birth, and, because of this cyclic quality, both death and birth are sacred. The afterlife begins after death, when the soul journeys south until it comes to the Ghost Road. This road leads to *Wagagi McKoce*, the spirit land. This is the place where all dead go, whether human or animal. Spirituality focuses on how to live in the here and now, not on a reward in the afterlife.

When a Dakota person knows that death is near, he or she will gather valuables and goods and distribute them to significant family members and friends. This is done to acknowledge the impending death and to show appreciation to the recipients for their relationships to the tribe member. When the person dies, an extensive gathering of family and friends takes place, and it is not unusual to have up to a thousand people attending a funeral service. As each person greets the family mourners, the mourners' expression of grief is renewed in intensity. Cutting of hair, cutting or scratching the forearms and face, tearing clothing, and wearing black are considered common and appropriate displays of grief.

Mexican-American Culture

The Spanish translation of grief has at least two distinct meanings: *dolar*, meaning pain, and *pena*, meaning worry. Mexican-Americans see grief as both an emotional and a physical process. Females exemplify the emotional and males the physical symptoms of grief. *Muerie*, or death, is followed by *luto*, or mourning. *Luto* is practiced more rigidly by first-generation Mexican-Americans than by members of the second or third generation. The first-generation mourners adopt a restricted lifestyle that can last up to two years. The women wear black, rarely smile, and pray daily. During the initial stages of *luto*, the women tend to be very emotional.

The second and third generations of Mexican-Americans began the practice of using professional funeral services. Unlike for first-generation mourners, their mourning period typically is shorter, dress is not restricted, and television and radio can be enjoyed during mourning. Prayer remains important and is seen as a sign of respect and a demonstration of the ongoing grief. Also, the family unit is very important to all generations of Mexican-Americans. There is a strong bond between the nuclear family and the extended one, and death of a loved one is seen as an important time to reconnect with relatives who might not be around routinely.

Even with the increased use of professional funeral services, Mexican-Americans maintain certain customs that assist in maintaining a cultural identity. Following a traditional Catholic philosophy, novenas are said during the nine-day period following the death, and candles are lit in church for the deceased. The religious influence and family cohesiveness are cultural factors requiring respect by professionals servicing this particular group.

THE INDIVIDUALIZATION OF FUNERALS WITHIN A CULTURE

The understanding of death and life and the normal grief process might seem odd in other cultures when compared with one's own. To work effectively with the bereaved from different traditions, it is necessary to step outside one's own cultural beliefs. It would be difficult, as well as inappropriate, to pretend to fully *understand* an individual's unique cultural perspective. A more practical course is to *respect* the customs and rituals of those being served in order to meet their needs.

Texts and literature provide a good starting point to gain respect and insight into other cultural beliefs. However, even within a specific culture, ethnic differences and economic distinctions can be found, as well as particular individuals who do not have past personal experience with death and dying. Another source of understanding is the person or people you are trying to help. Active curiosity and genuine interest are the key. Asking someone for assistance in learning and posing sincere questions are powerful tools toward understanding an individual's needs, expectations, and expressions of grief when they differ vastly from the normal patterns in one's own belief system (see Chapter 11).

In their book *Helping the Bereaved*, Alicia Skinner Cook and Daniel Dworkin (1992, p. 167) present the following guidelines for servicing a culturally diverse population:

1. Recognize cultural influences in your own life and how they affect your work.
2. Acknowledge your own limitations when working with culturally diverse groups. Be creative and explore alternatives for overcoming these limitations.
3. Be open to learning about cultural traditions and beliefs. Identify strengths from the person's cultural background and use them as resources in the process of service.
4. Appreciate the history and experiences of different cultural groups in the United States (e.g., refugees or first-generation immigrants) and identify areas of greatest vulnerability and strength.
5. Accept the wide variation in experiences of grief and ways of coping with loss.

6. Recognize that loss is a universal experience, having a profound effect on our lives regardless of our differences in language, lifestyle, and patterns of relating.

David Black, of Elton Black & Son Funeral Home in Union Lake, Michigan, shares this successful story. A Native American family, with its roots in two Southwest tribes, came to the funeral home. The family's twenty-four-year-old daughter had been tragically killed in an automobile accident. Unfamiliar with the family's customs, Mr. Black's staff ably "tackled" the situation. The family clearly communicated what traditions, customs, and rituals were most important, and the Black Funeral Home was able to accommodate many of the requests. The daughter's best friend came to the funeral home to prepare the special braid for her hair. The body lay in state at the parents' home for two days, then was returned to the funeral home for the final service. Family members brought firepots to the funeral home but were respectful of fire codes and brought asbestos pads. Throughout the entire funeral process, there was ongoing communication between the funeral professionals and the family. The respect for customs by the funeral home and the sharing of information by the family created a meaningful funeral experience.

What insights did the Black Funeral Home gain from this experience? Perhaps many, but most important was an appreciation for cultural diversity. After the funeral services were completed, a thank-you note was received at the funeral home. The family stated that "nothing could have been done better." It was a testament to this firm's sincere desire to be respectful and the family's ability to communicate its needs.

SUMMARY

While death and dying are universal, natural, and predictable, experience shows that the expression of grief is far from uniform around the world or even within a given culture. Although our society continues to diversify, it is still possible to distinguish groups by shared cultural traits. Even distinctive groups, however, have assimilated to varying degrees into the mainstream group's patterns. For example, as our country has evolved, funerals or wakes have moved from being held in private homes to the now-dominant practice of utilizing a professional funeral home. While certain customs and rituals have been maintained across generations, others have ceased to exist due to modernization, acculturation, and practicality. Therefore, respecting cultural traditions, as well as respecting the individual's wants and needs, is crucial in providing sensitive and professional funeral service (see Figure 2–1).

Throughout this chapter information is provided on (1) three general responses to death, (2) cultural diversity in the United States, (3) specific cultures and brief overviews of general cultural traditions, and (4) the cultural influence

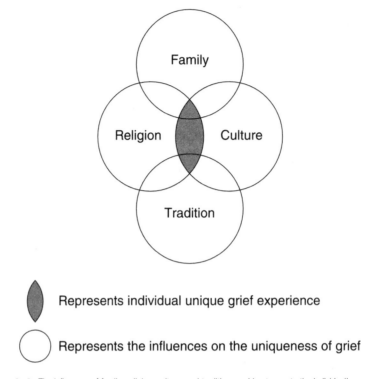

Represents individual unique grief experience

Represents the influences on the uniqueness of grief

Figure 2–1. The influences of family, religion, culture, and tradition combine to create the individual's own unique perspective, outlook, understanding, and acceptance toward the death of a loved one. (Dr. John D. Canine and Therese McNeil, Maximum Living Consultants, Inc., Birmingham, 1995)

balanced with assimilation. Cook and Dworkin's guidelines for serving culturally diverse individuals offer information that could be considered and applied by quality funeral professionals.

REFERENCES

Berger, A. 1989. *Perspectives on death and dying*. Philadelphia: Charles Press.

Black, D., of Elton Black & Son Funeral Home. January 1995. Interview.

Campbell, B. H. 1993. *Humankind emerging*, 6th Edition. New York: Harper Collins.

Candelana, E., and A. Adkins. October 1994. A Mexican-American perspective on death and the grief process. *The Forum Newsletter*. Association of Death Education and Counseling, 1–5.

Cook, A. S., and D. Dworkin. 1992. *Helping the bereaved*. New York: Harper Collins.

Craggett, F. T. 1980. A form critical approach to the oral traditions of the black church as they relate to the celebration of death. Ph.D. diss., Claremont School of Theology.

Fulton, R. 1965. *Death and identity*. New York: John Wiley and Sons.

Irish, D., K. Lindquist, and V. J. Nelson. 1993. *Ethnic variations in dying, death and grief.* Washington, D.C.: Taylor and Francis.

Narada. 1973. *The Buddha and his teachings.* Colombo, Sri Lanka: Vajirarama.

Rando, Therese. 1984. *Death, dying, and grief.* Champaign, Ill.: Research Press.

Raphael, B. 1983. *The anatomy of bereavement.* New York: Basic Books.

Sow, Alassane. February 1995. Interview.

U.S. Department of Commerce. 1993. *Statistical abstract of the U.S.*

Wass, Hannelore, Felix Berardo, and Robert Neimeyer, eds., 1988. *Dying: Facing the facts.* 2d ed. New York: Hemisphere Publishing.

White, J. L. 1984. *The psychology of blacks: An Afro-American perspective.* Englewood Cliffs, N.J.: Prentice-Hall.

Worden, W. L. 1992. *Grief counseling and grief therapy.* New York: Springer.

3

PROCESSING THE DEATH OF A LOVED ONE THROUGH LIFE'S TRANSITIONS

John D. Canine

Although we do not assume that infants think of themselves as "being" or "non-being," there is enough research to suggest that basic phenomena surrounding death are sensed by the child. For example, in 1961 Adah Maurer found that infants as young as six months already have an orientation toward existing and not existing. She cites the infant-adult interaction called "peek-a-boo" as the infant's exploration of appearance and disappearance, and further states that a "healthy baby is ready to experiment with these contrasting states" (Maurer 1961; see also Koocher 1973; Hoffman and Strauss 1985; Prichard and Epting 1992). As the infant gets older, "peek-a-boo" becomes "hide-and-seek," a childhood game that permits the participants to not exist (hide) so as to avoid the capture of the person designated as the seeker ("It"). Could the "It" be the personification of death? Nevertheless, most observers of infant and children agree that death-related themes conveyed through play, games, speech, toys, and pictures are prevalent. This is a notion that can benefit death care professionals when they are ready to learn about these early manifestations. This chapter discusses awareness of and perspectives on death from childhood through the later stages of life. These viewpoints on death are based on the research of psychologists, sociologists, and bereavements counselors. They provide fundamentals for death care professionals as they attempt to understand the needs of the bereaved.

CHILDHOOD AWARENESS OF DEATH

Nagy

It was Marie Nagy's well-known research regarding a child's gradual development of death concepts that first suggested three levels of awareness for children. These levels are

- Level 1 (birth to age five)—The child's perception of death is more "sensed" than "intellectualized." The dead are only less alive, more like a deep sleep. They are not void of sensation and functioning. Children at this level have a lot of questions about the body, casket, grave, cemetery, and so on. There is no connection with death being final. The dead are only temporarily gone.
- Level 2 (ages five to nine)—During this period the irreversibility of death is accepted by the child. There is an awareness that life is limited. This suggests a higher degree of mental development. However, children at this level manifest two other interesting characteristics. One is that death is viewed as a "person." It can be an old man, a clown, or simply a mysterious figure who makes the rounds at night. Second, the children believe a person can "luck out" and escape death. If a person is clever enough, death can be outwitted. Hence, the anxiety associated with the finality of death is lessened by giving the child some control over avoiding the "death person." Nagy believed that even at this age death is still "outside" the child.

TABLE 3–1. **CHILD AND ADOLESCENT CONCEPTS OF DEATH**

Piaget's Periods and Stages	Concepts	Developmental/Educational Status
II. Preparation and organization		
1. Preoperational thought (2–7 years)	Reversibility External causation (violence, accidents) Revival by various means	Preschool years
2. Concrete operations (7–11/12 years)	Irreversibility Cessation of functions Internal causation Universality Simple beliefs about life after death	Early school years Middle childhood years/preadolescence
III. Formal operations (11/12 years and over)	Religious and philosophical theories about the nature of death and existence after death	Adolescence

Source: Canine and Dates (1993).

- Level 3 (age nine and up)—At this point the child's ability to conceptualize and intellectualize death permits an understanding not only of finality but also of inevitability and universality. Everyone dies, and it cannot be avoided. (Nagy 1948; Cotton and Range 1990; Donders 1993)

Piaget

Most students of human development have turned to Jean Piaget for an understanding of how one level of mental functioning leads to another (Piaget 1965) (see Table 3–1). Some believe there is a conflict between Nagy and Piaget in the area of finality. Although Piaget had little to say about death, his developmental theory seems to suggest that a child would have to be older than nine or ten years to cognitively grasp the personal finality of death. However, it is important to point out issues on which Nagy and Piaget do agree, namely, during the ages of approximately five to eleven when children can comprehend what is real, universal, irreversible, and inevitable. Therefore, while children might struggle with the personal finality of death, they do see it as real. This point is supported by Canine and Dates (1993) in their analysis of drawings of death that were obtained from second and third graders in a Michigan elementary school.

Canine and Dates

The most significant aspect of the study reported by Canine and Dates (1993) was in the area of content coding. The following is an excerpt from their report:

> The drawings were coded according to the content of the pictures without regard to colors used to portray the content. This was accomplished by means of a

TABLE 3–2. **INDICATORS OF DEATH SYMBOLISM IN DRAWINGS BY SECOND- AND THIRD-GRADE CHILDREN**

Indicator	Frequency	Percent
Interpersonal violence:		
Indicated	11	13.0
Not indicated	73	87.0
Violence of non-personal nature:		
Indicated	9	11.0
Not indicated	75	89.0
Spirituality:		
Indicated	16	19.0
Not indicated	68	81.0
Pastoral/nature:		
Indicated	17	20.0
Not indicated	67	80.0
Funeral service:		
Indicated	35	42.0
Not indicated	49	58.0
Death as peaceful:		
Indicated	26	31.0
Not indicated	58	69.0
Deceased as distressful:		
Indicated	54	64.0
Not indicated	30	36.0
Deceased as retaining instrumental abilities:		
Indicated	40	49.0
Not indicated	44	52.0

content analysis of the drawings followed by the coding of each drawing inclusive of each content category. The interrater reliability of the three raters for content was 0.92 [see Table 3–2].

With respect to interpersonal violence, indicated on the drawings by one person doing harm to another, only 13 percent of the drawings viewed death as occurring through interpersonally violent means. Non-personal violence, depicted by a violent death as the result of an accident, was found in 11 percent of the drawings. No drawings had both interpersonal and non-personal violence. Thus, a full 22 percent of the drawings had views of death as violent occasions [see Figure 3–1].

Inclusion of spiritual signs, both religious and nonreligious, in the drawings appeared in 19 percent of the students' protocols, and indicated that most children of this age do not consider death as a spiritual event. Pastoral signs, or signs of nature, appeared in only 20 percent of the drawings. Indications of funeral preparations, funeral ceremonies, or interment appeared in 42 percent of the drawings [see Figure 3–2]. Consideration of spiritual, pastoral and funeral signs together indicates that most children surveyed often drew the deceased without any persons, deity or spirit, or inanimate surroundings. In fact, many of the drawings including

Figure 3–1. Twenty-two percent of children's drawings had views of death as violent occasions. (Canine and Dates 1993)

Figure 3–2. Forty-two percent of children's drawings related to funerals. (Canine and Dates 1993)

Figure 3–3. Forty-eight percent of children's drawings depicted the deceased possessing all body parts. (Canine and Dates 1993)

signs of funerals also included pastoral surroundings or some type of spiritual de-notion.

Only 31 percent of the children viewed death as a peaceful event, while 64 per-cent indicated that the deceased was in a distressed circumstance. Often, this was portrayed as the deceased yelling for help or crying.

The final category of content analysis was concerned with the portrayal of the deceased as having retained physical instrumentation such as arms, legs, eyes and ears. Somewhat under half (48 percent) of the children indicated the deceased as still possessing all body parts, while 52 percent indicated the deceased as missing instrumental abilities. [See Figure 3–3.] (Pp. 65–75)

Conclusion

Canine and Dates's research seems to support Nagy's and Piaget's findings that children struggle with personalizing death and seeing it as final. In six out of eight categories, the "not indicated" percentage was much higher than the "indicated." Was this because the children had no opinion on the subject surveyed? Did they have no opinion because they could not personally relate to the subject matter? As stated, most of the children "drew the deceased without any persons" (Canine and Dates 1993, p. 71). Why? Also, it seems significant that 64 percent said the dead were "distressed" and almost half said the dead had "physical abilities." Obviously, although death is real for these children, they do not view it as final. Nevertheless, while there is a need for more research on the subject of children and death, especially research that will utilize different methodologies, some basic conclusions can be drawn for the death care professional.

From early childhood through adulthood, the developmental phases from one age in life to another cause changes in human perceptions of death, resulting in different perspectives on death during each stage of life. First of all, how a child interprets death depends on many factors, as listed in the following:

- The developmental stage—Usually one can determine by age the mental developmental functioning of a child. However, maturation varies considerably, so age should be used as only an approximate guide to how well a child can reason. Generally, a child begins to conceptualize death at about age seven (Iig and Ames 1955; Reilly, Hasazi, and Bond 1983; Speece and Brent 1984, 1992).
- Personality—Each child has his or her own personality characteristics. A child who is highly communicative will probably talk about death. A child who is adventuresome is likely to ask questions about death. A child who has a strong bond and is close to his or her parents probably will "take on" the parents' attitudes about death at the expense of his or her own ideas and thoughts. Whatever makes a child unique also influences the way that child views death (Prichard and Epting 1992).
- Life experiences—When a child experiences a death or loss (especially the death of a parent or sibling) at an early age, it forces the child to cope. Whatever coping skills the child adopts, right or wrong, probably will influence the way he or she deals with loss the rest of his or her life. However, many other life experiences have the potential to affect a child's interpretation of death, such as illness, separation from loved ones, changes of environment, socioeconomic level, parental occupation, and so on. With this in mind, it is easy to understand why a child of a funeral director probably would have a concept of death unlike that of other children (Stambrook and Panker 1987).
- Emotional support—If a child has bonded to parents and other family members, and has the freedom to express feelings, chances are good that the anxiety associated with death will be lessened through communication of death-related issues. To this child, death education begins at home. For the death care professional, this means that any type of helping intervention, whether educative or therapeutic, can support and nurture the family values (Silverman and Worden 1992).

Second, the child's realization that death is personal and inevitable can be achieved through many different situations. The reality of death can be a spontaneous act of comprehension, like an "existential awakening," or a series of events that enable the child "to put things together" relative to the notion "I am going to die." Either way, death becomes real. In many cases the death care professional is challenged with helping the child balance this death awakening with the continuous pursuit of goals and dreams.

Third, when the child senses that the subject of death is forbidden, and his or her quest for understanding death is deferred, the potential for personal growth and development is hindered. When death is treated as an overwhelming catastrophe and not discussed, there seems to be enough evidence to suggest it will have a negative impact on the child's future.

YOUNG ADULTS

According to Piaget (Table 3–1), the young adult is capable of concepts of time, space, and causality. The adolescent can hypothesize, theorize, and personalize. In short, adolescence is when a fully developed mental apparatus is possessed by the child. As Wass and Stillion (1988) report:

> Adolescents formulate abstract ideas about the nature of death. For example, adolescents describe death as darkness, light, transition, or nothingness. They also formulate their own theologies about life after death which include belief in reincarnation, transmigration of soul, spiritual survival on earth, and spiritual survival at another level in a state of indescribable peace and beauty, in addition to beliefs about heaven and hell or total annihilation at death. These findings are consistent with Piaget's period of formal operations. Thus, research with healthy children and adolescents dispute an array of methodological problems seems to suggest that concepts of death develop generally in accordance with the Piagetian model of cognitive development. (P. 205)

Adolescence is a time of one's life. From a statistical standpoint, taking 1,000 males, fifteen years old, it is likely that 999 will reach the age of sixteen. For females the statistics are even better. Out of 2,000 females, fifteen years old, 1,999 will reach age sixteen. An adolescent can contemplate many years of life (Feifel 1977). However, there is a mortality rate even at this young age. Therefore, death-related thoughts and ideas need to be discussed.

In adolescence, as in childhood, personality and life experiences are important. Additionally, it is likely that males and females differ in their orientations toward death. An example of this is our society's encouragement of risk-taking behavior among young men. As Feifel states:

> Anthropological observations could be used to make a case that young men tend to be high risk takers in most, if not all, cultures. Yet there seems to be an especially lethal interaction in our own society between cultural incitements for young men to "prove" themselves and the means that are popular and available for these activities. Hazardous use of automobiles, drugs, alcohol, and unnecessary risks in athletic competition are among the modalities of life-threatening behavior encouraged by the attempt to establish that one is not "chicken," and can do all that is expected to demonstrate masculine powers . . . As more young women move into activities previously dominated by men, there is at least the

prospect for an increase in injury and death related to this risk-taking orientation. (1977, p. 33)

Feifel's point is well taken. Developmentally, adolescents have the mind to manipulate concepts to make rational decisions. An adolescent can understand the world in which he or she lives. However, being an adolescent is being somewhere between adulthood and childhood, which means, among other things, that decisions will be made that are not well thought out and that give the appearance of being childish. This is especially true of death-related issues. As we have discussed, an adolescent can understand death in a rational, reasonable manner. However, many death-related issues are "acted out" rather than being understood. For example, music has an important influence on adolescents, and rock music seems to be the choice. It is mass-produced and encompasses every area of our society. Rock music is marketed on MTV, radio, videos, tape cassettes, compact discs, and record albums. We can hear rock music in our homes, schools, places of business, health clubs, and even in our churches. Most sociologists agree that it started almost forty years ago as an expression of "counterculture," and continues to the present. In 1986 Attig provided a list of categories of death-related themes in rock music that includes

- Immortality
- Grief
- Suicide/homicide
- War
- Apocalypses
- Death via drugs
- Violence (including those of sexual nature)

In 1989 Wass, Miller, and Stevenson published an article entitled "Factors Affecting Adolescents' Behavior and Attitudes toward Destructive Rock Lyrics." Among their many findings, they state: "If indeed a portion of the adolescents are interested in rock music with destructive themes and do know the words of the lyrics, as our data suggests, the likelihood that they may be influenced is increased, especially if rock musicians serve as a role model" (p. 301).

In 1993 Plopper and Ness identified ninety death-related songs that have appeared in the Top 40 during the last thirty-seven years. They concluded the following:

- Death songs constitute a disproportionately popular subset of Top 40 music.
- Males dominate as the person who dies in the songs.
- Grief responses in the songs are confused and restricted.

Even with these findings, there still is an absence of research on adolescents' perceptions of rock music and the effect it has on their attitudes and behavior. However, it is obvious that this type of music provides an avenue for the young adult to express or act out death themes.

Another avenue to express death themes is games. Childhood games such as cops and robbers, cowboys and indians, and war have given way to more sophisticated video games that are popular among teenagers. Laser Tag is a game that includes a pistol, a holster, and a sensor that automatically records each "hit." It is a fair assumption that this toy simulates killing. On the other hand, Tech Force, Mortal Kombat, Cosmic Carnage, and Fatal Fury are all computer games that simulate war. In this age of the computer, we have little doubt that more video and computer games with a death theme will be marketed. The question is, what impact will they have on the values and attitudes of our young adults (Wass and Stillion 1988)?

Finally, adolescents are not limited in their expressions of death themes. From fairy tales, comic books, novels, and magazines to the care of pets, young adults explore the subject of death. It is up to the death care professional to pick up on these subtle expressions so that assistance can be given in understanding and accepting death.

MIDLIFE

The adult in the middle years usually has a focus on the immediate family as well as a concern for his or her family of origin. More people today have parents alive than at any other time in history. Hence, the middle-aged person feels the pressure from both sides. Nevertheless, how a middle-aged person copes with life and death depends on his or her development in the previous years. Whatever factors influenced a middle-aged person's thoughts on death, related issues will continue through the middle years. With few exceptions, this seems to be a safe assumption. However, some death issues seem to be unique to this time of life.

First of all, to be middle-aged and have to care for a dying parent can be very distressing. A parent who has lived a long time provides psychological insulation from an acceptance of mortality. The daughter finds it hard to live without the mother who has been there "forever." Of course, there is very little understanding from society when a parent dies. Everyone will grieve with a parent whose child dies unexpectedly, but not many people seem to encourage an intensive display of grief when a parent dies whose "time had come" or who lived a "fulfilled" life. Also, there is the issue of a mother being a burden to her daughter while she was dying. Or possibly mother and daughter had not gotten along through the years. In either case, it leaves the daughter with post-death conflicting feelings of guilt and liberation.

Second, the death of a parent also validates one's own mortality. After his father's death, one patient said to his therapist, "I looked into the casket and realized that is the *dead* state and I am in the *alive* state, but I am moving to the *dead* state." His statement is consistent with midlife reality, namely, that death is no longer uncommon, as opposed to when a person is young. The chance of dying during one's forties is about twice as great as in the previous decade, and will double again during that person's fifties (Feifel 1977). This phenomenon does not make one feel very secure, but it can be the impetus for developing a mature death-accepting attitude.

Third, the midlife adult must find some balance between a society that places value on youthfulness and a physical body that is getting older. As Feifel states, "Growing older is akin to growing deader" (1977, p. 38). Anxiety over physical changes (e.g., wrinkled skin, poor eyesight, extra weight) can lead to depression. The body that has been nurtured for so long now is experiencing "partial" death. The physical losses seem to mount with each passing year, bringing death closer and closer. If an individual tries desperately to hold onto a youthful self, further growth and development can be hindered. The midlife years should not be a time of looking back, which only promotes stagnation. Rather, the midlife adult should focus on the fact that "life is not over"; as long as there is life, there is growth. The middle years can be a time of redefining personal goals, interpersonal relationships, career objectives, and, of course, one's own mortality. In short, these are the years in which the self is "reborn."

GERIATRIC GROUP

It is difficult to define this group of Americans. To be a member of the American Association of Retired Persons, you must be at least fifty years old. Most companies still look at sixty-five years as retirement age. The government issues Social Security checks to men who are sixty-five years old and to women who are sixty-two years old. The situation becomes more complex when one moves from chronological age to levels of functioning. We may know someone who is "old" at forty years and someone else who is "young" at seventy. Should a college professor be retired at age sixty-five when her mind has more information stored than ever before, her intellect is sharp, and her years of experiences have made her very wise? One would think not. However, for the sake of convenience, we will refer to the geriatric population as those age sixty-five years and up.

Currently, there are over twenty-two million individuals in America who are sixty-five years or older. That is more than 10 percent of the population. Due to advances in science, medicine, and geriatric health care, the number of "elders" in our society will continue to increase. However, 71 percent of the 2,141,000 estimated deaths in the United States in a given year (1989) occurred in persons sixty-five years of age and older (National Center for Health Statistics 1990). Truly, death is associated with aging. How does the geriatric population view death? There is never a good time to die. Older people today are more active and have a higher level of functioning than at any other time in American history. They seem to place a lot of emphasis on life and living. For the last twenty years, studies have shown that death does not intimidate the old person. As early as 1966, Munnicks found that the aged come to terms with their finitude. Although they differed in their methods of coping, they seemed acutely aware and accepting of the closeness of death. More recently, Thorson and Powell (1988) found that "elders" had a lower death anxiety than younger age groups, but, more importantly, the meanings of death were different. Older persons were concerned about being in control and about life after death, whereas young people were attentive to the fear of pain, isolation, and the decomposition of the body.

From a practical standpoint, growing older should include preparation for death. This preparation can occur at the spiritual level through reflection and a review of one's life as well as thoughts on a better life hereafter. Or it can occur at the social level through the establishment of a will, making funeral arrangements, distribution of personal possessions, and saying "good-byes" to family and friends. Sometimes growing old means losing one's life mate.

In 1989 Kirschling and McBride found that widows experienced a greater loss of vigor and more physical symptoms than widowers. Women reported a high proportion of support from their ideas and beliefs. Men, on the other hand, had more evidence of denial. However, their study concluded that, despite differences in expressions of distress, widows and widowers used the same coping strategies. Nevertheless, this study, as well as others, provides evidence that older people perceive death and work through grief by establishing values, beliefs, and adaptive behavioral patterns. In essence, they are as prepared as they can be for death.

Death care professionals who are oriented toward helping older people cope with death-related experiences need to be alerted to those individuals whose behavior is maladaptive. The following lists some factors that cause difficulties for older adults when coping with the death of a loved one:

- Wanting to die and low self-esteem (Lund et al. 1986)
- Feelings of having contributed to the death in some manner (Murphy 1983)
- A pessimistic outlook on life in general (Rowe 1982)
- Limited support resources (Kirschling and Austin 1988)

Helping older people to cope with death-related transitions requires the death care professional to be focused on emotional needs, physical concerns, and realistic goals. While the aged might accept death with minimal anxiety, death-related issues bring them face-to-face with new situations that require instrumental problem solving in nearly every area of life.

SUMMARY

Nagy's well-known research regarding a child's gradual development of death concepts first suggest three levels of death awareness for children. This theory is supported by Jean Piaget's work in the area of childhood development. Also, Canine and Dates, in their 1993 study of children's drawings of death, support the fact that children seem to have an unsatisfied notion of death because they have not been challenged to personally relate to the subject. However, children at an early age do understand that death is real. How a child interprets death depends on the child's developmental phase, personality, life experiences, and emotional support.

In adolescence the child has the mental apparatus to comprehend death. However, adolescence is the time when behaviors vacillate between those of the adult and the younger child. Males seem to take more risks. Rock music is a channel for both males and females to express feelings about death and grief, yet adolescents are not limited to this avenue of expression. They also express their feelings through games, toys, literature, and the care of pets.

The midlife years are difficult because one is caught between caring for the immediate family and the family of origin. Watching a parent die or dealing with a sudden death of a parent reinforces one's own mortality. The midlife years are when the body experiences a "partial death." It is a time when physical limitations are quite noticeable.

The "geriatric group" is increasing in numbers, and generally seems to be accepting of death. However, they are faced with tremendous choices and decisions in confronting the death of their friends, their own grief, and their own death.

REFERENCES

Attig, T. 1986. Death themes in adolescent music: The classic years. In *Adolescence and death,* edited by C. A. Corr and J. N. McNeil. New York: Springer.

Canine, J., and B. Dates. 1993. Researching the need for death education in an elementary school curriculum. *Illness, crisis and loss* 3, no. 2: 65–74.

Cotton, C. R., and L. M. Range. 1990. Children's death concepts: Relationship to cognitive functioning, age, experience with death, fear of death, and hopelessness. *Journal of Clinical Child Psychology* 19:123–27.

Donders, Jacques. 1993. Bereavement and mourning in pediatric rehabilitation settings. *Death Studies* 17:517–27.

Feifel, Herman. 1977. *New meanings of death.* New York: McGraw-Hill.

Hoffman, S. I., and S. Strauss. 1985. The development of children's concepts of death. *Death Studies* 9:469–82.

Iig, Frances, and Louise B. Ames. 1955. *Child behavior.* New York: Harper and Row.

Kirschling, J. M., and J. K. Austin. 1988. Assessing support—the recently widowed. *Archives of Psychiatric Nursing* 2:81–86.

Kirschling, J. M., and A. B. McBride. 1989. Effects of age and sex on the experience of widowhood. *Western Journal of Nursing Research* 11:207–18.

Koocher, G. P. 1973. Childhood, death and cognitive development. *Developmental Psychology* 9:369–75.

Lund, D. A., M. F. Diamond, M. S. Caserta, R. T. Johnson, J. L. Poulton, and J. R. Connelly. 1986. Identifying elderly with coping difficulties after two years of bereavement. *Omega* 16:213–24.

Maurer, A. 1961. The child's knowledge of non-existence. *Journal of Existential Psychiatry* 2, 193–212.

———. 1966. Maturation of concepts of death. *British Journal of Medicine and Psychology* 39:35–41.

Munnicks, J. M. 1966. *Old age and finitude.* Basel, Switzerland: S. Karger.

Murphy, S. A. 1983. Theoretical perspectives in bereavement. In *Advances in nursing theory development,* edited by P. L. Chinn. Rockville, Md.: Aspen Systems.

Nagy, M. 1948. The child's theories concerning death. *Journal of Genetic Psychology* 73, 3–27.

National Center for Health Statistics. 1990. Births, marriages, divorces and deaths for 1989. *Monthly and Vital Statistics Report* 38, no. 12:1–20.

Piaget, J. 1965. *The child's conceptions of the world.* Edited by C. K. Ogden. Totowa, N.J.: Littlefield and Adams.

Plopper, Bruce, and Ernest Ness. 1993. Death as portrayed to adolescents through Top 40 rock and roll music. *Journal on Adolescence* 28:793–807, Winter 1993.

Prichard, S., and F. Epting. 1992. *Children and death: New horizons in theory and measurement.* Amityville, N.Y.: Baywood Publishing.

Reilly, T. P., J. E. Hasazi, and L. A. Bond. 1983. Children's conceptions of death and personal mortality. *Journal of Pediatric Psychology* 8:21–31.

Rowe, D. 1982. *The construction of life and death.* New York: John Wiley and Sons.

Silverman, Phyllis R., and William J. Worden. 1992. Children's reactions in the early months after the death of a parent. *American Journal of Orthopsychiatry* 62, no. 1:93–103.

Speece, M. W., and S. B. Brent. 1984. Children's understanding of death: A review of three components of a death concept. *Child Development* 55:1671–86.

———. 1992. The acquisition of a mature understanding of three components of the concept of death. *Death Studies* 16:211–29.

Stambrook, M., and K. C. H. Parker. 1987. The development of the concept of death in childhood: A review of the literature. *Merrill-Palmer Quarterly* 33:133–57.

Thorson, J. A. and F. C. Powell. 1988. Elements of death anxiety and meanings of death. *Journal of Clinical Psychology* 44:691–701.

Wass, Hannalore, David Miller, and David Stevenson. 1989. Factors affecting adolescents' behavior and attitudes toward destructive rock lyrics. *Death Studies Journal* 13, no. 3:287–301.

Wass, H., and Judith Stillion. 1988. Death in the lives of children and adolescents. In *Dying: Facing the facts,* 2d ed. Edited by Hannalore Wass, Felix Berardo, and Robert Neimeyer. New York: Hemisphere Publishing.

4

THE PSYCHOLOGY OF DYING

John D. Canine

CHAPTER OUTLINE

PSYCHOLOGICAL RESPONSES TO DYING

Beginning with Dr. Elizabeth Kubler-Ross and her book *On Death and Dying*, (1969), there has been widespread appeal to the notion that, once they realize death is close at hand, people go through several distinct psychological stages in response to their impending demise. Basing her observations on interviews with over two hundred limited life expectancy patients, Kubler-Ross presupposed that five stages were involved in the process of psychological response to dying. These stages are

1. Denial
2. Anger
3. Bargaining
4. Depression
5. Acceptance

This chapter aims to define and describe these stages, as well as bring to light the perspectives of other well-known authors on this subject. Responsibilities that dying individuals feel they must meet are recognized, and the role of the funeral director with the dying patient is reviewed.

Kubler-Ross

As human beings approach death, nature seems to prepare us for letting go of our need and desire to live our worldly existence, the only existence we have consciously experienced. When we learn that we have little time left on earth, we respond in a series of emotional reactions that eventually lead us to acceptance. These reactions are as follows.

Denial

When people discover they are dying from a terminal illness or condition, often their initial response is to deny the inevitable event in order to cope with the shock of finality. Such a reaction might cause a person to simply state, "It cannot be true." Usually, this is a temporary response that allows the individual time to collect him- or herself and deal rationally with the situation.

Anger

Once the patient has come to realize that death is close at hand, anger replaces the denial. The patient is angry because he or she feels unjustly chosen for death. Envious and resentful of those who will continue to live, the patient might say something similar to this: "Why couldn't this have happened to George? He doesn't deserve to live." Striking out at family members, doctors, and nurses is a typical reaction. In fact, anyone who approaches the dying person might feel the hostility the patient is experiencing.

Bargaining

Over time, people reach a stage at which they try to strike bargains with death. They begin to accept the inevitable and start looking to "extend the lease." They want to postpone death, so they bargain, most often with God, for more time to live as a reward for their "good behavior." They might say something like, "If I can just live through Mary's graduation next spring, then I won't ask for anything else."

Depression

The next stage a dying person moves into is depression over the loss of personal life. The purpose of this emotional state is to prepare the individual for full acceptance of death. For some people the depression spills over into other areas of life. They might be depressed about the loss of a job, money, future dreams, or their friends.

Acceptance

Finally, the dying individual fully accepts that he or she is about to die. At this time many people are void of feelings. They have not "given up," but they need time to rest before the end comes. Their interests might diminish, and they might want to be left alone in silence. At this stage in the process, the dying patient's family might need more help, patience, and understanding than the patient does (Kubler-Ross 1969).

Kubler-Ross was careful to make clear that not all dying patients move through these stages in this sequence. However, many health care workers, patients, and families of patients have interpreted her work in that way and have tried to force their understanding of "limited life expectancy" into a particular mold. It is not uncommon to hear people in the medical field talk about a patient who has not accepted his death, and question, "Why is this patient stuck in denial?" The implication is that he should go beyond denial to some other mode of coping so he can eventually accept his death.

Lofland

As a pioneer, Kubler-Ross put a great deal of effort into directing our attention to the emotional needs of dying patients and their families. However, there is very little scientific evidence to support the fact that patients proceed through definable stages. In fact, psychologist Edwin Shneidman (1973) writes:

> Indeed, while I have seen in dying persons isolation, envy, bargaining, depression, and acceptance, I do not believe that there are necessarily "stages" of the dying process, and I am not at all convinced that they are lived through in that order, or,

for that matter, in any universal order. What I do see is complicated clustering of intellectual and affective states, some fleeting, lasting for a moment or a day or week, set not unexpectedly against the backdrop of that person's total personality, his "philosophy of life." (P. 6)

Nevertheless, a "stage" approach to dying has made us aware of the prolonged period in which modern persons can "be dying." It is in this context that sociologist Lyn Lofland defined "dying scripts" to be individualistic, varied, emergent, and uncodified. She writes: "Being dying is relatively problematic because it is a role in the modern world, and such roles are frequently more akin to improvisational theater than to traditional drama. Parameters of some sort may be given . . . but within those, the actor has considerable freedom to shape the role's detailed stylistic enactment as he or she sees fit" (Lofland 1978, p. 49).

According to Lofland, "being dying" is being terminally ill or having a limited life expectancy. The "dying script" is how the dying patient decides to live out his or her last days. In attempting to understand the personal and social decisions the patient has to make, she suggests the use of "construction materials" such as space, population, knowledge, and stance.

Space
Lofland defines "space" as the area within one's life span that is set aside and dedicated to fulfilling the dying role. Logically, we could say that from the time of birth until the time of death we are moving toward extinction. However, most will choose a portion of space between the time of diagnosis (of a terminal condition or illness) and the time of death. Within this space there is an enormous amount of flexibility. Lofland cites the difference between two public figures' use of their space: journalist Steward Alsop and author Jacqueline Susann. Alsop wrote about his acute leukemia from the time he entered the hospital until his death. On the other hand, Susann shared the knowledge of her cancer with very few people and apparently committed nothing to paper concerning her movement toward death.

Population
Lofland's term "population" refers to the question of whether the patient chooses to play out the dying role alone or in the company of others who are dying also. Since many people die in a hospital surrounded by other patients who are dying, it might seem next to impossible to die alone. However, with the rising popularity of hospice (home palliative) care, it is possible for one to have some degree of privacy during the final days and at the moment of death.

Knowledge
An important issue for the dying patient is who will be told when this person is expected to die. Minimally, only the medical doctor and the patient would have this information. The question is, Who else should know? Conceivably, anyone and everyone might be told if the patient so desires. Since expressing one's feelings about

death is important, discussing it with selected individuals could be therapeutic. However, an anonymous letter to Ann Landers explains why discretion should be used when telling others about one's impending death.

> Dear Ann Landers: This may be one of the most unusual letters you have ever received. You see, I am dying, but don't become alarmed, and please don't feel sorry for me.
>
> After all, we are ALL dying. From the moment we are born, we are headed toward inescapable death.
>
> Three years ago, I learned I have chronic leukemia (I was 31 then). The doctor told me the truth at once because I insisted on knowing. The news came at a crisis time in my life. (I had just gone through a divorce and had young children to raise.)
>
> Would you believe I had to move out of town to a larger city because people would not accept me as a normal person? I was devastated, not by the disease, which has been controlled by drugs, but by the way I was treated.
>
> After I moved to this distant city, my life changed dramatically. No one here knows of my illness and I am keeping my mouth shut. I work part-time, attend college, have many friends, and am involved with community activities and participate in sports. What a pity that I had to move to a town where nobody knew me in order to live a normal life.
>
> Although I feel well, look fine, and am managing beautifully, I know it can't last forever. I dread the day my friends must be told of my illness. I don't want to be pitied. And, of course, I fear that I may be deserted as I was once before. (*Sacramento Union*, May 12, 1975)

Stance

As a dying person assumes her dying role in the philosophy by which she lived, her life will never be more significant. To some patients, their dying space offers a time to lean on religious beliefs. St. Paul wrote for the Christians, "Death, where is thy sting?" and "Death has been swallowed up in victory" (1 Corinthians 15:54, 55). To others, it is the time to show what years of education and rational thought have taught them. After all, death is inevitable; everyone dies, accepts it, and moves on. Still, for some people, the moments before death might be a time to mend broken relationships, confess wrongdoings, or cram as much pleasure into "being dying" as possible. To this end, "stance" is existential and its types are as many as human inventiveness can create. Lofland has given the patient a model that emphasizes choice as she constructs her "persona" during her "being dying." Lofland's greatest contribution to "being dying" is informing the patient that she can have some control right up to the time of death.

Contributions by Other Researchers

Kubler-Ross and Lofland are just two of many thanatologists, sociologists, and psychologists who have worked to define some aspect of the dying mode. The following are brief descriptions of conclusions drawn by other researchers.

In his essay on the living-dying process, E. M. Pattison (1978) simply divided the dying process into three clinical phases:

1. The acute crisis phase in which one learns of the terminal illness
2. The chronic living-dying phase
3. The terminal phase

In each phase the dying patient would have different initial responses.

Another researcher who has written extensively on death is A. Weisman. His greatest contribution is his definition of denial and what he calls appropriate death. Weisman (1984) concluded that there are three degrees of denial. First-degree denial is when the patient unequivocally denies the facts that have produced the diagnosis of being terminally ill. Although family and friends demand medical treatment, the patient steadfastly refuses and continues to disbelieve or ignore the advice of the physician. Second-degree denial is when the patient accepts the diagnosis with all its complications but refuses to believe the illness is terminal. This patient might even discuss the physical debilitation of the illness and be fully aware of the limitations caused by the disease. However, in the next breath this patient might discuss long-term career advancement plans. Third-degree denial is when the patient vacillates between "open acknowledgment of death and its repudiation" (p. 65). This patient might wake up one morning and plan his funeral, revise his will, and contact a hospice organization in preparation for his death. However, the next day he is angered by a chemotherapy treatment that interferes with his weekend plans.

From a psychological standpoint, denial does not always produce dysfunctionalism. In fact, Lazarus and Folkman (1984) reported that denial can be useful within the context of active coping strategies. In their opinion, "denial" needs to be further defined so that there is a clear understanding of favorable and unfavorable outcomes.

Weisman (1984) also developed the idea of "appropriate death." He writes: "I realized that not only some deaths were better than others, but that certain deaths were so fitting that they could be called "appropriate." These were not, of course, ideal deaths, nor particularly propitious, but they did share characteristics that were consistent with good coping and sustained morale. Appropriate death, in brief, was the opposite of suicidal death, in which an unhappy person appropriates death" (p. 80).

Weisman determined four factors that describe appropriate death:

1. The intrapsychic conflict of death is lessened.
2. The dying posture of the individual is consistent with his ego idea.
3. Important relationships are preserved or restored.
4. Basic instincts, hopes and wishes of fantasy, and goals for growth reemerge and give the patient some degree of fulfillment.

What is appropriate for one person will not necessarily be so for another. To some extent, the behavior of a person who is dying will mirror the times of his or her life when a crisis produced varied psychological responses. It is not uncommon for a dying patient to have a vast array of emotions such as rage, guilt, terror, surrender, heroism, and dependency. Nevertheless, how an individual behaves during a crisis will give clues to how the person will respond to dying. A death is appropriate if it is consistent with what a person has been, if it continues to promote what is meaningful and important to the individual, and if it maintains important relationships (Weisman 1984).

Sociologists Glaser and Strauss, in their book *Time for Dying* (1968), reported on the involvement of limited life expectancy patients with hospital staff members. They identified four "contexts of awareness." First, when a staff member knows of the patient's terminally ill diagnosis but does not share the information with the patient or family, a "closed awareness" exists. Since the research of Glaser and Strauss, there has been much more emphasis on full disclosure to consumers in many fields, including health care. However, if a closed awareness happens just once, it is once too often. The patient has a right to know about the diagnosis, prognosis, and treatment of the terminally ill disease. Second, a patient might suspect his or her illness through a variety of hospital information, such as the following:

- Indirect statements from the physician
- Comments overheard from the physician to other staff members
- Direct statements from hospital staff members (aides, nurses, social workers, etc.)
- Statements overheard from family and friends in the hospital room
- Changes in the behavior of others toward the patient
- Changes in medical care, procedures, medications, and so on
- Changes in the patient's physical location within the hospital

Third, the phase of "suspicion" is so unstable that it does not last long. Usually, it will give way to "mutual pretense." This happens when the patient and staff are quite aware of a terminally ill diagnosis but pretend it is not true. Even though mutual pretense is an activity that is not consistent with the patient's reality, Glaser and Strauss point out that it does serve a purpose. It enables the staff to keep a safe emotional distance from the patient, and it gives the patient more dignity and privacy. However, the danger of mutual pretense is the possibility of alienation, where the patient is left without any genuine relationships. Finally, "open awareness" occurs when both patient and staff are aware that the patient is dying and they openly acknowledge and discuss it. This permits the patient to "put his life in order" by taking care of practical matters such as finalizing a will, arranging for the funeral, caring for the children, saying good-bye to family and friends, and so on. Open awareness can place considerable strain on hospital staff who continuously work with dying patients. As Glaser and Strauss point out, there should be attention given to the psychological needs of the caregiver.

DUTIES OF THE DYING

In coping with a terminal illness, the patient is forced to perform some basic existential duties. These duties vary depending on the nature of the illness, the personality characteristics of the individual, and the environmental circumstances. Moos and Tsu (1977), Kalish (1970), and Rando (1984) have referred to these duties as "adaptive tasks." They are listed in the following:

1. The patient must arrange a variety of affairs, including the management of pain and discomfort for funeral arrangements. Each duty brings the patient one step closer to death.

2. The patient must adapt to the loss both of loved ones and of the self. The patient might be concerned about the survivors and what effect "my death" will have on them. Typical questions are: Will they be legally and financially vulnerable? Will they have replacement relationships? There is potential for bringing loved ones closer together if feelings can be openly and honestly discussed. At the same time, the patient must be attentive to the loss of her entire world as she has known it. Being responsible to personal loss can be terrifying to the dying individual.

3. The patient must manage her medical needs as well as balance her emotions. The choice of medical treatment and when it will begin and end often is left to the patient. The identification and expression of emotions about the disease and treatment are critical to maintaining her emotional equilibrium. All of this needs to be done with some degree of hope, even when it is limited by the realities of the illness.

4. The patient must plan for the future while anticipating the loss of various forms of sensory, motor, and cognitive abilities. Whatever time and energy the patient has left might be used for a vacation, general travel, or to visit friends. The patient should continue to plan for and enjoy life as long as possible. At the same time, the patient should make arrangements for a time when she will no longer be capable of carrying out her plans.

5. The patient must identify and cope with the death encounter. Living with the reality of death inevitably brings up concerns of immortality. Many patients are comforted through their religion; others are thrust into a "state of despair" when they face their own extinction. Although the research on the role of religion in the face of death has produced mixed results, generally it is agreed that the patient's will to live influences the dying process. If it is relinquished, for whatever reason, the patient might hasten death.

THE ROLE OF THE FUNERAL DIRECTOR WITH THE DYING PATIENT

To some extent the funeral director is a "caregiver" to the dying patient. When the patient faces the reality of his death and makes a conscious decision to plan his funeral, he will turn to the funeral director for counsel, care, and preplanning. There are some necessary prerequisites for those funeral directors who work with dying patients. These include:

- Coming to grips with one's own mortality (see Chapter 1).
- Understanding the grief process of a dying patient.
- Engaging in effective listening and responding appropriately. This includes non-verbal as well as verbal communication.
- A commitment to give a part of oneself to the dying patient and family.
- A knowledge of one's own personal limits; knowing how to avoid "burnout."

In preplanning the funeral, the patient has the assurance, witnessed by the funeral director, that he has performed what will be the final duty of his dying process. He will experience some control over his death by knowing what he wants for his funeral, how much it will cost, and where it will be held. The responsibility of the funeral is removed from the surviving family members, and, by discussing it frankly, the patient and family are better able to meet death when it comes. At the preplanning arrangement meeting, the funeral director can encourage the dying patient to make the funeral and burial fit his personal beliefs, standards, and lifestyle. It has been said in the funeral industry that the funeralization process should reflect the way the deceased lived. However, in light of this chapter, the funeral director might want to consider the way the patient is dying, and arrange the funeral to reflect the positive characteristics of the dying phase. For example, if the dying patient is working on restoring broken relationships, then the funeral might include the theme of forgiveness. If the dying patient was courageous in attempting to control his disease as well as his emotions, then the theme of tenacity, fortitude, and steadfastness might be encouraged as a major part of the funeral.

Nevertheless, the role of the funeral director in the limited life of the patient is significant. He or she should encourage the patient to talk about changes in attitude or perspective brought on by the illness, and should provide support and comfort for the patient during the preplanning meeting. Acceptance, clarity, candor, and compassion should be exemplified by the funeral director at all times. Each dying patient should be treated as an individual, with respect and recognition for his or her needs, fears, hopes, and expectations. This requires more than sensitivity from the funeral director. It calls for continued learning about the needs of the dying.

SUMMARY

Kubler-Ross pioneered work that focuses on the needs of the dying patient. Although her stages of the dying process are supported by little scientific evidence, they define the dying process in a manner that has enabled many individuals to gain understanding of limited life expectancy.

Lofland's attention to the "dying script" and the use of construction material such as space, population, knowledge, and stance emphasizes choice and gives the dying patient a feeling of control right up to the time of death.

Pattison divided the dying process into clinical phases. Weisman wrote about denial and "appropriate death." Glaser and Strauss defined "contexts of awareness" between hospital staff and the dying patient. The dying patient is forced to perform "adaptive tasks," which essentially are responsibilities that the dying person feels must be fulfilled. These tasks include arranging one's affairs, adapting to the loss of loved ones and the self, managing both medical and emotional needs, planning for the future, and coping with the death encounter.

The role of the funeral director with the dying patient is varied. As a caregiver, the funeral director might act as planner, adviser, and counselor. Working with dying patients requires certain personal prerequisites such as dealing with one's own mortality, understanding the grief process, learning to listen, and committing oneself to the role of caregiver.

REFERENCES

Glaser, B. C., and A. L. Strauss. 1968. *Time for dying*. Chicago: Aldine.

Kalish, R. A. *The onset of the dying process*. Omega, 1970, 1, 57–69.

Kubler-Ross, E. 1969. *On death and dying*. New York: Macmillan.

Lazarus, R. S., and S. Folkman. 1984. *Awareness of dying stress appraisal and coping*. New York: Springer.

Lofland, Lyn H. 1978. *The craft of dying*. Beverly Hills, Calif.: Sage Publications.

Moos, R. H., and V. D. Tsu. The crisis of physical illness: An overview. In *Coping with physical illness*, edited by R. H. Moos. New York: Plenum, 1977.

Pattison, E. M. 1978. The living-dying process. In *Psychosocial care of the dying patient*, edited by C. A. Garfield. New York: McGraw-Hill.

Rando, Therese. 1984. *Grief, dying, and death*. Champaign, Ill.: Research Press.

Shneidman, E. S. 1973. *Deaths of man*. Baltimore, Md.: Penguin Books.

Weisman, A. 1972. *On dying and denying*. New York: Behavioral Publications.

———. 1984. *The coping capacity: On the nature of being mortal*. New York: Human Science Press.

5

SOCIAL RESPONSES TO VARIOUS TYPES OF DEATH

John D. Canine

Our society, as all others, develops generalized responses to death and grieving through a variety of socialization processes, as well as unique characteristics that emerge and become established through population (demographic) norms. The goal of this chapter is to present an overview of how society develops its social responses to death and what it "expects" from us (and therefore what we often expect from ourselves) in responding to deaths of a particular type: parent, spouse, child, sibling.

More critically, the chapter goes on to examine how expected and generalized responses may differ greatly from what is experienced by an individual confronting an actual, specific death. These dichotomies can create stress and guilt among grievers who may think their emotions or thoughts are "inappropriate."

Throughout, the ability of the funeral professional to be alert and genuinely helpful to the bereaved is addressed, in terms of creating a secure atmosphere for families serviced, validating feelings that accompany individual circumstances, and offering direction and guidance to appropriate support groups and/or bereavement literature.

THE SOCIALIZATION OF OUR BELIEFS

We learn the organizing principles, ideas, beliefs, values, patterns, and norms of our culture through a variety of experiences and interactions with others. Many influences contribute to the socialization of the child into adult society: parents, peers, schools, day-to-day experiences and activities, television and movies, music and books, to name the most important. Death-related beliefs, values, and behaviors are "absorbed" through these means, as well.

As discussed in Chapter 1, Americans today do not experience death as directly and intimately as in previous eras. Preindustrial societies were characterized by high mortality rates (life expectancy between twenty and thirty years), and communities themselves were small and tightly integrated socially, economically, and politically. The death of an individual affected not only the surviving family members but the entire community, and, correspondingly, funeral and bereavement practices were highly ritualized. Within this structured tradition, it was understood that the entire community would participate in the mourning.

The industrial era and today's postindustrial society have seen a dramatic drop in mortality rates and a soaring increase in life expectancy. Additionally, the rise of "specialization" of work has led to what Blauner (1966) termed, "the bureaucratization of modern death control" (pp. 378–94), referring to the removal of the care of the dying and death itself into institutions, as opposed to the much earlier practices of keeping the dying at home, where they could be supported primarily by friends and family.

Today, death is distanced, sanitized, and often sensationalized; since it is no longer part of the normal routine of our lives, we are less able to identify our authentic beliefs and feelings around it—less able to cope with it. Consequently, our present-day ideas regarding death are even more vulnerable to outside influences, such as might be received from institutions that deal with death, the media, our peers, and the funeral industry itself.

Portrayal of Death in the Media as a Socializing Influence

Death is a staple theme and device used to attract attention to television, cartoons, and feature films. In both nonfiction and fictional contexts, however, the portrayal of death is often abbreviated, unrealistic, and distorted. Television news, for example, selects only the most unusual or violent deaths for inclusion in its broadcasts.

Viewers are likely to see only the most disturbing images of death's aftermath—perhaps the bodies, blood, the tangled wreckage of accident scenes, or the physical results of deliberate destruction (e.g., explosions or arson).

What news rarely, if ever, includes is the full range of additional human tasks that are required in the face of any death, regardless of its cause. Notification of family, contacting a funeral home, the emotional process of grieving, and the handling of the deceased's personal and business affairs are not considered part of the "story," thus denying audiences exposure to the many complexities surrounding real death.

Cartoons, with children as their primary audience, are notorious for their utterly distorted portrayal of death. A familiar example is the Road Runner cartoon series in which Wile E. Coyote is repeatedly blown up with dynamite, run over by a train, or smashed by a giant boulder, only to reappear in the next scene, fully recovered and ready to continue the chase. While on the one hand this is highly entertaining to children and perhaps adults as well, constant viewing of such material at an early age may lead children to internalize an unrealistic notion of death and its consequences. While there are developmental issues in childhood that may preclude an accurate comprehension of death, when a real death occurs within a family, it may be even more difficult to explain as a result of the distorted depiction to which children have been exposed.

Movies aimed at adults also remove the "realities" of death and dying, often showing us horrific, even preposterous, scenes related to killing and dying, or using death as a device for humor. Some notable examples are *Shallow Grave* (1995), *Weekend at Bernie's* (1989), and *The Trouble with Harry* (1955). Neither approach reflects the common experience of large numbers of people, thus perpetuating the myth of death as distant from our real lives.

In *Weekend at Bernie's*, sunglasses are placed on the title character's corpse, his arm is rigged to wave at people from a moving convertible, and his body is dressed to go to the beach. While the absurdity is obvious, audiences are entertained and "lured" into ignoring and denying such questions as embalming, notification of relatives, and funeral arrangements. Bernie seems almost "alive" to the moviegoer (it was a live actor playing "dead," incidentally), reinforcing an unrealistic view of what it means to be dead, and how survivors are to behave in response.

The Role of Peers as a Socializing Influence

Both children and adults learn responses to death through the language and intensity evidenced by their peers. On any school playground during any given recess period it would not be surprising to hear the words, "If you don't give that back to me, I'm going to kill you!" Children may hear this so often that the real meaning of "kill" is forgotten, or perhaps never learned in the first place. What a child really means, of course, is that he or she is going to "tell" on you or kick your shins.

Not until a child is actually faced with a death situation (whether of a pet or a family member) will words like "kill," "dead," or "die" begin to have a personal meaning. Parents should be alert to and calmly address any distorted ideas their children may express about death, in preparation for the child's first real experience.

Adult conversation includes references to death more frequently than is often realized. The repertoire of idiomatic expressions, slang, and cliché involving death is vast: "Over my dead body," "The comedian died out there," "That dress is a real killer," "This dessert is to die for," "I thought I'd die laughing," or "I'd kill for a car like that," are just a smattering of the ways in which we use death as a means of showing our intensity of feeling about a particular subject.

Nevertheless, such death references, collectively, may also serve to numb us to the actual pain, work, and grief associated with real death. Society has become so accustomed to these casual references that people who have recently experienced a significant death may feel wounded or trivialized by such messages. Unfortunately, contemporary social norms offer minimal guidelines or practice in sensitivity toward the newly bereaved. As one social commentator recently stated after the death of her sister, "Maybe we should reinstitute the custom of wearing black arm bands after the loss of a loved one. It's a signal that says, 'Treat me gently' " (Roberts 1994).

DEMOGRAPHICS OF DEATH

Death-related ideas and the social responses that arise around them are also influenced by the demographics of a society. Demography is the statistical study of human populations, and data that deal with mortality rates reveal many facts about the frequency and "distribution" of death among different groups within the society.

Here, we will examine mortality rates in America according to the three variables of age, gender, and race, and offer thoughts on how interpretation of such data creates patterns of socialized response and expectations. It should be noted that as these variables change over time, responses and expectations may change as well.

For example, the first national census in 1790 reported that only 2.7 percent of the population was sixty-five years or older. Today, more than 10 percent of the population is sixty-five or older, and projections for the time frame 2010 to 2030 indicate that the percentage will double to 20.5 percent, or approximately one person in five (Wass, Berardo, and Neimeyer 1988, p. 79). This longer life expectancy can be attributed to improved nutrition, sanitation, and medical technology, but with these changes in the age distribution of the population come shifts in how we look at the social structure—family, work, retirement, leisure, as well as the roles of government and the medical industry.

The single fact of the overall drop in mortality rates impacts society's general

TABLE 5–1. LIFE EXPECTANCY. EXPECTATION OF LIFE AT BIRTH, 1970 TO 1992, AND PROJECTIONS, 1995 TO 2010
[In years. Excludes deaths of nonresidents of the United States. See also Historical Statistics, Colonial Times to 1970, series B 107–115]

Year	Total			White			Black and Other			Black		
	Total	Male	Female	Total	Male	Female	Total	Male	Female	Total	Male	Female
1970	70.8	67.1	74.7	71.7	68.0	75.6	65.3	61.3	69.4	64.1	60.0	68.3
1975	72.8	68.8	78.8	73.4	69.5	77.3	68.0	63.7	72.4	66.8	62.4	71.3
1980	73.7	70.0	77.4	74.4	70.7	78.1	69.5	65.3	73.5	66.1	63.8	72.5
1981	74.1	70.4	77.8	74.8	71.1	78.4	70.3	86.2	74.4	68.9	84.5	73.2
1982	74.5	70.8	78.1	75.1	71.6	78.7	70.9	66.8	74.9	69.4	65.1	73.6
1983	74.6	71.0	78.1	75.2	71.6	78.7	70.9	67.0	74.7	69.4	65.2	73.5
1984	74.7	71.1	78.2	75.3	71.8	78.7	71.1	67.2	74.9	69.5	66.3	73.6
1985	74.7	71.1	78.2	75.3	71.8	78.7	71.0	67.0	74.8	69.3	65.0	73.4
1986	74.7	71.2	78.2	75.4	71.9	78.8	70.9	88.8	74.9	69.1	64.8	73.4
1987	74.9	71.4	78.3	76.6	72.1	78.9	71.0	66.9	75.0	69.1	64.7	73.4
1988	74.9	71.4	78.3	75.6	72.2	78.9	70.8	66.7	74.8	68.9	64.4	73.2
1989	75.1	71.7	78.5	75.9	72.5	79.2	70.9	66.7	74.9	68.8	64.3	73.3
1990	75.4	71.8	78.8	76.1	72.7	79.4	71.2	67.0	75.2	69.1	64.5	73.6
1991	75.5	72.0	78.9	76.3	72.9	79.8	71.5	67.3	75.5	69.3	64.6	73.8
1992 prel	75.7	72.3	79.0	76.5	73.2	79.7	71.8	67.8	75.6	69.8	65.5	73.9
Projections:[1] 1995	76.3	72.8	79.7	77.0	73.7	80.3	72.5	88.2	76.8	70.3	65.8	74.8
2000	76.7	73.2	80.2	77.6	74.3	80.9	72.9	68.3	77.5	70.2	65.3	475.1
2005	77.3	73.8	80.7	78.2	74.9	81.4	73.6	69.1	78.1	70.7	65.9	75.5
2010	77.9	74.5	81.3	78.8	75.6	82.0	74.3	69.9	78.7	71.3	66.5	76.0

[1] *Based on middle mortality assumptions; for details, see source. Source: U.S. Bureau of the Census, Current Population Reports, P25–1104.*

Source: Except as noted, U.S. National Center for Health Statistics, Vital Statistics of the United States, annual, and Monthly Vital Statistics Reports.

response to death. As discussed in Chapter 2, longer life expectancy (see Table 5–1), seems to have bolstered death-denying responses so that when an individual dies below the age "that is expected," the death can be more difficult to cope with and understand.

A look at the gender factor in American mortality rates reveals that women tend to live longer than men, by approximately seven years. While the causes for this difference remain subject to debate, the work of S. H. Preston (1968) suggests that when variables within lifestyles are examined (stress, diet, exercise, smoking, etc.), smoking has the highest impact on gender differentials (see Table 5–2).

Interesting as it may be, the demographic reality is that most women who marry can expect to be widowed. Social responses to and grief behavior of widowed men and women present a number of differences. Widowed men, for example, tend to remarry more often and more quickly than women (Berardo 1968, p. 192).

The third variable of significance in American mortality rates is race. The research of Kitagawa and Hauser (1973) indicates that within the U.S. population, Americans of Japanese extraction have the lowest mortality rates, while African-Americans demonstrate the highest. The next group most likely to die at an earlier-

TABLE 5-2. **DEATHS, BY SELECTED CAUSES AND SELECTED CHARACTERISTICS: 1991**

[In thousands. Excludes deaths of nonresidents of the United States. Deaths classified according to ninth revision of *International Classification of Diseases.*]

Age, Sex, and Race	Total[1]	Heart Disease	Cancer	Accidents and Adverse Effects	Cerebrovascular Diseases	Chronic Obstructive Pulmonary Diseases[2]	Pneumonia, Flu	Suicide	Chronic Liver Disease, Cirrhosis	Diabetes Mellitus	Homicide and Legal Intervention
ALL RACES[3]											
Both sexes, total[4]	**2,169.5**	**720.9**	**514.7**	**89.3**	**143.6**	**90.7**	**77.9**	**30.8**	**25.4**	**49.0**	**26.5**
Under 1 year old	36.8	0.7	0.1	1.0	0.2	0.1	0.6	*	(Z)	(Z)	0.4
1 to 4 years old	7.2	0.3	0.5	2.7	0.1	0.1	0.2	*	(Z)	(Z)	0.4
5 to 14 years old	6.5	0.3	1.1	3.7	0.1	0.1	0.1	0.3	(Z)	(Z)	0.5
15 to 24 years old	36.5	1.0	1.8	15.3	0.2	0.2	0.3	4.8	(Z)	0.1	8.2
26 to 34 years old	59.6	3.4	5.3	14.8	0.8	0.3	0.8	8.5	0.9	0.7	7.8
35 to 44 years old	88.1	12.4	15.9	11.8	2.5	0.7	1.4	5.8	3.6	1.6	4.6
45 to 54 years old	120.7	30.4	40.0	7.1	4.7	2.3	1.7	4.0	4.6	3.0	2.1
55 to 64 years old	248.1	75.0	94.2	6.6	9.7	10.4	3.7	3.2	6.0	7.0	1.2
65 to 74 years old	478.6	159.4	159.3	8.1	25.5	26.6	10.2	3.1	6.2	13.8	0.7
75 to 84 years old	607.5	228.9	139.4	10.1	49.4	33.7	24.6	2.4	3.5	14.7	0.4
85 years old and over	477.4	209.0	56.1	8.2	50.2	14.1	34.1	0.8	0.7	8.0	0.1
Male, total[4]	**1,121.7**	**380.0**	**272.4**	**59.7**	**56.7**	**50.5**	**36.2**	**24.8**	**16.3**	**21.1**	**20.8**
Under 1 year old	21.0	0.4	(Z)	0.6	0.1	(Z)	0.3	*	(Z)	*	0.2
1 to 4 years old	4.0	0.2	0.3	1.6	(Z)	(Z)	0.1	*	(Z)	(Z)	0.2
5 to 14 years old	5.3	0.2	0.7	2.5	(Z)	0.1	0.1	0.2	(Z)	(Z)	0.3
15 to 24 years old	27.5	0.6	1.1	11.5	0.1	0.1	0.2	4.1	(Z)	0.1	6.9
25 to 34 years old	43.7	2.3	2.6	11.6	0.4	0.2	0.5	5.4	0.6	0.4	6.2
35 to 44 years old	60.6	9.2	7.5	9.0	1.4	0.4	0.9	4.5	2.6	0.9	3.6
45 to 54 years old	76.0	22.5	20.0	5.2	2.6	1.2	1.1	3.0	3.2	1.7	1.8
55 to 64 years old	151.4	51.7	52.2	4.5	5.2	5.7	2.3	2.6	4.1	3.5	0.9
65 to 74 years old	275.9	97.8	89.9	4.9	13.1	16.2	6.0	2.5	3.7	6.4	0.5
75 to 84 years old	299.0	110.8	73.8	6.1	20.6	19.3	12.7	2.1	1.8	6.0	0.2
85 years old and over	158.8	64.0	24.3	3.1	13.1	7.3	12.1	0.6	0.3	2.3	(Z)
Female, total[4]	**1,047.9**	**351.0**	**242.3**	**29.8**	**86.8**	**40.2**	**41.8**	**6.0**	**9.2**	**27.9**	**6.7**
Under 1 year old	15.8	0.3	(Z)	0.4	0.1	(Z)	0.3	*	(Z)	(Z)	0.2
1 to 4 years old	3.2	0.2	0.2	1.1	(Z)	(Z)	0.1	*	(Z)	(Z)	0.2
5 to 14 years old	3.2	0.1	0.5	1.2	(Z)	(Z)	0.1	0.1	(Z)	(Z)	0.2
15 to 24 years old	8.9	0.3	0.7	3.7	0.1	0.1	0.1	0.7	(Z)	0.1	1.2
25 to 34 years old	15.9	1.1	2.7	3.2	0.4	0.2	0.3	1.2	0.3	0.3	1.6
35 to 44 years old	27.6	3.2	9.4	2.8	1.2	0.3	0.5	1.3	1.0	0.6	1.0
45 to 54 years old	44.6	7.8	20.0	1.9	2.2	1.2	0.7	1.0	1.3	1.4	0.5
55 to 64 years old	96.6	23.3	42.0	2.0	4.5	4.7	1.4	0.7	1.9	3.5	0.3

Age, Sex, and Race	Total[1]	Heart Disease	Cancer	Accidents and Adverse Effects	Cerebrovascular Diseases	Chronic Obstructive Pulmonary Diseases[2]	Pneumonia, Flu	Suicide	Chronic Liver Disease, Cirrhosis	Diabetes Mellitus	Homicide and Legal Intervention
65 to 74 years old	202.8	61.6	69.4	3.2	12.4	12.3	4.3	0.6	2.6	7.6	0.2
75 to 84 years old	308.5	118.0	65.6	5.0	28.8	14.5	11.9	0.4	1.7	8.7	0.2
85 years old and over	320.6	145.0	31.8	5.1	37.0	6.8	22.1	0.1	0.4	5.8	0.1
WHITE											
Both sexes, total[4]	**1,868.9**	**636.8**	**450.0**	**74.4**	**123.7**	**84.0**	**69.3**	**28.0**	**21.4**	**39.6**	**12.8**
Under 1 year old	23.7	0.5	(Z)	0.6	0.1	(Z)	0.3	*	(Z)	(Z)	0.2
1 to 4 years old	5.0	0.2	0.4	1.9	(Z)	(Z)	0.1	*	(Z)	(Z)	0.2
5 to 14 years old	6.3	0.2	0.9	2.7	0.1	0.1	0.1	0.2	(Z)	(Z)	0.3
15 to 24 years old	26.0	0.7	1.5	12.9	0.2	0.1	0.2	4.1	(Z)	0.1	3.2
25 to 34 years old	42.3	2.3	4.3	12.0	0.5	0.2	0.5	5.7	0.6	0.5	3.6
35 to 44 years old	64.0	9.0	13.4	9.2	1.6	0.4	0.9	5.3	2.6	1.1	2.4
45 to 54 years old	93.7	23.7	32.5	5.8	3.1	1.9	1.2	3.7	3.5	2.1	1.3
55 to 64 years old	205.3	61.8	80.2	5.4	7.1	9.3	3.0	3.0	5.1	5.2	0.7
65 to 74 years old	415.8	138.2	140.2	7.0	20.9	26.6	8.8	3.0	5.6	11.1	0.5
75 to 84 years old	546.6	206.6	125.2	9.2	43.8	32.0	22.3	2.3	3.2	12.4	0.3
85 years old and over	439.8	193.7	50.8	7.5	46.2	13.4	31.9	0.7	0.7	7.0	0.1
BLACK											
Both sexes, total[4]	**269.5**	**76.0**	**57.9**	**12.5**	**17.4**	**5.8**	**7.4**	**2.1**	**3.5**	**8.5**	**13.0**
Under 1 year old	12.0	2.2	(Z)	0.3	(Z)	(Z)	0.2	*	(Z)	*	0.2
1 to 4 years old	1.9	0.1	0.1	0.6	(Z)	(Z)	0.1	*	*	*	0.2
5 to 14 years old	1.9	0.8	0.2	0.8	(Z)	0.1	(Z)	(Z)	(Z)	(Z)	0.2
15 to 24 years old	9.3	0.3	0.3	1.9	(Z)	0.1	0.1	0.5	(Z)	(Z)	4.8
25 to 34 years old	15.7	1.0	0.9	2.3	0.3	0.1	0.3	0.8	0.2	0.2	4.0
35 to 44 years old	22.1	3.2	3.0	2.2	0.9	0.2	0.5	0.4	0.8	0.4	2.0
45 to 54 years old	24.4	6.2	6.5	1.1	1.4	0.5	0.5	0.2	0.8	0.8	0.7
55 to 64 years old	38.4	12.0	12.5	10.0	2.3	1.0	0.7	0.1	0.8	1.6	0.4
65 to 74 years old	56.4	19.3	17.1	10.0	4.0	1.8	1.2	0.1	0.6	2.5	0.3
75 to 84 years old	54.2	20.0	12.7	8.0	4.9	1.5	1.9	0.1	0.2	2.0	0.1
85 years old and over	33.1	13.6	4.7	0.6	3.4	0.6	1.8	(Z)	(Z)	1.0	(Z)

* Represents zero. Z Fewer than 50.

[1] Includes other causes not shown separately.

[2] Includes allied conditions.

[3] Includes other races not shown separately.

[4] Includes those deaths with age not stated.

Source: U.S. National Center for Health Statistics, Vital Statistics of the United States, *annual.*

than-average age is Native Americans, followed by Chinese Americans, followed by Caucasians. Further, the patterns reported between race and mortality are consistent with patterns regarding social class and mortality. Social class research, also by Kitagawa and Hauser, indicates that as education and income increase, mortality is reduced. While interpretation of this data may be debated, we do know that African-Americans, whose mortality is the highest, are more likely than other groups to live in poverty (see Table 5–3).

Although demographic data by themselves do not tell us how society regards any individual death, they suggest how general social responses may be shaped by the patterns of mortality in a given population. Certainly society reacts and thinks differently about the accidental death of a healthy, young mother than about the death of a ninety-year-old suffering from long-term illness.

The next section of the chapter will take a closer look at various types of societal and individual responses to specific, significant losses: death of a parent, spouse, child, and sibling. In each instance, implications for funeral professionals will be discussed.

SPECIFIC RESPONSES TO DEATH

Death of a Parent

Our society perceives the death of a parent as a natural event. It follows the "expected order" of things. Death of a parent is the most common loss in adulthood, with Lieberman and Borman (1979) finding in the year of their study that fully 5 percent of the U.S. population experienced this particular type of death.

Although most adult children are afforded the opportunity to become successful people directing their own lives prior to a parent's death, there remains the knowledge that the independent adult is still a "child" of the parent. Thus, as with every death, there are unique aspects to a parental loss. When a parent dies, the adult child experiences a loss of nurturing, guidance, and protection. There may also be the feeling that no one stands between adult children and their own death. They have suddenly, perhaps, become the "older" generation.

Variables exist that can intensify or complicate grief over a parent's death. A sudden or violent death can make the reality of the death more difficult to internalize and process, and this can be even more distressing when there is unfinished emotional business, ambivalence, or even feuding within the family.

Society's expectations, however, make little or no allowance for such untimely, unexpected, or violent deaths of a parent, generally regarding them as unproblematic. An adult child is expected to resolve his or her grief in the same manner as someone who has anticipated or been alerted to the coming loss.

Despite the relative frequency of parental death, surprisingly little research has been conducted regarding the specific impacts of these deaths on adult children.

TABLE 5–3. DEATH RATES, BY AGE, SEX, AND RACE: 1970 TO 1992
[Number of deaths per 100,000 population in specified group.]

Sex, Year, and Race	All Ages[1]	Under 1 Yr. Old	1–4 Yr. Old	5–14 Yr. Old	15–24 Yr. Old	25–34 Yr. Old	35–44 Yr. Old	45–54 Yr. Old	55–64 Yr. Old	65–74 Yr. Old	75–84 Yr. Old	85 Yr. Old and Over
Male[2]												
1970	1,090	2,410	93	51	189	215	403	959	2,283	4,874	10,010	17,822
1980	977	1,429	73	37	172	196	299	767	1,815	4,105	8,817	18,801
1990	918	1,083	52	29	147	204	310	610	1,563	3,492	7,889	18,057
1991[3]	912	1,024	52	29	148	204	312	605	1,525	3,439	7,689	17,800
1992[3]	902	919	47	26	145	200	325	587	1,482	3,360	7,538	17,656
White: 1970	1,087	2,113	84	48	171	177	344	883	2,203	4,810	10,099	18,552
1980	983	1,230	66	35	167	171	257	699	1,729	4,036	8,830	19,097
1990	931	898	46	26	131	176	268	549	1,467	3,398	7,845	18,268
1991[3]	926	861	46	27	128	176	269	545	1,444	3,350	7,642	18,021
1992[3]	917	755	43	26	124	173	285	531	1,396	3,271	7,479	17,888
Black: 1970	1,187	4,299	151	67	321	560	957	1,778	3,257	6,803	9,455	12,222
1980	1,034	2,687	111	47	209	407	690	1,480	2,873	5,131	9,232	16,099
1990	1,008	2,112	86	41	252	431	700	1,261	2,618	4,946	9,130	16,955
1991[3]	999	1,957	88	42	278	426	702	1,267	2,534	4,851	9,013	16,684
1992[3]	980	1,830	68	41	271	413	683	1,186	2,512	4,761	9,035	17,014
Female[2]												
1970	808	1,864	75	32	68	102	231	517	1,099	2,580	6,678	15,518
1980	785	1,142	55	24	68	76	159	413	934	2,145	5,440	14,747
1990	812	958	41	19	49	74	138	343	879	1,991	4,883	14,274
1991[3]	811	804	43	18	50	74	139	339	873	1,977	4,801	14,067
1992[3]	807	808	38	17	48	70	143	323	872	1,966	4,728	13,839
White: 1970	813	1,615	66	30	62	84	193	463	1,015	2,471	6,699	15,980
1980	806	963	49	23	58	65	138	373	876	2,067	5,402	14,980
1990	847	690	36	18	46	62	117	309	823	1,924	4,839	14,401
1991[3]	848	659	38	17	57	62	117	306	822	1,909	4,733	14,188
1992[3]	843	653	33	16	43	47	118	291	814	1,911	4,686	13,919
Black: 1970	829	3,369	129	44	112	231	533	1,044	1,986	3,861	6,692	10,707
1980	733	2,124	84	31	71	150	324	768	1,561	3,057	6,212	12,367
1990	748	1,736	68	28	69	180	299	639	1,453	2,868	5,688	13,310
1991[3]	745	1,581	71	28	73	159	304	633	1,400	2,854	5,707	13,259
1992[3]	741	1,601	63	26	72	155	318	619	1,458	2,700	6,629	13,719

[1] Includes unknown age.
[2] Includes other races not shown separately.
[3] Includes deaths of nonresidents. Based on a 10 percent sample of deaths.

Source: U.S. National Center for Health Statistics, Vital Statistics of the United States, annual; Monthly Vital Statistics Report, and unpublished data.

However, several studies do exist that indicate parental death can indeed be problematic. Research by Anderson (1949), Bunch (1971), and Birtchnell (1975) suggests the following potential reactions:

- A higher tendency toward suicide
- Increased rates of suicide attempts
- Higher rates of clinical depression

Although death of a parent creates significant psychological pain, a majority of adults who experience this loss are ultimately able to experience psychological growth and insight as a result. When parental deaths occur, funeral service professionals can be of great assistance in providing a form for the adult child to express the feelings of loss and to begin to find meaning, acceptance, and peace around the terminated relationship. General bereavement support groups facilitated under the direction of a funeral home can be a great resource for those suffering this type of loss.

Death of a Spouse

For ease of discussion, we will use the term "spouse" to refer to any significant individual with whom the griever has enjoyed a long-term partnering relationship. It is ironic that while our society appears to recognize the loss of a spouse (mate, partner) more than many other types of deaths, there as yet exists no widespread, established, accepted, consistent, supportive institution or process designed to assist and help integrate grieving widows and widowers into their changed social status.

As we learned from the earlier section on demographics, more women will spend more years as widowed people than will men, but initially there are some notable similarities in the grief issues and tasks faced by males and females following the death of a spouse. In spousal relationships, each person fulfills a variety of roles and functions, while sharing others. Spouses may comanage a home and coparent, deciding together how to allocate money, whose career or job may require priority, and when and where to spend leisure time and entertain themselves. Other couples may divide responsibilities more specifically, according to ability, inclination, or social stereotypes. Jobs such as yard work, financial record keeping, cooking, religious instruction of children, household repair, and even pet care may be seen as the "domain" of one spouse rather than the other.

After the death of a spouse, all these roles and functions must be assumed by the surviving partner. This can create overwhelming feelings of loneliness, inadequacy, anger, helplessness, and vulnerability, depending on the nature of the relationship that had been established with the deceased partner. These feelings can be further exacerbated if the surviving spouse must assume the sole responsibility of raising minor children.

This dramatic shift in life circumstances (whether abrupt or anticipated) is intensified by changes in how the surviving spouse is regarded by family, friends, and the community. When spouses have primarily shared social relationships with other couples, the surviving spouse may feel awkward (a "fifth wheel") or may discover that he or she no longer fits in with the pairs-oriented social order. Issues of sexual vulnerability, competition, and exploitation may arise. And if friendships had been defined by the deceased spouse's employment, there is the real potential that such social "belonging" may cease altogether.

The community may question how and when to include a surviving spouse in activities that had previously been shared by both partners, and these uncertainties may be compounded by a wide range of emotions and behaviors evidenced by the widowed themselves as they proceed through the grief process. Lund, Caterta, and Diamond (1986) found that the newly widowed exhibit a broad spectrum of feelings and responses to their new role, alternately demonstrating depression, guilt, or anger at being alone, and yet feeling pride, strength, or accomplishment in successfully handling the new challenges of performing and coping that widowhood presents.

The process of grieving a spousal loss is a long one, and intervention by funeral professionals at an appropriate time can serve to mitigate the heightened sense of isolation and loss of purpose that widowed people often experience. Referrals to support groups organized specifically for the widowed can be provided, as well as information on programs that focus on the (nonbereavement) needs of people coping with the death of a spouse. An excellent resource is the Widowed Persons' Service of the American Association of Retired Persons.

Whether facilitated by a mental health professional or a trained and caring volunteer, support groups tend to attract people whose goals and needs are likely to match the group's belief system and philosophy (Edelstein 1984). Support groups are valuable to a wide range of widowed people, offering opportunities to benefit from

- Similar goals of sharing
- Cognitive/informational goals of learning
- Modeling upon those who have had similar experiences
- Emotional support
- A safe environment in which to express feelings
- Linkages with others (Lieberman et al. 1979)

Death of a Child

The relationship between parents and children is the most intense of all—physically, psychologically, and socially. In intensity, the "unnaturalness" of a child's death perhaps looms largest in the grief and bereavement literature, since it violates society's expected order of events and robs parents of their personal link to the future, to continuity of family legacies, to their touch of immortality.

When a child dies, these precious connections die too. The intensity of parental grief bears no relation to the birth order, gender, circumstances, or age of the child or infant who has died. What is important are the meanings, hopes, values, needs, feelings, and expectations parents had invested in that child—or child-to-be. Indeed, even the most responsible of parents who have made provisions for life insurance, a will, and perhaps even their own funeral preplanning are unlikely to have considered or laid plans for the death of a child.

As Wolterstorff (1987) stated in his book *Lament for a Son:* "It's so wrong, so profoundly wrong, for a child to die before its parents. It's hard enough to bury our parents, but that we expect. Our parents belong to our past, our children belong to our future. We do not visualize our future without them. How can I bury my son, my future, one of the next in line? He was meant to bury me" (p. 16).

The experience of a child's death is so unnatural that, as a society, we are likely to display even stronger tendencies to deny the occurrence—our sensibilities assaulted by this seemingly impossible fact, our intimacy with death so diluted that we may even turn away from the grief-stricken parents. In fact, researchers (Lehman, Ellard, and Wortman 1986) suggest that the anxiety and uncertainty about the bereaved's specific experience result in would-be supporters falling back on stereotypical responses, for example: "You'll get over it," or "You'll have another one soon." It is also reasonable to think that the more tragic the circumstances of the death, the greater the anxiety would be for well-meaning supporters.

Compounding the parent's profound pain, sense of isolation, guilt, or helplessness may be society's expectation to grieve this death in a similar time frame and manner as might be appropriate for the death of a parent, mate, or sibling. This is unrealistic. Parents whose children die experience intense anger as well as a related phenomenon called "service guilt"—the feeling that they should have died first. Secondary forces come into play, as the parent realizes her or his own identity has changed, that is, to that of mother or father of a deceased child. The physical structure of the family is forever altered, along with the "foreseen" future that might have included graduations, marriages, and grandchildren that now will never be.

How does such a bereaved parent ever again answer the question "How many children do you have?" And how does such suffering begin to help surviving siblings deal with their own grief, questions or comments from friends, and the return to regular activities such as school and sports?

The answer is, not without great difficulty, and, in some cases, maybe never. The unwavering attention from family, friends, and death professionals is vital in cases of a child's death—and nowhere is such response likely to be more clumsy in the giving and more misunderstood or flatly rejected in the receiving. In truth, no one can relate to the experience unless it has happened to them, and the "average person" will probably not know where to seek appropriate support for him- or herself or a grieving loved one.

Referral to support groups created specifically for grieving parents is essential. Groups such as Compassionate Friends, Parents of Murdered Children, and Mothers Against Drunk Driving can offer the unique help and understanding that bereaved parents need and deserve. Groups of this nature provide parents a level of empathy, assistance, and closeness that is probably not available anywhere else in their daily experience. In addition to emotional support, these groups can often provide information, coping skills, and the opportunity to regain a sense of strength.

It should be noted that when a parent loses an adult child, there are three additional factors (Shanfield, Swain, and Benjamin 1986–87) that can affect the grieving process, beyond those already mentioned:

1. Nature of the death—sudden or anticipated
2. Gender and age of parent(s) and child(ren)
3. Aspects of the parent-adult child relationship

Due to the immense gulf between parents' response to the death of a child and society's response, it is all the more important for death care professionals to be aware of opportunities to be of service to families in this situation. First of all, professionals need to remember some of the reasons society responds differently than do the surviving family members. Lasch (1977) and Lifton (1979) have identified some of the problems:

1. The culture of individualism
2. The loss of looser social networks precipitated by the focus on close, nuclear families
3. Weakening of rituals

It is important for funeral professionals to reinforce the fact that what the parents are feeling is acceptable and normal, and that they are very probably going to experience a wide range of feelings at different times. It may also be possible, at an appropriate moment, to point out to them that society, in general, is uncomprehending of the overwhelming nature of their loss—that they should expect well-meaning people to inadvertently say or do the "wrong" thing.

When dealing with grieving parents, funeral professionals should stand ready and be prepared to repeat their willingness to offer appropriate information, support group referral, or follow-up consultation. They should, at all times, create an atmosphere of security, comfort, and accessibility.

Death of a Sibling

We will approach this section in the same manner as for the death of a parent—from the perspective of an adult loss. The information here can be also applied to a cousin, close friend, or in-law who was important in the griever's life.

From a societal view, this type of loss is probably the least acknowledged. Death of a sibling is seen as having less impact on surviving brothers and sisters, and therefore social response and attention are directed toward parents, spouses, or children of the deceased. Even a review of the literature reveals an absence of information regarding adults' response to the death of a sibling.

But it is not without emotional foundation that we reserve the compliment "just like a brother or sister," to describe only an individual who is enormously important to us. A bereaved sibling may have no memory of his or her life without the dead brother or sister. Shared parents, a shared home, and shared lives create an inextricable bond, one that may grow stronger (or blossom for the first time) during adulthood.

Unlike widowed people who can choose to remarry, a bereaved sibling can never replace the loss. It is uniquely devastating, creating a gap in the birth order and inevitably requiring a reorganization of roles for surviving brothers and sisters. Death of a sibling can be particularly problematic in a two-child family, as responsibilities toward surviving parents (and expectations of those parents) now shift onto the sole remaining adult child.

Death of a sibling may also constitute the first time an individual has faced the death of someone from his or her own generation, forcing a very personal confrontation of one's mortality. Concurrently, an adult child may wish to seek out surviving parents for security, comfort, and guidance during this painful time, but may feel this would be burdensome, inappropriate, or unseemly, since the parents are grieving as well.

In view of the lack of significance society places on sibling grief, it is very helpful for funeral professionals to "check in with" and identify the needs of surviving siblings. Healthy responses to the loss can be encouraged by referral to general bereavement support groups, where siblings can receive reassurance that their grief is important.

IMPLICATIONS FOR FUNERAL DIRECTORS

The four types of losses we have discussed in terms of the potential social and individual response have very direct implications for the environment, attitudes, and behavior funeral professionals should strive to employ in their dealings with the newly bereaved:

- The funeral director should recognize that society's perception of a death may not always "track" with the individual's response to it.
- The funeral director should be sensitive to any conflict mourners have between what is generally expected of them and what they actually feel. Validating mourners' feelings allows them to better clarify their own and others' needs.
- Availability at the funeral home of a variety of resources (support groups, workshops, counseling) for all types of losses is invaluable to clients.
- A small library of books at the funeral home dealing with death, dying, grief, and bereavement is a useful and helpful feature for families.
- Funeral professionals must always keep in mind that some individuals may have no previous experience with a death so close to them—if they have any experience at all. The entire funeral process and procedures may be unfamiliar, requiring clear, complete, and accurate communication.

SUMMARY

Our society has developed generalized responses to death through a variety of socialization processes. Among these are society's organizing principles, ideas, beliefs, values, and patterns of culture created through collective experiences. Two major influences on our responses to death are the media and the role of our peers. In recent years the media have affected us through the portrayal of death in abbreviated, unrealistic, and distorted forms. We are influenced by our peers through the permeation of death references in our everyday language. Such death references, collectively, may serve to numb us to the actual pain, work, and grief associated with real death.

Death-related ideas and the social responses that arise around them also are influenced by the demographics of society. Specifically, age, gender, and race have the most impact. In terms of age, the single fact of the overall drop in mortality rates affects society's general response to death. The gender factor comes into play through variables within lifestyles that might decrease the chances for a long life (e.g., stress, poor diet, smoking). Further, the patterns between race and mortality are consistent with patterns regarding social class and mortality. Basically, as education and income increase, mortality is reduced.

A closer look at our culture reveals various types of societal and individual responses to death. Death of a parent causes a loss of nurturing, guidance, and protection. Death of a spouse creates responses that require assistance in helping integrate widows and widowers into their new social status. Although the death of a child deeply strikes the heart of a parent, society often expects the parent to grieve in a similar time frame and manner as might be appropriate for death of a parent, mate, or sibling. This is unrealistic and must be understood by the death care professional. Finally, death of a sibling has long been the least acknowledged by society. In reality, it is uniquely devastating and requires profound support and compassion.

Society's various responses to death have direct implications for the funeral director. These include recognition of societal myths about individual responses to death, the need for sensitivity toward the mourners' perceptions of how society expects them to behave, and the importance of providing resources for grievers such as support groups, workshops, books, and so on.

REFERENCES

Anderson, C. 1949. Aspects of pathological grief and mourning. *International Journal of Psycho-analysis* 30:48–55.

Bank, S., and Kahn. 1982. *The sibling bond*. New York: Basic Books.

Berardo, F. 1968. Widowhood status in the U.S.: Perspective on the neglected aspect of the family cycle. *The Family Coordinator* 17:192.

Birtchnell, J. 1975. Psychiatric breakdown following recent parent death. *British Journal of Medical Psychology* 48, 379–90.

Blauner, R. Death and social structure, *Psychiatry,* 1966, 29:378–94.

Bruni, F. 1995. Deeply stylish. *Detroit Free Press,* March 3.

Bunch, J. 1971. The influence of parental death anniversaries upon suicide rates. *British Journal of Psychiatry* 118:621–25.

Donnelly, K. F. 1983. *Recovering from the loss of a child.* New York: Macmillan.

Edelstein, L. 1984. *Maternal bereavement.* New York: Praeger.

Frankel, V. 1963. *Man's search for meaning.* New York: Hemisphere Publishing.

Frogge, S. 1991. *We hurt, too.* Irving, Tex.: Mothers Against Drunk Driving.

Gibala, J. 1992. Funeral directors and AARP working together. *Florida Funeral Director,* November–December, pp. 20–21.

Kitagawa, E. M. P., and M. Hauser. 1973. *Differential mortality in the United States.* Cambridge, Mass.: Harvard University Press.

Lasch, C. 1977. *Haven in a heartless world: The family besieged.* New York: Basic Books.

LaTour, K. 1983. *For those who live.* Omaha, Neb.: Centering Corporation.

Lehman, D. R., J. H. Ellard, and C. B. Wortman. 1986. Social support for the bereaved: Recipients' and providers' perspectives on what is helpful. *Journal of Consulting and Clinical Psychology* 54, no. 4:438–46.

Lieberman, M., L. Borman, et al. 1979. *Self-help groups for coping with crisis.* San Francisco: Jossey-Bass.

Lifton, R. J. 1979. *The broken connection.* New York: Simon and Schuster.

Littlewood, J. 1992. *Aspects of grief.* New York: Routledge.

Lord, J. H. 1991. *No time for goodbyes.* Ventura, Calif.: Pathfinder Publishing.

Lund, D. A., Caterta, and Diamond. 1986. Identifying elderly with coping difficulties after two years of bereavement. *Omega,* 3, 231–24.

Osterweis, M., F. Solomon, and M. Green. 1984. *Bereavement reactions, consequences, and care.* Washington, D.C.: National Academy Press.

Preston, S. H. 1968. Analysis of a change in western mortality patterns. Ph.D. diss., Princeton University.

Rando, T. A. 1983. An investigation of grief and adaptation in parents whose children have died from cancer. *Journal of Pediatric Psychology,* 8:3–20.

Raphael, B. 1983. *The anatomy of bereavement.* New York: Basic Books.

Roberts, C. 1994. *Living with grief: Personally and professionally.* A National Bereavement Teleconference. Washington, D.C.: Hospice Foundation.

Shanfield, S. B., B. J. Swain, and G. A. H. Benjamin. 1986–87. Parents' responses to the death of adult children from accident and cancer: A comparison. *Omega,* 7, no. 4:289–97.

United States Bureau of the Census. 1994. *Statistical abstract of the United States, 1990.*

Wass, H., Felix Berardo, and Robert Neimeyer, eds., 1988. *Dying: Facing the facts,* 2d ed. New York: Hemisphere Publishing.

Wolterstorff, N. 1987. *Lament for a son.* Grand Rapids, Mich.: Wm. Eerdman Publishing.

6

SYSTEM COORDINATION APPROACH FOR THE DYING PATIENT

John D. Canine

Our society includes a variety of individuals, resources, and organizations that may, at different times, need to become involved in the dying process of a patient. For the purposes of this chapter, we will refer to any of these people or groups who have an impact on dying and death as a "system," and will attempt to show how systems can best interrelate while providing support for the terminally ill. The advantages of a death plan and the importance of good communication also will be addressed. Toward the end of the chapter there are some discussion questions based on case information; these should assist death care professionals in better understanding the full service—to clients and the community at large—that quality funeral firms are able to provide.

DEATH PLAN: ORDER OUT OF CHAOS

A "system," by definition, is a group of elements that interact and function together as a whole. All of us may be dependent at various times on the medical care

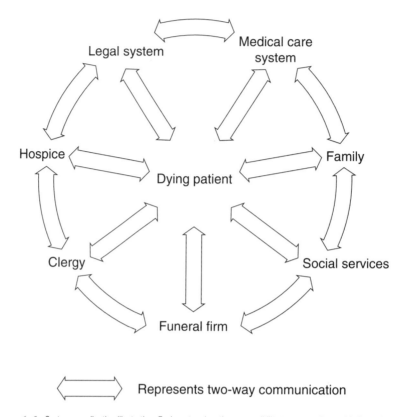

Represents two-way communication

Figure 6–1. System coordination illustration. Each system has the responsibility to communicate with the patient as well as with the other systems involved. (Dr. John D. Canine and Therese McNeil, Maximum Living, Birmingham, 1995)

system, an emotional support system, or the legal system. These, however, are only three of the systems that can easily become involved (perhaps even simultaneously) in the experiences of a dying patient—along with the family system, clergy or spiritual system, social services system, and funeral firm system.

The system coordination approach recommended here is designed to make the dying and death as personal, comfortable, rational, satisfying, and "accurate" as possible for the individual (see Figure 6–1). But this goal is not without its problems.

The worry and flurry that often follow a terminal diagnosis understandably create confusion and miscommunication as shock and denial set in. Many different people may have their own particular ideas on "what to do" for the dying patient. The patient may have strong ideas of his or her own, presuming the illness and treatment allow for clarity of thought. Too often, though, the patient can be ignored among the clatter and chatter of family members, nurses, friends, lawyers, clergy—and anyone else who gets into the act. At such a time, decisions are far too important to be made in an atmosphere of chaos, contradiction, and cacophony. The question of whether to continue medical treatment may arise, as may the question of removal to a hospice.

Each system, of course, has its own objectives, points of view, feelings, and concerns. Thus, it is not difficult to see the benefits of developing a death plan that will serve to coordinate the efforts of all the constituents in a way that satisfies the dying patient. A death plan, quite simply, is a commitment made by all systems to follow through on agreed-upon actions that support the dying patient. Some plans are more formalized than others and may be impacted by the nature of the illness, the complexity of the patient's personal and business affairs, and the number and relationships of involved family members. What is important about the death plan from a systems perspective is that it must clearly express the roles and responsibilities of each system and how they will interrelate on behalf of the patient.

Obviously, a death plan needs to be flexible. Adjustments, additions, and deletions may be required as the patient's situation changes. If one goal of the plan is proper care and support, adjustments may have to be made in terms of visiting the patient (who and when), exploring medical and environmental (housing) options, and dealing with the patient's personal affairs (paying bills, banking, etc.) if he or she is no longer able to handle such chores. Therefore it is vital that all systems agree to

- Share new information with other, affected systems
- Compromise
- Remain accountable to the patient and to other systems involved in the death plan

The following story is an example of how the lack of communication (sharing new information) caused conflict for a patient:

> In 1993, a sixty-five-year-old male with four adult children was diagnosed with lung cancer. The two children who live in the area were told of the situation, and the two out-of-town children were not. During a subsequent hospital admission for an infection, the two out-of-town children came to visit him in the hospital. The attending physician entered the room and began discussing the cancer as it related to the current infection. When the doctor left, the out-of-town children confronted their ill father with a mix of anger, hurt, and surprise. He said since they lived so far away, he didn't want to burden them with the bad news.

It is hard to blame the out-of-town children for their reaction, isn't it? And what sort of dynamic or framework does this situation set up between the four siblings? Between the out-of-town siblings and the doctor? What other thoughts, fears, or suspicions might be going through the minds of the out-of-town children? And, under the circumstances, how easy will it be for the "in-town" children to ask the others for help, should that be necessary? Most important, what are the possible ramifications for the dying patient?

If this family is to ultimately function in a system coordination approach for the dying patient, they will need to develop a death plan. In so doing, they will need to complete the following tasks:

- Identify each responsible system involved with the dying patient.
- Define the current and long-term goals, jobs, roles, and communication "paths" within the death plan.
- Determine methods for periodic "review" of the plan.
- Consult with the dying patient, allowing him as much control over the plan as he wishes to assume.
- Identify the dying patient's "representative," who ultimately coordinates and monitors the plan, assuring its implementation.

"WORKING" THE PLAN

The dying patient and his or her family are dependent on a number of society's systems to assure that the patient receives appropriate care, is able to "make the most" of the present life experience, and ultimately dies and is memorialized in a manner consistent with his or her wishes. The single most critical task to achieving these goals is communication. Consistent communication among the systems promotes a deeper and current understanding of the patient's (changing) needs. For example, if the patient asks her physician to place a "no code" order on her chart, this must be communicated to any other doctors involved and all shifts of the nursing staff. The hospital social worker and/or chaplain may also want this information. Family members may wish to take this as a signal to investigate or implement other services, such as a hospice or preplanned funeral arrangements. Without this constant sharing of information, families of dying patients and the professional systems who interact with them may encounter situations that create frustration, confusion, embarrassment, or open conflict—taking away focus and energy that are better spent on the dying patient.

The most favorable situation, of course, is when the patient himself is able to direct the plan. This allows the individual to maintain the positive feelings that come with empowerment, control, and self-reliance, as well as facilitates a healthy and realistic acceptance of the coming death. If the patient is not able to direct the plan, he or she may still be able to select an appropriate representative, gaining a sense of security and trust that the "preferred" person will be implementing his or her wishes and making "good" decisions. The role of representative can be filled by a family member, close friend, attorney, health care professional, or spiritual adviser. Regardless of who takes on the job, communication is still the essential task of the death plan. The designated representative must see to it that all systems are sharing information so they may function according to the plan agreements.

In addition, there are practical activities and techniques that people "working the plan" can use to share needed information and to help themselves, each other, and the patient. While the particular circumstances of every dying patient will be different, some possible, useful activities include the following:

- Have the patient (or someone close to the patient, if he or she is unable) make a list of favorite foods, flowers, music, or anything that might constitute an allowable special treat.
- Have the patient list his or her regular, monthly sources of income and expenditures, as well as bank information, or assign someone to do so.
- If practical, give the patient a tape recorder to record any thought, needs, concerns, or questions he or she may have; encourage faraway friends or relatives to tape a "letter" or greeting for the patient.
- Schedule regular discussions with physicians, nurses, hospice workers, or other appropriate individuals.
- Learn hospital procedures, visiting hours, overnight opportunities, and so on for families of dying patients, or assign this job to someone.
- Assemble resource information from other systems: home care assistance, meals-on-wheels, markets and pharmacies that make home deliveries, transportation services, hospice, funeral firms, appropriate clergy.
- Ask other systems (social workers, senior centers, religious institutions, funeral firms) how services to dying people interrelate in the community.
- Join or refer other system members to support groups that may be available through hospitals, hospices, or religious organizations.

As the death plan shifts into high gear and various tasks are completed, designated representatives should be sure to invite\all systems to use their initiative to explore any means or opportunity to meet the dying person's needs. And, as always, share the information!

PROFESSIONAL SYSTEMS COORDINATION: STANDARDS AND EDUCATION IN THE CARE OF DYING PATIENTS

Any professional system, regardless of its purpose, requires continuing education to meet the needs of its clientele. This is equally true for professional systems involved with dying and death. Many health care organizations and licensing boards require continuing education as a condition to maintain employment. But whether mandated or not, the constant updating of knowledge, information, and techniques based on new research and/or peer learning is extremely valuable in helping the professional system service dying patients and their families.

A number of organizations also establish written standards that, in their judgment, should be maintained in order to deliver a preferred level of professional assistance and care. An excellent illustration of this type of effort can be found in the second volume of the *Accreditation Manual for Home Care* (1995), by the Joint Commission on American Hospital Organizations (JCAHO).

The manual includes well-developed guidelines that deal with, on one side, continual assessment of patients' needs to accurately meet their needs and those of their families. Answers to the assessment can help professionals develop a death plan that is suited to the particular circumstances of the client being served, and indicate what additional systems may need to be included for optimum care. Assessment areas encompass the following:

- Severity of pain
- Patient's and family's religious or spiritual orientation
- Emotional needs and concerns, such as despair, depression, or fear, among patients and family
- Patient's and/or family's involvement in educational or support groups around the disease and/or dying
- Psychosocial status—social history, coping skills, family relationships, availability, and openness to use additional resources
- Caregiver options allowing adequate respite

Answers to the assessment process become the starting point for professionals within the system to deliver quality, established standards of care and performance. These individuals are required (the flip side of the guidelines) to be educated and proficient in the following areas:

- Concepts of death and dying
- Communication skills with dying patients and families
- Handling and helping with death in the home
- Psychosocial and spiritual issues related to death and dying
- Grief and bereavement
- Stress management for staff individuals involved in care of dying patients

Continuing education for death care systems professionals (classes, workshops, seminars) is often available through community colleges, colleges, and universities and their extension systems, most often through their departments of psychology, mortuary science, social work, and sociology. Departments of religious studies as well as seminaries may also offer educational opportunities for professionals in service to the dying and their families.

Professional associations and their local chapters (e.g., National Association of Social Workers, National Funeral Directors Association, and National Hospice Organization) are another source for standards, guidelines, and opportunities for ongoing professional learning (see Figure 6–2).

To summarize, the most important point for any death care systems worker or professional to remember is to respect the dying patient. Therese Rando, in her book *Grief, Dying, and Death* (1984), outlines principles that underlie all standards for dealing with the terminally ill:

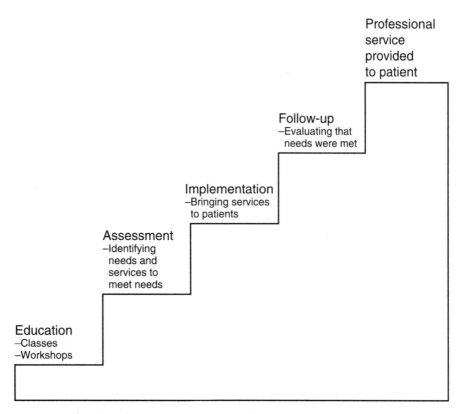

Figure 6–2. Steps for individuals in service provider systems. The goal of professional service can be reached by completing the objectives in each step. (Dr. John D. Canine and Therese McNeil, Maximum Living Consultants, Inc., Birmingham, 1995)

- These patients require highly competent professionals, skilled in terminal care.
- Pain should be controlled in all its respects. The patient should be kept as pain-free as possible, while remaining as alert and comfortable as possible.
- Staff must recognize that other services may need to be involved but that continuity of care should be provided whenever possible.
- The terminally ill patient's own framework of values, preferences, and outlook on life must be taken into account in planning and conducting treatment.
- The patient's wishes for information about his or her condition should be respected; the patient should be allowed full participation in the care and a continuing sense of self-determination and self-control.
- The patient should have a sense of security and protection; involvement of family and friends should be encouraged.
- Twenty-four-hour care must be made available seven days a week for the patient and family, when and where it is needed. (Pp. 294–95)

THE FUNERAL FIRM AS PART OF SYSTEM COORDINATION

Unquestionably, the funeral firm (home) and its staff have a major role to play in death plans for the terminally ill. The efficacy and success of the funeral home's involvement depend heavily on the commitment of the staff to develop and sustain a strong rapport with other related systems in the community and its internal continuing education mandate to stay abreast of changes and expansion in quality services available to dying patients and their families (see Figure 6–3).

Funeral firms must develop a strategy for their services. The first component of such a strategy should be determining exactly what the firm can and cannot do for a dying patient. Funeral home administrators and managers should ask themselves the following questions regarding their operation and services, in terms of both clients and employees:

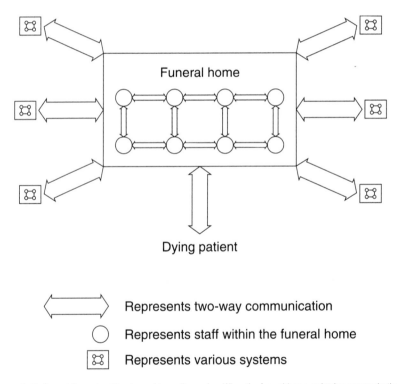

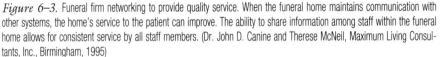

Figure 6–3. Funeral firm networking to provide quality service. When the funeral home maintains communication with other systems, the home's service to the patient can improve. The ability to share information among staff within the funeral home allows for consistent service by all staff members. (Dr. John D. Canine and Therese McNeil, Maximum Living Consultants, Inc., Birmingham, 1995)

- Who in the firm is responsible for establishing and monitoring the firm's procedures and policies?
- Are all staff members familiar with the firm's services, guidelines, and procedures?
- Does the firm have procedures in place for making prearrangements for a dying person?
- As changes occur within the firm's procedures, policies, guidelines, or scope of services, are dying clients and their families informed, so as to make any necessary adjustments in the death plan?
- When changes are made in a death plan, can the firm adapt smoothly?
- Does the funeral firm provide opportunities and information for its staff regarding continuing education in working with dying people and their families?

A second component of a funeral firm's overall strategic planning involves dissemination of information and communication with other systems that support dying patients. Funeral firms need to identify the full spectrum of organizations and institutions within the geographic area they serve and determine the "messages" (and image) they wish to convey, along with appropriate methods for that communication.

SUMMARY

Various individuals, resources, and organizations need to become involved in the dying process of a patient. A system coordination approach to the dying process can make the dying and death as personal, comfortable, rational, satisfying, and accurate as possible for the individual. Each system, of course, has its own objectives, points of view, feelings, and concerns. Thus, the development of a death plan that will coordinate the efforts of all the necessary constituents can be an important step in caring for the dying patient.

A death plan is a commitment made by all systems to follow through on agreed-upon actions that support the dying patient. It is vital that all systems agree to sharing new information, compromising, and remaining accountable to the patient and to the other systems involved. The single, most critical task to achieving the goals of the plan is communication. Consistent communication among the systems promotes a deeper and current understanding of the patient's needs. It is preferable that the patient direct the plan. However, if necessary, the patient should be the one to designate a representative to serve in this capacity. The designated representative must see to it that all systems are sharing information so they can function according to the plan agreements.

Any professional system requires continuing education to meet the needs of its clientele. The constant updating of knowledge, information, and techniques based on new research and/or peer learning is extremely valuable in servicing the dying patient. However, the most important point for any death care systems worker is to respect the dying patient. Principles are provided in this chapter for death care professionals to follow when dealing with the terminally ill.

REFERENCES

Bartlett, H. 1970. *The common base of social work practice.* New York: National Association of Social Workers.

Helmstetter, S. 1989. *Choices.* New York: Simon and Schuster.

Joint Commission on American Hospital Organizations. 1995. *Accreditation manual for home care.*

Kubler-Ross, E. 1969. *On death and dying.* New York: Macmillan.

Pincus, A., and A. Minahan, eds., 1973. *Social work practice, model, and method.* Ithaca, N.Y.: F. E. Peacock, Publisher.

Rando, T. 1984. *Grief, dying, and death.* Champaign, Ill.: Research Press.

Wass, Hannalore, Felix Berardo, and Robert Neimeyer, eds., 1988. *Dying: Facing the facts.* 2d ed. New York: Hemisphere Publishing.

7

LEGAL IMPLICATIONS FOR THE DYING PATIENT AND THE FAMILY

John D. Canine

As we go through life we assimilate personal property. At the time of death this personal property becomes the "estate." While most people are somewhat hesitant to confront the details of their deaths, they have a general idea of how they want their personal property distributed. However, the only way to be sure that family and friends will be financially and physically cared for is to distribute the estate according to the law. Arranging for the transfer of ownership of all of the deceased's personal property is a complex task in most cases. It should be undertaken with the assistance of an attorney and should be discussed long before the individual dies. It should also be pointed out that the disposition of a person's body is also regulated by law and varies from state to state. Therefore, where a person lives at the time of death controls the disposition of both personal property and the body. Thus, state laws have an impact on the family's planning, as does federal law, which is applied nationwide.

The purpose of this chapter is to acquaint the reader with the laws regarding disposition of personal property, the legal disposal of the body, and right-to-die issues. The reader should review the exact laws from his or her state, and any estate planning should be periodically reviewed and updated because of changes in the law.

DISPOSITION OF PERSONAL PROPERTY

Probate

The word "probate" comes from the Latin for "to prove." It refers to the court proceedings required to settle on the estate. A probate estate includes any property held in the deceased's name, which means joint assets are not included. When all assets were joint or plans were made for all assets to be distributed outside the will, an estate does not require settlement by the probate process. On the other hand, some of the estates settled through probate are quite complex and time-consuming. Under the supervision of the courts, the administration of the estate is handled by the deceased's personal representative. He or she is called either the executor or, if appointed by the court, the administrator. Usually the representative has thirty days to file the will with the court following the death. Once the court recognizes the will and the representative, it authorizes the management and transfer functions by the executor on behalf of the estate. The executor is responsible for taking an inventory of the estate, connecting assets, paying all debts and claims against the estate, paying taxes, arranging for the preparation of documents, distributing property to those who are entitled to it, and eventually closing the estate. In most states the executor will publish notices that all creditors who have claims against the estate must file them within a four- to six-month period. When that period expires, no further claims against the estate can be considered. The entire probate process can take anywhere from six to twenty-four months and, in some cases, longer (Dukeminier and Johanson 1983).

The Will

A person who writes a will is called a "testator." A will must be probated to be effective, and is considered the normal and legal manner in which one transfers personal property following death. In many states it is a crime to withhold a will. If a person has not prepared a valid will, he has died intestate. Sheryl Scheible explains in *Dying: Facing the Facts* (1988):

> Intestacy statutes are drafted and enacted by a state's legislators based on their assumptions of how a typical person would want his or her property distributed. The details of these statutes vary considerably between states, but general patterns of heirship exist. A surviving spouse and children are preferred heirs. If a child of a decedent has predeceased his or her parent, that child's children or other descendants take the decedent's child's share as representatives of their parents. In the absence of descendants, some states allow a surviving spouse to take the entire estate, while others apportion the estate between the spouse and the decedent's parents, if living. When a person dies leaving no surviving descendants or spouse, the property passes to the descendant's ancestor and descendants of those ancestors. . . .
>
> Except for a surviving spouse, only parties related to a descendant through bloodlines or by legal adoption are considered heirs; persons related by marriage, such as in-laws, or by informal relationships, such as cohabitants, foster children or friends, are excluded from intestacy statutes. The statutes often prohibit inheritance by persons only distantly related to a decedent. When an intestate person leaves no one who qualifies as an heir under the state's intestacy statute, the estate "escheats" or passes to the state. (Pp. 302–303)

Basically, Scheible's point is, if you don't write a will, the state will write one for you. And if you don't have a preference in terms of transferring personal property, the state will keep your property! The following are some facts concerning wills:

1. Any adult of "sound mind" is permitted to dispose of his or her personal property (estate) by will.
2. If the testator is influenced by another party to the extent the will does not represent his or her true intentions, it can be invalid.
3. A legal and formal will must be witnessed by at least two people.
4. Most states will recognize handwritten wills ("holographic"), but this is extremely risky and should not be encouraged.
5. A will is regarded as "ambulatory"—meaning it can be changed at any time prior to the testator's death. (Scheible 1988)

Trusts

A trust is a means by which an individual can share assets (primarily financial) with others without making an outright gift. For example, moneys can be placed in a fund by a third party, such as a bank, trust company, or individual experienced in managing and investing property, and the income and capital of that trust are distributed to the beneficiary in accordance with the guidelines established by the benefactor. The two most often stated reasons for a trust are (1) the assurance that funds will not be mismanaged by a relative and (2) the assurance that the money will be used for an exact purpose (e.g., college education).

The trust can be formal, managed and operative while the benefactor ("trustor") is still in good health. In fact, the trustor has a great deal of control over the distribution of funds both before and after death. If the trust is established after the trustor's death according to the instructions of the will, it is called a testamentary trust.

Flexibility is one of the major advantages of trusts. A testator might design a trust virtually any way he or she wishes. For instance, in providing for minor children, the trust might be set up as a single fund for all the children, or in separate shares. In a single-fund trust, the trustee is directed to provide for the needs of all children until the youngest child reaches twenty-one (or whatever age the parents determine). Although the youngest child did not have the benefit of the parents' love and encouragement as many years as the older siblings, at least their financial support will be available until the child reaches the specified age. Following the parents' death, a separate share trust can give older siblings a larger share than would be theirs under a single-fund arrangement. However, this is not always fair to the younger siblings. There still might be restrictions regarding disbursing of income, and eventually perhaps the principal of the trust at designated ages or life events such as marriage, birth of a child, purchase of a home, or graduation from college.

Money from the trust might come from the existing estate or a life insurance policy. Trusts usually are managed by a trust company or trust department of a financial institution, taking only a small percentage of the money for making the investments. The trustor can name anyone as trustee, himself included as long as he is alive. He can name successor trustees upon his death or the death of the original trustee.

Trusts are versatile and efficient and, if handled properly, can be a considerable tax savings. There are many trust options when planning an estate (Vail 1982).

Death Taxes

There are two basic types of taxes following a death: estate tax and inheritance tax. The purpose of these taxes is to generate revenue for the government and to restrict inheritance of great amounts of wealth. An estate tax is levied on the decedent's estate and paid by the executor from the estate before any assets are transferred to beneficiaries. On the other hand, an inheritance tax is imposed on individuals who receive property through inheritance.

The federal estate tax is based on the total assets of the estate minus the debts and deductions (spouse, children under twenty-one years of age, and charities). As of 1987, only estates valued at six thousand dollars and above are subject to the federal estate tax. It should be noted that the marital deduction applies if the decedent is survived by a spouse. Using it, one spouse can transfer an unlimited amount of property tax-free to the widowed partner.

Although a beneficiary does not have to pay federal income tax on gifts, most states will tax them either instead of or in addition to an estate tax. If an individual receives property that is taxed by the state, usually the tax is paid by the executor from the estate. Then it is deducted from the beneficiary's share. As one can see, estate planning is extremely complex, and professional estate planners should be consulted to minimize estate losses due to federal and state taxes (Scheible 1988).

DISPOSAL OF THE BODY

The disposal of the body following a death is a matter of social custom. Within American culture there is much similarity among individuals in the funeralization process. However, other countries and cultures watch in amazement as we select elaborate and expensive caskets, embalm and dress up our dead for display, and finally inter them in magnificent stainless steel and concrete underground vaults in a gardenlike cemetery. Some legal restrictions on disposal of the body are designed to protect the public health and safety. The law further tries to protect survivors from unfair funeral practices in the purchasing of goods and services relating to the funeral, burial, or some other disposition of the body. On the other hand, it is apparent that the law is either silent or uncertain in many areas of rights and duties in the disposition of the body and the entire funeralization process. The following discussion is intended to acquaint the reader with the way our culture treats its dead.

What to Do with the Body

Like all other legal rights, the control of one's body ends at death. Therefore, any requests a person might have expressed during his or her life about the death, funeral, burial, or cremation, either orally or written, might be considered but are not legally binding. After a death occurs, the right to arrange the funeral and plan for the disposal of the body is granted to the nearest relative, next of kin, a household member, or, in some cases, the executor of the estate. When there is a conflict over the intentions of the deceased or who should arrange for the disposal of the body, the courts have tried to intervene. However, case law in this area is very inconsistent and state statutes are inadequate.

Anatomical Donations

Since gifts of anatomical parts at death are a source of life to transplant patients, our society in general has taken kindly to those who choose to donate their bodies, in part or in whole, for legitimate medical purposes. The Uniform Anatomical Gift Act (1983) permits a person's request to donate an organ (or body) to be honored without the consent of the surviving family. The act also allows the following:

1. Any adult can donate an entire body or specific organ to any hospital, physician, medical school, or dental school.
2. The donation can be used for medical education, research, therapy, or transplant purposes.
3. The gift can be made in "general" or to a specific individual.
4. When an individual has not executed a donor card or the card cannot be found at death, family members can consent to an anatomical gift.
5. After the donation has been made, the body can be returned to the family for disposal or cremated (except for body donations).

The Uniform Anatomical Gift Act encourages states to have a short and simple form that can be included in the will. Some forms are so short they can be included on the back of a driver's license or senior citizen's card. Two witnesses are required, and the donor must be competent at the time the instrument is executed.

While the act has had some effect on increasing the number of organs available for transplant, many potential donors are still undiscovered. The demand for organs greatly surpasses the supply. It is currently illegal in all states to routinely remove organs without the consent of the donor or the survivors. Furthermore, if certain organs have been donated, it is illegal to remove other body parts.

There are still many issues—medically, ethically, and legally—to be worked out concerning anatomical gifts. However, at the present time in American culture, donation of a body and body parts is not only accepted but also appreciated.

Health Regulations

Most states have health restrictions concerning the disposal of a body. These regulations protect both the survivors and the general public. The following are some of the most common regulations:

- To control sanitation and prevent the spread of contagious or infectious disease, the location and operation of a funeral home are subject to certain restrictions.
- If the body is not disposed of within a certain amount of time, embalming is mandated.
- A burial permit might be required by a state or local health board.
- Local zoning laws might restrict the site in a cemetery.
- Some states have laws regulating the transportation of a body.
- Some states prohibit the scattering of crematory ashes.
- Most states have laws regulating the exhuming of a body. A body might be disinterred by a court order in a criminal case, or less frequently, in civil cases such as a suit brought on an insurance claim. (Scheible 1988)

Federal Trade Commission

Because individuals in the funeral service business work so closely with the general public, all states have regulations pertaining to the education, training, and licensing of funeral directors and embalmers. State agencies supervise sanitation, professional conduct, and advertising and business practices of the funeral profession. The funeral industry provides merchandise and service to over two million American families a year at an average cost of over $2,400.00. Since many individuals are emotionally distraught at the time of making funeral arrangements, and must make decisions on the purchase of expensive funeral items, federal regulations provide protection from deceptive funeral business practices (Roybol 1984).

The Bureau of Consumer Protection of the Federal Trade Commission began investigating the funeral industry in the early 1970s. As a result of this investigation, federal restrictions known as the "funeral rule" were enacted in 1984. As Scheible states:

> The rule requires full disclosure of costs related to funeral goods and services and requires the sale of individual items as an alternative to a complete package. Alternative prices of types of caskets and outer burial containers must be revealed, and the requirements imposed by both the law and the selected cemetery with regard to specific goods must be disclosed. Funeral providers may not make claims that expensive products are necessary for cremation. The provider must inform the consumer when embalming is not required by law and must make no inaccurate claims regarding any preservative effect of particular items. (1985, p. 317)

All funeral service items must be itemized with cost disclosure. By providing the consumer with full information regarding funeral services, the funeral professional is enhancing a more educated choice by the consumer as well as projecting a more positive business image in the community.

THE RIGHT TO DIE

Over the last few years there has been much social dialogue on the subject of euthanasia. Euthanasia, meaning "good" death, is taken from the Greek words for easy (*eu* as in euphoria) and death (*Thanatos,* the Greek god for death). In the past, if an individual did not die in an accident or commit suicide, then the death was considered "natural." However, with the ambiguity that advanced medical technology brings to prolonging life, and the lack of a clear definition of when death occurs, the public is confused as to what constitutes death with "unnatural interference." The purpose of this section is not to resolve the ongoing debate over the right to die but rather give the reader some thoughts on preserving life, preventing suicide, assuring the integrity of the medical profession, and protecting the patient's family members.

Many states have enacted "death-with-dignity" or "right-to-die" legislation.

These laws legitimize an individual's desire to decline life-prolonging treatment when death is imminent. The expression of this desire occurs through a document referred to as a "living will." Many organizations (e.g., Concern for Dying Education Council, Society for the Right to Die, Choice in Dying) have drafted living wills to disseminate to the general public. However, without state law, these wills are not legally binding, but still might offer some assurance that family and physician will honor a formalized stated intent. "Right-to-die" statutes vary from state to state; answers to the following questions will vary according to your state legislation.

1. Does the patient have to be terminally ill before executing a living will?
2. How many witnesses does the living will require, and do the witnesses have to be someone other than family and medical team?
3. Is the living will revocable?
4. Does the living will have a time limit?
5. What happens to the physician or medical team if they fail to comply?
6. What happens to patients who are comatose, incompetent, or of minor age?
7. What happens if the patient is a pregnant woman?

By 1986 many states had adopted the Uniform Determination of Death Act, which declares that an individual can be pronounced dead ". . . who has sustained either: (1) irreversible cessation of circulatory and respiratory functions, or (2) irreversible cessation of all functions of the entire brain, including the brain stem. A determination of death is to be made in accordance with acceptable medical standards." Since this definition of death is highly scientific and medical, it is open to debate by other nonmedical professionals, specifically the clergy, who believe in "miracles." Nevertheless, it is a beginning, and it does offer some protection as well as guidance for patient, physician, and family members.

The "right-to-die" issue has reached a pinnacle with the question of "physician-assisted suicide." According to Denzian (1992), on an average 5,800 Americans die each day. Over 75 percent of these deaths are timed or negotiated. Some hospitals will ask terminally ill patients if they have a death plan. Medicide, assisted suicide, planned death, and the new medical humanism are present everywhere in our culture. To some, a self-managed death is the only recourse against the impersonal and inhumane medical establishment. Life at any cost is no longer desirable. People are seeking a less expensive way to die, especially when the last days of life in an intensive care unit can cost in excess of one hundred thousand dollars. This is where Dr. Jack Kevorkian, a retired physician from Michigan, enters the scene.

Kevorkian

To Dr. Kevorkian, "positive" death is rooted in a new medical humanism that would allow a patient and family to determine death. The benefits are less suffering for the patient, less psychological and emotional pain for the family, and a savings in resources that would have been spent on prolonged care. However, these benefits do not counterbalance the loss of life. Hence, Kevorkian adds another benefit—the dying patient can time his death so that donated organs can save the life of another. Even after death occurs the individual (dying patient) can make a contribution to medicine, science, and the society of humankind.

Kevorkian makes a distinction between negative and positive death. Negative death is that which offers no benefit to science or medicine. Those would include "obligatory" (death row), "assisted" (euthanasia), and "optional suicide" (mental illness) types of death. To him, negative death is a loss without meaning or positive social consequences. On the other hand, positive death is merciful to the patient and a process that gives something of value to the "suffering humanity left behind."

In his book *Prescription: Medicine—The Goodness of Planned Death,* (1991), Kevorkian expands his theory of positive death. Some of the highlights of his theory are as follows:

- An orbitoria would be a suicide center centrally located, organized, and well controlled so that merciful dignified death could occur.
- Following a death at an orbitoria, ethical and experimental manipulations on the body would occur.
- The doctoring of death to achieve some sort of beneficial result is called obitiatry. Thus, a new medical practitioner would be born to administer obitiatry.
- Mercitron is the machine that will be used to bring merciful death to the patient.
- Every community would have a five-member group of medicide specialists who would make final decisions on who should be connected to the mercitron. All members of the group must agree before death can occur.

Obviously, Kevorkian's theory of medicide needs to be further developed before a reluctant and skeptical society accepts it. However, he has brought a great deal of attention and thought to the issues of death with dignity and the right to die. Listed in the following are some definitions of terms that are generally accepted in the medical profession concerning the subject of merciful death. (Note: Dr. Jack Kevorkian's terms of medicide are not listed because they are not to date generally accepted by the medical profession.)

- Mercy killing—A deliberate and empathic act to end the life of a person who is suffering terribly from an illness or condition that will probably end life soon anyway.
- Euthanasia—A decision not to interfere with the inevitable death process.
- Antidysthanasia—"Dys" means difficult or painful. Therefore, antidysthanasia means against a difficult or painful death.
- Active euthanasia—Taking a decisive measure that will lead to early termination of the life of a patient already close to death.
- Passive euthanasia—Failure to begin or continue treatment that would prolong the life of a terminally ill person.
- Direct and positive euthanasia—A deliberate act to shorten a life, such as injection of a large volume of air directly into the bloodstream.

- Indirect and negative euthanasia—Allowing death to occur unimpeded by medical intervention.
- Voluntary euthanasia—The patient consents to, or even requests and cooperates in, bringing his or her life to an early death.
- Involuntary euthanasia—Shortening a patient's life for reasons of mercy without his or her consent.

The following questions are often asked by patients and their families. The responses are consistent with the law in the State of Michigan, and were prepared by the national organization Choice in Dying, Inc. (Choice in Dying 1994). Other states must be contacted regarding their laws, which do not necessarily match those in Michigan.

In Michigan, Whom Should I Appoint as My Patient Advocate?

Your patient advocate is the person you appoint to make decisions about your medical care if you become unable to make those decisions yourself. Your patient advocate may be a family member or a close friend whom you trust to make these serious decisions. The person you name as your patient advocate must be an adult who clearly understands your wishes and is willing to accept the responsibility of making medical decisions for you. (A patient advocate may also be called an "attorney-in-fact," "agent," or "proxy.")

You can also appoint a second person as your alternate patient advocate. The alternate will step in if the first person you name as patient advocate is unable, unwilling, or unavailable to act for you.

How Do I Make My Michigan Designation of Patient Advocate for Health Care Legal?

The law requires that you sign your designation in the presence of two witnesses, who also sign the document to show that you voluntarily signed the designation in their presence and that you appear to be of sound mind and under no duress, fraud, or undue influence. These witnesses cannot be any of the following:

- Your spouse, parent, child, grandchild, or sibling
- A person who stands to inherit from your estate, either by law or through a will
- A physician or patient advocate
- An employee of your life or health insurance provider
- An employee of your treating health care facility
- An employee of a home for the aged, if you are a patient in that facility

Should I Add Personal Instructions to My Michigan Designation of Patient Advocate for Health Care?

The answer to this question is no. Although space is provided where you may list limitations on your patient advocate's authority, Choice in Dying advises you *not* to restrict your patient advocate's authority. One of the strongest reasons for naming a patient advocate is to have someone who can respond flexibly as your medical situation changes, and can deal with situations that you did not foresee. If you add limitations to this document, you might unintentionally restrict your patient advocate's power to act in your best interests. Instead, we urge you to talk with your patient advocate about your future medical care, and to describe what you consider to be an acceptable quality of life. If you want to record your wishes about specific treatments or conditions, you should use your Choice in Dying Living Will.

In Michigan, What If I Change My Mind?

In Michigan, you may revoke your designation at any time and in any manner, regardless of your ability to make medical decisions. If your revocation is not in writing, you are required to have a witness to your revocation who must sign a written description of the revocation and, if possible, notify your patient advocate. Your designation is automatically revoked under any of the following circumstances:

- Your death occurs.
- Your patient advocate resigns or is removed by a probate court for failing to act in your best interest (unless you have appointed an alternate).
- You execute a subsequent designation.
- You have explicitly made a provision for revocation in your document.
- You name your spouse as your patient advocate and your marriage ends (unless you have appointed an alternate).

What Other Important Facts Should I Know?

In Michigan, other important facts include the following:

- Due to restrictions in the Michigan state law, a patient advocate does not have the authority to decide to withhold or withdraw life support from a pregnant patient.
- Your patient advocate and alternate (if any) must receive a copy of your document and must date and sign an acceptance to the designation before he or she makes medical decisions on your behalf.
- If you have religious convictions that prohibit you from being examined by a physician, you can add instructions to your designation stating that you do not wish to be examined by a physician. You must state in your designation how it shall be determined when your patient advocate has authority to make decisions on your behalf.

In Michigan, How Do I Make My Living Will Legal?

Because Michigan does not have a statute governing the use of living wills, there are no specific requirements to make your Choice in Dying living will legal. Choice in Dying recommends that you sign your living will in the presence of two adult witnesses. Your witnesses should not be any of the following:

- Related to you by blood or marriage
- Beneficiaries of your estate
- Your health care provider or an employee of your health care provider
- Your health care agent or proxy

Can I Add Personal Instructions to My Living Will?

Yes. In Michigan, you can add personal instructions in the part of the document called "Other directions." For example, if there are any specific forms of treatment that you wish to refuse that are not already listed on the document, you may list them here. Also, you can add instructions such as "I do not want to be placed in a nursing home," or "I want to die at home." If you have appointed a patient advocate, it is a good idea to write a statement such as "Any questions about how to interpret or when to apply my declaration are to be decided by my agent."

What If I Want to Revoke My Living Will?

You may revoke your living will in Michigan at any time by doing any of the following:

- Executing a new living will
- Tearing, burning, or otherwise destroying your document
- Notifying your doctor orally or in writing of your intent to revoke your document

What Do I Do After I Have Completed My Documents?

1. Your Michigan Designation of Patient Advocate for Health Care and Choice in Dying Living Will are important legal documents. Keep the original signed documents in a secure but accessible place. Do not put the original forms in a safe-deposit box or any other security box that would keep others from having access to them.
2. Give photocopies of the signed originals to your patient advocate and alternate patient advocate, to your doctor(s), family, close friends, clergy, and anyone else who might become involved in your health care. If you enter a nursing home or hospital, have photocopies of your documents placed in your medical records.
3. Be sure to talk to your patient advocate (and alternate), your doctor(s), clergy, and family and friends about your wishes concerning medical treatment. Discuss your wishes with them often, particularly if your medical condition changes.

4. If you want to make changes to your documents after they have been signed and witnessed, you must complete new documents.
5. Remember, you can always revoke your Michigan Designation of Patient Advocate for Health Care or your Choice in Dying Living Will.

The moral, ethical, and medical questions that are raised from the right-to-die issue go far beyond the scope of this chapter. There are no easy answers. The concerned student can only continue to try to understand. As Arthur Zucker states: "To seek a clear and easy answer is only to ensure a dissatisfaction which is more likely to lead one astray than is the tortuous path to legitimate understanding" (1988, p. 343).

SUMMARY

Upon death, our personal property becomes the "estate." Laws governing estate planning, including probate (court proceedings required to settle an estate), wills, trusts, and taxes, vary from state to state. It is important to review and understand the exact laws in your state.

The disposal of the body following a death is a matter of social custom. The American way is called a funeral. Funerals incorporate body preparation, viewing, caskets, vaults, and burial or cremation. In 1983 the Uniform Anatomical Gift Act was passed; it permits an individual to donate an organ or body for legitimate medical purposes. There are also state laws regulating the disposal of the body. Most states control the location of a funeral home, embalming, site of burial, transportation of a body, cremation and ashes, exhuming, and location of the cemetery. In 1984 the federal government passed funeral industry restrictions known as the "funeral rule."

Right-to-die issues have raised many moral, ethical, and medical questions concerning euthanasia. With the 1980 Uniform Determination of Death Act, the federal government took a step toward defining death. Although open to debate, the act does offer protection and guidance for a patient, physician, and family members. Jack Kevorkian has kept the right-to-die debate very much "alive" with his emphasis on physician-assisted suicide, or what he calls "positive" death. However, the debate is far from over, and currently American society has no clear definition as to a patient's right to die.

REFERENCES

Choice in Dying. 1994. *Michigan: Advance directive guide*. New York: Choice in Dying.
Denzian, Norman. 1992. The suicide machine. *Society Magazine*, July/August, pp. 7–10.
Dukeminier, J., and S. M. Johanson. 1983. *Wills, trusts, and estates*. Boston: Little, Brown.
Funeral Industry Practice (Funeral Rule). 1985. 16 C.F.R. 453.
Kevorkian, Jack. 1991. *The goodness of a planned death*. New York: Prometheus Books.

Roybal E. R. 1984. *A guide to funeral planning.* Washington, D.C.: U.S. Government Printing Office.

Scheible, Sheryl. 1988. Death and the law. In *Dying: Facing the facts,* 2d ed. Edited by Hannalore Wass, Felix Berardo, and Robert A. Neimeyer. New York: Hemisphere Publishing.

Uniform Anatomical Gift Act. 1983. 8A U.L.A. 15.

Uniform Determination of Death Act. Supp. 1986. 12 U.L.A. 270.

Vail, Elaine. 1982. *A personal guide to living with loss.* New York: John Wiley and Sons.

Zucker, Arthur. 1988. The right to die: Ethical and medical issues. In *Dying: Facing the facts,* 2d ed. Edited by Hannalore Wass, Felix Berardo, and Robert A. Neimeyer. New York: Hemisphere Publishing.

Section II

PSYCHOSOCIAL ASPECTS OF GRIEF

8

UNDERSTANDING THE BASIC TASKS OF GRIEF

John D. Canine

The bonds between and among human beings have been described as "the background to bereavement" (Raphael 1983, p. 2). What this means is that, because we are human and form attachments, we will, without exception, experience loss in its many forms. Infants, for example, exhibit signs of distress when their mothers leave the room, and even older children may cry or fuss when left with a baby-sitter for a parents' evening out. The anxiety of this perceived abandonment or separation is relieved when the mother "reappears."

As adults, we become attached to people, places, things, and situations. One person may genuinely "love" a home and delight in its improvement and decor, while someone else may be devoted to an antique automobile, a sailboat, a job, or sandlot baseball. No matter whether our attachments are fixed on people, abstractions, activities, or ideas, the feelings, experiences, and satisfactions derived from these bonds contribute meaning to our lives.

When these "objects" or "situations" are lost to us through death, catastrophe, or social or economic changes, our lives are profoundly altered. We can be laid off or "outplaced" from a longtime job. The dream house we built after years of planning can be destroyed by fire, flood, or earthquake. Leisure activities, like golf, travel, or camping, may need to be curtailed due to ill health. And most difficult of all, people we love will leave—through one means or another.

We hurt. We mourn. And it is necessary to grieve so that we may reorder our lives around the enormously empty space that seems to fill our path.

This section of the book will explore prevalent theories and goals regarding the grief process as they are understood and practiced in American culture. The nature, conflicts, and objectives of "grief work" and the role of death care professionals in facilitating "good" grief will be also be addressed. This chapter defines grief and mourning in the context of a loved one's death and goes on to explain several constructs (with minor differences) of the process, goals, and outcomes of healthy mourning.

GRIEF AND MOURNING: DEFINITIONS

Although the terms "grief" and "mourning" are often used interchangeably, they are not always considered synonymous. Various researchers and clinicians make the distinction that grief is a normal *reaction* to loss, while mourning is the *process* of adjustment and adaptation to the loss.

Notably, Raphael defines grief as "the emotional response to loss; the complex amalgam of painful affects including sadness, anger, helplessness, guilt, despair." Mourning, however, is defined as "the processes whereby the bereaved gradually undoes the psychological bonds that bound him to the deceased" (1983, p. 33).

Rando distinguishes between grief and mourning, although more subtly. She places grief in the context of the "overarching process of mourning" and calls it a "transitional phase" (Rando 1984, p. 16). She expands on Raphael's definition, calling grief "the process of psychological, social, and somatic reactions to the perception of loss" (p. 15), implying that grief is a *normal*, continuing condition that manifests itself in the emotional, social, and physical realms of the griever's life.

She notes that the absence of grief is (in most cases) abnormal, and that grief can be expected as a reaction to many kinds of loss, not just death alone. Her expanded definition posits that grief is based on the unique, individual perceptions of the loss by the griever—in other words, it is not necessary that the loss be recognized or validated by others for a person to experience grief.

From Rando's standpoint, both grief and mourning are processes, although mourning (the "overarching" process) is driven by the social and cultural influences to which the griever is exposed. Whether viewed as a reaction or a process, grief is regarded as the natural accompaniment to loss, be it death of a pet, divorce, loss of a job, or death of a lifetime friend. Because humans cannot insulate or protect themselves from loss, grief is universal. As Rando states, it is the process that allows us to let go of that which was and be ready for that which is to come" (1984, p. 17).

CHARACTERISTICS OF GRIEF

As with the definitions of grief, there are a number of valid and acceptable descriptions of what grief "looks like" when a loved one dies. A basic beginning is offered by Lindemann (1944), who has identified five characteristics of grief:

1. Somatic (bodily) distress
2. Preoccupation with the image of the deceased
3. Guilt
4. Hostile reactions
5. Loss of patterns of conduct (inability to function as before the loss)

A sixth characteristic noted by Lindemann as present in some grievers was the documentation of bereaved persons "develop[ing] traits of the deceased in their own behavior."

These general characteristics, however broad, do not exist in a vacuum and may vary tremendously in their severity and duration, due to a myriad of other factors. The "uniqueness" of a person's grief will be influenced by:

1. How the bereaved perceives the loss
2. The bereaved's age
3. The age of the person who died
4. The degree to which the bereaved was prepared for the death
5. The bereaved's inner strength and outer resources
6. The nature of the relationship with the person who died (Couldrick 1992, p. 1521)

A detailed examination of grief characteristics is offered by Worden (1982), who, based on research studies as well as his experience in working with the bereaved at Massachusetts General Hospital, arranged Lindemann's five normal grief characteristics into four major categories:

1. Feelings
2. Physical sensations
3. Cognitions
4. Behaviors

This model allows for effective exploration of a wide range of experiences that may occur with bereaved individuals, both in their thinking and in outward manifestations.

Among the feelings that may be present in normal grief are sadness, anger, guilt, self-reproach, anxiety, loneliness, fatigue, helplessness, shock, yearning, emancipation, relief, and numbness (Worden 1982, pp. 22–23). Physical sensations may include hollowness in the stomach, tightness in the chest or throat, shortness of breath, oversensitivity to noise, weakness of the muscles, lack of energy, dry mouth, and a sense of depersonalization.

A common initial cognition among grievers is disbelief—an unwillingness to acknowledge that the loss has occurred. It is not unusual to hear a griever say, "Mother can't be dead, I just saw her yesterday," or, "This cannot be happening." Disbelief normally gives way to confusion. Grievers often review the events leading up to and surrounding the death, sometimes questioning themselves and others about ways in which the death might have been prevented or trying to find sense or "logic" in what took place.

Another typical cognitive response is preoccupation with thoughts of the deceased. This may extend to ruminating to oneself or verbalizing with others on the entirety of the relationship with the deceased.

A further cognitive reaction may be a deeply felt "presence" of the deceased, occasionally via auditory or visual means. Some grievers claim to have heard the voice or seen the physical form of the dead person, and, while some authorities refer to these occurrences as hallucinations, such reports are not necessarily considered "out of bounds" of normal grief reactions. Rather than dismiss them as wild imaginings on the part of bereaved people, some experts think they may merit further scientific study.

Adding emphasis to the notion that in American culture there is a wide range of normal responses to grief is an extensive list of behaviors (sometimes contradictory) that are frequently seen among the bereaved. These behaviors include sleep and/or appetite disturbances, social withdrawal, absentminded behavior, restless overactivity, crying, sighing, searching and calling out, dreaming of the deceased, avoiding reminders of the deceased, visiting places or carrying objects that remind the survivor of the deceased, or treasuring objects that belonged to the deceased.

How long these feelings, physical sensations, cognitions, and behaviors persist will depend on the unique factors present in the individual loss, such as the nature and length of the relationship with the deceased, how the deceased died, and the amount of social and cultural support the griever receives.

STAGES OF GRIEF

Various authorities view the mourning process, with its universal and particular characteristics, as consisting of stages or phases. Death care professionals should heed Engel's (1964) caution that grief is a "healing process that can be interfered with by unsound interventions, suboptimal conditions . . . or a lack of individual coping mechanisms" (p. 93). Any serious attempt to increase the comprehension of and compassion toward the bereaved must consider the stages of grief that have been variously identified. Engel offers a six-step model consisting of the following:

1. Shock and disbelief
2. Developing awareness
3. Restitution
4. Resolving the loss
5. Idealization
6. The outcome

Stages 1–3 generally occur soon after the death has taken place. At this time the mourner is "stunned and incredulous. He attempts to protect himself against the effects of the overwhelming stress by being numb, and tries to block out recognition of the loss and painful feelings." As the shock and disbelief wear off, the mourner's awareness of the loss gradually increases. "Crying is typical, and involves both the acknowledgment of the loss and regression to a more helpless state" (Rando 1984, p. 26).

The restitution stage relates to various funerary rituals that evoke social support from family and friends, acknowledge the life and relationships of the deceased, and encourage the expression of feelings by the bereaved. In this context, crying is not only a normal, personal response to the loss but an expected behavior in Western cultures.

Stages 4–6 of Engel's model occur more gradually. Resolution takes place as the bereaved person proceeds to review the death itself and focus a great deal of mental and emotional energy on the deceased and their entire relationship. A frequent result of this stage—stripping the deceased of any negative qualities—leads to the subsequent stage of idealization. Here, the griever suppresses any and all negative thoughts and emotions about the deceased and may experience guilt—for any real or imagined past offenses, for the death itself, or simply for surviving.

Some bereaved people never get beyond this idealization stage. Yet Engel's stage 6 indicates the road toward a healthy accommodation to the loss wherein the griever comes to a place where there is less and less preoccupation with the deceased in *all* of its aforementioned forms. Sadness, anger, guilt, ambivalence, and idealization are ameliorated. As Rando puts it, "Successful mourning takes a year or more, with successful healing being evident in the ability to remember comfortably and realistically both the pleasures and disappointments of the lost relationship" (1984, pp. 26–27).

TASKS OF MOURNING

Regardless of which model of the stages of grief is employed, there is relative agreement in Western societies that a set of basic tasks must be completed for successful mourning to take place. These basic tasks are part of an overall process that can be called "grief work." Stated simply, grief work is the "cognitive process of confronting a loss, of going over the events before and at the time of death, focusing on memories and working toward detachment from the deceased. It requires an active, ongoing, effortful attempt to come to terms with loss" (Stroebe 1993, pp. 19–20).

Interpreting Lindemann, Stroebe suggests that grief work involves reliving, thinking through, and breaking down each "item" of the shared relationship between the bereaved and the deceased, and feeling whatever pain this process may produce. Gradually, the griever raises the question "How can I do that with somebody else?" And gradually, the collection of activities that shaped the "unit" of the deceased and the survivor can be seen as "pieces" that may or may not be possible to "pick up" with other people (Stroebe 1993, p. 21).

Perhaps no one has done more than Worden (1982) to categorize and describe the key requirements necessary for healthy grief work, as well as noting their potential difficulties and pitfalls. Death care professionals will do well to appreciate the difference between "stages" of grief and "tasks" of mourning, as there are no guarantees that individuals will move in some natural fashion through the stages of grief, neatly accomplishing the tasks along the way. Indeed, helping professionals should be alert and prepared with questions for their grieving populations to discover where an individual might be "stuck" (in a stage or with a task) to best determine interventions and/or counseling direction.

The following is a review of Worden's four primary requirements for successful completion of grief work.

Accept the Reality of the Loss

The first hurdle or "job" the survivor faces is acknowledging and accepting the truth of the loss. Many people attempt to deny this reality through a variety of mechanisms, which may include calling out to the deceased, searching for the deceased in familiar locations, or refusing to accept the circumstances that led to the death. Denying the facts of the loss can vary in degree from slight distortion to full-blown delusion. In the case of stillbirth or neonatal death (where the deceased is, in a sense, unknown to the parents), enlightened hospital staffs encourage the baby's parents to name the baby, dress it, and hold and spend time with it so that a "reality check" is able to occur before saying good-bye.

In any death, however, acceptance of the reality of the loss is facilitated by seeing or being with the dead body. Grief counselors and funeral service providers encourage mourners to observe, touch, and even photograph the body if they wish. Each activity helps the bereaved accept the truth of the death, and arrive at the knowledge that reunion is impossible.

Experience the Pain of Grief

Allowing the full expression of pain resulting from the death of a loved one is central to an ultimately successful resolution of grief. However, this task may be so difficult for some people that they attempt to avoid it by employing a variety of strategies that accomplish nothing more than delaying or suppressing needed relief. This may eventually lead to complicated grief, or, later on, seemingly inappropriate expressions in response to subsequent losses.

One avoidance strategy is buying into the subtle, but prevalent, societal discomfort with outward displays of mourning. Crying may be confined to private moments, while one maintains an outward "face" (or even belief) that finds it unnecessary to demonstrate grief. This dichotomy (the "stiff-upper-lip" school of coping versus the authentic anguish that grievers feel at various moments) can detach the bereaved not only from their pain but from valid sources of support as well.

Professionals and laypeople alike who find observing or participating in expressions of grief awkward or distasteful should know that they are, in effect, discounting the griever's pain, subtly inferring that it has little importance, and run the risk of inhibiting the overall resolution of the grief process.

Another avoidance strategy is what is sometimes called taking a "geographic cure." This usually involves physically removing oneself through travel from the old environment of which the deceased was a part. A close cousin of this strategy is making major life-changing decisions, such as selling a longtime family home and/or moving far from the location that holds memories of the lost loved one.

Other strategies may involve "postponing" the grief in hopes that it will "go away," displacing the feelings in other directions (complaining of difficulty at work or in other relationships), or indulging in compulsive spending and/or eating behaviors (Wolfelt 1993). Additional strategies include engaging in overwork, oversocializing, or overinvestment in the lives of others, or even becoming romantically involved (where spousal loss is concerned) in another relationship prematurely. There is as much truth as irony in the comment of one experienced therapist who casually observed, "Women grieve. Men replace."

Potential consequences of avoiding the pain of grief cannot be underestimated. They include depression, physical reactions, substance abuse, delayed (or displaced or explosive) expressions of pain, or experiencing the avoided pain in response to (and on top of!) a subsequent loss. It is fair to say that pain cannot be suppressed indefinitely, and that it will manifest itself sooner or later in one form or another.

Adjust to an Environment in Which the Deceased Is Missing

This requirement for completion of successful mourning inherently contains a wide variety of meaning and can represent a wide range of "work," depending on the bereaved's relationship with the deceased. In cases of close friendship, or even colleagues at work, it may be extremely difficult for the griever to accustom him- or herself to the loss of the deceased's presence, availability, support, or personality attributes that were relied upon and enjoyed.

In spousal situations where the deceased and the bereaved lived in the same house, adjusting to the environment after death is especially problematic. Every room, their contents, and even the neighborhood may trigger reminders and painful cues that the loved one, along with his or her activities and roles, is no longer there. The sense of emptiness, of missing the person, and the initial sense of helplessness (particularly for long-term spouses) may require a lengthy period of adjustment. Supportive family, friends, and professionals need to watch for grievers who become rooted in such helplessness, refusing to learn new skills or accept new responsibilities, preferring instead to lean on others rather than make an effort to devise new ways of operating and functioning in their altered environment.

Withdraw Emotional Energy and Reinvest It in Another Relationship

This final requirement for healthy mourning may be the hardest, particularly when the lost loved one is a child or a spouse. Bereaved people may feel that rechanneling emotional energy into a new child or a new romantic love relationship is somehow a betrayal of the deceased. Not only can this create an emotional "tug-of-war" within the bereaved (should there exist real opportunities for starting life again), but it also presents a task that may be approached and avoided repeatedly, with no definitive resolution ever taking place.

Not to be ignored in this discussion of concluding good grief work is the element of fear. To find the freedom and the courage to love again also means the bereaved runs the risk of experiencing another devastating loss. Satisfying, loving relationships require that we be vulnerable and squarely recognize the fact that life is uncertain. Few people find this easy.

MORE ABOUT MOURNING

The trajectory from initial grief through its healthy resolution is neither straight nor smooth. Societal and familial attitudes, as well as the circumstances of the loss, can exert tremendous influences on how any given individual makes his or her way through the work of grieving the death of a loved one. It is an enormously strenuous process, entailing, as Rando notes, "not only grieving for the actual person that is lost, but also for all of the hopes, dreams, fantasies and expectations the griever held for that person and their relationship." Unfortunately, contemporary American society discourages people from displaying their feelings or talking about their losses—expressions that would greatly assist them in realizing that their reactions are both acceptable and appropriate, and that would facilitate their working through the tasks of mourning.

By way of academic interest, Lindemann constructed three "tasks" of grief (subscribed to by Rando), which parallel Worden's and consist of (1) emancipation from the bondage of the deceased, (2) readjustment to the environment in which the deceased is missing, and (3) formation of new relationships.

This chapter will conclude with a construct that may add to the understanding of the concrete and psychological efforts confronting a bereaved person. We will use, as a sample case study, the fictional situation of a happy couple married more than fifty years. He is a physician, she a musician. They began dating in high school, married after college, and had two children together. As mentioned at the beginning of this chapter, human bonds are created whenever there are shared feelings, activities, and experiences. We'll walk through Lindemann's three tasks with this couple in mind.

Emancipation from Bondage of the Deceased

The bonds that humans establish with each other, with objects, and with abstractions (such as power and prestige) give rise to real and lasting beliefs and responses in how they conduct their lives. According to Rando, "There is an emotional bond between the person and whoever he cares about that develops as that individual invests his psychic and emotional energy in the loved one. . . . When one of these people dies, the remaining person has to withdraw the emotional energy that was invested in the person who is no longer alive" (1984, p. 18).

With our fictional couple, over the years their bonds were woven into a rich and colorful tapestry that included the teenage years, courtship, and their roles as newlyweds, parents, and individual professionals. For the vast majority of their lives they identified themselves as partners, experiencing all the ups and downs that relationship implies. Bondage, in this case, does not mean they were "slaves" to each other, but instead that they were freely and voluntarily indebted to each other to perform certain roles and responsibilities, and to provide mutual support and approval.

Now he is dead. She must begin to understand, unravel, and undo these complex, complicated bonds. "This does not mean that the deceased is forgotten or betrayed. The relationship . . . still exists in a very special way in the heart and mind of the griever. . . . The energy that previously went into keeping the relationship with the deceased alive now must be channeled elsewhere, where it can be returned" (Rando 1984, p. 19).

Readjustment to the Environment in Which the Deceased Is Missing

It was only a short illness, but the widow is now alone for the first time in more than half a century. She is no longer "his" wife, but an elderly woman living alone. The activities they shared may no longer be attractive or even interesting to her. They may now serve as "red flag" reminders of her loss and pain.

Further, she is faced with responsibilities he always carried out, be it yard work, automobile maintenance and repair, or the position as primary family breadwinner. Any or all of these issues may loom (realistically or unrealistically) large in the process of her adjustment. The transition to self-sufficiency may prove to be understandably clumsy or actually impossible, depending on her personal emotional, intellectual, and physical resources. And regardless of the degree of success or accommodation she ultimately achieves, the task is likely to prove taxing in many arenas.

She may find it difficult (or unnecessary) to maintain her former daily routine—which had been structured around him. She may experience sleep disturbances, seek "escape" in television or alcohol, not return phone calls, or take to visiting the grave excessively. Her grieving children, who themselves want comfort, may be reluctant to intrude on *her* pain.

She may not know what's expected of her when the accountant calls about the taxes, what to ask when the stockbroker calls about the portfolio, or what to do when the travel club calls about renewing the membership. She must face and make decisions about his clothes, his tools, his toys, his papers.

She may become frustrated or angry, may appear preoccupied or sad, or may throw herself into activities that previously held only mild enjoyment. There are many environments to which the bereaved individual must adjust, many "firsts" (holidays, anniversaries) she must confront without the loved one's participation or support.

Formation of New Relationships

As we know, the energy once invested in the deceased must now be redirected toward people and/or activities that can return the investment. Our widow will need to recognize and pay attention to what provides pleasure and satisfaction to her as a solo player in the game of life instead of part of a team. She may rediscover interests she had abandoned or "let slide" while a wife and a mother of growing children. She may buy season tickets to the local theater, begin volunteering at the local library, or share meals with single friends for whom she had little time while busy being a wife. She may find she's genuinely fascinated with that stock portfolio and may subscribe to the *Wall Street Journal* and join an investment club. And, of course, she may begin attending dances or social or athletic events where she will meet "appropriate" men, and perhaps eventually form a serious attachment or even remarry.

Forming these new relationships requires both time and the appreciation that life is meant to be lived in the present—not in the past, and not saved for "someday." She may initially struggle with a sense of guilt or betrayal when she finds herself involved, laughing, or having a wonderful time while her husband of fifty years lies cold in his grave.

In order to complete her mourning and make the most of the rest of her life, our widow must come to realize that her enjoyment in being alive does not mean that she has forgotten or is being disloyal to her beloved spouse. The history and love they shared were real—but he is no longer available to her. She must find a new way, new avenues that meet her needs, not to recapture what she has lost but to refashion a life that has taken a different turn.

TIMETABLES FOR RECOVERY

The only universal agreement among grief experts regarding timetables for recovery is that there isn't one. The mourning process, as we have seen, is complex, unique to each person, and will be influenced by a wide set of variables. When relationships are close (parent, spouse, sibling, child), a year seems to be the *minimum* time for the process to come anywhere near a resolution.

While historically the social mores of Western culture have often dictated one-year periods of mourning, the effort of "grief work" and the back-and-forth nature of the stages of grief as we now understand them suggest that our society is often too impatient with grievers and may place too much pressure on them to "get over it" and "get on" with their lives.

Depending on the circumstances of the death, some mourners may be able to decathect and form new relationships more readily. This might happen in situations involving a long terminal illness that created opportunities for anticipatory grief. But as mentioned earlier, investing too quickly in new relationships may be an avoidance strategy that concerned family members and professionals should watch out for.

Successfully working through the tasks of grief may be the most difficult job a person ever accomplishes. At the same time, it may reward the individual with levels of wisdom and compassion he or she would otherwise have never known.

SUMMARY

Experts define grief as a reaction to loss, with mourning viewed as the overarching process of which grief is a part. However, the two terms are and can be used interchangeably. Lindemann defined five characteristics of grief: (1) somatic or bodily distress, (2) preoccupation with the image of the deceased, (3) guilt, (4) hostile reactions, and (5) loss of patterns of conduct. The manifestation and degree of these characteristics are driven by a variety of factors, including the nature and duration of the bereaved's relationship with the deceased, their ages, the circumstances of the death, the amount of preparation the survivor was able to bring to the loss, and the inner and outer resources the bereaved can call upon for support.

The basic tasks of grief were presented according to two models. Worden's model constituted four tasks: (1) accepting the reality of the loss, (2) experiencing the pain of grief, (3) adjusting to an environment in which the deceased is missing, and (4) withdrawing emotional energy and investing it in another relationship. Similarly, Rando bases three tasks on Lindemann's work: (1) emancipation from the bondage of the deceased, (2) readjustment to the environment in which the deceased is missing, and (3) formation of new relationships.

There is agreement that successful mourning depends on many variables, including the expectation or suddenness of the death, as well as the internal and external sources for support available to the bereaved. It is also generally agreed that there is no specific timetable for the healthy completion of grief work, but that at least one year is required.

REFERENCES

Couldrick, Ann. 1992. Optimizing the bereavement outcome: Reading the road ahead. *Social Science Medicine* 35, no. 12:1521–23.

Ellard, John. 1968. Emotional reactions associated with death. *Medical Journal of Australia* 1, no. 23:979–83.

Engel, G. 1964. Grief and grieving. *American Journal of Nursing,* 64:93–98.

Jacobs, S., S. Kasl, C. Schaefer, and A. Ostfeld. 1994. Conscious and unconscious coping with loss. *Psychosomatic Medicine* 56:557–63.

Levy, L., K. Martinkowski, and J. Derby. 1994. Differences in patterns of adaptation in conjugal bereavement: Their sources and potential significance. *Omega* 29, no. 1:71–87.

Lindemann, E. 1944. Symptomatology and management of acute grief. *The American Journal of Psychiatry,* 101:141–48.

Rando, Therese A. 1984. *Grief, dying and death: Clinical interventions for caregivers.* Champaign, Ill.: Research Press.

Raphael, Beverly. 1983. *The anatomy of bereavement.* New York: Basic Books.

Stroebe, Margaret. 1993. Coping with bereavement: A review of the grief work hypothesis. *Omega* 26, no. 1:19–42.

Tagliaferre, L., and G. Harbaugh. 1990. *Recovery from loss.* Deerfield Beach, Fla.: Health Communications.

van Gennep, Arnold. 1960. *The rites of passage.* Chicago: University of Chicago Press.

Wolfelt, Alan D. 1993. Identification of grief avoidance response patterns: A growing phenomenon. *The Forum* 18, no. 1.

Worden, J. William. 1982. *Grief counseling and grief therapy.* New York: Springer.

Zisook, S., and S. Schuchter. 1993. Uncomplicated bereavement. *Journal of Clinical Psychiatry* 54, no. 10:365–72.

9

CIRCUMSTANTIAL FACTORS INFLUENCING GRIEF

John D. Canine

CHAPTER OUTLINE

As readers know by now, the manner in which individuals grieve and how the grieving process is resolved depend on myriad circumstances that will be as diverse as the individuals themselves. People handle loss in personalized ways, based on factors that can be grouped as psychological ("internal") and sociological ("external"). In addition, various physiological factors may come into play in many individuals as they move through the stages of the mourning process. This chapter examines these three categories of variables and relies, to a great extent, on the work of Rando (1984), Raphael (1983), and Worden (1982).

PSYCHOLOGICAL FACTORS: THE BIG PICTURE

It should be remembered at the start that, in general, the circumstantial differences involved with every death and every survivor may provide a positive or negative influence (or no influence at all!) on how the bereaved handles the grief process. A factor that strongly influences one individual may have little or no impact on another. Yet each factor we will discuss *can be* significant and should be considered when dealing with bereaved populations.

Raphael gives us a broad approach to the psychological "determinants of grief," grouping them into three "umbrella" categories:

1. The preexisting relationship between the bereaved and the deceased
2. The type of death
3. Previous losses

We will briefly examine the general aspects of these categories before moving on to Rando's more detailed breakdown of psychological influences.

The Preexisting Relationship

Who was the deceased? Who is the survivor? Were they colleagues at work, siblings, members of the same bridge club, or deeply in love? What are their ages and genders, and how long were they involved? The greater the bereaved's dependence on the dead person (for identity, survival, or social standing), the greater the chances that grief will be intense and the outcome of mourning may be less than optimal.

Worden suggests that, when considering the nature of the relationship, three factors should be addressed: the strength of the attachment, the security of the attachment, and the ambivalence of the attachment. He notes that the greater the love, the stronger the reaction to the loss. And in relationships characterized by high levels of ambivalence, the bereaved may focus on guilt-provoking behaviors and attitudes they once exhibited toward the dead person. This can greatly influence the outcome of the mourning process. For example, a normal, essentially well-adjusted college student may feel appropriately sad at the loss of an elderly aunt who died of natural causes, but the extent and duration of the mourning process will probably be relatively short. But if the student's mother, in whose professional steps she hopes to follow despite intense disagreements between them, dies suddenly, the nature and length of the grief work will be far deeper, more complicated, and may require professional help.

Type of Death

The specific circumstances of the death will influence how each mourner will grieve. If the death was natural and those involved had advance warning, grievers may have had the opportunity to engage in actions and gestures with or toward the dying person that enhanced the relationship and facilitated closure.

Research has shown that when deaths are sudden or are considered "untimely," it is frequently more difficult for loved ones than when death is anticipated. This is especially true in cases where the deceased is a child or young person, or where the death was a result of violence. Survivors of homicide victims and suicides are particularly challenged in terms of grief work and bereavement outcomes.

Previous Losses

This category refers to ways in which the bereaved mourned—or perhaps failed to mourn—prior losses. Even if the present situation is the first loss through death the griever has experienced, indications of his or her potentially healthy mourning can be inferred from reactions to other life-changing events, such as divorce, change in residence or employment, birth of a child, or economic reversals.

It is not the number or severity of previous losses or life changes that determines their effect, but rather how the bereaved perceived and responded to those events. Was he open and unashamed of expressing his feelings? Did she repress her feelings, fearing social disapproval? Did he try to "escape" or "deny" the situation? Did she confront the real circumstances head-on? Where previous losses were not completely grieved, it will not be surprising if resolution of the current loss is complicated by the unresolved issues "hanging on" from the earlier unexpressed or uncompleted grief.

PSYCHOLOGICAL FACTORS: A MORE FOCUSED VIEW

In contrast to Raphael's large "umbrella" categories influencing the grief process, Rando (1984) identified twenty separate factors that impact the psychological component of bereavement. What follows is an adaptation of her list, along with brief comments on the potentially positive or negative developments that may be triggered in the griever as a result.

Meaning of the Loss

Because each relationship between any two people is unique, no two people will grieve in precisely the same way. The individual's perception of the loss will be the force driving the grieving process. The death of a dear friend and confidant may be more difficult for someone than the death of a parent for whom the individual held little affection due to early abuse. Societal standards (vis-à-vis what relationships "should" be more painful) in the final analysis provide no guidelines. Only through efforts to understand the unique nature of the relationship can we make sense of the magnitude of the individual's loss and the extent of his or her grief.

Qualities of the Relationship

Whenever someone dies, the bonds between the deceased and the griever must be undone. But what do those bonds look and feel like to the survivor? The stronger or tighter the bonds, the more difficult they will be to sever—regardless of whether the relationship was a healthy or an unhealthy one.

The degree of ambivalence must be considered, as it may detour the straight-line trajectory that grief in clearly defined relationships is likely to follow. For example, it is quite possible that a husband separated from his wife and contemplating divorce will in some ways have a more difficult mourning upon learning that she has been killed in a car accident than would a husband who has lived together happily with his spouse for many years.

When examining relationships with the deceased, it is important to realize that the bereaved is often experiencing two losses. Most obvious, of course, is the loss of the person, which can be referred to as the object loss. Less obvious, but still significant, is the loss of the individual's role (role loss) in conjunction with the person who has died. For example, a wife becomes a widow, an adult becomes an orphan, a business partner becomes a sole proprietor, a dedicated caregiver becomes a free agent.

Roles of the Deceased

Imagine a mobile hanging from a ceiling. When one part of the mobile is moved, all the other parts move in response. When a member of a family or other social system dies, the removal of this "piece" throws the system into a state of disequilibrium. The known and expected dynamics are disrupted.

This state of disequilibrium builds another layer of complexity onto the grieving process. There is more to be done than simply grieve the lost family member, friend, or colleague. The roles that the deceased occupied must be parceled out to other members of the family or social circle. Day-to-day practicalities must be handled, with new roles and responsibilities assigned, assumed, or accepted. Depending upon who died, someone must now pay the bills or maintain the automobiles. Someone may need to take over the primary child-rearing responsibilities. In a work situation, someone must now set the goals, order supplies, or determine job assignments. The extent to which these roles are shouldered and mastered will affect the system's overall grieving process and determine how soon and how smoothly it returns to functioning in a new state of equilibrium.

Age of the Griever

There are immense differences between the way an adult deals with grief and the way a child deals with grief. Their concepts of death and their levels of experience with loss will be vastly different. Teenagers who have suffered a serious loss will exhibit a range of behaviors that may be puzzling and disturbing to caring adults.

While grief reactions and strategies for dealing with children who have lost a loved one will be covered in a later chapter, it is interesting to note here that research has shown that younger widows and widowers (under the age of forty) tend to have a more difficult time accepting their loss than do those who are older and have enjoyed longer relationships when widowhood occurs.

Griever's Sex-Role Conditioning

In American culture it is traditionally expected that males will maintain an outward appearance of calm and control, while females are permitted a wider range of emotional display. Grievers may judge themselves and their behavior according to the degree to which they have been conditioned to accept these stereotypes. For example, a man who cries while speaking of his dead mother may feel he has "broken down," and might feel embarrassment, shame, self-disapproval, or humiliation. Indeed, he may be supported in those judgments by the reactions or responses from the people around him. Contrarily, a woman's lack of tears under similar circumstances might actually generate disapproval, and she herself might question her inability or disinclination to cry when recalling memories of her mother.

Fortunately, as we move into the twenty-first century, sex roles and accompanying behaviors are slowly changing. A man who cries at his wife's funeral is more socially accepted, although that tolerance may disappear if he cries too long, too loudly, or too often in front of too many people. A woman who can speak honestly, intimately, and candidly about her dead husband without shedding a drop may no longer be considered "cold." Nevertheless, an individual's sex-role conditioning still determines his or her perception of how someone of that gender "should" behave. Such conditioning runs strong and deep, and should be considered against whatever "mask" the mourner may appear to be wearing.

Deceased's Unique Characteristics

Here we turn our attention not to the nature of the relationship with the deceased or the roles that were played but to the kind of person the deceased was. How old was he, and what opportunities or lessons had he gained from living? Did she have a sense of humor? Was he alcoholic? Was she selfish and indifferent? Would he give you the shirt off his back? Was she a menace to society, or eternally cheerful and optimistic? It should not be difficult to appreciate how these variables contribute to the psychological ease or disease of the grieving process.

In most societies the natural order of things dictates that older people die before younger ones. The death of an infant, child, or young adult is therefore seen as a violation of nature, as a lost opportunity, and it is often grieved more intensely than, say, the death of a ninety-year-old great-grandmother. It would be a mistake, however, to assume more vigorous grief based solely on the deceased's age. An argument could be made that the loss to society of the great-grandmother's wisdom and tenderness is greater than the loss of a newborn, whose future was simply a blank page.

Returning to the "type" of person who has died and is being mourned, we can readily agree that society may care little when a convicted murderer is put to death by state-sanctioned lethal injection but will simultaneously respect that his family will feel and grieve the loss.

Death care professionals should appreciate that even in seemingly "ordinary" losses, there will be unique elements of the deceased's personality, attitudes, or predilections that will be missed and mourned by the survivors. It could be something as profound as unflagging encouragement to others in pursuit of a goal, or something as mundane as regular apprisals of the baseball standings. But it was something the deceased did, offered, shared, or represented that will now be absent from the griever's daily life.

Griever's Mental State

It is often said that past behavior is the single best predictor of future performance. This holds true for the grieving process. How an individual has handled crises in the past will largely determine how the current death crisis will be handled as well. Individuals use the coping mechanisms that are familiar to them or that have been effective in the past—whether or not these mechanisms are healthy.

In Chapter 8 we examined some unhealthy coping behaviors employed by bereaved individuals to avoid the pain of grief. It should be remembered that the psychological factors that lead to these behaviors are already in place before the death—whether they manifest in obsessive rumination, geographic cures, substance abuse, prayer, intellectualization of the death, or intense involvement with other people and/or activities. Further, it should be recognized that within the normal realms of mental health and personality development, the death of a loved one "upsets the apple cart" of life and presents adjustment difficulties. Bereaved people, in general, should be trusted to have the skills needed to put the death in perspective and experience a lessening of pain and despair as time goes on.

Griever's Maturity and Intelligence

It will come as no surprise that the more mature and intelligent the bereaved individual, the more likely he or she is to possess and employ the needed coping mechanisms and skills to be able to insightfully work through and resolve the loss satisfactorily.

Previous Experience with Loss

While Western society generally accepts the adage that practice makes perfect, familiarity with loss and death does not automatically enable the bereaved to manage sequential or later losses better than someone experiencing death for the first time. The manner in which earlier major losses were resolved (or not resolved) will play an important part in how the current loss is managed. Previous, unresolved losses may resurface and resonate for the griever concurrently with the newest loss, thus complicating and impeding the mourning process.

Further, the experience of multiple loss, such as might occur when several family members die in a plane crash or natural disaster, can produce what is known as "bereavement overload." This can render survivors numb and unable to face the enormity of what they have suffered, and may disturb their ability to function effectively during any future loss situations.

Cultural Elements Affecting the Griever

Every culture has its own unique and specific norms for grieving the dead. The way in which an individual grieves will be greatly influenced by exposure to how members of his or her social, ethnic, or religious group typically handle their own grief. Some groups encourage loud, overt displays of grief, while others do not. Some religions have open caskets at funerals; others strictly forbid the practice.

As one's social contacts multiply, people enter into and become members of various groups—family, work group, social group. We learn, from our earliest days, how group members are supposed to behave, and (assuming we wish to "maintain" our membership) we adhere to the group's rules of conduct. Following the rules makes it easier to know what to do in specific situations; it helps people avoid potentially embarrassing missteps and helps them feel comfortable in awkward situations. This principle applies to the rules different groups have regarding mourning, including its length and acceptable means of expression.

Arnold van Gennep, in his seminal work *The Rites of Passage* (1960), describes in great detail the funerary and mourning practices of a variety of cultures, both ancient and modern. "Mourning," he writes,

> which I formerly saw simply as an aggregate of taboos and negative practices . . .
> now appears to me to be a more complex phenomenon. It is a transitional period

for the survivors, and they enter it through rites of separation and emerge from it through rites of reintegration [rites of the lifting of mourning]. . . . Mourning requirements are based on degrees of kinship and are systematized by each people according to their special ways of calculating that kinship. (Pp. 146–47)

This systematization of rites and behavior helps grievers "know what to do" and affirms their continued membership in the cultural group.

Fulfillment of the Deceased's Life

Derinda's grandfather was seventy-seven when he died. But beforehand he told his family that he loved them and had had a wonderful life and a rewarding career, that he had done all the things he'd wanted to do, and that he had no regrets. His family mourned his loss, of course, but were greatly comforted by his serenity and their knowledge of his inner peace and satisfaction.

Kevin had a little brother who was only six when he died of cancer. The child had been ill most of his short life. The grief Kevin and his parents felt, and their talks about the tragedy that his brother never had a chance to grow up, continued to cause Kevin sadness about "what might have been" nearly twenty years later.

While these two situations are extreme in their circumstances, they are not abnormal in the reactions they provoked. More commonly experienced is the "gray area" in which grievers question whether their loved one was truly happy, truly fulfilled, had truly accomplished her goals or lived according to his principles. The degree to which bereaved people can satisfy themselves that their loved ones died in a state of relative contentment is an important psychological factor in their ability to mourn with a successful outcome.

Context of the Death

The immediate circumstances of the death are an important component of the grieving process. Was the griever prepared for the death? What was the cause of death? Where did the death occur? The answers to these and other questions will have a profound impact on the bereaved and how he or she carries out resolution of grief. Certainly, the ideal context (or "death surround," as it is sometimes called) would be that of an elderly person who had lived a rich, full life and died quietly while sleeping, surrounded by loved ones who had all resolved their unfinished business and said good-bye. Such a set of circumstances makes it easier for the bereaved to accept the loss and resolve their grief.

As we know, many deaths unfortunately occur in heartrending fashion, involving long-term illness, pain, and suffering, or under sudden, violent circumstances. The death surround may also reveal surprising information previously unknown to family members, such as might occur in a situation of fatal drug overdose or a husband dying in his mistress's bed. Such contexts may produce significant obstacles to loved ones' straightforward resolution of grief.

Preventability of the Death

Uncertainty about the preventability of a person's death can profoundly affect the severity of mourning and how long the grief process may last. Consider these two, vastly different situations:

Tom died of a heart attack while on a business trip. His colleagues later noted that Tom's skin had taken on a gray pallor and he was experiencing shortness of breath, but no one had called for assistance. Tom drove away from the final meeting session and died at the wheel of his car minutes later. His widow, understandably, was bewildered about why no one had acted to help Tom, or to stop him from getting into his car when all agreed he had appeared ill. She read and reread the police, ambulance, and emergency room reports, as if by some force she could change the outcome. She remained convinced for many months that Tom's death could have been prevented. This interfered mightily with her ability to accept and resolve her loss.

Jeanne, on the other hand, lost her eighty-six-year-old husband, Charlie, to terminal cancer. From initial diagnosis to the moment of death, she and his doctor exhausted all medical options, and she provided him with the finest care available. His pain was managed effectively, and family and friends spent time with him during his final days. Knowing that everything that could be done *was* done, Jeanne was able to view Charlie's death as inevitable. In contrast to Tom's wife, who clung to the belief that her husband's death could have been prevented by the prompt action of his colleagues, Jeanne's path was clear to heal and work directly toward a resolution of grief that held no risk of becoming prolonged.

Timeliness of the Death

Probably no one would hypothesize that there is a "good" time for a person to die. But there are times that are perceived as more terrible, more sad, or "worse" than others. As already discussed, the death of an infant, child, or young adult is generally considered in our society to be more "tragic" than the death of an elderly person. But timeliness can also refer to the fact that anyone—young or old—can have activities, work, contributions to society, goals, or dreams that are left incomplete by the death.

We can simply look at the deaths of well-known people to understand this concept. Examples that come quickly to mind include John F. Kennedy, John Lennon, Mozart, Anne Frank, Abraham Lincoln, Alexander the Great, Arthur Ashe, Marilyn Monroe, Charlotte Brontë, Lord Byron, James Dean, and Martin Luther King.

Another determinant of timeliness may be the status of the deceased's relationship with another person or group of people. John and Dorothy married late in life, he in his seventies, she in her sixties. The marriage was celebrated by their families, and they were enjoying what was expected to be the first of many travels when John died suddenly of a heart attack on a Caribbean cruise. Dorothy grieved

John's death "all the more" because she felt they had just begun their life together.

Expectation of Death

Although we have already covered the related factors of preventability and timeliness of death, there are broader issues that encompass both of these psychological
determinants. In general, an expected death allows the dying person and the be-
reavers some time to anticipate and gradually accept the idea of death prior to its
occurrence, and to finish the personal, emotional, and/or professional "business"
between them and to say their good-byes.

Sudden death (regardless of preventability, timeliness, or the death surround)
makes such tying up of loose ends impossible, and may leave the bereaved in denial, devoid of resources, or totally overwhelmed. It is important to note, however,
that there is little, if any, difference in the *depth* of grief in expected or unexpected
deaths. Anticipated deaths simply provide survivors with an early warning, permit-
ting loved ones a "head start" on imagining the idea of life without the other
person.

Length of Illness

While anticipated deaths give the bereaved a small advantage over those who experience a sudden loss, some data demonstrate that extended illnesses can produce
poor bereavement outcomes. Caring for a dying person takes time, patience, love,
energy, and devotion. One's own life may have to be "put on hold." It can be
physically and emotionally exhausting for the caregiver, who may become isolated
from others as the illness progresses, and may come to resent and/or blame the
dying loved one or others who they perceive as not doing their share to help. As
the illness ebbs and flows, the caregiver may experience anger, frustration, hope,
grief, giddiness—an emotional roller coaster, if you will, whose ride will only end
when the loved one finally dies. Depending on the duration of the illness and the
degree of involvement in it, these ambivalent feelings can turn into strong feelings
of guilt and remorse after the death has occurred.

Involvement with Dying Person

This psychological factor may be seen as a "subcategory" of the previous one. It
has been observed that anticipatory grief may propel the bereaved in either of two
directions. First, it may bring the bereaved closer to the dying person, allowing the
opportunity to heal past hurts, disclose important information or secrets, come to
terms with each other's real or perceived flaws, and experience warmth and loving
closeness.

The second possibility is that the bereaved may pull away from (or feel pushed
away by) the dying person. This resulting distance can stem from a variety of underlying sources: It could be the bereaved's own fears regarding mortality; it could

be a rush to "get over" the inevitable and minimize pain before death actually occurs; or it might be truly rooted in the dying person's own denial, anger, or frustration. Another possibility is an "altruistic" attempt on the part of the dying person to detach from loved ones in a misguided effort to spare them pain.

Secondary Losses

Secondary losses are defined as those that occur after, and as a direct result of, the loved one's death. This relates to the second and third psychological factors discussed earlier: the unique qualities of the relationship, and the roles that were fulfilled by the deceased and the bereaved.

The volume and intensity of these secondary losses are critical to how well the griever will move through the stages and tasks of mourning. How willing (or unwilling), equipped (or ill equipped), and prepared (or unprepared) is the survivor to undergo the myriad of changes that occur following the death? These losses can involve moving from a longtime home, giving up a set of friends, living on a reduced income, lowering of social status, no longer feeling important and needed, relinquishing dreams of the future, or no longer feeling supported and safe. The degree to which the griever is invested in any of these secondary losses will impact his or her ability to resolve the mourning process.

Additional Stressors

No one lives a life without occasional crisis, and many people live lives under recurring stress. These conditions make heavy demands on us both emotionally and physically. When a loved one dies, and other crises are in progress (or follow shortly thereafter), the bereaved individual often has no choice but to split his or her emotional energy between the competing situations—often to the detriment of both.

Let us consider, as an example, the psychological struggles of a woman who experiences the sudden death of her husband, and a month later is laid off from her job in an auto factory. At the same time, her teenage son is growing more rebellious and out of control (she suspects drug use), and her daughter in college becomes pregnant. There is no question that this woman's ability to pay attention and give time to her grief process is severely compromised by the nature of the concurrent stresses in her life.

These twenty psychological factors that influence the ability of the mourner to come to a satisfying readjustment or renewal of his or her life should be ever in the forefront for those who interact with or service bereaved populations. They can even be used to create a checklist that certain medical, mental health, hospice, or funeral professionals might find useful in understanding their clientele.

An ancillary psychological issue to mention before moving into the external (sociological) factors is one that has been termed the problem of "payoff." This refers to certain bereaved individuals who derive such pleasure from the attention and sympathy they receive as mourners that the grieving process is actually extended in order to avoid losing the attention.

SOCIOLOGICAL FACTORS

Sociological factors are those that are "outside" the bereaved; they include the social structure of the family and the overall society around the bereaved, which consists of any and all structures of which the bereaved is a member (i.e., work group, church, community organizations, hobby groups, ethnic associations). These sociological "memberships" and their responses to a death can greatly assist or inhibit the overall grief process and the nature of its outcomes.

Stated simply, social support is an important ingredient in the successful resolution of a person's mourning. It is difficult to do this work and complete the basic tasks in a vacuum without the benefit of encouragement and love from others.

Raphael notes sociodemographic factors such as age, gender, cultural heritage, and ethnic and/or religious affiliations as determinants in how grief may proceed. She adds to this list both the deceased's and the bereaved's occupation and economic position. These factors all influence the level and type of response the bereaved is likely to receive from family members and the external social support network (Raphael 1983, p. 63).

Clearly, for helping professionals, it is beneficial to have some knowledge of the bereaved's background with respect to these social variables. As a guide, we can examine Rando's (1984) identification of four sociological factors that affect bereavement.

Available Support Systems

The way in which the bereaved and the deceased are perceived by members of the social groups in which they play a part will be a major determinant in the level of support that the group offers the bereaved. If the bereaved (or the deceased, for that matter) was a marginal member of the group—for example, a relatively new employee at a large company—it is likely that there will be a minimal show of support. On the other hand, had the deceased (or the bereaved) been a longtime employee who participated in many activities inside and outside the workplace, chances are that members of this social structure will offer more substantial and meaningful levels of support.

We can interpret this factor in several ways. The length of the relationship may result in people knowing and caring about one another at deeper levels, or a long association may simply stimulate a greater sense of duty and obligation on the part of the social group. At the opposite end of the spectrum are those who are bereaved as a result of suicide or AIDS. So strong are the social stigmas regarding these deaths that it is not uncommon for loved ones of these victims to be given only minimal, intermittent, or even no social support whatsoever.

We recognize that ambivalence on the part of a griever is a psychological factor in determining the outcome of mourning, but it is also important to recognize the impact of sociological (external) ambivalence. When Sam died suddenly of a stroke, he and his longtime wife, Molly, were legally married but separated, while he had taken up residence with a new girlfriend. Molly was naturally shocked and distraught by his death, but she willingly participated in carrying out the funeral arrangements in concert with Sam's family. Although the funeral was well attended by family, friends, and colleagues of them both, the situation was sufficiently awkward that many people declined or demurred from offering Molly a normal show of sympathy and support. Finding itself in doubt, the social structure did nothing. Many "would-be" grievers were so angry at Sam that they felt the death was "deserved," could not appreciate Molly's pain, and told her to just "forget" about him and put the experience behind her. Others never acknowledged the death at all. As Rando states,

> When the griever does not receive the nonjudgmental compassion and support of concerned others, she loses a vital aid to handling the difficult confrontations demanded in grief work. The tasks of grief work require the encouragement, empathy and sustenance gained from positive relationships. Lack of support usually leads to difficulty in the successful resolution of grief. (Rando 1984, p. 54)

Clearly, the "death surround" creates sociological implications as well. In a well-known, recent example, the families who lost loved ones in the April 1995 bombing of the Oklahoma City Federal Building received an extraordinary outpouring of support from people from one end of the United States to the other. This included "official" support from the governor of their state and even from the president of the entire nation. Similar support is frequently demonstrated for those who are bereaved following other types of tragedies over which the survivors had no control, such as plane crashes, or natural disasters such as hurricanes, floods, and earthquakes.

Ongoing social support—beyond the period immediately following the death(s)—is also helpful in reaching successful outcomes. In many instances the outpouring of initial attention to grievers dwindles to a trickle or dries up completely in the weeks and months following the loss. And often, the bereaved chooses to withdraw from potential sources of support. This common dynamic is usually counterproductive, since it occurs during the time frame in which the difficult task of adjusting to the environment without the loved one is taking place.

Cultural Background and Context

As discussed, knowing what is expected as a mourning member of a sociological group can be helpful and comforting to bereaved people. Different groups, as we know, have different standards and expectations for behavior during the grieving process. Following these sociological dictates can greatly aid an individual's grief resolution.

The British, for example, generally take pride in their ability to be publicly undemonstrative about their grief. Mediterranean ethnic groups, by contrast, are less reserved and permit wider latitude in their expressions of grief, which may include wailing, crying, and screaming.

Van Gennep (1960) provides a detailed description of how the Kol of India bury their dead, in funeral rituals in which it is expected that "the women cry, the men are silent." Social mores are different for the Todas of Indonesia, who expect that "mourning lasts five months for a man and four months for a woman. . . . The female relatives make a doll in the image of the deceased, and they dress, wash and feed it every day for two-and-a-half years if the person was a man, or for two years if it was a woman" (van Gennep 1960, pp. 150–51).

One of the difficult facts of life for death care professionals and some bereaved people is that, in the United States, there are no universally accepted funerary, grief, or mourning rituals and practices. The diversity and multiculturalism that characterize this country leave many people confused and uncertain as to how to behave as a griever, or as a supporter of those in mourning.

Socioeconomic Status

Particularly for women in traditional, one-income family arrangements, the loss of a breadwinning spouse can bring major complications to the grieving process. In addition to losing her mate, such a woman has lost her economic security and per-haps her social position within the community. The urgency to meet the basic needs—food, clothing, and shelter—can result in the bereaved "shelving" her grief process until these daily needs are met and an economic equilibrium is reestab-lished. With more and more American families dependent upon two incomes for survival, younger widows and widowers become particularly vulnerable to eco-nomic upheaval when a spouse dies.

Funerary Rituals

A funeral ceremony, regardless of religious or ethnic orientation, is, at its heart, a rite of separation. Its purpose is to assist the bereaved in accepting the loved one's death and to afford society an opportunity to acknowledge the loss. As has already been discussed, these rites will vary widely among different cultural groups and may further be affected by the sex, age, and social position of the deceased.

Funerals that are designed to assist the griever in accepting the reality of the loss and permit the expression of the grief that accompanies it can be significantly helpful in the overall bereavement outcome. Conversely, the absence of any sort of funeral rite can inhibit the process by encouraging denial that the death has taken place and leaving the survivors "nowhere to go" with their grief.

PHYSIOLOGICAL FACTORS

The bereavement process is affected not only by the psychological state of the griever and the external influences of society but also by physical factors. As we know, mourning is strenuous work. The following are some common physical issues that have been identified as potentially affecting bereavement outcomes.

Drugs and Sedatives

Physicians frequently prescribe sedatives or tranquilizers to grievers who display dramatic symptoms in the belief that such medications will help them for the short term. Mild doses may, in fact, assist the griever in reducing excessive anxiety or obtaining needed sleep and should not be considered problematic. There is evidence, however, that the chemically induced "numbing out" of one's feelings has a negative effect on the bereavement process. According to Rando (1984),

> Often the bereaved are drugged during the wake and funeral, the precise times at which they should be encouraged to give vent to their emotions. This leaves them to confront their loss later on, at times at which there may not be the social support that is usually available during the initial period following the death. (Pp. 55–56)

Also to be considered is the issue of nonprescription (illegal) substances and alcohol. Alcohol consumption is a socially accepted adult activity in our culture, and many people believe there is no harm in the bereaved having a drink or two to "steady the nerves." This social permission, however, may in some cases lead to subtle abuse of alcohol, where the griever begins drinking routinely to block feelings of sadness and despair, or perhaps for help in getting to sleep. In addition to "deferring" the pain necessary for grief work, the potentially addictive consequences of this behavior are well known. The same is true for the use of illegal narcotics, such as cocaine, marijuana, and crack.

Nutrition

After experiencing the shock of a death, it is common for many people to lose their appetite and feel unable or unwilling to eat. Gastrointestinal disturbances are common as well. Good, balanced nutrition, however, is important to maintain strength and is critical to the bereaved's ability to function effectively in the days and weeks following the loss. Admonitions to grievers to "eat a little something" are well founded.

Rest and Sleep

A normal by-product of the grieving process is the experience of some type of sleep disturbance. This can include difficulty in falling asleep or staying asleep, or it may manifest in sleeping for abnormally long periods of time, perhaps as an escape from painful feelings. Where sleeplessness is an initial problem, grievers may be encouraged to participate in some light exercise to "tire them out," or to use a mild, sleep-enhancing tranquilizer.

Exercise

Most people are aware of the enormous emotional and physical benefits brought about by exercise. A bereaved person in particular should not abandon his or her regular exercise routine, and absent such a regimen, should be encouraged to begin one. Exercise promotes the production of endorphins, chemicals in the human brain that create feelings of well-being. Exercise is also known to diminish levels of aggression and anxiety, and to relieve symptoms of depression (Rando 1984, pp. 55–57).

Overall Physical Condition

Grief places tremendous burdens on the human body. The bereaved's overall physical health at the time of the loss will be a determinant in how well the body handles the stress of grieving. Prompt attention to *any* physical anomaly during this period is a must.

SUMMARY

This chapter has explored the psychological (internal), sociological (external), and physiological factors that influence the grieving process. Each individual experiences loss differently based on his or her psychological makeup, and on the type and level of social support received from family and friends. Factors such as the nature and intensity of the relationship between the bereaved and the deceased, the bereaved's level of maturity and intelligence, the personal qualities of the deceased and how he or she died can all affect—positively or negatively—the bereavement outcome.

When working with people who are grieving, awareness of these psychological, sociological, and physiological factors teaches us to follow two crucial caveats: First, assume nothing; second, resist the urge to pass judgment.

Taking a griever's situation at face value ultimately may not serve his or her best interests. Often, what is seen on the surface may not reflect the truth of what the person is experiencing. Further, there is a natural tendency to assess others' behavior based on personal experience and standards. Your background and the bereaved's, particularly with respect to membership in cultural, ethnic, and/or religious groups, may be vastly different. What appears unusual or even abnormal to you may be perfectly normal in the context of the griever's life.

REFERENCES

Rando, Therese A. 1984. *Grief, dying and death: Clinical interventions for caregivers.* Champaign, Ill.: Research Press.

Raphael, Beverly. 1983. *The anatomy of bereavement.* New York: Basic Books.

van Gennep, Arnold. 1960. *The rites of passage.* Chicago: University of Chicago Press.

Worden, J. William. 1982. *Grief counseling and grief therapy.* New York: Springer.

10

COMPARING AND CONTRASTING REACTIONS TO LOSS

John D. Canine

CHAPTER OUTLINE ....

....

Until about 1960, only Sigmund Freud and a few others had developed theories about the process of grief as a reaction to loss. In 1917 Freud approached the issues of grief by studying depressive illness in adults. In 1944 Erich Lindemann wrote his benchmark study defining the physical aspects of grief, and in 1961 John Bowlby defined the grief process as a result of his study of children and attachment behavior. In the early 1970s C. M. Parkes combined these theories with clinical results to further define the process of grief as a reaction to loss. This chapter will discuss some of the writings of the pioneers of bereavement studies and provide insight into the progressive development of theories about grief. It is worthwhile to note that Freud developed the original idea that grief is a normal, universal, and necessary response to loss—an idea that has provided a foundation for all other writings. The early writers of bereavement studies focused on differing aspects of grief reactions: Freud, the psychoanalytic; Lindemann, the physical; Bowlby, the relational; and Parkes, the clinical.

FREUD

In 1917 Sigmund Freud, in his classic psychoanalytic study "Melancholia and Mourning," described grief as "a task carried out bit by bit, under great expense of time and (cathectic) energy, while all the time the existence of the lost object is continued in the mind" (Freud 1957, p. 126). He proposed that grief is a process by which libido (energy) is withdrawn from a love object. Freud viewed libido as a quantity of energy that undergoes transformation. Since he believed that no one willingly abandons a "libido position," this leads to an internal struggle. He concluded that grieving is a process of reliving memories until the internal struggle of withdrawing from a love object is complete.

While describing this process as "work," Freud refers to the grief process as one that absorbs the energies of the ego: "In grief we found that the ego's inhibited condition and loss of interest was fully accounted for by the absorbing work of mourning" (p. 127). Freud suggests that the process of removing energy from a love object is accomplished by reliving memories, which requires attention from the individual's ego. "The fact is, however, that when the work of mourning is complete, the ego becomes free and uninhibited again" (p. 127). Freud believed this idea to be essential to the process of grief so that the individual can let go of a love object and form new emotional attachments. This idea is fundamental to the view of grief as a normal, appropriate, and necessary process. Additionally, it provided the foundation for psychiatrists to later develop ideas about normal versus pathological grief.

Another essential aspect of Freud's definition is the description of grief as a painful process. He considered this process a "painful one, but necessary to complete the work of mourning" (p. 126). Although he described it as difficult to explain, he believed it to be natural and necessary. Freud termed this "extraordinary pain" and linked it to the testing of reality, the realization the loved object no longer exists, and the struggle the libido encounters to withdraw from its attachment to the object.

LINDEMANN

Erich Lindemann's 1944 article "Symptomatology and Management of Acute Grief" is the most influential single piece of writing on the topic of physical expressions of grief. Basing his beliefs about normal grief reactions on interviews and psychotherapy with over one hundred bereaved persons who had lost family members in the catastrophic fire at the Cocoanut Grove Night Club, Lindemann developed a description of physical aspects of normal grief reactions. One set of symptoms common to all the people he interviewed included "sensations of somatic distress occurring in waves lasting from twenty minutes to an hour at a time, a feeling of tightness in the throat, choking with shortness of breath, a need for sighing with an empty feeling in the abdomen, lack of muscular power and an intense subjective distress described as tension or mental pain" (p. 141). After developing this description of the physical aspects of grief reactions, Lindemann believed this symptomatology to be uniform and essential to the grief process.

Like Freud, Lindemann also suggested that the grief process is "work" and addressed the issue of pain. He believed that the duration of a grief reaction depends on the success with which a person does the "grief work," namely, "emancipation from the bondage to the deceased, readjustment to the environment in which the deceased is missing, and the formation of new relationships" (p. 142). Furthermore, he believed that many individuals try to avoid the pain connected with the grief process because of the intense distress associated with the expression of emotion necessary for grief work.

It was from this idea that grief is a process that requires work and pain that Lindemann described the typical reaction to bereavement and then delineated what he believed to be pathological forms of grief. What he called "delayed" grief was the most striking and most frequent reaction of this sort: "If the bereavement occurs at a time when the individual is confronted with important tasks and when there is necessity for maintaining the morale of others, he may show little or no reaction for weeks or even much longer" (p. 144). During the period of delay, the bereaved person may behave quite normally or may show symptoms that Lindemann regarded as distorted forms of grief. These include the following:

1. Overactivity without a sense of loss
2. The acquisition of symptoms belonging to the last illness of the deceased
3. Progressive isolation from friends and relatives
4. Furious hostility toward a specific person
5. Wooden formality hiding intense anger
6. Enduring loss of pattern of social interactions
7. Self-punitive behavior (such as excessive generosity)

According to Lindemann, reactions such as these can be transformed into normal reactions with psychological intervention. Lindemann believed it was possible to settle an uncomplicated and undistorted grief reaction in a period of from four to six weeks, and that psychological intervention during this time frame could transform a distorted reaction into a normal grief reaction.

In addition to defining the physical aspects of grief, Lindemann was the first to recognize and use the term "anticipatory grief." He describes this as a genuine grief reaction in people who had not experienced a bereavement but who had experienced separation, for instance, the departure of a member of the family into the armed forces: "The patient is so concerned with her adjustment after the potential death of a father or son that she goes through all the phases of grief—depression, heightened preoccupation with the departed, a review of all the forms of death which may befall him, and anticipation of the modes of readjustment which might be necessitated by it" (p. 148).

Lindemann suggests that while this reaction can serve as a safeguard should the death actually occur, it may inhibit continued involvement if the death does not occur and the loved one returns to be reunited. He illustrates this phenomenon with the example of the soldier who returned from the war and complained that his wife did not love him and had demanded a divorce. Lindemann interpreted this action as grief work done too effectively.

BOWLBY

John Bowlby (1980) derived his theory about the process of grief from a relational viewpoint, the result of his clinical studies and the formation of his well-known attachment theory. The four aspects of the attachment theory are strength of attachment, security of attachment, reliance, and involvement. The goal of attachment behavior is to maintain certain degrees of proximity to or communication with the person to whom the individual is attached. Since the goal of attachment behavior is to maintain an affectional bond, any situation that appears to endanger that bond will elicit action to preserve it. The greater the threat of loss, the more intense and varied the actions will be to prevent it. Like Freud and Lindemann, Bowlby proposed that healthy mourning is a process of withdrawal of investment in the lost person and preparation for making a relationship with a new one.

Basing this theory on the attachment bond, in 1961 Bowlby developed three phases to describe the grief process: the urge to recover the lost object; disorganization and despair; and reorganization. In 1980 he revised his schema by adding a phase to the beginning, which he felt was omitted from his original theory. The four phases are as follows:

1. Phase of numbing that usually lasts from a few hours to a week and may be interrupted by outbursts of extremely intense distress and/or anger
2. Phase of yearning and searching for the lost figure, lasting some months and sometimes for years
3. Phase of disorganization and despair
4. Phase of greater or lesser degree of reorganization

As did Freud and Lindemann, Bowlby (1980) addressed the issue of the pain of grief, describing it as inevitable. In contrast to Freud, who attributed the pain of grieving to the ego's internal struggle of reliving memories, Bowlby traced this pain to the idea of identification with the loved person. Based on his attachment theory, he believed temporary absence from a loved person results in pain (p. 25). He concluded, "The urge to regain the person lost is powerful and often persists long after reason has deemed it useless" (p. 27).

This conclusion prompted Bowlby to investigate other issues relating to the psychological nature of the grief process, which included motivations that are present in mourning and how anxiety and anger are related to mourning. Like Lindemann, Bowlby approached these issues by investigating healthy mourning: "The more detailed picture we obtain of healthy mourning the more clearly are we able to identify the pathological variants as being the result of defensive processes having interfered with and diverted its course" (p. 31). This idea is the same as that of Lindemann, who, in describing the various morbid reactions, regards them as exaggerations or distortions of the normal grief process.

Bowlby believed the motivation for mourning to be attributable to the difficult experience of pain resulting from the insatiable nature of yearning. He describes this as a change that occurs as the griever begins to register the reality of the loss. He states: "This leads to pangs of intense pining and to spasms of distress and tearful sobbing. Yet, almost at the same time, there is a great restlessness, insomnia, preoccupation with thoughts of the lost person combined with a sense of his actual presence, and a marked tendency to interpret signals or sounds as indicating that he has now returned" (p. 86).

Bowlby suggests that anger and anxiety are intertwined with one another during this yearning and searching phase of the grief process. He believed this to be a normal aspect of this early phase of mourning because the bereaved person alternates between two states of mind: "On the one hand is belief that death has occurred with the pain and hopeless yearning that entails; on the other hand is disbelief that it has occurred, accompanied both by hope that all may yet be well and an urge to search for and to recover the lost person" (p. 87). Bowlby asserts that this conflict within a person not only arouses anger toward those held responsible for the death, but also results from frustrations encountered during fruitless searching.

Exploring this view further, Bowlby suggests that the urge to search and recover varies greatly from person to person and gradually diminishes over time. Moreover, he describes this urge as essential because the bereaved person is impelled to search and recover the person who has gone. "Whereas some bereaved people are conscious of the urge to search, others are not. Whereas some willingly fall in with it, others seek to stifle it as irrational and absurd" (p. 87). Bowlby believed that many features characteristic of pathological forms of mourning can be understood as resulting from the active persistence of this urge to search, which tends to be expressed in a variety of disguised and distorted ways. Essentially, Bowlby formed the same conclusion as Lindemann: that pathological mourning results from the individual's attempt to avoid the pain of grieving.

PARKES

C. M. Parkes (1972) writes from a clinical viewpoint and defines grief as "the only functional psychiatric disorder whose cause is known, whose features are distinctive and whose course is usually predictable" (p. 6). While comparing the theories of Freud, Lindemann, and Bowlby with his own clinical conclusions based on the Harvard Bereavement Study, which reports how a sample of Boston widows and widowers coped with bereavement, Parkes describes the experience of grief as a normal reaction to overwhelming loss. Additionally, he believed "grief symptoms start after a loss and then gradually fade away, they involve a succession of clinical pictures which blend into and replace one another" (p. 6).

In describing grief as a normal reaction to loss, Parkes addressed Lindemann's ideas about the physical aspects of grief in stating:

> Grief may not produce physical pain but it is very unpleasant and it usually disturbs function. On the whole, grief resembles a physical injury more closely than any other type of illness. The loss may be spoken of as a "blow." In many respects grief can be regarded as an illness. But it can also bring strength. Just as broken bones may end up stronger than unbroken ones, so the experience of grief can strengthen and bring maturity to those who have previously been protected from misfortune. (P. 5)

Parkes referred to Lindemann's description of somatic distress as a constellation of reactions he termed "pangs." Parkes believed that they are the most characteristic single response to grief. Adding sobbing and crying to Lindemann's description, he says these pangs begin shortly after the death—a few hours or a few days later—and occur less frequently with the passage of time (p. 6). Parkes attributed the "pangs" of grief to the yearning and searching that constitute separation anxiety. As did Bowlby, Parkes believed that the personal bond between a mother and child is the basis for this anxiety.

Additionally, while Parkes agreed with Lindemann's description of normal grief reactions, he disagreed with his idea that the grief work could be accomplished within a short period of time and that psychological interventions could produce results in four to six weeks. He believed this to be an oversimplification of the bereavement process. Based on his conclusions drawn from the Harvard Bereavement Study, Parkes believed that the forces of bereavement usually operate over a much longer time that is more appropriately labeled a "period of life transition" rather that a "life crisis" (as defined by Lindemann) (p. viii).

Parkes proposed that Freud's theory had been criticized on the grounds that his "libido," which he thought of as a kind of relational energy, was a confusing concept. However, Parkes believed, even if we omit libido from the formulation, we are still left with the notion of grief as a struggle between opposing impulses, one tending toward realization of loss and the other toward retention of the loved person. Another view proposed by Bowlby and Parkes in 1970 is recognition of the similarity between the mourning behavior of adults and young children. They describe a clearly discernible tendency among many adults who are separated from those they love to cry out, to search out restlessly for the lost person, to attack anything or anybody who impedes this search, and to find some way of "keeping alive" memories of the person they have lost.

Parkes concluded that resistance to change and a reluctance to give up possessions, people, status, and expectations are the basis of grief. He believed how a man copes with the challenge of change in his life will determine not only his view of the world but his view of himself: "It is no exaggeration to assert that personality is both a resultant and a determinant to change" (p. 120). From this idea,

Parkes (1972) developed criteria to describe the determinants of the outcome of bereavement. These include antecedent determinants (childhood and later life experiences, previous mental illness, relationships with the deceased, and the mode of death); concurrent determinants (sex, age, personality, religion, and cultural and familiar factors); and subsequent determinants (social support or isolation, secondary stresses, and emergent life opportunities) (p. 121). Parkes identified seven features that he considered major aspects of grief reactions:

1. A process of realization—The person moves from denial or avoidance of recognition toward acceptance.
2. An alarm reaction—Anxiety, restlessness, and the physical accompaniments of fear.
3. An urge to search for and to find the lost person in some form.
4. Anger and guilt, including outbursts directed against those who press the bereaved toward premature acceptance of the loss.
5. Feelings of internal loss or self-mutilation.
6. Identification phenomenon—The adoption of traits, mannerisms, or symptoms of the lost person, with or without a sense of his or her presence within the self.
7. Pathological variants of grief, that is, the reaction may be excessive and prolonged or inhibited and inclined to emerge in distorted forms.

While concluding that pain is an essential aspect of the grief process, as did Freud and Lindemann, Parkes also spoke about love: "The pain of grief is just as much a part of life as the joy of love, it is, perhaps the price we pay for love, the cost of commitment" (p. 5). What is remarkable about the process of grief as a reaction to loss is not only the number and variety of responses that are engaged but also the way in which they tend to conflict with one another. Loss of a loved person gives rise to an intense desire for reunion, a cry for help, anger at his or her departure, and, later, to some degree of detachment. No wonder it is painful to experience and difficult to understand.

SUMMARY

This chapter addresses early bereavement studies and provides insight into the process of grief while focusing on four differing aspects of grief reactions: psychoanalytic, physical, relational, and clinical. Fundamental to the development of current theories of grief as a process is the idea presented by Sigmund Freud that grief is a normal, universal, and necessary response to loss. Freud defined the grief process as a process whereby emotional energy is withdrawn from a love object so the individual can form new emotional attachments. He viewed this as natural and necessary. Additionally, Freud termed this process "grief work," because the individual's ego relived memories as a means of withdrawing emotionally. Freud viewed this as "extraordinarily painful."

In 1944 Erich Lindemann presented the first writings about physical reactions to loss. Lindemann viewed grief as a painful but essential psychological process and delineated between normal and pathological grief. In addition, he identified distorted or delayed reactions as pathological and defined anticipatory grief reactions.

John Bowlby has suggested that grief is a normal result of how an individual conceptualizes affectional bonds, a result of his attachment theory. Bowlby believed that the pain of grieving results from the individual's searching and yearning for the lost loved one. Bowlby also identified pathological variants of the grief process and proposed a theory about the grief process consisting of four phases: numbing, searching, disorganization and despair, and reorganization.

C. M. Parkes combined these theories with clinical results from the Harvard Bereavement Study. He believed that resistance to change is the basis of grief reactions and identified seven major aspects of grief reactions: realization, alarm reaction, urge to search, anger and guilt, feelings of internal loss, identification phenomenon, and pathological variants.

REFERENCES

Bowlby, J. 1961. Processes of mourning. *International Journal of Psychoanalysis* 42:317–40.
———. 1980. *Attachment and Loss.* Vol. 3. New York: Basic Books.
Glick, J., R. Weiss, and C. Parkes. 1974. *The first year of bereavement.* New York: Wiley.
Lindemann, E. 1944. Symptomatology and management of acute grief. *American Journal of Psychiatry* 101:141–48.
Parkes, C. M. 1972. *Bereavement: Studies of grief in adult life.* New York: International Universities Press.
Parkes, C. M., and R. Weiss. 1983. *Recovery from bereavement.* New York: Basic Books.
Rickman, J. 1957. Mourning and melancholia In *Standard edition of the complete works of Sigmund Freud.* Vol. 14. London: Hogarth Press, pp. 124–40.

11

MANIFESTATIONS OF GRIEF

John D. Canine

The term "stages of grief" refers to a process that describes personal manifestations of grief. This process involves universal tasks that those in mourning will work through in some form and at some time during their period of bereavement. Freud termed this process "grief work" (Freud 1959).

As Chapter 10 discussed, as early as 1917, Freud, in "Melancholia and Mourning," distinguished between normal grief and depression. He believed grieving was an attempt by the bereaved to withdraw energy (libido) from the loved one who died. He differentiated between "cathexis" (the attachment of an individual to a significant other) and "hypercathexis" (the process of eventual separation from the significant other). He further believed that as a grieving individual relived past experiences in the form of memories, feelings for the deceased would become so strong and real that they would provide a sense of permanent connection. The result for the griever is acceptance of the physical loss and a desire to form new attachments.

In 1961 psychiatrist John Bowlby defined the goal of attachment behavior as an individual's way of maintaining proximity or communication with the person to whom the individual is attached. Bowlby observed attachment behavior in many species, causing him to theorize that attachment is an organism's way of keeping in touch with its caretaker and thus reducing the risk of harm. His research further defines Freud's original thought and suggests that any situation that appears to endanger an individual's bond of affection (attachment) will elicit action to preserve it. Therefore, if a griever maintains *any* intense emotion over the death of a loved one, he or she will often appear to receive some gratification from it. Why? In reality, the emotion keeps the griever from having to face the loss all at once and permits a gradual acceptance of the death. In time, this acceptance permits the formation of new relationships.

Over the years, bereavement studies have produced many theories similar to Freud's and Bowlby's that demonstrate an individual's "grief work" (see Figures 11–1 to 11–3). However, none identified specific conditions that grieving individ-

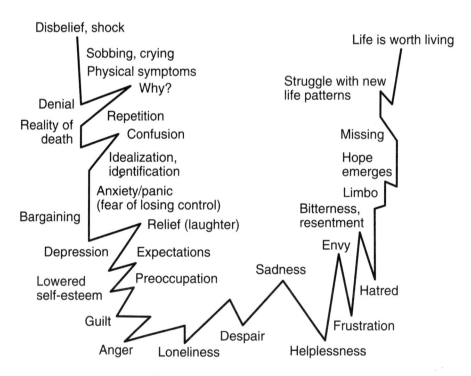

Figure 11–1. Experiences of grief. (Hope for Bereaved, 1342 Lancaster Avenue, Syracuse, New York 13210; taken from Hope for Bereaved handbook.)

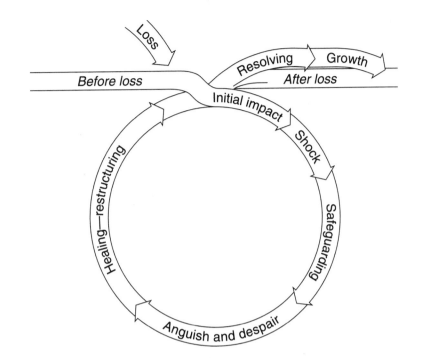

Figure 11–2. Grief growth cycle. (Donna O'Toole, Rainbow Connections, 1986)

uals experience until Erich Lindemann's 1944 benchmark grief research based on the Boston Cocoanut Grove fire. In this study Lindemann demonstrated that acute grief was a normal reaction to adverse, stressful situations. Because so many in the fire shared the same loss experience at the same time, he was able to identify consistent reactions toward that loss. From studying survivors' feelings regarding the experience at Cocoanut Grove, Lindemann identified five general emotional conditions of grief: guilt, hostile reactions, somatic distress, preoccupation with the image of the deceased, and changes in normal behavioral patterns.

STAGES OF GRIEF

Through his work Lindemann developed a theory of grief that consists of three major stages: the urge to recover the lost object, disorganization-despair, and reorganization (Lindemann 1944). He defined these more specifically as follows:

1. Shock-disbelief—This first stage is the urge to recover the lost object. It is characterized by a person's inability to accept the loss and, for some, absolute denial that the loss ever occurred.

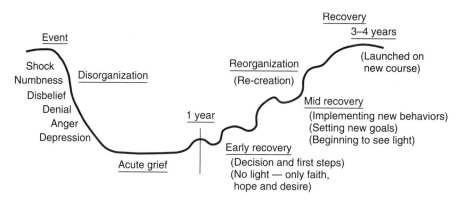

Figure 11-3. Levels of grief recovery. (Dr. William Jones, Oakland University, 1990)

2. Acute mourning—In the second stage, disorganization-despair, there is an intense preoccupation with the image of the deceased. Typical symptoms are acceptance of the loss, disinterest in daily affairs, crying, insomnia, loneliness, and loss of appetite.

3. Resolution of the grief process—The third stage, reorganization, is a gradual reentry into the activities of daily life and a reduction in the preoccupation with the image of the deceased.

Every individual who grieves has had a unique relationship with the deceased. The grieving person's mental state, personality, and relationship with the deceased are all factors in the successful resolution of the grieving process. For some individuals there are clear, outward signs of grief. For others there are none, which could lead to a false belief that the person is working through his or her loss. Ultimately, each grieving person has his or her own unique process for working through grief within the framework of specific phases of grief.

In 1990 John D. Canine designated five major stages of grief. These are

1. Denial
2. Numbness
3. Searching
4. Disorientation
5. Resolution

Canine identified specific behaviors of the grieving person that correspond to each of these "stages of grief." It is important for the bereavement professional to understand these behaviors so appropriate strategies for best servicing grieving families can be developed.

From the moment of death, the grieving survivor engages in an emotional

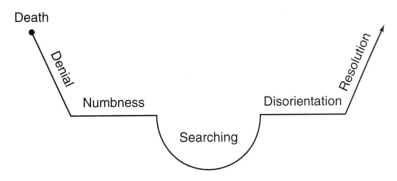

Figure 11–4. Stages of grief. (Dr. John Canine, Maximum Living Consultants, Inc., Birmingham, 1989)

journey, initially in a downward spiral (see Figure 11–4). This progression downward begins with denial.

Denial

"There must be some mistake . . ." This is a typical response from someone in the denial stage. As described in the *American Psychiatric Glossary,* "denial is a defense mechanism, operating unconsciously, used to resolve emotional conflict and allay anxiety by disavowing thoughts, feelings, wishes, needs, or external reality factors that are consciously intolerable" (Stone 1988).

This state is usually temporary, and allows the individual time to deal rationally with the loss. Denial behavior acts like a shield, protecting the bereaved from the realities of the death. Denial reactions to a loss can range from withdrawal and isolation to the inability to actualize the death. However, denial behavior is manifested in various ways depending on the individual.

In her book *No Time for Goodbyes* (1990), Janice Harris-Lord describes "fight" or "flight" denial. "Fighters" sometimes physically attack the person who has delivered the terrible news of the death. On the other hand, those whose reaction is "flight" either run away or faint to escape the pain. Lord's term "frozen fright" describes those who become speechless upon the news of the death.

It is possible that during the denial stage, the funeral director will have a great deal of interaction with the individual or family. The director can enhance the grief process by suggesting meaningful rituals that will assist the griever in actualizing the loss. The following are a few such rituals:

• Choosing clothes for the deceased
• Asking the family to assist in writing the obituary
• Involving the griever in planning the funeral
• Making a collage of pictures of the loved one
• Allowing the family to assist in the closing of the casket
• Asking the family to take part in scattering of the ashes

Numbness

The numbness stage is a psychological state that allows some survivors to organize and carry out the social activities of the funeral week. When observers of the grieving person comment, "She is doing so well," it is actually the mechanical behavior of the numbness stage that gives the illusion of composure. Within this fog of numbness, the individual is fatigued, has poor concentration, and can experience nausea, difficulty in breathing, tightness in the chest, and loss of appetite. In this stage the bereaved is stunned but still able to take part in the funeralization process.

During this stage it is the responsibility of the funeral professional to help the bereaved help themselves. This can be done best by providing structure and definition to the funeral. Also, the funeral professional can show understanding when the survivor's acceptance of the death is minimal, producing a variety of emotions. Often, the griever's most arduous task during the numbness stage is decision making. The process of grief renders decision making enormously difficult, and the griever might look to the funeral director for assistance. In this situation, here are some suggestions to assist the bereaved:

1. Since grieving individuals often are unaware of the options for funeral services, explain the various alternatives open to them.
2. Do not force bereaved individuals into any choices that appear to contradict their stated needs.
3. Respect the choices made by the bereaved.
4. Make sure that the mode of disposition is one that is acceptable to the mourners.
5. Be sensitive to the fact that some decisions made by the bereaved could be regretted later. A sensitive funeral director will encourage the family to make only the decisions that are necessary.

Searching

The third stage, searching, is described as falling into the "pit." It is initially characterized by overwhelming doubt. The griever questions the circumstances surrounding the loss while at the same time doubting his or her ability to go on with life. It is during this stage that anger, guilt, and a generalized panic are paramount. The griever is tortured by an inability to trust anyone or anything. The emotional pain seems to be never-ending.

However, working through the feelings associated with the searching stage is absolutely necessary to successfully complete the grief process. Angry feelings must be released in an appropriate manner. Internalizing anger or directing it inappropriately can lead to lowered self-esteem, depression, conflict in interpersonal relationships, and stagnation in the grief process. Here are some appropriate ways to discharge anger:

1. Hit a pillow.
2. Kick a bed.

3. Yell and scream. (A parked car makes a good scream chamber.)
4. Play a competitive sport.
5. Hit a punching bag.

Like anger, guilt feelings also must be released. Guilt is felt by people who, before the death, wanted harm to come to the deceased. Discharging one's guilt can be accomplished by the following:

1. Verbally reviewing and discussing with someone the circumstances surrounding the death.
2. Journal writing. (This is good for angry feelings too.)
3. Thinking through one's feelings with a focus on objectivity. Looking more objectively at the situation surrounding the death.

However, before assuming that guilt is *the* emotion being experienced, a grieving person should consider that the emotion might be regret. It is important to recognize the difference. For example, intentionally harming someone usually causes a feeling of guilt. On the other hand, regret carries no harmful intentions. It is the realization that something might have been done differently if there had been a second chance. So, instead of guilt, the feelings actually might be regret.

In the "search" to recognize and accept the pain involved in this phase of grieving, crying is an important mechanism for working through this stage. Although an individual might cry throughout the grief process, it is in this stage that crying can be most intense.

William Frey, a University of Minnesota biochemist, conducted a study on adult crying. By studying two specific neurotransmitters that are present in tears, Frey discovered that crying can be a chemical (enkephalin) release for stress. When an individual is sad (grieving), enkephalin is produced by the brain and has an opiate effect on the body. Once it has done its job, enkephalin is removed from the body as waste through the individual's tears.

Dr. Frey's research (1983) offers a physiological explanation of why people feel better after crying—removal of waste and a release for stress. Considering society's traditional attitude that crying be suppressed, particularly in men, this evidence has significant implications. Research tells us that, in fact, crying can be a positive step toward rising out of the "pit." Thus, crying is a healthy response to grief for both women and men. More will be said about tears, as well as anger, guilt, and anxiety, in later chapters.

In summary, the searching stage is a very difficult phase of the grieving process. It is a time when the funeral director might have limited interaction with the family of the deceased. However, when interaction occurs, a wonderful opportunity emerges to be empathetic, supportive, and encouraging toward the bereaved. Also, it is a time to consider possible referral to a mental health practitioner. In *Dying: Facing the Facts* (1988), Robert Fulton writes: "It would be beneficial if the funeral director would come to be seen as a participant in a community's mental health network. This view would not only support those practices which historically have served human needs, but it would also strengthen the movement within the funeral service itself and play a positive part in helping with the burdens of bereavement" (p. 270).

Disorientation

Having "hit bottom" in the searching stage, the bereaved is ready for the move upward toward resolution. Disorientation is a time when the bereaved fluctuates between wanting to look back (searching) one day and want to move forward (resolution) the next. This dichotomy creates tension and anxiety while the individual is deciding which direction to take. This adds feelings of confusion to the worthlessness and loneliness the grieving person has experienced since the death. As in previous stages of grief, the griever still looks to the memories of the deceased to maintain some degree of attachment. It is difficult to think in the present, let alone the future. However, disorientation becomes the time when the griever has healed sufficiently to begin experiencing pleasurable moments and start to plan for the future.

The decision to move ahead with one's life is done without the support of the loved one who has died. Therefore, the griever might second-guess him- or herself with even the most minor of choices. If the decision-making process becomes too tense and confusing, the bereaved might "shut down," deciding not to make any choices or decisions at all. This attitude prohibits a "future" and renders life meaningless. Both active and passive suicidal tendencies seem to be prevalent in this phase, especially among the elderly.

Most funeral directors will have little influence over the griever in the disorientation stage. If, however, a bereavement aftercare program is part of the funeralization process, tremendous insight into this stage can come to the griever through dialogue (telling life stories) in a support group setting.

Resolution

Once the griever decides "there is a future for me," he or she can move quickly into resolution. This does not mean the past is forgotten. It simply means memories that best exemplify the loved one are retained without intense attachment. This promotes a new and healthy relationship with the deceased, and permits goals for the future.

What is resolution? Most grievers find it hard to define. However, there is a "letting go" of the loved one along with a renewed interest in life. Laughter, pleasurable activities, and a willingness to change and forgive characterize this stage. With it comes a clear understanding that life is to be lived one day at a time.

During this journey through grief, an individual has struggled but has made new discoveries about life. The choices, the bereaved has learned, are to live a life that is barren, broken, and bitter, or to work toward healthy, productive living. One's "grief work" is most successful when behavior following bereavement is at a higher level of functioning than before the death occurred.

Generally, funeral directors do not have the opportunity to observe families in the resolution stage. However, it is important to note that family members might return to the funeral home weeks, or even months, after the funeral to validate or clarify information they learned during the funeral week while in a state of denial or numbness. Once again, the funeral director can play a supportive role in this information-seeking process. Most grievers do not move through the stages of grief in a clear, well-defined manner. There are moments of advancement and regression. Since different family members grieve differently over the loss of the same person, it is important for the funeral professional to understand that sensitivity and awareness of the various manifestations of grief are crucial. During a funeral arrangement meeting, many family members can be present. Each had his or her own unique relationship with the deceased, and each will bring different perspectives, responses, and requests to the arrangement process.

These differences continue throughout the funeralization process as well as the grief process. With this in mind, the funeral professional can acknowledge the family differences yet, at the same time, promote unity, encourage compromise, and offer insight into the stages of grief.

SITUATIONS OF DEATH

All death is difficult, but there are five situations that make a death very difficult to deal with as we move toward resolution. These five situations are categorized as sudden, premature, intense relationship, violent, and death when no body is found.

Sudden Death

"The shock and injustice of losing someone you love to a sudden, violent, and senseless death can result in grief with a wider range and depth of feelings and which lasts longer than for survivors of anticipated non-violent death" (Harris-Lord 1990). This statement by Janice Lord in her book *No Time for Goodbyes* points out that although death is difficult to cope with under any circumstances, mourners of an unanticipated death need special attention. Accepting the loss of a significant other person is never easy. When death occurs suddenly, as with a heart attack or car accident, it is extremely difficult to accept.

When a person anticipates the death of a loved one, as with a long illness, some of the grief work is done before the death occurs. In this situation it is more likely a person will experience normal patterns of grief after death. Therese Rando suggests in *Loss and Anticipatory Grief* that "the more anticipatory grief behavior engaged in prior to death, the less abnormal grief was present following the death" (Rando 1986).

However, when there is a sudden death, there is no time for a person to prepare for the loss. Without a period of anticipation, the emotional devastation for the survivor following the death is usually greater than if there is anticipatory grief. For the survivor of sudden death, emotions are raw and accepting the loss is risky. The survivor is not ready for the sudden detachment. Therefore, the period of denial could be quite long since avoiding the loss often feels better than riding an emotional roller coaster.

This case study offers an example of sudden death. After reading the case, discuss the questions that follow.

CASE STUDY #1

A seventy-year-old man, John, had been to his cardiologist for an annual physical. After running a variety of tests, the doctor declared that John was not only physically fit but had the heart of a young man. One week later, John and his wife were at the airport, ready to fly to their vacation spot. As John carried the suitcases to the check-in counter, he suffered a massive heart attack and died in his wife's arms.

Discussion Questions

1. What kind of emotional response do you think John's wife had to his death?
2. John's wife had many questions haunting her after John died. What would you imagine those questions to be?
3. What could a funeral professional do to support John's wife during the funeralization process?

Premature Death

There is an old proverb that says, "The greater the expectation, the greater the disappointment." When we expect our loved ones to live a long life and instead they die unexpectedly, disappointment runs deep. John's death can be considered a premature as well as a sudden death because he did not live to the average life expectancy. An American male's life expectancy is approximately 71.5 years of age; an American female's is about 78. When a person dies before the expected time, it is considered premature.

Most grief counselors agree that the most troubling premature death is the death of a child. *If one loses a parent, he loses some of his past. If one loses a spouse, he loses some of his present. But, if one loses a child, he loses some of his future* (Canine 1990). Since our future holds the hope of expectations being met, the loss of a child (loss of the future) leaves one with great disappointment over many unfulfilled expectations.

In the next case study, both parents lost a significant part of their future.

CASE STUDY #2

Sally and Tom had planned to have three children. After having two baby boys, they were hoping the third child would be a girl. Much to their delight, the birth of Susan completed the family. Tom adored his sweet little daughter. Sally especially had great expectations for the fun she and her daughter would have with growing up, proms, and weddings. Tragically, Susan was killed in a car accident at the age of thirteen. Afterward, reflecting on what a beautiful teenager Susan was becoming, Tom jokingly said, "I just wanted to keep 'the boys' away."

Discussion Questions

1. In losing their child, how did Sally and Tom lose their future?
2. What kind of loss did Susan's brothers experience in their sister's death?
3. What can a funeral professional do to help soften the blow for Sally and Tom?
4. Is there anything a funeral professional can do to assist the brothers in their grieving? Explain.

Intense Relationship

Why do we grieve? Because we love. As long as people are bonded to each other in a caring and loving way, people will continue to grieve. When that love is lost, any relationship with a deep loving bond can be considered intense. The greater the intensity of the relationship, the greater the intensity of the grief. Not only can a marriage relationship be intense, but a young child dependent on parents, an elderly woman dependent on her son, and sisters whose parents have died are all examples of potentially intense relationships.

The next case describes an intense relationship. Use the questions that follow to engage in discussion on the impact of intense relationships on the grief process.

CASE STUDY #3

Mary and Jim had been married fifty-two years. They had no children, and were completely dependent on one another for personal support. They worked, played, and worshiped together. They truly lived their lives with and for each other. Even simple routines became significant, such as Jim's daily stop at home for lunch with Mary. That's why, when Jim died, Mary realized, "I suddenly felt that half of my life had been cut away."

Discussion Questions

1. Why did Mary's dependency on Jim make her grief so intense?
2. Do you think Mary's grief might have been abnormal? Explain.
3. What could a funeral professional do to demonstrate sensitivity toward Mary's emotional state during the funeralization process?

Violent Death

There are two types of violent death: homicide and suicide. Violent death not only shocks the survivors, it also disrupts the natural stages of grieving.

Simply stated, homicide is murder, the killing of one human being by another. In 1991 approximately twenty-five thousand reported homicides occurred in the United States (Bureau of Crime Statistics Reporting 1991). For each homicide, there are seven to ten close surviving family members. Frequently, a homicide case does not come to trial for five to seven years. This is what makes life so difficult for the survivors. They are unable to grieve because there has been no resolution to the case. To make matters worse, each time the case is brought to court, the survivors must reexperience the acute grief they initially felt.

Interestingly, in order to function "sanely" in this situation, a survivor might fantasize about what he or she "would, could, or should do" to the murderer. Revenge becomes important to the survivors. Is it normal to think of doing to the murderer what was done to the victim? *Yes*. Fantasizing about revenge not only is normal but can be healthy. An enormous amount of energy is released as the survivor works through the grief process. This allows the survivor to function.

Another reaction the survivor might have to a homicide is withdrawal into a deep emotional depression. At this point some individuals might benefit from professional counseling.

The other type of violent death, suicide, is the intentional killing of oneself. Although suicide is committed for different reasons, it is the ultimate act of control. This is why anger and rage are normal reactions to suicide early in the grieving process. After all, the control was taken from the hands of the survivors and placed into the hands of the suicide victim.

There is almost no preparation for grieving in suicide death. Occasionally, the victim leaves a note. Generally speaking, however, very few suicide victims do so. Because suicide offers little or no information about the death, the grieving period is abnormally affected. The lack of understanding in most suicide cases leaves the survivors with guilt that is difficult to rationalize. Questions regarding what could have been done, or what wasn't done, must be resolved in the survivor's mind so the survivor can progress unencumbered through the stages of grief.

Statistics tell us that most individuals who commit suicide really want to live, are not crazy, have not inherited the tendency, and would seek help if directed to it

(Coleman 1979). However, when one is faced with a real situation in which a family member or close friend has committed suicide, there is little comfort in these statistics. The survivors must find supportive people who will listen and not make judgments. They have already judged themselves enough.

Read the next case, which describes a violent death. Then discuss the questions that follow.

CASE STUDY #4

Bill was fifteen years old. He had two very strong, domineering parents. They wanted a lot for him and expected as much from him. Also, their very strict guidelines were regularly enforced to ensure that these expectations were met. Bill often resisted and rebelled, but only in small ways. Over time, the conflicts between him and his parents grew into major proportions. It was after one such conflict that Bill went to his bedroom, put a shotgun to his chest, and pulled the trigger. He left a note saying: "I am in charge. I am in control."

Discussion Questions

1. How do you think Bill's parents felt after his suicide?
2. What kinds of questions do you think Bill's parents needed to resolve in order to work through their grief?
3. What would you anticipate Bill's parents' behavior to be during the funeralization process?
4. What could a funeral professional do to lighten their burden?

When No Body Is Found

To move through the grief process toward finality and closure, it is important for loved ones to actually see the body in its "dead" state. It provides the griever with a point of reference for each stage in the grieving process. When the body of the deceased is not seen, or in some cases not even recovered (e.g., death at sea, MIAs, violent accidents), the mourner might wish, hope, and even fantasize that the loved one is *not* dead. Grief work is neglected, and the griever stagnates at a particular "stage of grief," unable to move on in the process.

The next case study describes a death that occurred several years ago. Use the discussion questions to consider the implications of the death.

CASE STUDY #5

Dan was told by the United States Navy that his son was presumed dead in the Pacific Ocean due to a boating accident. The body had not been recovered. For years, Dan hoped that somehow his boy was still alive. Every time the phone rang, he fantasized that it was his son, calling to say he was O.K.

Discussion Questions

1. Why was it so difficult for Dan to believe that his son was dead?
2. What would help Dan break through his emotional paralysis to complete the grieving process?
3. What could a death care professional do to help Dan work through his grief?

These five "situations of death" make up only one of the variables that can affect the grief process. As discussed in Chapter 2, other circumstances or situations surrounding death can have a dramatic effect on how an individual progresses through the five stages. Therefore, depending on the many factors that could influence grief work, it is important for the death care professional to be aware of the uniqueness of each person's grief.

SUMMARY

Throughout this chapter on manifestations of grief, basic information has been provided on (1) a brief history of grief studies, (2) Canine's five stages of grief, and (3) the five abnormal situations of death. The key to the information presented in this chapter is how it can be applied during the funeralization process to assist families and friends of the deceased.

In this regard, special attention should be paid to the suggestions listed for funeral professionals. These are for your reference as well as a source for generating ideas in helping the people you will serve someday. In addition, the discussion questions are intended to offer an opportunity to begin exploring the many different kinds of situations you might encounter as a funeral professional. The purpose of this information is to demonstrate the kind of sensitivity and creativity that can become an integral part of any funeral professional's service delivery.

REFERENCES

Bowlby, John. 1961. Processes of mourning. *International Journal of Psycho-Analysis* 42:317–40.

———. 1980. *Attachment and loss: Loss, sadness and depression*. Vol. 3. New York: Basic Books.

Canine, John D. 1990. *I can, I will*. Birmingham, Mich.: Ball Publishers.

Coleman, William. 1979. *Understanding suicide*. Elgin, Ill.: Cook Publishing.

Freud, Sigmund. 1959. Mourning and melancholia 1917. *Collected Papers.* Vol. 4. New York: Basic Books. p. 152–170

Frey, William. 1983. Crying behavior in the human adult. *Integrative Psychiatry* 1:94–100.

Fulton, Robert. 1988. *Dying: Facing the facts,* ed. Hannalore Wass. New York: Hemisphere Publishing Corporation.

Harris-Lord, Janice. 1990. *No time for goodbyes.* Ventura, Calif.: Pathfinder Publishing.

Lindemann, Erich. 1944. Symptomatology and management of acute grief. *American Journal of Psychiatry* 101:141–48.

Rando, Therese. 1986. *Loss and anticipatory grief.* Lexington, Mass.: D. C. Heath.

Stone, Elizabeth. 1988. *American psychiatric glossary.* Washington, D.C.: American Psychiatric Press.

12

WHY SOME PEOPLE DO NOT GRIEVE

John D. Canine

Grief is natural and normal. Yet, for a variety of reasons, some people do not seem to grieve. That is, they are psychologically blocked from grieving. People who do not manifest grief have one or more life experiences that prevent them from moving through the normal grief process. In this chapter we will discuss variables that can prevent normal grieving, and work against the resolution of a loved one's death. This resolution is the goal of the grief process. It allows a person to "let go" of the deceased and accompanying emotions that can otherwise interfere with healthy functioning.

The chapter also discusses the four important variables that can obstruct the grieving process:

1. Past losses
2. Death surround
3. Social issues
4. Abnormal grief response

PAST LOSSES

Oftentimes, when someone dies, a survivor is not able to grieve because unresolved emotional issues regarding a death in the past are creating a psychological block. In the following example, consider the impact of Jim's suppressed grief over the years.

CASE STUDY #1

Jim, a thirty-two-year-old insurance agent, and his wife, Diane, have one child to whom Diane devotes most of her time. Each week, Diane and her son would visit Grandma to make sure she had what she needed. Recently, on one of these visits, Diane found her mother dead, sitting in a living room chair. Although her mother had not been feeling well lately, Diane did not expect her to die this suddenly. Diane and Jim were grief stricken following her mother's death.

After a few months of unsuccessful attempts at working through their grief, Diane and Jim went to see a counselor. In the first session Diane discovered for the first time that Jim had found his own parents dead in their home fourteen years earlier. This was the root of his despair over his mother-in-law's death. Since then, he had used denial and avoidance to cope with that tragic scene. Jim's unresolved grief was preventing him from talking about his mother-in-law's death. With Diane responding to the counselor's request to discuss their recent grief, Jim no longer could use his denial and avoidance as coping mechanisms.

People who have been troubled with complicated grief reactions in the past are prone to having them in the future. According to Simos (1979) "Past losses and separations have an impact on current losses and separations and attachments, and all these factors bear on the fear of future loss and separations and the capacity to make future attachments" (p. 27). Obviously, Jim had difficulty dealing with his mother-in-law's death because he was still burdened by the loss of his own parents. His coping mechanisms of denial and avoidance were no longer effective. With the constant encouragement from Diane and the counselor to talk about his losses and grief, Jim realized how many feelings and emotions he had buried and not addressed.

Thus, past losses can have a bearing on future losses. This is true of multiple losses as well. Multiple losses result in what Kastenbaum (1969) termed "bereavement overload." This happens when there is an overwhelming amount of grief in a short period of time. The bereaved person psychologically shuts down and does not appear to grieve. Frequently, this happens with the death of an entire family or where there are several losses in a short period of time. These are the kinds of historical factors that can affect one's ability to grieve. Past losses include other areas of concern that have yet to be researched. For example, when a child loses a parent and has no opportunity to discuss this loss with someone, the child will cope with whatever mechanisms are available at that particular age or level of development. The danger lies in these mechanisms' setting potential unhealthy psychological and behavioral patterns for the child's grief in the future (Vaillant 1985).

In addition, some evidence suggests that a person's mental health has some bearing on whether a person can or cannot grieve. For instance, if a person is inclined toward depression or dysthymic disorder (depressive neurosis), he or she will become depressed and somewhat dysfunctional instead of manifesting healthy grief. If this has been a reaction in the past to losing a loved one, it is likely to become a pattern with future losses (Worden 1991). The first time a person experiences the death of a loved one is the most important time to work through the grieving process. The avoidance of grief not only can impact future bereavement but also can set the stage for anger, frustration, and depression over other types of losses during one's life.

THE DEATH SURROUND

"Death surround" is a term applied to the circumstances surrounding the death of a loved one that affect the survivor's ability to grieve. Often these circumstances underscore intimate feelings between the deceased and the survivor that create troubling emotional aftereffects for the survivor. Take the case of Richard and his father.

CASE STUDY #2

When Richard was forty-two years old, his father, twenty years his senior, stopped by Richard's house one day to discuss a fishing trip they were planning in the near future. During their conversation these two men, who were similar in nature, broke into a heated argument. Angry at Richard, the father grabbed his coat and bolted out the door. Richard was just as furious. Richard's father stormed into his car and had driven only a couple miles when he and another driver collided. The father was killed in the crash.

At first Richard was unable to grieve the loss of his father. Knowing he should be grieving, Richard sought counseling. During the course of his counseling, he began to realize how much he was like his father, a man who did not express emotion or grief. In fact, he was so much like his father that Richard had equated his father's death with the termination of his own existence. Richard felt that he himself had died. After exploring the relationship he had with his father, Richard began to understand the anger and the guilt, and how these related to his own feelings of nonexistence.

Anger and guilt are major issues emerging from the death surround. These are powerful emotions that can prevent a person from grieving. Thinking about the relationship with the deceased and dwelling on the death can evoke anger toward that person for disharmony in their relations, or even anger at the deceased for dying. At the same time, a person can feel guilt over quarrels and disputes. For example, Richard felt the last argument with his father was his own fault. He reasoned that if he had stopped the argument, his father would not have died an untimely death.

There are other issues involving the death surround. One is Richard's feeling of self-extinction. Even though they argued, Richard and his father had developed a special bond that came from their sameness. In many ways they were as one. Just as Richard was affected by his father's inability to grieve, he intimately identified with the ending of his father's life—he too had died. Another issue of the death surround is when the circumstances of the loss are uncertain, such as a death at sea or a homicide where no body is found, but there are signs of foul play. These types of situations leave the mourner with uncertainty about the loss. Without closure to the circumstances of death, the survivor becomes confused. This person asks, "Did he die? Or didn't he?" The survivor cannot work through the grieving process while in the throes of uncertainty.

The loss of a loved one in a highly dependent relationship also can create difficulty in the survivor's ability to grieve. In such a relationship the loss of the deceased is not just the loss of that person; it also represents a loss of personal security for the survivor. The survivor's self-image changes from that of a strong person (through the previous support of the deceased) to the earlier weak and needy self who longs to be rescued. According to Horowitz et al. (1980), most people experience a sense of helplessness following the death of a mate, but this is not the deserted and defenseless feelings felt by those who were overly dependent. In a healthier person the loss does not reduce the positive aspects of self-image. A balance of the positive and negative image factors is maintained. But the self-image of a person who has been dependent beyond normalcy can collapse when affected by needy and desperate feelings. These circumstances can prevent a highly dependent survivor from working through the grief process.

SOCIAL ISSUES

Grief is a social process. It is best dealt with in a social setting where people can support and encourage each other to experience and express their grief. Without a support system, people tend to suppress their grief.

CASE STUDY #3

Having just completed medical school at age twenty-seven, Tammy became pregnant. Her boyfriend was the father. Six weeks into the pregnancy, Tammy had an abortion. Afterward, she became irritable and tense, and created constant conflict with her boyfriend. Although she had been a devout Christian, Tammy dropped out of her Bible study group. Finally, having been constantly on edge with her Christian friends, she decided to see a counselor. During counseling Tammy uncovered a host of psychological issues that haunted her while she was making the decision to have an abortion. Making this decision alone was more than she could bear. She learned that sharing her fears and concerns with others could have helped her through this difficult time.

Having suppressed her feelings, Tammy experienced a complicated grief reaction due, in part, to her loss of social support. Lazare (1979) outlined three conditions that might produce such reactions. He determined that a complicated grief reaction can occur when any of the following is true:

1. The loss is socially unspeakable.
2. The loss is socially negated.
3. There is an absence of social support.

The first condition, when the loss is socially unspeakable, occurs in cases of abortion, suicide, and AIDS. What these events have in common is a personal fear of wrongdoing and the consequent rejection by friends and relatives. The woman who aborts cannot talk to her friends for fear they will reject her if they perceive abortion as a wrongdoing. The family of a suicide victim is afraid others will discover family dysfunction and cut off their association with the family. Or an AIDS victim and his or her loved ones might fear social rejection due to prejudices regarding sexual preference, a characteristic sometimes associated with family dysfunction. When these circumstances surround death, the survivors often have inappropriate grief responses.

The second social issue that complicates grief is when the loss is socially negated. In other words, people pretend the death or loss did not happen. The result of this pretense is an entire array of suppressed emotions that sooner or later manifest themselves in bleak, depressed moods of intrapsychic conflict and conflict with others. For Tammy, the denial of her loss led to social withdrawal. Because she internalized and suppressed her feelings, she thwarted the emotional discharge she so badly needed. She believed her friends would disown her if they knew the truth, never thinking they could care about her while disagreeing with her actions.

Third, Lazare postulated that complicated grief response can occur when there is an absence of social support. In assuming there would be little support for her actions, Tammy avoided social contact. Another example can be found in Parkes's (1972) study of widows in London. His findings showed a correlation between those who were the most angry following the husband's death and those who were the most socially isolated. Worden (1991) also noted this relationship between anger and social isolation. Parkes's study illustrates that when a widow's (or widower's) anger drives away family and friends, that person becomes isolated from an important support group. One of the widows in the study was a young woman with three children who, initially, experienced support from many of her friends. Six months later, she was angry beyond words because no one called her anymore. Apparently, the initial anger she felt toward her husband's death was affecting her other relationships. This absence of social support can increase the pain of loss, intensify the grief, and interfere with the resolution of death.

ABNORMAL GRIEF RESPONSES

Following the death of a loved one, some people exhibit abnormal behavior regarding the loss. William Worden (1992) identifies this behavior as "abnormal grief response" (i.e., chronic, exaggerated, delayed, and masked). Others refer to it as "pathological grief" or "unresolved grief." In the fourth edition of the American Psychiatric Association's *Diagnostic and Statistic Manual,* abnormal behaviors related to grief are referred to as "complicated bereavement." Whatever the label, abnormal or pathological grief is "the intensification of grief to the level where the person is overwhelmed, resorts to maladaptive behavior, or remains interminably in the state of grief without progression of the mourning process towards completion. . . . It involves processes that do not move progressively toward assimilation or accommodation but, instead, lead to stereotyped repetitions or extensive interruptions of healing" (Horowitz et al. 1980, p. 1157).

Chronic Grief Reaction

Abnormal grief response manifests itself in several conditions. One of these Worden refers to as "chronic grief reaction." This happens when a person's grief does not come to finality or closure. Day after day, the person's grief is fresh as if the loss had just occurred. Often there is a linking object, a constant reminder of the deceased, that the survivor touches or holds on a regular basis. For example, one widow started every morning by opening her closet and breathing in the fragrance of her deceased husband's favorite shirt preserved in his favorite cologne. Every day began with fresh grief. This ritual kept her in a chronic state of grief. People who perform these types of rituals tend to make statements such as these: "I'll never recover. This grief will go on and on." Or, "If I don't get help, I'll just sink and never make it back." Another response indicative of chronic grief is the yearning for a relationship that never was (Paterson 1987). What the relationship might have been is idealized, and the person mourns what he or she would never have.

CASE STUDY #4

At age twenty-nine Mary had her first child, Samantha, who lived six months and then died of sudden infant death syndrome (SIDS). After Samantha's death, Mary spent every morning with a cup of coffee, looking out the family room window while holding Samantha's blanket to her cheek. This grief ritual continued day after day. With the blanket against her cheek, Mary would think about all the things she had wanted to do with Sam, the places they would go, Sam's first date, driving a car, college, first job, marriage—all those occasions typically shared by mother and daughter.

Mary was in the grip of a chronic grief reaction. This kind of grieving is abnormal and can go on indefinitely. Mary needed professional assistance to help provide closure to her grief.

Exaggerated Grief Response

Abnormal grief behavior also takes the form of exaggerated grief response. This behavior is a maladaptive reaction to the death of a loved one, with the grief rooted in "angst," a word meaning despair. Martin Heidegger, in his book *Being and Time* (1962), defined this existential angst as an anxiety toward nonbeing or nonexistence. This grief is objectless, which makes it even more intense.

CASE STUDY #5

Marilyn was the mother of three children, two of whom were twins. One of the twins died at age four. Afterward, Marilyn started having panic attacks when driving, and often felt alone when in the company of friends. She began feeling abandoned, isolated, nauseous, and even developed diarrhea. Finally, she went for counseling and was diagnosed as having exaggerated grief response.

In an exaggerated grief response, the mourner has "runaway angst." The despair is out of control and manifests itself in maladaptive behaviors or psychiatric disorders. Three types of reactions are associated with this behavior:

1. Depression/despair (i.e., when life seems hopeless)
2. Phobias (e.g., thanatophobia—fear of death; feeling alone when in the company of others; fear of touching the loved one's bed)
3. Post–traumatic stress disorder (e.g., multiple losses such as those of Vietnam veterans who existentially relive their wartime losses)

A person suffering from exaggerated grief response might show signs such as reading obituaries every day, frequently mentioning death in general conversation, wearing darker colors (black), making comments like "I deserve to die too," or "I should have died instead of my child."

Delayed Grief Response

If you draw a large circle, place a black dot in the middle, and call the dot physical loss, that is what healthy people grieve and mourn (see Figure 12–1). Healthy grief is for the loss of the physical person—the touching, holding, kissing, conversation, and being together. If you draw several Xs around the perimeter of the circle, those are called secondary losses. These range from family conflict to lawsuits, loss of income to loss of social status—just about anything associated with loss of a loved one. The key to healthy grieving is focusing on the primary loss—the deceased. If the focus is transferred to secondary losses, then the actual process of grief is delayed.

CASE STUDY #6

A five-year-old boy wandered into his neighbor's backyard one day. The gate had been left open, and the ladder to their aboveground pool was in place. The boy climbed the ladder, fell into the pool, and drowned. The boy's parents filed a lawsuit against the neighbors, which was in litigation for the next four years. When the case was resolved, they decided to go for counseling. As they talked about their son's death, at first the therapist thought the death had occurred in the past few days. The parents' grief was so fresh not because of chronic reaction but because of a delayed reaction.

There are other reasons why a person might delay grief. For instance, the loss might be overwhelming, such as the death of someone very close and important to the survivor. We grieve because we love. The more intense the love, the deeper the grief. Sometimes delayed grief response is seen after a second loss. When the emotional response to the first death is not fully expressed, there can be excessive grief following the second death, and it can last for years. This excessive grief could occur even if the second death is that of a pet. Or excessive grief might happen while watching a friend grieve. There even are times when watching a movie could trigger this psychologically unhealthy emotion. Obviously, grief responses can be delayed when the griever does not express enough emotion after the first loss. When we inhibit, suppress, postpone, or delay our grief, we do a disservice to ourselves. Inevitably, those feelings will surface.

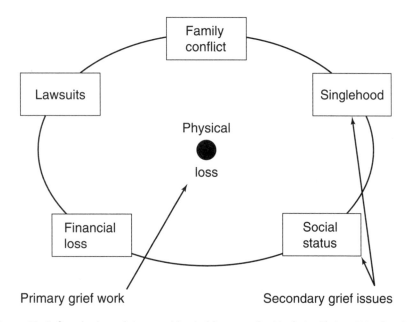

Figure 12–1. Secondary issues that cause a delayed grief response. (Dr. John Canine, Maximum Living Consultants, Inc., Birmingham, 1995)

Masked Grief Response

Maladaptive behaviors following a loved one's death are not always a symptom of grief. People who are incapable of expressing emotion might exhibit symptoms of grief that, in reality, cover up abnormal behaviors that existed before the loss. This is called "masked grief response."

CASE STUDY #7

Kathy and her husband, a Vietnam veteran, had one child and were hoping to have more. However, when Kathy was twenty-eight her husband died of liver cancer directly connected to his exposure to Agent Orange, a chemical used in weapons in Vietnam. Kathy's grieving period lasted longer than normal. Thinking her grief would never end, she consulted a counselor. After six or seven sessions, her therapist realized that Kathy no longer was grieving even though she had problematic symptoms and behaviors.

Upon further examination, the therapist uncovered the foundation of Kathy's distress. Apparently, in her formative years, Kathy called her mother "Aunt" and called her aunt "Mother"; she knew neither a father nor a father figure; and she was repeatedly sexually abused by cousins, uncles, and other family members.

People with masked grief response rarely reveal their grief. Typically, these people do not cry, do not show anger, and usually throw off guilt. They appear to be void of emotion. The masked grief response is a behavior acquired during the early years of personality development. According to Freud, a normal, healthy personality develops an id, an ego and a superego. The id represents basic human drives such as the need for food, warmth and sex. The ego is the self, which is developed through choices and decision making. Its goal is to make peace between the id and the superego, which is the conscience or value system (see Figure 12–2).

The problem that results in masked grief response is a defective ego that does not develop normally. Helene Deutsch (1937) suggested that a defective ego cannot withstand the strain of mourning. If this is so, grief will be disguised by other types of behavior, particularly narcissism. When this happens, a person's ego migrates toward the id, focusing on the self without any influence from the conscience, or superego. In Kathy's case, after a few weeks of therapy, the therapist noticed she had been to the hairdresser a couple of times a week, manicured her fingernails, improved her facial makeup, bought a sports car, and otherwise dramatically changed her world in a "selfish" way. Kathy was manifesting her grief through these narcissistic behaviors.

Figure 12-2. Personality (from Freud). (Dr. John Canine, Maximum Living Consultants, Inc., Birmingham, 1995)

In addition to narcissism, a defective ego can hide grief in a somatization disorder, or psychosomatic complaints, where there are symptoms of physical problems but no physical origin. Grief is converted into physical symptoms that can range anywhere from minor complaints to severely chronic disorders with no organic findings. These maladaptive behaviors emerging from a defective ego are another form of masked grief response.

FOR THE DEATH CARE PROFESSIONAL: CHARACTERISTICS OF COMPLICATED GRIEF

Death care professionals are wise to alert themselves to the behaviors of their clients that may indicate complicated or abnormal grief. These are signs that become indicators for special management of client needs. However, before decisions for client handling can be determined, it is important to understand bereavement issues and characteristics.

One issue is bereavement outcome. For example, following research on widows and widowers, Parkes and Weiss (1983) identified factors that were most likely to predict the effects of bereavement. Among these factors are the following three circumstances that can lead to pathological grief:

1. Sudden, unexpected, and premature deaths that thrust survivors into unanticipated grief
2. Survivors who reacted toward the deceased with ambivalence, expressed intense anger and/or self-reproach, and, as a result, generated conflicting grief
3. Survivors who had an overly dependent relationship with the deceased, who responded to their loved one's death with an intense yearning that developed into chronic grief

Parkes and Weiss identified five issues that can help the death care professional understand the needs of clients with these characteristics. These issues, listed here in order of importance, together can predict the bereavement outcome at thirteen months as well as a pattern for future outcomes.

1. The survivor's degree of yearning. A few weeks after the death, the survivor demonstrates intense yearning for the deceased, indicative of an abnormally dependent relationship.
2. The survivor's altered view of his or her own death three or four weeks following the loss. There is a wish for one's own death.
3. The time frame of the terminal illness. This issue is closely related to reactions of unanticipated grief.
4. The social class of the survivor. Social class can have a profound affect on the grieving process. For instance, the environment of either lower or upper social class can provide a lack of resources or specific kinds of stresses. Although people of lower socioeconomic status grieve similarly to those of higher status, the outcome is less successful. Interestingly, social class can affect the outcome of grief without changing its course.
5. Duration of marriage. Although the impact of the term of marriage on grief can be determined only in conjunction with other factors, shorter marriages appear to be easier to relinquish than longer marriages. However, longer marriages do not necessarily cause abnormal grief.

In responding to the needs of their clients, death care professionals can watch for characteristics of complicated and abnormal grief and use them to determine actions that are supportive. These characteristics are as follows:

1. The inability to speak of the deceased without expressing fresh emotion
2. Intense expressions of grief triggered by relatively minor events
3. Holding onto material possessions belonging to the deceased and/or preserving the environment as it was just before the death
4. Physical symptoms similar to those of the deceased before death; severe depression; acute guilt; or self-destructive behavior
5. Radical changes in one's lifestyle following the death, such as excluding friends and family or avoiding social activities
6. Phobias about the deceased's illness or death itself, including thanatophobia, the fear of death
7. Inability to visit the grave site or participate in death-related rituals or activities; avoidance of all funeral ceremonies; difficulty in celebrating holidays; ignoring laws

Circumstances that interfere with the resolution of one's grieving process have notable implications for the death care professional. For example, some widows and widowers are at a high risk of complicated grief reaction and loss of social support. Recent studies have shown that early intervention in their bereavement results in the successful reduction of damaging effects. However, early intervention does not necessarily help those who are at low risk or in selected groups (Parkes 1980; Parkes and Weiss 1983). Therefore, effective intervention requires knowing which widows and widowers are at high risk.

SUMMARY

This chapter has explored circumstances that can prevent people from grieving in a healthy manner. These circumstances cause people to suffer complicated grief reactions or abnormal grief responses. Four important variables that can interfere with the grief process are (1) past losses, (2) death surround, (3) social issues, and (4) abnormal grief response. People who have not resolved past losses, especially those burdened with "bereavement overload," are likely to experience complicated grief reactions to future deaths. Yet to be determined are the effects of childhood losses on future bereavement and the role of mental illness in complicated or abnormal grieving.

The death surround refers to the circumstances surrounding a loved one's death that affect the survivor's ability to grieve. These circumstances arouse intimate feelings toward the deceased that create troubling emotional aftereffects. Major problems for the survivor attributed to the death surround are anger, guilt, feelings of self-extinction, abnormal dependence on the deceased, and lack of closure to the grieving process.

Social issues that can produce complicated grief reactions occur when (1) the loss is socially unspeakable, (2) the loss is socially negated, and (3) there is an absence of social support for the bereaved. Grief is a social process. People need family and friends to provide support and encouragement for experiencing and expressing their grief.

Abnormal grief responses are maladaptive behaviors resulting from intense, overwhelming grief that cannot progress to resolution. Sometimes these abnormal responses are referred to as pathological grief or unresolved grief. Typical conditions of abnormal grief response are (1) chronic grief reaction, (2) exaggerated grief response, (3) delayed grief response, and (4) masked grief response. These are behaviors involving specific emotional effects that often require therapeutic intervention in order for the bereaved person to complete the grieving process.

The implications for death care professionals begin the need to be alert to signs of complicated or abnormal grief among their clients. A thorough understanding of bereavement issues associated with anomalous behaviors is essential to providing appropriate care and support. These issues include bereavement outcome as well as grief behaviors and characteristics.

REFERENCES

Deutsch, H. 1937. Absence of grief. *Psychoanalytic Quarterly* 6:12–22.

Heidegger, Martin. 1962. *Being and time.* New York: Harper and Row.

Horowitz, M. J., N. Wilner, C. Marmar, and J. Krupnick. 1980. Pathological grief and the activation of latent self images. *American Journal of Psychiatry* 137, 1157–1162.

Kastenbaum, R. 1969. Death and bereavement in later life. In *Death and bereavement,* edited by A. H. Kutschen. Springfield, Ill.: Charles C. Thomas.

Lazare, A. 1979. Unresolved grief. In *Outpatient psychiatry: Diagnosis and treatment,* edited by A. Lazare. Baltimore, Md.: Williams and Wilkins.

Parkes, C. M. 1972. *Bereavement: Studies of grief in adult life.* New York: International Universities Press.

———. 1980. Bereavement counseling: Does it work? *British Medical Journal* 281:3–6.

Parkes, C. M., and R. S. Weiss. 1983. *Recovery from bereavement.* New York: Basic Books.

Paterson, G. W. 1987. Managing grief and bereavement. *Primary Care* 14:403–15.

Simos, B. G. 1979. *A time to grieve.* New York: Family Service Association.

Vaillant, G. 1985. Loss as a metaphor for attachment. *American Journal of Psychoanalysis* 45:59–67.

Worden, William. 1991. *Grief counseling and grief therapy.* New York: Springer.

13

THERAPEUTIC STRATEGIES FOR THE BEREAVED

John D. Canine

CHAPTER OUTLINE ....

Bereavement is a condition that is as individual as the people who are experiencing it. To know the circumstances of death and the potential reactions of the griever to the loss is a step forward in understanding the griever's bereavement needs. Whether the griever responds to a loved one's death with normal, healthy grief behaviors or complex, dysfunctional ones, there are therapeutic strategies that can help the griever move toward resolution of the death. The strategies discussed in this chapter fall into four categories:

1. Reaching out to the bereaved
2. Rituals of bereavement
3. Resolving complicated grief
4. Expectations for closure

The death care professional can gain significant insight into the griever's behavior and needs by employing these strategies.

REACHING OUT TO THE BEREAVED

Reaching out to the bereaved can be a challenge when assisting people through the grief process. To fulfill this challenge, the death care professional can follow specific actions toward a positive growth experience for the bereaved. First, the caregiver must be physically present and emotionally available to the griever. When physical and emotional caring is given early in the bereavement period, poor behavioral coping patterns can be avoided. Once these patterns have emerged, however, reaching out can become more difficult and the person's ability to complete the grieving process can be obstructed. Berlinsky and Biller (1982) suggested therapeutic intervention immediately following the loss. This allows the caregiver to step in and assist the griever in focusing on one problem at a time. Also, practical matters related to the loss can be resolved before progressing to more complicated emotional issues.

Encouraging the griever to actualize the loss—to accept it as real—is a second strategy in reaching out to the bereaved. This can be done by asking the individual to revisit the scene of the death, whether it be the hospital or the place of an accident or some other site. Another option is to revisit the place where the doctor or police officer brought word of the loved one's death. These actions are a beginning. Then we must encourage the griever to talk about the death. This keeps denial and avoidance at bay. An example of denial is walking into the funeral home and saying, "Oh my God, this can't be true. It didn't happen." An example of avoidance is walking away after the funeral saying, "I guess it's true, but I'm not going to think about it anymore." When encouraging the griever to talk about the death, we can start by asking questions such as these:

- What type of cancer did the deceased have?
- How did your last day with the deceased begin?
- What were your thoughts at the beginning of that day?
- How did the two of you meet?
- What is your fondest memory of the deceased?
- How have you been since the death?
- Are you experiencing any overwhelming emotions such as anger or guilt?

Also, it is important to ask the griever what kinds of grief tasks may not be completed. Reminding this person about these tasks can serve as a stimulus toward taking action.

Giving permission to feel and grieve is an essential message that can impel the bereaved to enter into the grieving process. The opportunities for giving permission are plentiful, Lazare (1979) explains, especially in those moments when the griever's voice cracks, lips begin to quiver, eyes mist, or physical trembling appears. By giving the bereaved permission to cry, grieve, and feel all the emotions that are rising to the surface at that moment, the death care professional can begin to interact with the griever. Consider this example.

CASE STUDY #1

As soon as Kristen sat down in her counselor's office, she said, "I don't want to talk about my husband." The counselor replied, "O.K. I understand that. I'd like to ask you a question, though. How did you and your husband meet?" Kristen talked for fifty-five minutes about how she and her husband met. During the course of that conversation, the counselor gave Kristen permission to cry, to be angry, and to feel guilty.

As with Kristen, that critical moment can come when a person consciously does not want to grieve. But if someone gives permission by asking a question or simply stating permission, the bereaved will start grieving.

To be decidedly helpful in reaching out to the bereaved, the death care professional must encourage the individual to be realistic. What does this mean? In our approach to the bereaved, we must be empathetic, that is, understanding the loss from the griever's perspective. Therefore, any assistance or intervention we provide must be appropriate in regard to the person's loss and the relationship with the deceased. In being realistic, we share with the griever the fact that nothing takes away the pain and longing. Simply stated, we grieve because we love, and the loss of that love causes pain. However, there are many unhealthy issues surrounding grief that can be resolved by taking a realistic approach. These include the following:

- Feeling an obligation to stop grieving and go on with life to please someone else—This is *not* realistic. The helpful approach is to encourage the individual to feel and react to his or her sadness.
- Taking little time to grieve—This can be harmful to the individual. In reaching out, we allow the griever as much time as needed to grieve. A person must be free from the pressures of time. On the other hand, we must not let the griever believe that the length and intensity of grief have value or special meaning, such as a deep love for the deceased.
- Conflicting emotions about the death—There are times when the griever becomes confused about the emotions associated with grief and personal feelings for the deceased. For instance, a person might misconstrue feelings of grief with the sacrificial caring for the deceased before the death. Here, the death care professional can offer clarity by explaining the difference. To care for another person is a symbol of love and an act of sacrificial giving. On the other hand, grief after the death of a significant other is caring for oneself, and a time to establish a new relationship with the deceased. Case Study 2 is an example.

CASE STUDY #2

Jessie, who had taken care of her mother for ten years, was fifty when her mother died at age eighty. Jessie said she could not imagine a relationship with her mother without caring for her. The counselor explained that the caring relationship was over and Jessie needed to return to the prenursing relationship she had before her mother became ill.

This focus on the more appropriate, interdependent love was a healthy step for Jessie. It allowed her to establish a new and different kind of relationship with her mother once the grieving process was completed. This is one of the goals of grief work.

- The need for continuous grieving—This is a myth. In fact, the individual is wise to take breaks from the grieving process. Some people describe grief as waves of the sea coming and going. When the tide is out, the griever would do well to take a break by focusing on something else for a while.
- The fear of talking about the death—The death care professional can help the griever conquer this fear by encouraging conversation. Once the individual begins talking, the experiences with the deceased might be repeated many times over. This behavior is normal. It helps the individual gain control over the grief, and it is an important part of decathexis, or detachment.
- Exposing personal defenses—Often, bereaved individuals will hold on to feelings of anger and guilt, using these emotions to defend themselves against working through their grief. Sometimes these individuals will endure these feelings hop-

ing to preserve the relationship with the deceased. The death care professional must be careful in exposing these defenses.

- Pain—The painfulness of the loss needs to be openly addressed with the griever (Raphael 1983). Discussing the pain can feel like opening a wound. But we do the griever a favor by encouraging him or her to confront the pain.
- Sitting and thinking about the death—Passivity during grief can lead to depression. The griever needs physical activity to renew the energy required to work through a healthy grieving process. Frequently, physical activity will assist in releasing pent-up emotions. A supportive caregiver encourages daily physical activity and helps the griever select one or more activities that are appropriate.
- Unfinished business—It is realistic for the griever to have unfinished business with the deceased. Unfinished business consists of either unresolved feelings, such as conflict or anger, toward the deceased or more practical uncompleted tasks, such as an unfinished basement. The death care professional can help the griever identify any unfinished business and plan to complete it. For instance, when one woman's husband died, his renovation work in their kitchen was left unfinished. She realized she would not be able to resolve her grief until the kitchen renovation was completed. When the new kitchen was finished, she dedicated it to her husband by hanging a plaque on the kitchen wall in the presence of their friends.

The following are additional strategies that can be used by the death care professional to encourage the griever to be realistic:

1. The griever must be reminded of the goal for successfully completing grief work. Although pressure to do so will be counterproductive, a gentle periodic reminder can keep the griever on track.
2. We must encourage the griever to be hopeful. In reaching out, we can work with the individual's value system to establish hope. If the griever is spiritually linked to a specific religion such as Christianity or Judiasm, supporting those values can summon up hope. Knowing there is a light at the end of the tunnel can be a powerful motivator for the bereaved.
3. Providing an environment for the bereaved to promote use of the individual's coping skills is healthy. Whether the griever has a normal or complicated grief response, setting up special environments can trigger the use of these skills. The kinds of environments the griever needs are those that facilitate self-nurturing such as planting a tree in the name of the deceased, dedicating completion of a job the deceased started, standing at the grave site talking to the deceased, or exploring reasons for the unhealthy use of drugs or alcohol.

When the griever's actions signal that he or she is not doing well, the individual should be encouraged to seek private counseling. Even in normal grief, it can be important to validate the healthy aspects of mourning. In some instances just one counseling session is sufficient; for others extended therapy might be the answer. Also, we need to encourage the bereaved to join support groups. Researcher David Spiegel (1993) applauds the value of support groups in his comment: "I am a great believer in self-help groups . . . it means being able to tolerate the very strong feelings that arise when people have to give up their ability to do things. Grieving for people you have cared about who have died, and facing your own fears of dying, and handling pain—those kinds of issues require focused attention. They require a serious effort to allow people to share what they are feeling inside so that they feel comfort and supported when they do" (p. 161).

RITUALS

Bereavement rituals, which are practiced by all societies in a variety of ways, have one common theme. They have tremendous therapeutic value in areas of transition, that is, moving on with one's life. Rituals provide healing, continuity, and balance if the griever believes there is meaning in them (van der hart 1983).

Moreover, Rando (1984) offers, "A ritual is a specific behavior or activity that gives symbolic expression to certain feelings and thoughts of the actor or actors, individually, or as a group. It may be habitually repeated or a one-time occurrence" (p. 104). An example of a ritual is the committal service (see Figure 13–1),

The living and the dead leaving
the land of the living to commit the
dead to the land of the dead.

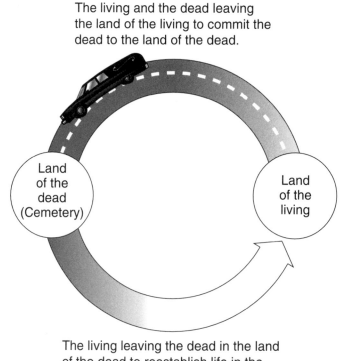

Land
of the
dead
(Cemetery)

Land
of the
living

The living leaving the dead in the land
of the dead to reestablish life in the
land of the living without the dead.

Figure 13–1. The ritualistic purpose of the committal. (Dr. John Canine, Maximum Living Consultants, Inc., Birmingham, 1995)

in which we take the deceased from the land of the living to the land of the dead (cemetery). We, the living, commit the deceased to another state. We have a processional or parade acknowledging our commitment, then get back in our cars and journey back to the land of the living to live without the one who has died. This is the outward symbol of what we do during the grieving process. In our grief, we let the loved one go to the life hereafter, then we journey back to the land of the living and form new relationships. The committal service happens in the first two or three days after the loss, when the mourners are deep in grief, so it is not easy. But we leave the land of the dead to start our life again. The journey back is what we must strive to complete.

Rituals are an essential element in our journey through the grief process. They provide various means of expressing emotions and talking through our feelings. Rituals give us permission to discharge our distress over the loss. More specifically, rituals permit the following:

- A well-defined acting out—For instance, sending flowers for the funeral, contributing to a memorial fund, delivering special, home-cooked dishes to the home of the bereaved, and helping with the funeral arrangements are all actions we might take to demonstrate support, comfort, and caring. Through these actions, we try to beautify death to make it more palatable. Rituals allow us to experience the closeness we had with the deceased one more time. We celebrate passing into life after death, sensing that our loved one is moving on to a better life. "Better is the day of the man's death than the day of the man's birth" (Ecclesiastes 7:1). Rituals bring us comfort. They initiate the acceptance of our loss.
- Expression of feelings—During the ritual, we can express feelings that we might otherwise withhold. Rituals provide an environment in which grieving and crying are acceptable.
- A rehearsal of the entire grief process. Every ritual is a miniature grief process. It channels grief into a defined activity with a beginning, an ending, and a well-defined purpose.
- Healthy interaction with the deceased—It is nearly impossible to participate in a ritual without thinking of the deceased, especially one that focuses on an object or idea associated with the deceased. For example, before death, the deceased might have asked others to pray for him if he died. The ritual might entail prayers for the deceased during mass each week. In doing "what my loved one wanted," the bereaved exercises a healthy interaction with the deceased that can promote healing.
- Full acceptance of the loss—Engaging in a ritual happens only when the bereaved have begun to accept the loss. Otherwise, the ritual does not occur. The existence of a ritual is a sign of healthy progress.

RESOLVING COMPLICATED GRIEF

William Worden (1991) makes a distinction between grief counseling and grief therapy. He states:

The goal in grief therapy is somewhat different from the goal of grief counseling. The goal of grief counseling is to facilitate the task of mourning in the recently bereaved in order that the bereavement process will come to a successful termination. In grief therapy, the goal is to identify and resolve the conflicts of separation which preclude the completion of mourning tasks in persons whose grief is absent, delayed, excessive, or prolonged. Grief therapy is most appropriate in situations that fall into these three categories: (1) The complicated grief reaction is manifested as prolonged grief. (2) The grief reaction manifests itself through some masked somatic or behavioral symptoms. (3) The reaction is manifested by an exaggerated grief response. (P. 79)

In prolonged grief, therapeutic techniques address problems for people who are consciously aware that, after suffering the loss for many months or even years, they are not coming to an adequate resolution of their grief. Usually, prolonged grief occurs because the griever has not completed all the tasks in the grief process. On the other hand, masked grief speaks to individuals who have no idea what is causing their somatic or behavioral symptoms. The fact is they ignored their own grief at the time of the loss, not allowing themselves to feel or express grief. This inhibition transformed their grief into somatic or behavioral disorders. As a result, their grief is unresolved. Finally, therapy for exaggerated grief response deals with behaviors such as excessive depression, excessive anxiety, or other types of normal grief behavior that have become exaggerated. A specific definition of exaggerated grief response is hard to pinpoint since the behaviors are an extension of normal grief, which in itself has a wide array of responses. Essentially, the normal grief behaviors are so exaggerated that the griever becomes dysfunctional, possibly to the point of psychiatric disorder.

Although Worden's book is a handbook for the "mental health practitioner," it can be used by all death care professionals in understanding complicated grief. It can be helpful especially for the funeral director who sponsors a bereavement aftercare program or has sustained personal contact with the family following the loss. For example, a funeral director in a small community might see the bereaved family often in informal settings.

The following guidelines can be used to assist those suffering from complicated grief. They can be valuable tools for funeral directors, counselors, pastors, volunteers, or anyone assuming the caregiver role.

Be Aware of the Difference between Normal Grief and Complicated Grief

These two conditions require different kinds of assistance. Professional therapy might be required for someone with complicated grief. According to Raphael (1983), as quoted by Rando (1984), "In 'focal psychotherapy' there is an assessment of the particular form of pathological bereavement response and specific treatment to manage it and address the etiological process involved. The goal is to convert the pathological bereavement response to one in which the individual is able to grieve more appropriately or more normally" (p. 108). Raphael believed that the optimal time for preventive intervention is two weeks to three months after the loss. In other words, the person who is reaching out to a griever suffering from complicated grief has a responsibility to suggest that an assessment be conducted by a qualified professional to determine if a pathological bereavement response exists and recommend specific treatment to manage it. At the same time, the etiologic issue or origin of the condition must be addressed. The goal is to help the individual grieve more appropriately.

Before Assisting the Bereaved, Confirm the Desire for Help

In helping people through their grief, we are not taking them hostage, nor do we hold a position of authority. If the griever does not want help and assistance is forced, additional complications could occur, as illustrated in this scenario.

CASE STUDY #3

Paul and Jason were brothers who grew up in a family with close relationships among its members. They enjoyed each other's conversation, but they never discussed their feelings, nor did they openly demonstrate affection toward one another. Upon reaching adulthood, Paul and Jason continued to remain close friends. When he was thirty-three, Paul was killed in an avalanche while on a ski vacation. Jason's reaction was severe shock. His despair was apparent during the funeral. Afterward, one of Jason's friends persistently encouraged him to talk about Paul's death. Jason refused. After several weeks, Jason blew up and told his friend to leave him alone. Jason hasn't talked about Paul since then.

Helping a person through the grief process is effective only with the griever's permission. Obviously, Jason was not ready to discuss Paul's death. Although well intentioned, his friend's persistence was driving Jason away. People must be ready for and open to a caregiver's assistance. Otherwise, it is not helpful. As caregivers, we must wait for the griever to signal a desire for help.

Encourage the Griever to Talk about the Deceased

Invite the griever to talk about the deceased in a positive way with positive feelings. At the same time, explain that expressing negative feelings and experiences is just as important. Urge the griever to remember the total person both in thought and in conversation. Also, if the griever is a victim of multiple losses, suggest that the conversation focus on one loss at a time. Separating the discussions of multiple losses allows the griever to better manage his or her grief.

Encourage the Griever to Consult a Physician

The griever should arrange for a physical exam. Grief symptoms can be similar to disease symptoms. For example, anxiety can cause an upset stomach, nausea, and a tight chest. These are symptoms of certain viruses and diseases as well.

Suggest an Evaluation of Incomplete or Complicated Grief

If the grief is absent or delayed, it might be that the griever is focused on a secondary issue. For instance, the griever could be fearful of the pain, unable to withstand the pain, or overwhelmed by emotions such as anger, guilt, or anxiety about the death and unable to deal with them. On the other hand, if the grieving is continuous, perhaps the griever was highly dependent on the deceased. Or there could be a linking object disturbing the griever since the object symbolizes the relationship the griever had with the deceased and is prohibiting "moving on" (Volkan 1972). In cases of exaggerated or masked grief, extreme emotions can cause distorted grief. For example, a person might have anxiety over his or her own death or loss, therefore exaggerating the grief. Another example is the overwhelming guilt some people associate with the death that causes low self-esteem or feelings of inadequacy. This type of masked grief response occurs when an individual has an underdeveloped ego or not enough ego strength to withstand mourning. Assessment and evaluation of these factors can aid in working with the bereaved.

Offer Assistance in Overcoming Complicated Grief

CASE STUDY #4

A couple of German origin had a glass of beer every night before they went to bed. For the first couple of years after the husband died, the wife continued to pour him a glass of beer. This was a sign that she was not accepting her loss.

The death care professional can assist individuals with complicated grief with the following actions:

- *Encourage the griever to accept the loved one's death.* Some individuals become involved in fantasy thinking in which they imagine the loved one has not died but simply has gone away.
- *Explore the griever's relationship with the deceased.* Determine what kind of relationship the griever had with the deceased. Ask what roles each of them played in the other's life. This is very important because the death might have caused enormous complications for the survivor. For example, the survivor might be de-

pressed and angry that the deceased is not around to do such tasks as buying a car or balancing a checkbook. Also, exploring the relationship holds clues to the kind of future relationship the survivor eventually would like to have with the deceased. Encourage the griever to avoid ambivalence about the relationship.

- *Encourage the griever to try new skills.* The griever must be held accountable for learning new skills. Undoubtedly, there are skills that have not been tried, especially in the area of forming new relationships. This helps the individual move forward into a new life.

- *Overwhelming emotions of anger and anxiety need to be identified and expressed.* These emotions need to be redefined in order to limit the impact on the loss. In some cases these emotions can be eliminated. If not, they must be redefined to prevent dysfunctional behavior. These emotions can be placed in a healthy context. For instance, if the griever is feeling guilty about an unhappy situation with the deceased, the guilt can cause dysfunctional behavior like excessive crying, constant thinking about the loved one, or interminable searching for ways to right the wrong. To help, the caregiver can walk the griever through a ritual such as going to the cemetery, writing and reading a letter to the loved one, even having the letter witnessed by someone and burying it with the deceased. Then the caregiver can point out how the guilt caused the individual to channel the grief through a ritual. The griever examined the guilt, felt it, and resolved it. Now the guilt has been used in a healthy context. It can be laid aside and will no longer interfere with the individual's progress.

- *Assist the griever in giving up linking objects.* This might take some time. People cannot surrender linking objects until they are ready to do so. However, letting go of linking objects is symbolic of letting go of the person who died. It can be useful for the griever to project life in the future without the burden of grief. Abandoning linking objects is a big step forward.

- *When the time is right, encourage the griever to say good-bye to the deceased.* Be careful not to pressure the griever in this regard. Saying good-bye too soon can result in prolonged grief. Be sensitive to the griever's readiness for separation from the loved one. Then be available in the future for "bad days."

Lazare (1979) recommended that the caregiver prepare a checklist for offering assistance to those with complicated grief response. A sample checklist is provided in Figure 13–2.

EXPECTATIONS FOR CLOSURE

As the bereaved move toward resolving the death of a loved one, the death care professional can expect closure of the grief process. These expectations include four behaviors the bereaved will experience as separation from the deceased: acceptance of feelings, detachment from the deceased, reestablishment of relationships, and restoration of wholeness in one's life.

CHECKLIST

Individual's Name: _____

Questions	Yes	No	Note/Comments
1. Have the depressive symptoms disappeared when talking or thinking about the loved one?			
2. Has the time sense gone back to normal?			
3. Is there a change from a bitter sadness to a sweet sadness?			
4. Is there more balance when discussing the loss? (Ex: "Oh, this can't be true!" is replaced with "It is true. People do die.")			
5. Does the individual enjoy holidays again?			
6. Has the searching for the lost loved one discontinued?			
7. Does the individual relate better to others?			
8. Is there a healthier relationship with the deceased?			
9. Is there movement toward solution of outstanding problems? (Parkes and Weiss 1983)			
10. Is the level of functioning comparable to prebereavement?			
11. Does the survivor have the ability to socialize effectively?			
12. Is there a positive and realistic attitude toward the future?			
13. Is the health back to prebereavement levels?			
14. Do they have the ability to cope with future loss?			
15. Is their level of self-esteem appropriate?			

Figure 13–2. How do I know I'm better? (Dr. John D. Canine, Maximum Living Consultants, Inc., Birmingham, 1995)

Feelings

The end of the grieving process comes with the acceptance of the various emotional responses to death and the loss. The bereaved experience a wide range of emotions, from anger to deep sorrow. Each individual wages a personal battle, resisting the tragedy that fate has thrust upon him or her. Over time, through healthy grieving, the bereaved begin to accept their plight. The death care professional can expect that grievers will do the following:

- Accept the feeling of outrage toward the separation that was forced upon them because of the death.
- Accept the feeling of being a child again, expressing feelings and emotions.
- Accept the need for counseling or a support group to lend assistance during the grieving process.
- Accept the need for a physical exam due to anxiety over the loss; even accepting the occurrence of physical symptoms.
- Accept the confusion experienced during the grief process. The expectation for closure is to end that confusion; to clearly understand past behavior and hope for the future.

The expectation for closure is that the bereaved will deal appropriately with all the anxiety issues accompanying the loss. In moving toward closure, the griever will move past the anxiety and resultant depression, and self-esteem will be renewed. However, Barlow and Cerny (1988) observed that people who suffered repeatedly from anxiety because of personal loss became vulnerable to severe depression and needed professional help. Also, Kast (1988) noted that people with low self-esteem are inclined to further reduce their self-image following a loss. They are likely to have complicated grief reactions that can lead to chronic depression. This also relates to issues of pathology. Wegner (1988) discerned that people who are depressed before a loss are more likely to encounter one negative thought after another after the loss until a perception of hopelessness develops. In pathological grief, this condition becomes even more complex.

The expectation for closure challenges the bereaved to give up this hopelessness and transform negative thoughts of death and loss into more positive energy. The death care professional can assist the bereaved by encouraging healthy activities and supporting the notion of a future of hope and renewed spirit. For those with difficulty coping with their grief, the caregiver has a responsibility to recommend professional counseling.

Detachment

The pivotal point of detachment, or decathexis, means the griever gives up the physical, intellectual, emotional, and spiritual investments with the deceased. All attachments have been severed. Following decathexis, the griever is ready to form new relationships and can go on with life. Bondage with the loved one ceases, and new patterns of social interaction and support are established. The griever gives up linking objects as well as transitional objects (items acquired during the grieving process that bring comfort and take the place of linking objects). During this time of detachment, journaling is important not only for therapeutic value but as a means of observing one's own progress toward detachment during the grieving period. Writing down one's thoughts and feelings allows the griever to look back and feel a sense of accomplishment. Detachment is a time to discontinue dependency needs on the deceased. For example, the griever might have depended on the deceased for such practical needs as car repairs or home-cooked meals, or may have depended on that person for conversation and comfort. Also, detachment might require forgiveness for the loved one regarding past incidences of conflict. Detachment does not mean that we stop loving and living. It means that those feelings and emotions associated with loving and living are channeled in a different direction. The griever must learn to live alone as a whole person.

When detachment occurs, the griever looks toward other relationships, using the "Three Cs" for reconnecting with others: companionship, commonality, and commitment. Companionship is necessary during detachment to fill the void of loneliness and adjust to living without the deceased. Companionship during or following grief that offers commonality will be most helpful. Relationships that share common values and interests are most likely to succeed. A relationship of commonality allows the griever to focus on newer relationships while not dwelling on the old one or comparing one with the other. Finally, commitment to a new life can bring lasting, lifetime relationships.

Reestablishment

Another expectation for closure is adapting to a world without the loved one. This reality must be confronted in order to complete the grieving process. As the bereaved move toward closure, they understand their feelings, learn to live with them, and focus on behavior. They must accept the fact that the loved one cannot be replaced. However, in forming new relationships, the void left by the loved one can, to some extent, be filled. Feelings for the loved one cannot be substituted, but other people can fill the void and replace the emptiness. The griever can adapt behaviors and skills for forming new relationships and engaging in new activities. The primary benefit of reestablishment is renewed energy. As the bereaved recover and move toward closure, they have more energy to invest in new relationships and activities.

In establishing new relationships, the griever must be cautioned about entering ill-advised relationships, including physical or sexual relationships, before letting go of the loved one. Another caution is against addictive behaviors such as overeating, drugs, alcohol, and medications. The need to fill the void left by the deceased can cloud one's judgment regarding appropriate behaviors and healthy relationships. For some, this need can be filled by a pet if the griever is not ready for full separation from the deceased. A dog, cat, or other pet can be therapeutic. In addition, support groups such as church, professional organizations, or recreational groups can provide the social interaction necessary for making new friends. Some of the renewed energy of reestablishment can be directed toward expressing appreciation to those who gave assistance and support during the grieving period.

Restoration

Restoration means closure placed on the past life with the deceased and a positive outlook for one's future life. To enhance the future, the death care professional can offer these guidelines to the bereaved (Lauer and Lauer 1988):

1. *Be responsible for your own future.* Everyone experiences losses sooner or later. Take responsibility for your own life. Do not relinquish control of your future to others.
2. *Believe in yourself.* Recognize the value within yourself as a whole and independent person. Confirm that you are a worthy individual without the deceased.
3. *Maintain a balance in caring for yourself and others.* Some people care primarily for themselves, but some care more for others. For all of us, balance is the key.

4. *Identify resources for creating a healthy future.* Whether the resources are internal (e.g., coping skills) or external (e.g., support groups), ask questions and search for information to find those resources that can assist in renewing your life.

5. *View problems and mistakes as learning experiences.* All people make mistakes and create problems for themselves. This is normal and natural. Use these situations to change behaviors and actions.

6. *Look for the silver lining.* When undesirable situations arise, search for positives that might result. Although the death was not meant as a learning experience for you, take time to figure out the positive aspects.

7. *Empower yourself to complete the grieving process.* Talk to yourself, push yourself, do what it takes to persevere toward resolution of your grief. Look for alternative actions to take when progress slows down.

8. *Develop an awareness of your progress.* Pay attention to signals from others about your condition. Focus on the world outside yourself to diminish self-absorption. Bypass obsolete attitudes for newer opportunities.

9. *Rebuild your life.* Use your internal and external resources to redirect your character into new, appropriate values and behaviors.

10. *Actively engage in living.* Become an active participant in your own life. Confront your pain and challenges instead of passively avoiding them.

SUMMARY

This chapter has presented therapeutic strategies for the death care professional to use in assisting people through their grief. Specifically, in reaching out to the bereaved, the griever can be encouraged to actualize the loss, accepting it as real. The caregiver can help the individual to talk about the death and discuss memories of the deceased. Also, it is important to give the griever permission to feel and grieve and to be realistic about the loss. If the griever does not show signs of progress in the grief process, private counseling can be recommended.

An understanding of bereavement rituals is valuable information for the death care professional. Rituals can provide healing, continuity, and balance in the life of the survivor, and can offer various means of expressing emotions and talking through feelings about the loss. More specifically, rituals permit a well-defined acting out, an expression of feelings, a rehearsal of the entire grief process, a healthy interaction with the deceased, and a full acceptance of the loss.

It is useful for caregivers to be aware of people who suffer from complicated grief reactions. In these situations grief therapy, which might be an appropriate recommendation, can identify and resolve the more profound conflicts of separation. Grief therapy is most valuable when the grief reaction is manifested as (1) prolonged grief, (2) masked somatic or behavioral symptoms, or (3) an exaggerated grief response. The caregiver can make use of the following guidelines in assisting people with these complications:

- Be aware of the difference between normal grief and complicated grief.
- Before assisting the bereaved, confirm the desire for help.
- Encourage the griever to talk about the deceased.
- Encourage the griever to arrange a physical exam and consult with the physician.
- Suggest an evaluation of the areas where the individual's grief is incomplete or complicated or both.
- Offer assistance in overcoming complicated grief.

As the bereaved move toward resolving the death of a loved one, the death care professional can have certain expectations for closure of the grief process. The caregiver can expect to see four behaviors in the grieving individual: (1) the acceptance of feelings, (2) detachment from the deceased, (3) reestablishment of relationships, and (4) restoration of wholeness in one's life. Understanding these behaviors will allow the caregiver to direct the griever toward healthy separation from the deceased and building a new future.

REFERENCES

Barlow, David H., and Jerome A. Cerny. 1988. *Psychological treatment of panic.* New York: Guilford.

Berlinsky, E. B., and H. B. Biller. 1982. *Parental death and psychological development.* Lexington, Mass.: D. C. Heath, Lexington Books.

Kast, Verena A. 1988. *A time to mourn: Growing through the grief process.* Einsiedeln, Switzerland: Dainon Verlag.

Lauer, Robert H., and Jeannette C. Lauer. 1988. *Watersheds: Mastering life's unpredictable crises.* Canada: Little, Brown.

Lazare, A. 1979. Unresolved grief. In *Outpatient psychiatry: Diagnosis and treatment,* edited by A. Lazare. Baltimore, Md.: Williams and Wilkins. Pp. 498–512.

Rando, T. 1984. *Grief, dying and death.* Champaign, Ill.: Research Press.

Raphael, B. 1983. *The anatomy of bereavement.* New York: Basic Books.

Spiegel, David. 1993. Therapeutic support groups. In *Healing and the mind,* edited by Bill Magers. New York: Doubleday.

van der hart, O. 1983. *Rituals in psychotherapy: Transition and continuity.* New York: Irvington.

Volkan, V. A. 1971. A study of a patient's "re-grief work" through dreams, psychological tests and psychoanalysis. *Psychiatric Quarterly* 45:225–73.

———. 1972. The linking objects of pathological mourners. *Archives of General Psychiatry* 27:215–21.

Wegner, Daniel M. 1988. *Whitebears and other unwanted thoughts.* New York: Viking.

Worden, William. 1991. *Grief counseling and grief therapy.* New York: Springer.

14

PSYCHOSOCIAL FUNCTIONS OF FUNERALS

John D. Canine

From the earliest of times, humankind has practiced death ceremonies. These ceremonies generally are referred to as funeral practices and, more often than not, reflect a society's philosophical and religious values. The Egyptians, Greeks, and Romans all used funeral practices to encourage solidarity among members of society. Thus, while funeral rituals might be created by psychosocial tasks demanded by death, they are controlled by social factors, such as the extent and type of social organization, and the demography within it (Pine 1972).

This chapter explores funeral rituals, the history of funeral practices in American culture, the psychological and social functions of funerals, types of funerals, and suggestions for ways the funeral director can interact with the bereaved to meet their psychological and social needs.

GENERAL TYPES OF FUNERAL RITUALS

Since no member of a society lives in a social vacuum (for example, learning speech habits and the meaning of life from each other), the death of one individual is traumatic for all of the survivors. Hence, death ceremonies and funeral rituals are important in meeting the social and emotional needs of the mourners, and even with the deritualization of grief in recent years, there seem to be certain universal needs that are met through basic rituals. These rituals are similar in every society, and are as follows:

1. Religious or other types of ceremonies are enacted, which usually include rites or observances associated with the occasion.
2. Visual contact with the deceased is encouraged, most often occurring with the body lying in a casket and the face and body exposed. Viewing the body usually happens in the funeral home, but, in some instances, it occurs at the place of death, at a neighborhood meeting place, or at the deceased's home.
3. A procession, or family parade, occurs, allowing a public display of grief and accompaniment of the deceased to a final resting place.
4. A gathering of relatives and friends follows the death to provide emotional support for the bereaved. This is known as social support.
5. There is financial expenditure, such as flowers or fund contributions, that allows the bereaved to communicate their sorrow with a measurable means of support.
6. The body is prepared by a sanitary method for permanent placement in the grave.

Since death disrupts relationships and social groups in general, all societies should develop some forms of controlling its impact. There is a necessity for some form of a funeral ritual to address the psychological and social needs that are manifested by the survivors of death.

HISTORY OF FUNERAL PRACTICES

In the United States prior to 1830, the deceased had been laid out at home, sometimes in a roughly made pine box. Other times, the body was washed and dressed in clean clothes, then laid on a table or bed for viewing. The vigil, "wake," or lying in state, was derived from an ancient Hebrew practice that served the functions of a precaution against a premature burial, an act of piety, and an occasion of prayers for the dead. The practice also provided an opportunity for those who had been present at the death to clear themselves of the suspicion of foul play, and a chance for all interested parties to witness whether an equitable distribution of property had been made. After the wake, the body was carried by family and friends to the church cemetery. Occasionally, a horse-drawn carriage was used, but more often mourners would walk in parade fashion from the house to the grave site with the wooden box on their shoulders. Sometimes a band would play. Since bodies were not embalmed, most funeral ceremonies occurred within twenty-four hours of the death.

Since America was a "melting pot" society, there were many variations of the funeral ceremony. For example, with the Italian American funeral, various components of the funeral and burial rituals function to placate the soul to render its reluctant, usually involuntary, and frequently violent departure from this world, as amicably as possible, and to forestall any possibility that it might return to disturb those who remain behind. Useful objects, such as matches and small change, would be placed near the body, and objects of which the deceased had been particularly fond were put in the pine box. The body would be carried out of the house feet first: by not seeing the door as it left, it would not be able to locate it later. The procession to the cemetery would traverse various paths, returning to the house by a different route to confuse the soul's sense of direction: the wailing and lamenting that had begun at the time of the death were forbidden upon the return trip lest the soul be distracted from its otherworldly journey and return.

With the funeral over, the mattress of the deathbed was taken out and washed, and a meal was prepared by neighbors for the family and friends. Thus were the funeral activities concluded until the Day of the Dead (November 2), when a mass would be celebrated, the grave visited, and food left out on the table. Since the soul was thought capable of observing and experiencing what transpires on earth and its departure had been a forced one, it sought constantly to return and thus had to be coaxed and persuaded to remain in the next world (Mathias 1974).

From 1830 to 1920, America was immersed in an intellectual movement that manifested itself in the kind of rational and spiritual thinking that initiates social change. Inventions paved the way for automation and systemization of the workforce. Businesses formalized their processes and services into a new type of professionalism. In the wake of this trend toward industrialization, science, medicine, religion, philosophy, and education developed new ideas and specialized approaches to working and living. For example, the artisan or furniture maker who had built plain box coffins as a sideline gradually made a specialized business. This person fine-tuned the craft to give the coffin an aesthetic appearance, a symbolic gesture toward honoring death, while others designed new ways to beautify death. For the most part, Americans turned these new practices into acceptable customs that redefined society's view of death (Farrell 1980). These new trends provided an opportunity for Americans to deritualize death and distance themselves from the painful event. The developing power of technology and science to explain and control the ability to extend human life contributed to this new set of attitudes.

In addition, secularization was brought on by modifications in the medieval theology of death previously perpetuated by the church. According to Farrell (1980), religious thought in the nineteenth century migrated from the morbid, medieval notions of death to ideas developed from the logic and reason inherited from the Age of Enlightenment. The theology of death was influenced by the new romanticism and adapted from scientific naturalism. The new thinking was employed in the development of romantic, gardenlike cemeteries. Dealing with a person's death was considered a repugnant set of tasks to endure; thus the romantic and more spiritual customs came to replace the previous emphasis on the biological aspects of death. Farrell concluded that the accumulation of these factors turned American attitudes toward death in another direction. He also noted that the general entrepreneurial growth in this country fostered the development of the funeral business and the insurance industry.

The result of these social and economic changes, along with the evolution of death, was an industrial commercialism that intensified the association of social status with the new type of services being provided by funeral businesses. For instance, artistic embalming, decorative coffins, and a "parlor" atmosphere replaced funeral services held in the crowded home of the deceased (Cowell 1985). All in all, according to Farrell (1980), the new American funeral practices changed four basic elements:

- Treatment of the body
- The burial container
- The funeral environment
- Funeral procedures

Traditional funerary treatments and preparations for the deceased's body, which were previously done by family and friends, were replaced in the twentieth century by outsiders whose profession was to handle those duties; subsequently, they were labeled "undertakers." Embalming became the preferred standard for preserving the body and improving its appearance. This became a form of protection that disinfected the body and prevented long-term decay. It also resolved the issue of premature burial. The underlining spirit of these rationales was well illustrated by one undertaker who advised colleagues that "one idea should always be kept in mind, and that is to lay out the body so that there would be as little suggestion of death as possible" (Farrell 1980, p. 160). To enhance this notion, coffins were no longer built to conform to the deceased's body but were designed in a standard rectangular shape that took the focus away from the individuality of death. Also, before the 1900s, funeral vigils and viewing of the body traditionally took place in the deceased's home. From there, the survivors proceeded to the church for the memorial service, followed by a trip to the cemetery for the burial. After the turn of the century, funeral directors suggested the need for a town center that would accommodate the deceased's family in preparing the body, providing a common place for the vigil and funeral service, while at the same time serving as a receiving point for bodies that were being sent home from another state. To further interest people, by 1920 funeral homes established a cheerful atmosphere that was aesthetically pleasing to their clients. This helped families deal with their loss by removing the practical burdens of death. Hence, taking the funerary duties out of the home, thereby lightening the physical and emotional load, gave affirmation to the services provided by the funeral industry.

Along with this shifting paradigm came changes in the funeral service itself. Generally, in the funeral home, the family assumed a more passive role while the funeral director provided a brief service that focused on consoling the survivors. Interestingly, the death care profession unknowingly contributed to a general suppression of grief: "It was as if grief were a contagious disease, a needless and shameful will, a manifestation of abnormal self-indulgence, and a sinful objection to the divine will" (Farrell 1980, p. 179). Other related customs changed as well, such as a shortening of the time frame for wearing mourning clothes.

In summary, the advent of twentieth-century industrialization and expansion of innovation removed the ugliness and fear of death while simultaneously reducing its sting through aesthetic enhancements and distancing its reality.

THE POSITIVE FUNCTION OF FUNERALS

Basically, the contemporary American funeral consists of five elements:

1. Visitation of the deceased—The community's opportunity to express sympathy and support for the bereaved
2. The rite of passage—A ritual to address the needs of the mourners; a religious orientation for 75 percent of them (Rando 1984)
3. A funeral procession—A parade to the cemetery symbolizing the living transporting the deceased to the land of the dead, then returning to the land of the living to reestablish themselves without the loved one
4. Disposal of the body—A symbol of the survivors' emotional separation from the deceased
5. The commitment to death—Committing the loved one's body to its final resting place (Raether and Slater 1977)

The primary purpose of a funeral is embedded in the rite of passage for both the deceased and the bereaved. During the service, the deceased is symbolically transferred from his or her surviving social community to the "afterlife," then is physically placed in the land of the dead through burial or cremation. For the bereaved, the funeral is the initial step toward separation from the deceased—the beginning of the grief process and the reestablishment of a place in the social community without the loved one. Generally, the survivors relationships with the deceased are starting to diminish (van Gennep 1960). Also, funerals are held as an affirmation of the dead person's life. They validate life itself, act as a testimony to one's existence, and assure the survivors that their own lives will be honored as well—that they will not have lived in vain. This is why survivors engage in ceremonies for their deceased loved ones. The funeral is their last chance to publicly recognize the deceased, pay their respects, and spend a final, personal moment with their loved one (Kastenbaum 1977). Thus, funerals primarily are for the living, to meet specific needs of the bereaved, and, in a larger sense, address society's need to confirm the value of life.

PSYCHOLOGICAL BENEFITS OF FUNERALS

Funeral rituals speak to the needs of individuals by providing psychological and social opportunities for them to work through the grief process. These psychological benefits are as follows:

1. Funeral rituals impose the reality of death upon the bereaved. The understandable reluctance of the survivors to accept the loss is confronted by the ceremony and burial of the physical body. Viewing the body is the first confirmation of death, participating in the memorial service is the next step, and watching the casket lowered into the grave is the final reality that, in fact, death has occurred. Some people are disturbed that funeral directors hold a "viewing" because it causes painful reactions. However, this confrontation has a necessary purpose in rudely awakening the griever to the finality of the loss. Without the conscious realization that death has actually occurred, especially following an accidental or sudden death, the griever becomes susceptible to denial of the loss. At the same time, viewing the body allows the griever to solidify pleasant memories of the deceased's physical wholeness, particularly in cases of bodily disfigurement due to accident or violence.

2. Funeral rituals validate and legitimize the griever's feelings of loss. They offer the bereaved social acceptance and support for their emotional response to death.

3. Funerals offer the survivors an environment conducive to the expression of grief. This allows the mourners a public opportunity to act out emotions and behaviors necessary for working through the grief process, for example, confessing wrongdoing, demonstrating love, and taking care of unfinished business. All these can be a part of the funeral ritual.

4. Funerals rekindle memories of the deceased, a necessary aspect of decathexis, or detachment. Mourners can begin to revisit their involvement with the deceased, a process that is necessary to effectively complete grief. Each story told, each incident remembered, and each emotion shared with others assists in the process of decathexis.

5. Funerals initiate thoughts about life without the deceased. During the grieving period, the mourner will struggle to find a new relationship with the deceased based on memories of the past. The funerary rituals provide a springboard into this new relationship.

6. Funerals allow the opportunity for input from the community, which becomes a living memorial to the deceased and helps the griever form an integrated image of the deceased. This is a singular psychological benefit to the mourner. Tributes paid to the deceased emphasize the worth of that individual and establish that he or she is worthy of the pain currently felt by the mourners.

7. Funeral rituals themselves contain many of the elements that constitute psychological therapy. The activities involved in these rituals allow the griever to "act out" feelings of loss and separation. This acting out provides a therapeutic release for the individual's emotions in the form of safe and socially acceptable behaviors.

SOCIAL BENEFITS OF FUNERALS

Funeral rituals provide numerous social benefits to the bereaved. These benefits are as follows:

1. Funerals allow community-wide support for the mourners. The community displays its empathy for the mourners, thereby strengthening social support for these individuals. This implies a sense of shared loss through which a willingness to help the mourners through this difficult time is communicated.

2. Funerals provide social interaction through meaningful, structured activities where the mourner is thrust into a newly defined social role. These activities redirect the mourner from dwelling on inner pain to focusing attention outside the self. This is particularly helpful in light of the sociological changes that have reduced the bereavement period in America and removed the special markings that identified mourners, such as black armbands or mourning clothes. Since there are no guidelines for how a mourner should behave, the funeral can provide some structure.

3. Funeral rituals assist the bereaved individual in initiating the process of social reintegration. Through its attendance at the funeral, the community opens its arms to offer social support for the griever and extend concern for the individual's well-being. As the griever accepts these comforting actions, a new identity emerges for the griever (e.g., a wife becomes a widow) and a new relationship is established between the griever and the community in which the griever assumes a new social position. The validation of this emerging identity begins during the funeral.

4. Funerals assist the community in grieving the loss of one of its members. Just as the funeral rituals have therapeutic benefits for the mourner, they also have a purpose in helping the larger community adapt to the imprint that death leaves on society. The community also must deal with its grief.

5. Funerals validate the continuity of life when, following the death and final commitment, society lives on and continues to move forward. Evidence of this fact can be seen all around us. When national celebrities die, society mourns the loss, then resumes its normal activities; when a rabbi dies, the congregation bands together to find a new spiritual leader; when a Little League player dies in a car accident, the team goes on to play. The funeral, while it honors the dead, is a testimony to the living.

6. Funerals are a reminder to society that every individual will die someday, and participation in funerary rituals repeatedly confirms one's future mortality. In the meantime, each member of society becomes a vehicle of anticipatory grief, the accumulation of which impacts the community through participation in the funeral rites of its members (Rando 1984).

7. Funerals serve as a channel through which the community communicates its belief system regarding life and death. The rites of passage provide an occasion for society to demonstrate its values and underlying beliefs.

PSYCHOLOGICAL BENEFITS OF GRAVE GOODS

Regardless of the type of funeral chosen, or the method of disposition of the body, a frequent and important aspect of funerals involves artifacts that are associated with the loved one and included in the casket or in the grave. These personal items are of sociological interest, and are sometimes known as "grave goods." Grave goods have been of intense interest and speculation for many years to scientists who study the theological and philosophical values of societies of old. Although the disturbance of graves from past cultures and civilizations remains an ethical (and sometimes legal) issue, grave goods are still with us as an important feature of modern funeral practice, as Elliott's 1990 study of funeral directors proves.

Grave goods can provide benefit to the mourner as a way of either connecting or disconnecting with the deceased. Funeral directors report that approximately two-thirds of burials include some kind of artifact, with personal jewelry accounting for 85 percent of such items (see Table 14–1). This means that only one-third of the burials involve a corpse that is simply clothed. Forty-six percent mention other types of personal possessions, while 24 percent note nonpersonal effects, such as a rosary, which a mourner might choose to "give" as a final gift. See Table 14–2 for a list of some of the most unusual items funeral directors reported having been asked to include with a deceased loved one.

Of further note is the request for placement of such artifacts within the coffin, suggesting that location indicates an intensity of feeling about the particular object and the relationship it represents to the deceased. It is generally expected that funeral directors handle the placement of such objects, with one director stating unequivocally, "Make no mistake, when it's requested, we do it. In fact . . . it is considered unethical not to enter any legally allowed artifact presented by relatives for burial along with their dead" (Elliott 1990, p. 604). The law (and good busi-

TABLE 14–1 GRAVE GOODS LISTED BY MORTICIANS AS "TYPICAL"

Family photographs	Jewelry, wedding bands, or rings
Costume jewelry rosaries	Letters from the family
Flowers	Small crosses and hearts
Eyeglasses	Handkerchiefs
Crucifixes	Shawls
Masonic aprons	Sprigs of evergreen
Favorite hats or boots	Lodge pins
Mother's pins and rings	Bibles
Military caps with medals	Dolls
Stuffed animals	Cigars

Source: Elliott (1990).

ness practice) is only part of it. Motivation for mourners to include grave goods can range from pure sentiment (10 percent) to a genuine perception or belief in how the article will correlate with the deceased's state of happiness in the afterlife. Sending a loved one to the hereafter with possessions or gifts that are perceived to benefit him or her can be a source of comfort or satisfaction to a griever.

Funeral directors should be prepared to expect inquiries from loved ones regarding what items make appropriate grave goods, although most directors say they prefer having the survivors select them. They may, however, provide recommendations for the timing of the placement of an item or symbol in a casket or grave. Elliott's survey is important for both funeral directors and clergy to under-

TABLE 14–2 GRAVE GOODS LISTED BY MORTICIANS AS "UNUSUAL"

Food	Set of wrenches
Pet dog	Deck of cards
Fishing rods	A rock
Stuffed toy animal	Cigarettes
Cans of beer	Old jeans and sweater
Pictures	Bottles of whiskey
Shot glasses	Minnesota Twins baseball
Letters from the family	Pets
Cowboy hats	Cowboy boots
Toys	Snuff
Shillelagh (nightstick)	Ballpoint pen
Cocktail stir sticks	Fishing hat
Motorcycle jacket	Boat paddles
Tennis racket	Set of golf clubs
Radios tuned to a favorite station	

Source: Elliott (1990).

stand. First, the inclusion or placement of grave goods can be seen as a last act of love. Second, burying objects with the dead can also help bring closure to the relationship for other grievers. Third, it might help them feel close to their loved one in a manner that promotes healthy mourning (as if they have performed a worthwhile act that will be acknowledged in the afterlife). Finally, it might simply provide a useful way to say good-bye.

TYPES OF FUNERALS

Funerals in America today have several common, traditional characteristics. Typically, they are held in the presence of the body (open or closed casket), involve a visitation period and/or wake, and take place over approximately a three-day period. As Rando (1984) has reported, about 75 percent of funeral ceremonies include a religious component. We can expect a procession to a committal service at a chapel or grave site, followed by a final procession away from the location where disposition of the body has taken place.

Cremation, the burning of a body, represents another significant mode of body disposition, and offers several different opportunities for a ritual, while not necessarily varying greatly from traditional funerals involving burial. First, cremation can occur immediately following a death, with no accompanying ritual or ceremony. This is known as an immediate disposition. Second, cremation might follow the normal activities of traditional visitation and funeral service, but instead of taking the body to a cemetery, the family accompanies it to a crematorium. A third way of handling a cremation is to cremate the body first, then follow up with a memorial service at the funeral home or a designated chapel at a later date. I, however, am reluctant to recommend the immediate disposition mode as an "equal" option from a psychological standpoint, as it might potentially lead to a more complicated grief reaction among mourners. Subsequent to cremation, several methods of handling the remains are available:

1. Inurnment—Ashes are placed in a container made of metal or stone.
2. The urn can be maintained privately, or buried or placed in a type of mausoleum called a columbarium.
3. Ashes might be strewn or scattered at a location that is meaningful or appropriate to the deceased or the survivors, according to the legal permissions or prohibitions enacted by individual state governments.

As stated by Irion (1974), cremation involves pros and cons for the grievers. On the positive side, cremation assists in recognizing the finality of the death. Second, it is quick, clean, and inexpensive, affording the sanitary aspect of fire, as opposed to the decaying (and lingering) aspect of burial. Third, it contains an important element of "naturalness." As the Bible says, "Ashes to ashes, dust to dust." This message makes sense and feels appropriate to many people.

On the negative side, cremation, particularly if immediate disposition is involved, can allow grievers a quick avenue to "escape" grief and try to ignore their real need to mourn. Any attempt to move too hastily back into life without their loved one can be psychologically dangerous. Second, cremation might provide an angry mourner a way to "act out" at the deceased. The very nature of burning suggests destruction, and Irion notes cases where this appeared to be a motivation in choosing cremation. Third, cremation might be chosen in direct opposition to the wishes of the deceased, in yet another attempt to display anger or rebellion. When cremation is the expressed wish of the deceased (or the preferred, healthy decision of the family), the memorial service becomes an important element of the total funeral process. This service performs much the same function as a funeral service where a burial is involved, except that it tends to be more positively focused on the life and values of the dead person, rather than focusing on the dead body.

At a memorial service, the body is usually not even present and the activity is taking place three to four days after the death. The personality and energy of the deceased are honored, rehabilitated, and fondly remembered for the good years and good acts of his or her life. Survivors are able to go away with pleasant images, strong reinforcement of their investment in the individual, and renewed respect for the capabilities and influence of their loved one. This is especially important after a long-term illness or a decline in the deceased's ability to function. Whatever the disposition of the remains, survivors need to feel an identity with the deceased, a pride at sharing some aspects of a life together, and a sense of being custodians of values, talents, or traits that the loved one possessed.

Another type of service can be one the deceased has planned in advance by him- or herself. This can include preselected readings, music, and even decisions regarding the people who will perform these activities. Others simply may want family and friends to come together for a quiet evening to remember the individual in any manner in which they feel comfortable. It might also include entertainment, recordings, readings, or refreshments prearranged by the person who has died, or someone chosen to act on his or her behalf.

A final, common type of service is best described as multiple services; and this situation comes into play when the deceased has ties or history in more than one location. More than one gathering in more than one place might be advisable or necessary—and family members might need a day or two for travel and/or to coordinate multiple arrangements. In the event friends in another state hold a service independently or simultaneously with another memorial activity, it should be fully noted and reported to the family, who can take comfort, satisfaction, and gratitude from the additional acknowledgment of their loss.

TWENTY SUGGESTIONS FOR FUNERAL DIRECTORS

In view of the various types of traditional funerals that are commonly handled by modern funeral directors, there is value in summarizing some general ideas and considerations that should come to mind with every death:

1. The job of funeral directors is to make the funeral as meaningful and personal as possible to both the deceased and the bereaved.
2. Inquire and stay aware of the value, expectations, religious preferences, and style of the family.
3. Ask the grievers how they want the deceased to be remembered.
4. Explain their options. As consumers, they are likely to be unaware of choices of services and the sequence of funeral activities available to them (see Chapter 10 for more information on this).
5. Try to broaden involvement to include other family members besides the immediate ones. Not only do they need to feel important, but somewhere along the line you might need their assistance or influence.
6. Encourage the bereaved to include affected children in funeral rituals. Omitting, ignoring, or pushing children aside can be damaging for the present and for future situations.
7. Funeral directors should understand the cultural values, expectations, philosophical and religious tenets, and customs and socioeconomic norms that operate in their clients' communities.
8. At all times, invite the bereaved to ask questions and attempt to answer them as fully and honestly as possible.
9. Listen carefully to the specific needs of the grievers. Help them determine and clarify their own needs for the funeral, whether it be assembling photographs, selecting musicians, or choosing grave goods.
10. Offer and allow grieving families more than one opportunity to spend private time with the body—for talking, remembering, touching, reflecting, praying, or even arguing. They don't have to be swept along in an arbitrary ritual "timetable."
11. Invite mourners, particularly mothers whose children have died, to help you prepare or dress the body. This can defuse resentment or contribute to a strong need for participation.
12. Respect any choice made by the bereaved. At a very profound level, it is ultimately "their" funeral to direct, not yours.
13. Encourage grievers to express their feelings—but don't force it. Listen. Validate. And help them to feel normal, as long as it does not appear to preclude resolution of the grief process.
14. Recognize and be alert to the fact that various family members will react differently to the funeral event and will have different needs based on their personal relationship with the deceased.
15. Be sensitive to the fact that you might be one of the few people to observe and understand the needs and dynamics of the whole family and its support system. Make appropriate suggestions and recommendations based on your knowledge.
16. Recommend that the bereaved reach out for support and love from friends or family as needed.

17. Remember that some people might regret decisions that are made in a time of crisis. Funeral directors would be wise to question and affirm family members' decisions and their possible consequences. But they should be sure to do this in a caring and sensitive way.

18. Funeral directors need to integrate into the larger community. They should join local civic, cultural, and charitable organizations that enable them to understand and participate in the life of their cities or towns.

19. Funeral directors must not become "surrogate sufferers." This means they should avoid becoming a "sponge" for the problems and pain of the people they serve (Nichols 1983).

20. Do not be surprised or offended at hostility that mourners sometimes display. The funeral industry has received some negative publicity that might provoke or seemingly "permit" bereaved individuals to take out their anger on funeral directors. Such behavior should not be taken personally.

SUMMARY

Death ceremonies and funeral rituals are important in meeting the social and emotional needs of the survivors. These basic rituals seem to meet certain universal needs. In fact, research has shown that rituals are similar from one culture to another.

Since the early 1800s, many changes have been made in customs corresponding to funeral rituals in America. Funerary practices have changed as well. Prior to 1830, the deceased had been laid out at home, sometimes in a roughly made pine box. Now, however, customs and practices surrounding the four basic funerary elements are dramatically different. Significant changes have been made in (1) the treatment of the body, (2) the burial container, (3) the funeral environment, and (4) funeral procedures.

The advent of twentieth-century industrialization and innovation removed the ugliness and fear of death experienced in previous decades while simultaneously reducing its sting through aesthetic enhancements. The primary purpose of the contemporary American funeral is embedded in the rite of passage for both the deceased and the bereaved.

Funeral rituals speak to the needs of the survivors by providing psychological and social opportunities for them to work through the grief process. These rituals provide numerous social benefits to the bereaved, such as structured activities for interaction with other people. Also, a frequent and important aspect of engaging in rituals involves artifacts that are associated with the loved one and are laid in the casket or grave. These are known as "grave goods." Grave goods can provide benefit to the mourner as a way of either connecting or disconnecting with the deceased.

Funerals in America today have several common characteristics. Typically, they are held in the presence of the body, involve a visitation period and/or wake, and take place over approximately three days. If the body is not laid in a casket, other modes of body disposition are used: cremation, inurnment, burial in a columbarium, or scattered ashes. Although the body is not included in memorial services, survivors are able to go away with pleasant images, strong reinforcement of their investment in the deceased, and renewed respect for the capabilities and influence of their loved one.

REFERENCES

Cowell, D. 1985. *Funerals, family, and forefathers: A view of Italian-American funeral practices.* Bethesda, Md.: Baywood Publishing.

Elliott, J. 1990. *Funerary artifacts in contemporary America.* New York: Hemisphere Publishing.

Farrell, J. J. 1980. *Inventing the American way of death.* Philadelphia: Temple University Press.

Irion, P. 1974. To cremate or not. In *Concerning death: A practical guide for the living,* edited by E. Grollman. Boston: Beacon Press.

Kastenbaum, R. J. 1977. *Death, society, and human experience.* St. Louis: C. V. Mosby.

Mathias, E. 1974. The Italian-American funeral: Persistence through change. *Western Folklore* 33:35–50.

Nichols, R. V. 1983. Professionals and the funeral: Do we help or hinder? *Newsletter of the Forum for Death Education and Counseling* 6:6–7.

Pine, V. R. 1972. Social organization and death. *Omega* 3:149–53.

Raether, H. C., and R. C. Slater. 1997. Immediate postdeath activities in the United States. In *New meanings of death,* edited by H. Feifel. New York: McGraw-Hill.

Rando, Therese. 1984. *Grief, dying and death.* Champaign, Ill.: Research Press.

van Gennep, A. 1960. *The rites of passage.* Chicago: University of Chicago Press.

15

THE FAMILY: GRIEF CHARACTERISTICS AND CONFLICTS WITHIN THE FAMILY SYSTEM

Shirley A. Brogan

CHAPTER OUTLINE ....

....

We know that coming to terms with the death of a family member is a highly individualized experience. At the same time, in the context of the loss of one of its members, family members continue to relate to one another, and in so doing each person's grief pattern influences the experiences of others and the functioning of the family unit. In this chapter we will look at characteristics of the family system and how they influence the family's grief response. These include family structure and communication, emotional expression, spirituality and religious beliefs, internal and external resources, and family stage of life when death occurs. We will then look at death as a family crisis and potential conflicts that may arise. The chapter concludes with suggestions for help to assist families to move through grief and normalize the process.

THE FAMILY SYSTEM: COPING WITH GRIEF

Family Structure

In the 1990s and on into the twenty-first century, death care professionals working with bereaved families will encounter a variety of family structures. The structures define the relationships. A *nuclear family,* for example, is defined as a husband, wife, and their biological children, living together as a unit. A *remarried family* is a unit created by the marriage of one or both adults who have been married previously. This family is also known as a *stepfamily,* or *blended family. Siblings,* or children in this family, can be (1) *biological siblings,* with the same two parents; (2) *half siblings,* with one biological parent in common; or (3) *stepsiblings,* coming together through remarriage of a biological parent. An *extended family* is a married couple and their children, plus relatives of other generations, such as grandparents, aunts, or uncles. Members may be living together in one household, such as a grandmother with a married daughter's family, or in close proximity, such as brothers living in homes on the same street. There may also be *unmarried partners* living together, often in long-term relationships that would produce intense grief with a loss.

While looking at the structure, or who makes up the family unit, family activities, or tasks, are also significant. Families exist for a number of reasons. The most basic task is to provide food, clothing, shelter, and security for their members, particularly offspring. Families will also teach, maintain discipline, give direction, and motivate. Families have several possible ways of governance: (1) patriarchal, where the father figure rules the household and/or extended family; (2) matriarchal, where the mother rules her family; or (3) egalitarian, where both father and mother have equal rights, duties, and governing power.

The family also creates roles for its individuals: significant roles may include parent of a young family, family patriarch or matriarch, or a "special" child or bearer of the family legacy (someone to take over the family business, or carry on a family tradition of musical or sports achievement). Death calls for reorganization of family roles. This could be on an instrumental level, when task-oriented functions, such as family breadwinner, need to be redistributed, or on an emotional level, as when the deceased was the family's emotional barometer, peacekeeper, or nurturer (Kissane and Bloch 1994). With regard to the prior functioning of the deceased in the family system, the greater the role, the greater the loss. A family will respond differently to the loss of a young parent than to the loss of an elderly grandparent, or to the loss of a leader and caretaker than to that of a quarrelsome troublemaker (Walsh and McGoldrick 1991).

Kantor and Lehr (cited in Goldenberg and Goldenberg 1985) identify three basic family types representing the way the family interacts internally and with the outside world:

1. Open family structures are essentially democratic and allow honest exchange within the family and with outsiders. There is a sense of order with flexibility; adaptation takes place through consensus, individual rights are respected, and loyalty to self and to the family is expected.
2. Closed family structures have rules and a hierarchical power structure which demands that individuals subordinate their needs to the good of the group. Rigid daily schedules are likely to be followed. The family seeks stability through tradition, unlike open families, which foster adaptability.
3. Random family structures are fragmented, and these family members are more likely to "do their own thing," which may or may not be connected to what others are doing. There are few, if any, rules. The family fosters exploration through intuition.

Dealing with grief, the open family structure would most likely provide tolerance, which Walsh and McGoldrick (1991) state is needed for different responses within families and for "the likelihood that some members will be out of phase with others, given differences in the meaning of the relationship and different coping styles" (p. 10). In closed family structures, rigidity and loyalties may disallow feelings as they relate to grief and may block communication. In addition, "Overidealization of the deceased, a sense of disloyalty, or the catastrophic fear of another loss may block the formation of other attachments and commitments" (p. 12). A random family structure may inhibit the sharing of the reality of the death and the experience of loss. Again, Walsh and McGoldrick (1991) note that families need clear information and open communication about the death: "Inability to accept the reality of the death can lead a family member to avoid contact with the rest of the family or to become angry with others who are moving forward in the grief process" (pp. 8–9).

Looking at three continua that further describe the family network, Walsh and McGoldrick (1991) identify the following:

1. Family cohesion and differentiation of members. At one extreme, the family structure is one of enmeshment, at the other extreme, disengagement.

   Enmeshed families demand a united front, and individual differences are regarded as disloyal or threatening. Members may have difficulty with subsequent separations, holding on to other family members at normal, developmental transition stages. An adult child, for example, may be discouraged from leaving a widowed parent to live independently, get married, or accept a promotion that involves relocation to another town. Disengaged families may avoid the pain of loss through distancing and emotional cutoffs. Members are left isolated in their grief and fending for themselves.

2. Flexibility. At one extreme, the family structure is rigid, at the other, it is chaotic.

Rigidity in families can make it difficult for members to modify set patterns to accommodate loss and needed role changes. In chaotic families, the confusion may make it difficult to maintain enough leadership, stability, and continuity to manage the transitional upheaval.

3. Communication. Family communication can be open or closed (secrecy).

Open communication of needs, feelings, and experiences promotes trust, support, and acceptance of a range of responses. Secrecy surrounding the loss interferes with mastery of the grief experience. "When communication is blocked, the unspeakable is more likely to be expressed in dysfunctional symptoms or destructive behavior" (Walsh and McGoldrick 1991, p. 17). These might include delinquency, abuse of drugs or alcohol, or physical illness.

The Family's Accepted or Expressed Emotions and Their Level of Intensity

Most families, through values, behaviors, and styles of living often passed through generations, have acceptable emotions and ways of expressing them. In one family, stoic nonexpression of feelings may be considered a strength. Feelings may be allowed to some family members but not to others. For example, a father can get angry and swear, but children are punished for doing the same. Some family members will express feelings together, while others will hide responses until they are alone. Staudacher (1991) notes that most men find it easier to mourn by themselves. They go to the grave site by themselves, often at regular intervals at a specific time. They won't show fear or insecurity. They see crying as "falling apart," even though crying can be a signal to other members of the family, particularly children, that it's acceptable to grieve, that you share others' sadness and loneliness, and that you loved the person who died. Families can experience a range of feelings depending on each person's relationship with the deceased and the implications of the death for the family unit. Mixed feelings of anger, disappointment, helplessness, relief, guilt, and abandonment may be present (Walsh and McGoldrick 1991). Feelings may also be expressed in a piecemeal fashion: one family member expresses all anger, another only sadness, another is numb (Reilly cited in Walsh and McGoldrick 1991).

Family Spirituality, Religious Beliefs and Practices

In research to discover what modern healthy families had in common, Curran (1983) identified fifteen traits, one of which was that healthy families had a shared religious core. Faith in God plays a functional role in daily family life and strengthens the family support system. Parents feel a strong responsibility for passing on the faith in positive, meaningful ways. Another trait is that healthy families have a strong sense of family in which rituals and traditions abound. Brown (1988) states that all families have personal and/or religious rituals or customs that help them mourn. They can be clues as to how the family deals with death as well as how family members function together. Rituals mark the event and reflect the philosophical and spiritual beliefs in which the family is grounded. Belief systems may be deepened, renewed, or changed as a result of loss. Families with a strong faith may mistakenly believe they have no need to mourn. However, having faith can mean we have the courage to allow ourselves to mourn (Wolfelt 1992).

Family Resources

The family's capacity to grieve, to create and/or carry out rituals, and to adapt to life without the deceased is influenced by the family's internal and external resources. Family finances may dictate decisions about funeral options, burial places, and other ritual events. Questions will come up about basic living needs in the months and years that follow: Was the deceased an important financial resource to the family, that is, the breadwinner? How will bills be paid now? Is life insurance or pension money available? The family may experience a change in financial status, with a reduced income or loss of employee benefits.

Connection and status in the community may also be significant. A family with close, longtime friends in its church, neighborhood, or community will have resources to help with emotional and physical needs—providing encouragement, hugs, and love as well as a hot meal, baby-sitting, or help mowing the lawn. A family isolated in a new location, or because of its own closed system, may exhaust itself. The number of persons in the family system and the degree of extended family closeness will also make a difference; an adult only child living far from aunts, uncles, or cousins, for example, will not have the same support dealing with both terminal illness and death of a parent as someone who has brothers or sisters and other relatives who are nearby and willing to help.

Cultural norms regarding bereavement also dictate family resources and responses. These norms help create the backdrop for mourning, the guidelines for what's expected and acceptable, and the rituals to facilitate, or possibly hinder, the grief process. Families with German heritage sometimes show a more stoic approach to loss. Italian families might be more expressive of their feelings (Wolfelt 1992). Those of British ancestry may prefer a "no muss, no fuss," rational approach. Irish families consider death the most significant life-cycle transition, and families go to great lengths to give the deceased a "good send-off," openly grieving and viewing the wake as a kind of party. The Hindu culture also looks at death as another phase of the life cycle, bringing about the rebirth of a human being (McGoldrick et al. 1991).

Many other customs and mourning styles occur. African-Americans, like the Irish, place great importance on "going out in style," with the funeral and its expense the final opportunity the family has to let the deceased have dignity and status. African-Americans emphasize funeral attendance. In Jewish families, by contrast, there are more important life events than a funeral. While perhaps not attending the funeral, family and community members will pay a condolence call (shivah) to the home (McGoldrick et al. 1991). Wortman and Silver (cited in McGoldrick et al. 1991) state: "The dominant American norm is that a certain, moderate level of emotional expression, and even depression, is 'required,' but that this should last only for a 'reasonable' period of time—perhaps a year or two for the death of a close relative."

Family Life Cycle and Loss Experience

Stages of the family life cycle have been identified by many authors and researchers. Developmental tasks, transitional periods, and changes in family status have been mapped out; Carter and McGoldrick (1988) have created one schema (see Table 15–1). Death can have a significant impact on the progress of these stages. The impact of the loss of a parent will be different if the deceased parent is young, at midlife, or elderly. Grieving the loss of a spouse will differ the couple was in a new marriage, a long-term relationship, or a remarriage. Sibling loss can be affected by the age of the deceased, the age of the sibling, and the birth order. For the most part, experts believe the farther along in the life cycle, the less the degree of family stress associated with serious illness and death. Death at an older age is seen as a natural process (Walsh, cited in Brown 1988). AIDS-bereaved families commonly have lost a loved one when young, out of phase with the normal life cycle (Michael 1994).

One way to help a family look concretely at the impact of its losses is through the construction of a genogram (McGoldrick and Gerson 1988) (see Figure 15–1). This is like a "family tree," done in counseling to help families see relationships over generations. A genogram was used in the following case study (see Figure 15–2).

CASE STUDY #1

Grace, age thirty-nine, was experiencing depression and significant loss of energy following the stillbirth of her son David. Her husband, Robert, forty-one, and son Robert Jr., sixteen, were supportive, but also had gone back to work and school. Grace was home alone. In her initial interview with a grief counselor, Grace reported she had had three other miscarriages, one before Robert's birth and two after. Grace said she was especially close to her mother, Donna, who also had experienced two miscarriages and a stillbirth.

When the counselor did a genogram, Grace looked surprised, then began to cry. She saw both the pattern of loss and the potential size of the family she might have had if her mother's pregnancies, as well as her own, had resulted in healthy births. She became aware of the "ghosts" in her life, and of the unresolved grief that she and her mother shared.

DEATH AS A FAMILY CRISIS

Webster's defines crisis as "an unstable state of affairs in which a decisive change is impending." Looking at grief and loss in the family system, the key words in this definition are "unstable" and "decisive change." Walsh and McGoldrick (1991)

TABLE 15–1. THE STAGES OF THE FAMILY LIFE CYCLE

Family Life Cycle Stage	Emotional Process of Transition: Key Principles	Second-Order Changes in Family Status Required to Proceed Developmentally
1. Leaving home: Single young adults	Accepting emotional and financial responsibility for self	a. Differentiation of self in relation to family of origin b. Development of intimate peer relationships c. Establishment of self re work and financial independence
2. The joining of families through marriage: The new couple	Commitment to new system	a. Formation of marital system b. Realignment of relationships with extended families and friends to include spouse
3. Families with young children	Accepting new members into the system	a. Adjusting marital system to make space for child(ren) b. Joining in childrearing, financial, and household tasks c. Realignment of relationships with extended family to include parenting and grandparenting roles
4. Families with adolescents	Increasing flexibility of family boundaries to include children's independence and grandparents' frailties	a. Shifting of parent child relationships to permit adolescent to move in and out of system b. Refocus on midlife marital and career issues c. Beginning shift toward joint caring for older generation
5. Launching children and moving on	Accepting a multitude of exits from and entries into the family system	a. Renegotiation of marital system as a dyad b. Development of adult to adult relationships between grown children and their parents c. Realignment of relationships to include in-laws and grandchildren d. Dealing with disabilities and death of parents (grandparents)
6. Families in later life	Accepting the shifting of generational roles	a. Maintaining own and/or couple functioning and interests in face of physiological decline; exploration of new familial and social role options b. Support for a more central role of middle generation c. Making room in the system for the wisdom and experience of the elderly, supporting the older generation without overfunctioning for them d. Dealing with loss of spouse, siblings, and other peers and preparation for own death. Life review and integration

Source: B. Carter and M. McGoldrick, "Overview—The Changing Family Life Cycle: A Framework for Family Therapy," in The Changing Family Life Cycle: A Framework for Family Therapy, 2d ed., edited by B. Carter and M. McGoldrick (New York: Gardner Press, 1988), pp. 3–28. Copyright 1988 by Gardner Press. Reprinted with permission.

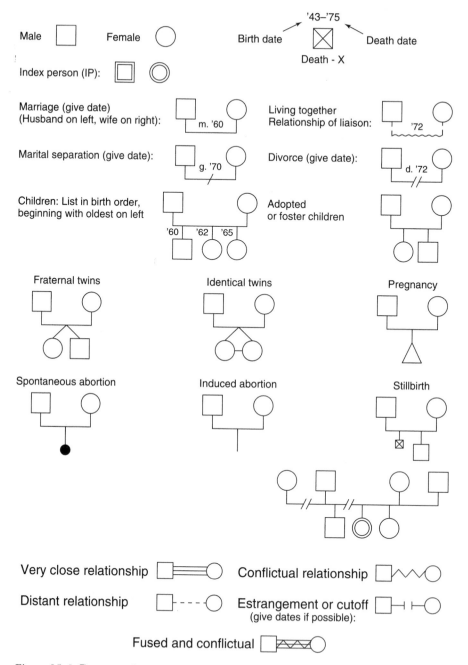

Figure 15–1. The genogram format uses symbols to describe basic family membership and structure. Significant others who have lived with or cared for family members should be recorded on the right side of the genogram, with notation about who they are. (Brogan 1995) *Note:* Genogram format symbols reprinted from M. McGoldrick and R. Gerson, "Genograms and the Family Life Cycle," *The Changing Family Life Cycle: A Framework for Family Therapy,* 2d ed., edited by B. Carter and M. McGoldrick (New York: Gardner Press, 1988), pp. 164–87. Copyright 1988 by Gardner Press. Reprinted with permission.

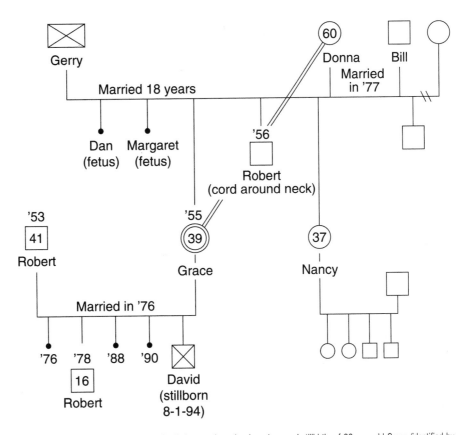

Figure 15–2. Genogram depicting family losses, through miscarriage and stillbirth, of 39-year-old Grace (identified by double circles). She was seen by a grief counselor shortly after the stillbirth of her son David. (Brogan 1995)

state: "Of all life experiences, death poses the most painful adaptational challenges for the family as a system and for every surviving member, with reverberations for all other relationships" (p. xv). They further note:

> Death poses shared adaptational challenges. Adaptation does not mean resolution, in the sense of some complete "once and for all" coming to terms with the loss. Rather, it involves finding ways to put the loss in perspective and to move on with life. Adaptation has no fixed timetable or sequence. . . . meanings of any death are transformed throughout the life cycle, as they are experienced and integrated with life experiences. (Pp. 7–8)

They define two major tasks that promote adaptation: (1) shared acknowledgment of the reality of death and the experience of loss; and (2) reorganizing and reinvesting in other relationships and life pursuits.

Several factors can influence the family's adaptation. Terminal illness may be depleting both emotionally, especially for primary caregivers, and financially, putting other family needs, such as a new house or college education, on hold. The family may be confronted with the dilemma about maintaining life support efforts or approving organ donation in a situation of brain death.

With sudden, accidental, or violent death, the family must deal with the shock, disbelief, and unanticipated, abrupt changes in lifestyle. There is no time to prepare for loss, to deal with unfinished business, such as making peace after a quarrel, or to say good-bye. With violent death, there may be trauma from body disfiguration that may recur in family members' dreams and memories. In homicide deaths, bereavement may be ongoing when members have to deal with time-consuming court cases or believe justice has not been served. In a major disaster, a loss that appears random and senseless may create insecurity and feelings of vulnerability.

Other types of deaths may not be grieved openly. These include suicide, drug overdose or alcohol-related deaths, or other deaths due to circumstances family members may not want to talk about. There may be a sociocultural context—the impact of combat deaths influenced, for example, by society's acceptance of war involvement, or AIDS deaths looked on as involving innocent victims or those who "brought it on themselves" through lifestyle choices (sexual practices or intravenous drug use) (Walsh and McGoldrick 1991). With suicide, anger and guilt can pervade family relationships, particularly when members blame themselves or others for the death, thinking they could have prevented it. Social stigma around any death contributes to family shame. Promotion of a family secret, likely to occur following suicide or deaths such as those related to AIDS or those connected with illegal activity, serve to uphold the family's pride but at the expense of completing the grief work (Bowlby-West, cited in Kissane and Bloch 1994). Secrecy inhibits family communication and can isolate the family from outside social support. For example, at a time when AIDS families need spiritual rituals and affirmations from a religious support group, they may fear seeking those comforts because of professed church attitudes (Michael 1994).

Some deaths may not be grieved by family members, because the loss is minimized or not acknowledged. An example is the loss of a child due to miscarriage, stillbirth, or infant death. A sensitive hospital staff may give time for the family to be with and hold a stillborn child. A family may give the child a name, have a funeral, and bury the body in a cemetery plot. Other blocks to the normal expression of grief may occur when the relationship is not acknowledged, as with the death of ex-spouses, unknown fathers, or homosexual or unmarried companions; the loss is not recognized, as with prenatal loss, selective abortion, giving a child up for adoption, or infertility; or the griever is not recognized, as with the very young, the very old, or the mentally disabled.

In a study of forty-nine families who lost a child to cancer death, McClowry et al. (1987) identify what they call the "empty space phenomenon" in the bereaved family. They quote from an interview with one mother nine years after her son's death:

We moved things out of his room . . . probably much too soon. Then we had a hole that kept moving within that house. Because his room was empty, we put some bookcases and things in there from the living room. . . . Then that end of the living room was empty. So we moved a picture down from upstairs and then there was a hole upstairs. I mean, we moved the absence . . . all the way around, and there was no getting rid of it. And if you bought something new, it would have been to fill that hole. . . . There is an emptiness still. I haven't found anything that would substitute or fill it, but it's receded. The emptiness is within me now instead of that empty arm feeling. (P. 371)

The researchers report that families were able to create current productive and happy lives, but there was a qualitative change as the loss was integrated and seen as "an incentive to cherish other significant relationships and treasure daily events as a special gift" (p. 371).

POTENTIAL CONFLICTS

All of the family characteristics we have discussed previously, such as structure, roles, adaptability, communication, expression of emotion, spirituality, resources, stage in family life cycle, and experience with loss, come to bear when members deal with potential conflicts. The following are some examples of stresses that might occur.

Before Death

Caring for a terminally ill family member can cause strain in several areas. Brown (1988) reports a shift in health care philosophy and services available to the terminally ill, moving from a pathological view, with care delegated to the hospitals and experts, to a more normative and acute view, placing care and decisions on the individual and the family. This has increased the use of hospice and/or home care. While it has been generally shown that this increased contact with dying relatives has brought strength to the family, conflict can occur about such issues as who will care for the one who is ill, how the tasks will be divided, how openly the diagnosis of the illness and the prognosis are discussed, and what decisions are made about heroic measures and organ donation.

Family members with unresolved issues, what counselors call "unfinished business" with the dying person, will have difficulty making decisions. These may include funeral prearrangements. Established family roles may dictate who does what, for example, the oldest son takes charge of funeral details, or the family may have to redistribute tasks.

At Time of Death

Who was present? Where did the death occur? What were the circumstances of the death (accident, violent death, suicide, death at home "in her sleep")? Conflict can occur for family members who were not present, not notified immediately, not permitted to view the body at the hospital or home before it was taken to the funeral home, and so on. One task of mourning is to accept the loss as real. The way family members facilitate this for each other, as with parents and grandparents spending time with a stillborn infant in the hospital, can be significant to the grief process as well as to future relationship dynamics.

Funeral decisions and activity can also cause stress, as the family delegates responsibilities, accepts each other's coping styles, and deals with feelings and expectations about those who are not present.

Bereavement and Mourning

Changes can occur in family relationships, bringing closeness or further strain (Myers 1986). One area of potential tension involves distribution of a parent's estate. In carrying out this task, family members are dividing up a financial inheritance, as well as family heirlooms. Angel (1987) has one suggestion to create a different, positive emotional atmosphere: siblings take part of the estate and dedicate it to a charitable cause in memory of the parent or parents. This should be something that was important to the deceased. This is done (1) to provide funds for worthy causes, (2) to identify these causes with the deceased's memory, and (3) to remind heirs that the estate was created by the deceased through that person's own labor. As Angel reminds us, "Inheritance is a gift from parents, not an entitlement" (p. 137).

There can be varying impact with the distribution of possessions or heirlooms. Meyers (1986) describes the awkward experience of Mark when he and his siblings divided up their mother's possessions. All of Mark's siblings were married and had children; he was single and had kept close to his hometown, his mother, and the family house. He reports that, as they divided things up, what struck him was that they were dividing his home.

There may be gaps in family functioning—parenting, companionship, giving advice/mentoring, basic tasks like who cooks or cleans the gutters—to be filled in following a death. Conflict may occur if there is an assumption of inappropriate roles, such as the parentification of a child following the death of a parent (Bowlby-West, cited in Kissane and Bloch 1994), or if someone gets the message to take over as an exact replacement for the deceased. There may be distancing as contacts with family of origin subside and individuals become patriarchs and matriarchs of their own families. Unmarried children may find themselves on their own, without strong family connections (Angel 1987).

Remarried families may struggle with unresolved grief from the loss of individuals, as well as loss of the previous family structure. As founders of the Stepfamily Association of America and specialists on working with remarried families, Visher and Visher (1982) state that remarried families formed following the death of a spouse have a better statistical chance of lasting than those with an ex-spouse still living. However, children in these families may have to deal with a greater sense of loss and loyalty conflicts. Families need to give themselves enough time to mourn the person who has died. This may be a longer time for children than for an adult seeking to ease the pain and loneliness of being single (and a single parent) again. Sometimes families can end up idealizing the person who died, and this makes connection with other potential partners or stepparents difficult. When older couples remarry, there may be money and inheritance questions that cause conflict. Persons about to remarry should talk to their adult children, inform them about the contents of the will, and get their children's reactions if comfortable doing so. Let family members choose items before disposing of them; what is insignificant to one may be a special memento to another.

CASE STUDY #2

John, age sixty-seven, died after a ten-year battle with cancer. He and his wife, Emma, just missed their forty-eighth wedding anniversary, which was five days after his death. They prearranged his funeral six months ago. John's oldest son, Alex, has been distant from his father ever since he left the family business eight years ago and moved with his wife and two daughters to Nebraska to become a farmer. Linda, their middle daughter, is single and has spent a great deal of the last two years helping her mother care for John. Liz, the youngest adult child, is a young mother of two, with a third child on the way.

Emma, Alex, Linda, and Liz have all lost John, but the relationships and the losses are not the same. Emma has lost a husband of forty-eight years, a lifelong companion and spouse who was also an organized head of the household. She'd been learning to do most of the important tasks, like manage finances, while John was ill, but now he won't be there for advice. Alex knew he was expected to take over the family business, something that Liz's husband, Dale, and George, Alex's cousin, have now done, but he wished his father could have seen how successful his farm had become and accepted how happy he was. Linda is now worried about her mother, and has put a career change and a move to Denver on hold to spend more time with her. Liz, excited about the upcoming birth of her child, is also concerned about her mother's well-being, but her own pregnancy and care of her two children take much of her physical and emotional energy.

Many factors will affect the mourning of each person in this family. Emma will deal with the loneliness and adjustments to living by herself; Alex with the loss of a chance to repair a relationship; Linda with the relief, and guilt for the relief, of no longer having to care for her father. She may, however, transfer her energies to her mother's welfare, continuing to put her own life "on hold." Liz will have to deal with the inherently conflictual processes of mourning a loss and parenting a new infant her father will never see.

HELPFUL GRIEF INTERVENTIONS

Families can be assisted in their coping with grief and loss through several methods. Support groups can help family members normalize their experiences by hearing how others are doing. Groups and family counseling with a therapist experienced in grief and loss can create a setting for families to express needs and feelings, especially if family communication patterns make this difficult. Worden (1991) states that the family interacts as a unit even though individuals will not be working on grief in the same way. "When the counselor can assess the feelings of all the family members, the probability is greater that the grief counseling will be effective and that equilibrium will be restored to the family unit" (p. 131). A family session devoted to a family life review, with a genogram, family photos, scrapbooks, and other mementos, can facilitate acceptance of the reality of the current loss and possibly the discover of legacies of previous losses and unresolved grief. There are many current self-help books that families can share to provide information on the grief process and written exercises or activities that can be tools for healing.

SUMMARY

When a family has a loss, each person's grief pattern influences the experiences of others and the functioning of the family unit. Death care professionals working with a bereaved family will see a variety of family structures: nuclear family, remarried family, extended family, or unmarried partners living together. Siblings, or children in families, can be biological siblings, half siblings, or stepsiblings. Families exist for a number of reasons. They provide food, clothing, shelter, and security for their members. They teach, maintain discipline, give direction, and motivate through patriarchal, matriarchal, or egalitarian governance. The family creates physical and emotional roles for its individuals, which change when death occurs. Families interact in three basic patterns—open, closed, and random—which affect adaptation to loss and change. Families also vary in cohesion, flexibility, and communication style. Other influencing factors include accepted emotions, religious beliefs and family rituals, internal and external family resources and support, and the point in the family's developmental cycle at which the death occurs.

Death as a family crisis produces a painful, unstable state followed by decisive change. Two major tasks for the family are (1) to share acknowledgment of the death and (2) to reorganize and reinvest in other relationships and life pursuits.

Conflict can occur before the death, at the time of death, and in the period of bereavement that follows. While increased contact with death brings strength to the family, conflict can occur about such issues as who will care for the one who is ill, how the tasks will be divided, how openly the diagnosis of the illness and prognosis are discussed, and what decisions are made about heroic measures and organ donation. At the time of death, conflict can occur for family members who were not present, not notified immediately, or not permitted to view the body before it was taken to the funeral home. Funeral decisions and activity can also cause stress, as family members delegate responsibilities, accept each other's coping styles, and deal with feelings and expectations about those who aren't present. As the family mourns the death, changes can occur in family relationships, bringing closeness or further strain. There can be varying impact with the distribution of possessions or heirlooms. There may be gaps in family functioning, conflict over role changes, and separation as contacts with family of origin subside and individuals become patriarchs and matriarchs of their own families.

Families can be assisted through support groups, family counseling with a therapist experienced in grief and loss, and current reading to provide information on the grief process and written exercises or activities that can be tools for healing.

REFERENCES

Angel, M. D. 1987. *The orphaned adult: Confronting the death of a parent*. New York: Human Sciences Press.

Brown, F. H. 1988. The impact of death and serious illness on the family life cycle. In *The changing family life cycle: A framework for family therapy*, 2d ed., edited by B. Carter and M. McGoldrick. New York: Gardner Press.

Carter, B., and M. McGoldrick. 1988. Overview: The changing family life cycle—A framework for family therapy. In *The changing family life cycle: A framework for family therapy*, 2d ed., edited by B. Carter and M. McGoldrick. New York: Gardner Press.

Curran, D. 1983. *Traits of a healthy family*. Minneapolis: Winston.

Goldenberg, I., and H. Goldenberg. 1985. *Family therapy: An overview*, 2nd ed. Pacific Grove, Calif.: Brooks/Cole.

James, J., and F. Cherry. 1988. *The grief recovery handbook: A step-by-step program for moving beyond loss*. New York: Harper and Row.

Kissane, D. W., and S. Bloch. 1994. Family grief. *British Journal of Psychiatry* 164, no. 6:728–40.

McClowry, S. G., E. B. Davies, K. A. May, E. J. Kulenkamp, and I. M. Martinson. 1987. The empty space phenomenon: The process of grief in the bereaved family. *Death Studies* 11:361–74.

McGoldrick M., and R. Gerson. 1988. Genograms and the family life cycle. In *The changing family life cycle: A framework for family therapy*, 2d ed., edited by B. Carter and M. McGoldrick. New York: Gardner Press.

McGoldrick, M., R. Almeida, P. Hines, E. Rosen, N. Garcia-Preto, and E. Lee. 1991. Mourning in different cultures. In *Living beyond loss: Death in the family*, edited by F. Walsh and M. McGoldrick. New York: Norton.

Michael, S. 1994. Counseling the AIDS bereaved family: Awareness of complicated grief and ethical concerns. *Michigan Journal of Counseling and Development* 23:17–20.

Myers, E. 1986. *When parents die*. New York: Penguin.

Rando, T. A. 1984. *Grief, dying and death: Clinical interventions for caregivers*. Champaign, Ill.: Research Press.

Staudacher, C. 1991. *Men and grief: A guide for men surviving the death of a loved one, a resource for caregivers and mental health professionals.* Oakland, Calif.: New Harbinger.

Visher, E., and J. Visher. 1982. *How to win as a stepfamily,* 2d ed. New York: Brunner/Mazel.

Walsh, F., and M. McGoldrick. 1991. Loss in the family: A systemic perspective. In *Living beyond loss: Death in the family,* edited by F. Walsh and M. McGoldrick. New York: Norton.

Wolfelt, A. D. 1992. *Understanding grief: Helping yourself heal.* Muncie, Ind.: Accelerated Development.

Worden, J. W. 1991. *Grief counseling and grief therapy: A handbook for the mental health practitioner.* New York: Springer.

16

CHILDREN: MAKING SENSE OF SEPARATION AND LOSS

John D. Canine

CHAPTER OUTLINE

The word "dead" is never any harder to say than when an adult is speaking it to a child. Adults think that children will not understand death, or that it will be too great an emotional burden for them. On the contrary, as discussed in Chapter 3, death education is important at every developmental level and age. Why? Because, from the time of birth on, death is a part of the child's life. It may be the death of a family member, a pet, a friend, or a schoolteacher. It may be death on a television show, in a nursery rhyme, or in a comic book. It may simply be a question the child asks about a funeral procession ("Look, Mommy, at all those cars. Is it a parade?"). A child is never too young to learn about death, and learning about death will enable the child to better understand grief. The purpose of this chapter is to discuss how children (from birth to adolescence) can comprehend the enormous emotional confusion that death can bring, and how the death care professional can assist them.

TEN THINGS TO TELL A CHILD ABOUT THE DEATH OF A LOVED ONE

Tell the Child as Soon as Possible About the Death

It is important to start with what the child knows. For example, if a grandfather had been going to the hospital for chemotherapy treatments, then one might begin a conversation with the child by saying, "Do you remember all those trips Grandfather made to the hospital?" When appropriate, it is also important to touch the child. This gives the child a sense of security. In his article "Death Education from the Beginning" (1979), Robert Slater shares an interesting story:

> Dr. B. J. Kennedy, the Chief Oncologist at the University of Minnesota Hospital, . . . was asked by a sophomore medical student how old a child should be before the child was told that he/she had a life-threatening illness. . . . Dr. Kennedy was not stymied for a second by the question from the medical student. He said, "It is impossible for me to tell because any child who has cancer and has a limited life span is sitting in my lap when I tell the parents. (P. 7)

Finally, when telling the child about the death, one should be gentle and trustful, and should choose a place that is comfortable, safe, and familiar.

Be Truthful

A child can sense dishonesty. Do not make up stories that will have to be changed later. This only confuses the child and promotes emotional instability. Also, withholding information can be a threat to the child. Emphasis needs to be placed on the facts, for example, "dead is dead" and "buried" means "in the ground." Even if the loved one was cremated, or died by an act of suicide or homicide, it should be explained to the child as clearly as possible. Euphemisms such as "passed away," "expired," or "departed" should be avoided because they are less than honest.

Share Only the Details the Child Is Ready to Hear

Children will actualize a crisis much like an adult. Therefore, to make it real in their mind, they need a logical explanation of why the person died. However, they may not be ready emotionally or cognitively to accept all the facts surrounding the death. For example, if an older brother dies in a car accident in which he is decapitated, the child certainly needs to know about the accident and possibly see the car. However, the details about the decapitation should not be shared with the child until she is able to understand it. It has been my clinical experience to have children mentally reprocess the information about the death of a loved one at each developmental level. It is not uncommon for a child in later life to ask a parent, "Tell me again how my brother died." This provides the adult with the opportunity to deliver information that was previously not shared. As discussed earlier, truthfulness is very important, but it should be balanced with the child's readiness for the details.

Encourage the Child to Express Feelings

A child will experience stages of grief very similar to those of adults. However, the child relies upon the adult for permission to "feel" the loss during each stage. The best way for a child to learn how to identify, own, and express feelings is to hear and watch an adult do so. For the first few years children get their understanding of grief through their senses, not through their intellects (Ilg and Ames 1955), so it is important for adults to "feel" their grief in the presence of the child. Cry together, get angry together, be sad together, and, most importantly, don't be afraid to hold each other.

Take the Child to the Funeral

Seeing is believing, and even young children should be able to view the body. The following are some thoughts about taking a child to the funeral:

- The child does not have to be present during all of the visitation hours.
- If the casket is on a bier, the child may have to be lifted up to see the body.
- The child should have the security of having an adult present at all times.
- The child should be allowed to touch the body but should not be forced to do so.
- The child should not be allowed to "roam" the funeral home.
- The child should be allowed to participate in the rituals for the purpose of expressing grief and recalling the event in later life.
- The child should be able to observe those who are mourning.

Take the Child to the Cemetery, Even If the Person Is Already Buried

The child will find some degree of comfort in knowing where the body is buried and how to get there. Like adults, children need to direct their grief feelings toward the appropriate object. Doing so lessens the child's emotional disorganization. In many cases this will be the person who died. The grave site can be where the child makes "contact" with the loved one. Furthermore, periodically taking the child to the cemetery lessens the chances of the child denying or avoiding the death.

Let the Child Tell Others about the Death

Often when children are accompanied by an adult and the child is questioned about how the loved one died, the adult will respond and "talk over" the child. This creates anxiety in the child. The child feels more in control and has greater understanding of the loss when he or she can explain it to another person. Adults should be silent and let the child speak.

Encourage the Child to Talk about the Loss

When a child talks about the death, not only are feelings generally expressed, but if the child has incorrect ideas about any aspect of the loss, it can be brought to the attention of the adult and corrected. The following case illustrates this point:

CASE STUDY #1

Bobby was ten years old and was brought by his mother to a counselor after his father's sudden death. Mother did not think Bobby was talking enough about his father. The counselor asked Bobby how his father died. Bobby's response was, "He ate too much ham." The counselor was momentarily stunned by the answer but proceeded to inquire as to what Bobby meant by "too much ham." It seems as though Bobby's father had "gorged" himself at dinner. Moving away from the table, he started to complain about feeling "stuffed," and confessed that he should have "stopped eating the ham." Later in the evening he had pains in his chest and trouble breathing. He still complained about eating too much ham. Shortly after Bobby went to bed, his father had a heart attack and died. However, no one told Bobby what *really* caused his father's death. The counselor asked the mother to go to the library and get a book about the heart. Together, mother and son read a medical explanation of what happened to Bobby's father. The next week Bobby explained to his counselor that his father had cardiac arrested—he had died of heart failure. If the counselor had not asked how Bobby's father died, Bobby's misconception that his father's death was caused by eating too much ham might not have been discovered. However, because Bobby was encouraged to talk about his loss, the error in his thinking about the death of his father was corrected.

Be Available to Answer the Child's Questions

If the child is encouraged to talk about the loss, tell stories about the one who has died, and remember happy and unhappy times together, then there will be questions. The questions may focus on life, death, spiritual values, relationship, and so on. The child may simply want to know why the loved one had to die. Regardless, adults need to answer each question as sincerely and accurately as possible (Costa and Holliday 1994), and with the understanding that some questions cannot be answered. To do this, the adult needs to spend time with the child. What is important is not so much the ability to answer each and every question but being available to discuss each concern as it arises.

Never Say "You Shouldn't Feel Like That"

The child should be encouraged to express anger, sorrow, loneliness, fear—any feeling the child has should be accepted. If the child is told "not to feel" by the adult, the message the child receives is one of coping with loss by emotionally "playing dead." This type of repression potentially creates interpersonal conflict in later life due to the child's inability to communicate emotions.

STAGES OF GRIEF FOR CHILDREN

Every child's grief is unique to his or her circumstances and situation. However, some grief responses can be considered "norms." As in adults, these normal responses can be defined as stages. As Claudia Jewett (1982) says, "Though there may be overlapping, skipping around, or returns to previous stages, each phase has a number of components that follow in a somewhat predictable order" (p. 22).

Shock

The child's first reaction to death is generally a lack of sensation. It is like watching an event that is happening to someone else. This numbness can lead to withdrawal. Observers of the child may notice little physical activity, loneliness, sadness, and a "flat" facial expression, lasting for a few hours to a few days. As the reality of the loss begins to register, the child may alternate between crying/sadness and anger/irritability. During this stage it is not uncommon for the child to "protest" the loss. For example, the child may say to the surviving parent, "Daddy did not die," or "Daddy is at work." Nevertheless, the painful experience of grief has begun, and child's ability to move through the process will determine the outcome.

Alarm

Children look to adults for safety and security. When someone close to them dies, their world becomes less safe. This feeling is intensified after the death of a parent. However, feelings of vulnerability, separation anxiety, depression, and immobilization are characteristic of most childhood losses (Vida and Grizenko 1989). Furthermore, many children experience bodily tension, sweating, dryness of mouth, shortness of breath, bowel and bladder relaxation, and physical exhaustion when discussing the death. Insomnia is common in the alarm stage (Koocher 1983).

When your trust in the world is shaken, it is difficult to let your defenses down and sleep. John Bowlby, in his book *Attachment and Loss* (1980), reported that following a loss many children experienced acute night terrors, a desire to sleep with a parent or sibling at night, and a fear of the dark.

Disbelief

Have you ever seen a child in a threatening situation close her eyes? Or, when a small child is greeted for the first time by a very "large" adult, have you noticed he may put his hands over his eyes and pretend the person is not there? Disbelief is a conscious or unconscious defense the child uses to avoid, prevent, or reduce anxiety. It is akin to denial. The child uses disbelief to reject the reality of the loss. In some cases the child tries to "forget," which enables an exclusion of feelings that rightfully go with the loss. Also, some magical thinking goes with disbelief, such as "Mommy did not die, she will come to my bedroom tonight and tuck me in," or "This cannot really be happening, because if it were I would feel bad, and I don't so it's not really happening." It should also be noted that occasionally children will use disbelief at some time during the grief process to allow for a reprieve from the pain and work of mourning.

Yearning

CASE STUDY #2

Randy was soon to be sixteen years old. He and his father had been looking at cars to buy for his birthday. It was a good time for both of them. However, shortly before Randy's special day his father was killed in a snowmobile accident. For months Randy could not even think of buying a car. Finally, he started to look again. He found a car he liked, purchased it, and immediately drove to the cemetery. He later told his counselor that he drove his car right on top of his father's grave and said, "Well Dad, I got the car I wanted. What do you think of it? I wish you were here." He and his counselor both cried.

This story illustrates the intense longing a child has for the dead loved one to return. Even though Randy was older, it is normal for all children to yearn, wish, and hope that the loss will "go away" and that the one who has "left" will come back. The conflict between letting go of that which has been lost and the wish to hold on to it can have a positive effect on the child. It is the process of working through ambivalence that enables the child to identify conflicting impulses, practically learn to live without the one who has died, and eventually understand the reality of the separation. Sometimes, however, a child will temporarily give up a skill that was mastered earlier in the developmental process because of intense yearning. This return to the behavior of an earlier age is called regression. A younger child may begin again to wet the bed, suck a thumb, or cry for a bottle. An older child may want to sit on Mother's lap or cling to Daddy (Van Eerdewegh 1982). The child's regressive behavior should not be a cause for panic. It should be a signal to the adult that the child needs some special attention in working through the grief process.

Searching

Searching for something that is lost seems reasonable enough. The tongue explores the place where the tooth has been lost. And, of course, one will go back to the same spot to look over and over again for an item that has been lost. Searching for someone who has died seems compulsive and irrational, yet we all do it, especially children. Psychologist Claudia Jewett (1982) says the following are the three basic elements to this stage:

1. Preoccupied and intense thought about the lost person, involving a compulsion to speak of him, to review a lifetime of memories about him, and to ignore anything not relevant to his presence.
2. A sense of waiting for something to happen and a direction of attention to places where the person is likely to be found.
3. Restless, sometimes aimless moving around with an inability to sit still, and constant searching for something to do, a scanning of the environment.

As in adults, the searching stage for the child can last for months. The effort to find the lost loved one and restore the bond may wane when the child is not successful (Silverman, Nickman, and Worden 1992). However, as Bowlby (1980) discovered, "Evidence shows that, at perhaps increasingly long intervals, the effort to restore the bond is renewed; the pangs of grief and perhaps an urge to search are then experienced afresh. This means . . . attachment behavior is remaining constantly primed and that, in conditions still to be defined, it becomes activated anew" (p. 42). This stage will end when the child realizes that all attempts to restore the lost relationship with the one who has died are unsuccessful. Only then will the child relinquish the searching behavior and begin to explore and form new relationships.

Disorganization

Grief is hard work. To try and understand emotions like sadness, guilt, shame, and anger is extremely demanding on the child. Grief takes energy. Sometimes the child cannot keep up. Hence, the child's life becomes disorganized in social activities, domestic responsibilities, and schoolwork. Observers of the child may see him or her walking around aimlessly, withdrawn, daydreaming, unable to complete simple tasks or follow directions, ignoring school assignments, and fighting with friends. It is a matter of focus, and the child is focused on the enormous pain of separation and loss. There is very little energy left for anything else.

Resolution

The quality of "being determined" or the ability "to persevere" is resolution. This is the child at the end of the grief process. A whole, healthy person emerges from grief ready to live and enjoy life again. The child is no longer preoccupied with the loss. There is decreased anger and irritability. There is a return to stable eating and sleeping patterns. There is an ability, once again, to focus on schoolwork and other responsibilities. The child has greater understanding of death and its finality. And, most importantly, he or she is able to freely love again.

These stages of grief are not given for the purpose of defining a timetable with specific points of when a child should be "better" or eventually "over" grief. They are given to better assist the death care professional in understanding the grief process a child goes through. They should be used by adults who allow and encourage children to move toward their grief, not away from it, keeping in mind, that our best gift to our children is ourselves, with the assurance that life will go on. As Earl Grollman (1970) writes:

> The most important gift you can give your children at this time is the feeling that life continues despite pain. Death, "the loss of innocence," can either lead you to the edge of the abyss and threaten your existence with meaninglessness and futility; or you will start to build the bridge that spans the chasm with things of life that still count—memory, family, friendship, love. When you have sorted out your own feelings, you will be better able to understand your troubled children who come to you laden with questions and beset with fears. (P. 71)

THE GRIEVING CHILD: DEATH CARE PROFESSIONAL INTERVENTIONS

In responding to the needs of a grieving child, the death care professional must provide acceptance, attention, sincerity, empathy, patience, and tolerance, while at the same time giving an appropriate response, and sometimes counsel, to the child's behavioral, physical, and emotional conflicts. If the child is given the opportunity to understand and cope effectively with the loss, it can be a valuable learning experience that will enhance personal growth and development. The death care professional "sets the stage" for this positive grief experience. In the next few pages, to better describe the interaction between the death care professional and the grieving child, we will give a child's grief response (CGR) with the appropriate death care professional response (DCPR).

CGR: The child is shocked and in disbelief. He says, "Mommy is not dead." "If I pretend this is not happening, then it won't." He is walking around in a daze, and it is difficult to communicate with him.

DCPR: It is important to keep the child connected to family and friends who will love him and support him. It is equally important to involve the child in every phase of the funeralization process. Encourage the child to view the body with the family and to take part in the funeral rituals. Also, accept the disbelief as a natural part of the grief process.

CGR: There is an outburst of emotion from the child. Caregiving adults are very upset because they have never seen the child act in this manner. The child says, "I am angry at Daddy for dying." "I hate the doctor for letting him die." "I will never go to the doctor again."

DCPR: The first thing to remember is that when a child has outbursts of emotion it is a sign that he feels the environment is safe. The fact that the child can act out what is being felt is a credit to the "listening" and "observing" adult. It is important not to punish the child or try to make him feel guilty about the outburst. The expression of feelings during the outburst is healthy, and the adult should work at accepting all feelings while not judging them good or bad. If anger and the associated feelings are not expressed and are turned inward by the child, then depression and withdrawal may occur. At this point, the child may need professional help.

CGR: "I didn't like Mommy, I'm glad she is gone." "I wish I could have given Mommy a hug and kiss at the hospital. That would have made her better." "Mommy didn't love me, that is why she died." These are statements of self-blame and guilt. Children are egocentric. They believe the world revolves around them. Therefore, they believe they can make something happen, sometimes just by thinking it will happen. When it does not, they feel guilty and blame themselves.

DCPR: The child needs to understand that all of us have wished our parents would go away at some time or another. This is a natural feeling. The child should be encouraged to talk about the loved one in a realistic manner, remembering both the good and the bad times. The adult should stress that conflict between two people is normal, and that being angry or upset with someone does not make the person die. The child should also be helped to understand there are many things in life over which we have no control. Finally, the adult needs to reinforce that the child is lovable and very important to others, and that she has herself with a full life ahead to do the things she wants to do.

CGR: "I'm sad today, I don't want to play." "Leave me alone." "If Daddy died and left me, what if Mommy dies? Where will I be?" These are statements of sadness, loneliness, and fear. It is understandable why the child is sad—she misses the loved one. If the person who died had a lot of interaction with the child, there will be feelings of emptiness and loneliness. And of course, if *Daddy* can die, anyone can die and leave the child. This fear may be rooted in the child sensing her own mortality.

Figure 16–1. Five feeling faces.

DCPR: Adults must be sensitive to the many different feelings a child has during the grief process. Accepting the feelings is accepting the child. The child may have trouble expressing intense grief feelings. Adults can help by encouraging the child to draw, write, and play. To simply sit down and talk about the "Five Feeling Faces" (see Figure 16–1) can be of great benefit to the child (Jewett 1982).

It is important to remember that the child is very sensitive to rejection during the grief process. If the adult is struggling with personal grief feelings and finding it difficult to assist the child, it will be noticeable and can potentially cause more emotional confusion for everyone. On the other hand, when the adult is honest about personal feelings and can still provide an atmosphere of warmth, acceptance, and understanding, it benefits all concerned.

CGR: Occasionally, after a long illness, children have a sense of relief that the loved one died. It is not uncommon that individuals will pray that a family member or friend will "die soon and peacefully." When that happens, there is a sense of relief and sometimes satisfaction. If a child is not permitted to express feelings of relief, or later becomes confused about the feeling, it can create an emotional struggle between guilt and peace of mind.

DCPR: This is the time for the adult to understand and utilize the child's (family) value system. For example, if the family believes in God and heaven, then the child can be helped to understand that the loved one is safe with God and has no more pain in heaven. Hence, the child's feelings of relief are appropriate and do not imply a lack of love for the one who died. However, a word of caution: no matter what the family values are, feelings of relief are normal, so the child should never be made to feel guilty. And, if the adult uses the family values, staying within the parameters is of utmost importance.

CGR: "Mommy, since Daddy died, I'm scared. Can I sleep with you?" "Daddy, I'll be home early from school tonight so I can fix you dinner and clean the house." These statements represent two extreme types of behavior. A child sleeping with a parent is usually regressive behavior, and a child who wants to care for the surviving parent is assuming the role of the dead adult. The former finds safety and security in returning to a former developmental level. The latter gives up childhood to rush ahead to adulthood. Although both behaviors are normal during a child's bereavement period, they need to be addressed by an adult.

DCPR: Any regressive behaviors manifested by the child should not be repressed, but rather understood, and an effort should be made by the adult to reduce the contributing factors. After the death of the father, if the child wants to sleep with her mother, the chances are good that she is afraid. The adult should understand the fear and take measures to lessen it (e.g., keeping a light on all night in the child's room). Any "adultlike" behaviors manifested by the child should be discouraged. The child should be directed toward childhood activities and encouraged to enjoy them. Every effort should be made to show the child that in time loved ones will be cared for as well as they were before the mother's death (e.g., the father hires a cleaning company to clean the house once a week).

In conclusion, Alan Wolfelt (1983) has given some general suggestions concerning children and grief. They are as follows:

1. *Be a good observer*. Receptively attend to a child's behavior by maintaining eye contact and a responsive posture. Usually more growth occurs in exploring questions than attempting to provide quick answers.

2. *Respond in an empathetic manner.* Make your baseline helping response the reciprocal empathetic understanding, acknowledging the explicitly expressed feelings of the child and reasons or experience behind them.

3. *Allow the child to express feelings and thoughts.* Do not attempt to "over understand" the child, particularly in fields related to psychological data. It is better to allow the child to communicate depth of understanding to you, rather than attempting to "diagnose" what the child is thinking and feeling.

4. *Respond to the child in language that he/she can understand.* Be simple and direct. Begin at the child's level and remember that attitude is more important than words. What is said is not as important as the emotional meaning communicated to the child.

5. *Respond to the impact of events on the child (internal frame of reference) rather than to external facts only.* Remember—reality is for the child the world as he/she perceives it.

6. *Respond in a voice, tone, and intensity that reflect the affect expressed by the child.*

7. *Develop your skill in recognizing and responding to minimal cues of the child.* Check out the accuracy of your understanding with the child, but in such a way that the child can modify or change your perceptions in the reaction. If you are aware that the child is experiencing feelings, even though your awareness is from the child's nonverbal behavior, feed this back to the child in a supportive, non-threatening permissive manner.

8. *Express your own feelings that are natural to the situation.* This will provide the child with a basis for expressing feelings.

9. *Accept the child's questions.* Do not try to attach adult meanings to the child's questions. Usually the child's questions are quite simple and factual.

10. *Be patient and available.* Do not expect a child's reaction to the experience of death to be obvious and immediate.

11. *Provide reassurance through action as well as words.* Remember—the child is part of the family. Reassurance comes from the presence of loving people. Children feel secure in the care of gentle arms and loving tenderness.

12. *Learn to tolerate and feel at ease during reasonable periods of productive silence.* Generally speaking, acceptance, reflection, and silence often result in increased understanding. Oftentimes the child needs permission to talk at his/her own pace, not to be talked to.

13. *Maintain a continuing dialogue with children about death as the opportunity arises* (i.e., death of a pet, news events). Do not wait or plan for "one big tell-all."

14. *Create a healthy relationship between you and the child.* Recognize your helping-healing ambition and attempt to create a relationship with the child which is basically a healthy one.

15. *Select and adjust your procedures according to the child.* Remember—no one procedure or formula will fit all children, either at the time of a death experience or during the period that follows. (Pp. 89–90)

SUMMARY

Adults will not find it easy to discuss the subject of death with a child, especially the death of a family member or friend. However, there are ten things that a child needs to hear from an adult about the death of a loved one. They range from telling the child as soon as possible about the loss to never saying "you shouldn't feel like that." These ten items assist the child in understanding and coping with grief from the time of death on, and can offer the adult some guidance in the areas of how, when, and where to discuss the death.

Just like adults, children move through stages of grief. The stages identified in this chapter are shock, alarm, disbelief, yearning, searching, disorganization, and resolution.

Finally, the death care professional or adult needs to be aware of certain behaviors manifested by the child that require intervention. Many, but not all, of these behaviors are identified at the end of this chapter, with a suggested adult response.

REFERENCES

Bowlby, John. 1980. *Attachment and loss.* Vol. 3. New York: Basic Books.

Costa, L., and D. Holliday. 1994. Helping children cope with the death of a parent. *Elementary School Guidance and Counseling* 28 (February):206–13.

Grollman, Earl. 1970. *Talking about death: A dialogue between parent and child.* Boston: Beacon Press.

Ilg, Frances L., and Louise B. Ames. 1955. *Child behavior.* New York: Harper and Row.

Jewett, Claudia L. 1982. *Helping children cope with separation and loss.* Boston: Harvard Common Press.

Koocher, G. P. 1983. *Grief and loss in childhood.* In *Handbook of clinical child psychology,* edited by C. E. Walker and M. C. Roberts. New York: Wiley.

Silverman, P. R., S. Nickman, and W. Worden. 1992. Detachment revisited: The child's reconstruction of a dead parent. *American Orthopsychiatric Assoc., Inc.,* 62, no. 4:494–503.

Slater, Robert. 1979. Death education from the beginning. *Thanatos* 5, no. 1 (winter 1979):5–8.

Van Eerdewegh M. M., M. P. Bieri, R. H. Parilla, and P. O. Clayton. 1982. The bereaved child. *American Journal of Psychology* 140, 23–9.

Vida, S., and N. Grizenko. 1989. DSM-III-R and the phenomenology of childhood bereavement. *Canadian Journal of Psychology,* 34, 148–55.

Wolfelt, Alan. 1983. *Helping children cope with grief.* Muncie, Ind.: Accelerated Development.

17

A RESPONSE TO CONTEMPORARY FUNERAL PRACTICES

John D. Canine

Although it has been over thirty years since her book was released, Jessica Mitford's 1963 attack on the funeral industry, *The American Way of Death,* still has an impact on contemporary funeral practices. In the 1970s the Federal Trade Commission conducted an intense investigation into the funeral industry, which resulted in numerous changes (see Chapter 7). However, many Americans still complain about the traditional funerary rituals as well as the funeral director. This chapter is a response to Mitford's major criticisms, a look at alterations in funeral customs due to social change, and a positive statement about the future of the funeral service.

MITFORD'S CRITICISMS

According to Mitford (1963), "The most therapeutic funeral . . . [is] the one arranged under circumstances guaranteeing a maximum profit" (p. 91). Mitford seems to imply throughout her book that funeral directors place profit ahead of feelings. In fact, in her opinion, funeral directors live in a dreamworld: "The funeral men live very largely in a dream world of their own making" (p. 225), and are incapable of feeling for the people they serve. Mitford further comments: "You must start treating a child's funeral, from the time of death to the time of burial, as a golden opportunity for building good will and preserving sentiment without which we wouldn't have any industry at all" (p. 228). These are strong accusations from a long time ago. However, these complaints are as alive today in the public mind as they were thirty years ago.

The funeral process is a "rite" of separation and integration that requires the funeral director to be aware of the emotional and social needs of the family. In most cases the funeral director does see the funeral as much more than a commercial transaction. Many studies (Glick, Weiss, Parkes 1974; Binger 1969) have pointed out that a responsible funeral director plays a valuable role in the psychosocial reestablishment of the griever. As one family stated in the Binger report, "Experience with grief reactions makes them [funeral directors] skilled in offering solace to grieving families." More recently, studies on widows and widowers (Lieberman and Borman 1982) cited the "helpfulness" of funeral directors in getting through the initial stages of grief. And, again, it was parents who stated that funeral directors were "supportive" and "understanding" when their children died (Cook 1981, 1983).

A second criticism of funeral directors is that they take advantage of people when they are vulnerable. "Some undertakers take advantage of the grief-stricken for financial gain," (Mitford 1963, p. 265). Granted, funeral directors work with people who are emotionally unstable because of grief. And yes, this makes them vulnerable. However, there are many "vulnerable" situations in life (e.g., a patient whose physician offers the choice of biopsy to determine whether a growth is malignant). Funeral directors are professionals who specialize in funerary rituals, and they may be the only professionals who are criticized for performing the functions they are supposed to perform. Once the "vulnerable" patient makes the decision to have the biopsy, we are not critical of the physician for performing the surgery. As Fulton (1976) states:

> It is of interest here to mention that statistics suggest that people are prepared to pay for a wedding, on the average, twice what they pay for an average funeral, and this without benefit of "wedding insurance." We know of only one published statement condemning the uneconomical behavior of parents at this festive occasion and know of no charges publicly made of exploitation by the dress-making industry, catering industry or Brewers Association of America in connection with the wedding. (P. 171)

A third criticism by Mitford (1963) is that funeral directors do not understand the funeral needs (social norms and customs) of the communities they serve: "In their relations with the community as a whole, the funeral men carry on a sort of weird shadowboxing, frequently wildly off the mark" (pp. 239–40). On the contrary, funeral directors put forth a great effort in meeting the personal needs of each family they serve while, at the same time, trying to operate a business for profit. Let's not forget that within our American democratic, capitalistic system, every individual has the right to operate a legal business for profit. The greatest challenge for the contemporary funeral director may be to find harmony between meeting the funeral ritual needs of the diverse people being served and financially supporting a family. The inadequacies in funeral service are more a problem of our culture than of the funeral director. It is more likely that the funeral director has inherited a faulty death system. Philosophically, there is little unity among those who would try to define a purpose for American funeral practices. In the following, some of those definitions of funeral practices are given to illustrate the lack of unity.

Durkheim (1954) emphasized the role of ritualized behavior in promoting and maintaining social norms. To Durkheim, ceremony was a collective expression of sentiment, and he interpreted certain attitudes and rituals as "objectified sentiments." Malinowski (1954) viewed ceremonies associated with death as a part of the institution of religion that bestowed upon individual men and women the gift of mental integrity, a function he believed was also fulfilled with regard to the whole group. Mandelbaum (1959) examined death rites in five widely separated cultures and concluded that funeral customs serve "manifest" as well as "latent" functions. Manifest functions refer to those activities associated with mortuary rites that are most readily apparent, such as the disposal of the body, assistance to the bereaved, the public acknowledgment of the death, and assertions of the continued viability of the group. Mandelbaum argues that participation in the funeral ceremony, the procession, the partaking of food and other social exchanges, as well as the mourning and keening, all add to the sense of being a part of a larger social whole, just as the order of precedence in the conduct of the ceremony reminds one that there is structure and order in the social system. Finally, he regards the funeral as a "rite of passage." It not only marks the completion of a life and separation of the dead from the world but also reaffirms the belief in the immortal character of human existence.

Van Gennep (1961) assigned the greatest importance to the rituals associated with death because he found that funeral rites that had as their express purpose the incorporation of the deceased into the "world of the dead" were characteristically the most extensively elaborate. Fulton (1976) found that a majority of the American public surveyed was favorably disposed toward present-day funeral practices and the funeral director. The majority of respondents also viewed the funeral as providing a meaningful emotional experience for survivors. Moreover, more than half of the respondents viewed the funeral director as a professional person or as one who combined a professional service with a business function.

So, who is right? Is it Durkheim and his "objectified sentiments," Malinowski and the "institution of religion," Mendelbaum with his "manifest and latent" functions, van Gennep and his "world of the dead," or Fulton and his "meaningful emotional experience"? Based on our American culture, they all are right. It has been said that America's strength is in her diversity. Contemporary funerals in America are different things to different people (Fulton 1967). It is up to the funeral director to understand that diversity and to promote it through diverse funeral practices. From memorial societies to "drive-by viewings," the majority of funeral directors are doing their best to meet the needs of the people they serve.

Finally, Mitford (1963) was critical of the funeral industry for not educating the consumer about its merchandise and the funeral options available to them. She suggests a "go-between" counselor who can work with the funeral director and the family: "Experienced staff members could provide much needed advice to the bereaved and even serve as intermediary to the mortician" (p. 281). Of all her criticisms, this could have been the most reasonable and significant. However, in the last thirty years many changes have been made to help educate the general public about the funeral industry and its practices. A full disclosure of funeral goods and services as a part of the FTC's "funeral rule" has already been mentioned.

However, many funeral directors have gone a step further and, through their state associations, have published booklets explaining their practices. In Michigan, for example, the table of contents in a funeral information booklet offers such listings as "Things you should know," "Choices to be made," and "Visit the funeral home," as well as a glossary of terms and code of ethics. There is even a section on "how to file a complaint"! (Michigan Funeral Facts 1993). Very few industries have opened themselves up to the scrutiny of the American public like the funeral industry has in the past few years. Furthermore, the concept of preplanning a funeral (pre-need) permits a consumer to examine preferred funeral practices without the emotional unsettledness that grief brings. In this regard, Mitford was no "prophetess"; she wrote, "If funeral directors insist on soliciting pre-need funerals, they are in part prearranging the funeral of their profession" (p. 91). The fact is, pre-need for the funeral industry has been a way for funeral directors to do the following:

1. Educate the consumer
2. Protect against rising funeral expenses
3. Ensure the consumer's merchandise and service desires
4. Enhance the consumer's emotional and financial peace of mind when thinking about death
5. Ensure future business by connecting families to a particular funeral firm

One might say the future of the funeral industry is in pre-need. The funeral firms that expand their "market share" through programs like bereavement aftercare and pre-need (see Chapter 3) are the firms that will survive and grow into the next century.

ALTERATIONS TO FUNERAL CUSTOMS DUE TO SOCIAL CHANGE

As with any culture, the customs of American society change with the needs and demands of the population. The most radical changes occur when we push our limits or extend beyond our reach. Over time, people adjust their customs as they adapt to change, including those associated with funerary practices. Here is what social and industrial changes have meant to American funeral traditions.

Twentieth-century America has been an era of industrial and social revolution that has caused a prodigious break from the past, resulting in a transformation in the way we live and work. Technological advances, urbanization, social reorganization, and the secularization of society are the products of our modern age. The emotional mark of these events has left Americans with few strong personal attachments. Increased mobility, advances in medicine, and computerized technology have widened this emotional gap. As a result, social bonding has lost its status in American society. Thus, the need for a time, a place, and community sharing of grief has been replaced with the desire for a convenient, simple funeral visitation and service.

In the previous century, American life revolved around the extended family, where relatives, religion, and a sense of community fostered feelings of belonging and stability. Rituals and celebrations of important events were common, everyday occurrences: "Ritual provided cultural prescriptions for formal patterns of behavior to guide and sustain the individual during confusing and chaotic periods of transition" (Rando 1984, p. 176). However, mobility, an effect of the Industrial Revolution, interrupted this stability by taking people to new frontiers and offering the chance to expand one's horizons. Although mobility brought new, exciting opportunities, it also took families and friends away from each other. The lure of new adventures drove away the desire for interdependence. With families and friends living miles apart, people became less likely to spend time together following a death and share their grief. As technology developed, especially computerization, and new opportunities made themselves available, medical science made numerous advances culminating in additional changes to funerary customs. For example, medicines, surgical techniques, and fast response to medical emergencies have extended the lives of those with previously terminal illnesses. The lengthening of illness before death has allowed more occasions of anticipatory grief in which the survivor silently works through much of the grieving process in anticipation of the death. This has decreased the need for funeral services or arrangements of any kind. "If too much decathexis occurs prior to the death, the survivors may feel they have already said good-bye and do not require a funeral service" (Rando 1984, p. 176). When this happens, grieving individuals can be robbed of the social and community support they need to work through their loss.

Another impact on funerary practices has been legislative rulings for undertaking functions, such as embalming. These laws have diminished involvement of the family in funeral arrangements and rituals. The funeral director takes care of responsibilities and tasks associated with the death that the family used to fulfill, while the family and friends attend the viewing, the service, and, sometimes, the burial ceremony. Afterward, they dash off to their busy lives. This "get in, get out" syndrome seems to complete the bereavement obligation. Little time is taken to mourn the death or share the sorrow with others. Consequently, the lack of social bonding and interaction with funerary duties opens a wide door for denial and the rejection of bereavement rituals.

Since death has become a remote aspect of American life, the behaviors associated with bereavement have changed radically. In turn, the customs surrounding death have been adjusted to accommodate modern attitudes, and funerary practices have changed accordingly. In reaction to the alterations of funerary rituals, some have launched criticisms at funeral directors and their businesses. While some of these may be valid, funeral directors cannot be rebuked for adapting to social trends. "Moreover, doing away with funerals may result in a culture with even more juvenile death-denying ways, haunted by unresolved guilt, pent up anger and half-finished relationships" (Cassem 1976, p. 20).

The loss of socialization has prompted what Volkart (1957) called the "high vulnerability in bereavement." Decades ago, children and adults frequently gathered for bereavement rituals and events. The deaths of friends, neighbors, and extended family were observed with the same attention and shared togetherness as a birth. Before the industrialization of America, life and death were acknowledged and ritualized as one cycle in an integrated process. However, this perspective no longer exists. In contemporary society, even communications have advanced so far that there is little occasion for people to gather together. However, without social bonding, an individual's need for emotional connection is unfulfilled. No matter what a person's age, this missing link is tantamount to an impairment in one's emotional development. Thus, many Americans are unprepared for the death of a loved one. Bereavement is intensified because people lack the emotional skills to cope with such a loss.

To say that the funeral industry offers little substance and value to society is to negate the significance of human need for social and emotional support following the death of a loved one. Without the traditional rituals to help people work through their anger, hostility, guilt, and anxiety, people tend to seek out unhealthy ways of expressing these pent-up emotions such as psychosomatic illness or violent acts toward others (Fulton 1976). Hence, death care professionals who offer assistance to the bereaved in developing meaningful rituals that will help them work through the grief process are essential to the health and lifeblood of our communities.

A POSITIVE STATEMENT ABOUT THE FUTURE OF FUNERAL PRACTICES

Despite all the criticism of funerary practices, funerals are here to stay. The form, structure, and function of the American funeral may be modified in the future, but the rite of passage is necessary after the death of a loved one. As Rando (1984) states, "The passing of that person must be recognized, his survivors must be supported as they start a new life without him, and they must be reintegrated into the community, which itself must reaffirm its continuity after the loss of a member" (p. 190). The future of the funeral in our American culture is rooted in its ability to provide diverse settings in which both private sorrow and public loss can be expressed and shared. It is not only a vehicle by which society can state a death has occurred but also one that proclaims that a life has been lived. However, funerals require direction, and in the future, as at no other time in the history of the American way of death, funeral directors will give meaning to the rite of passage. The funeral director will not only design the "business" of funerals (i.e., market-driven product and program development, value versus price, and creative expansion of market share) but will orchestrate the funeral to "catalyze acute grief responses, prescribe structured behaviors in a time of flux, and encourage recognition of the loss and development of new relationships with both the deceased and the community" (Rando 1984, p. 190). In the future, the funeral director will have to wear many different hats to provide a "full-service" program of funeral practices to the people being served.

The following are some categories of funeral service that the reader can use as a checklist to validate knowledge in each area.

Business

1. Understanding the history of American birth rate from 1909 to 1993 (see Figure 17–1).
2. Understanding the American death rate, actual from 1909 to 1993 and projected to the year 2033 (see Figure 17–2).
3. Adjusting to regulatory pressures (FTC and state law).
   - Embalming
   - Autopsies
   - Cremations
   - Pricing of merchandise (caskets or containers)
   - Cemetery requirements
   - Pricing of services
4. Death away from home or overseas (i.e., transporting the body).
5. Means of disposition (e.g., burial, entombment, scattering of ashes).
6. Body or body parts donation.
7. Insurance-funded funeral plans (pre-need).

Death Education

1. Association for Death Education and Counseling (ADEC). This association welcomes funeral directors.
2. A library of death education books, journals, and literature. These resources should be in the funeral home and accessible to the general public.

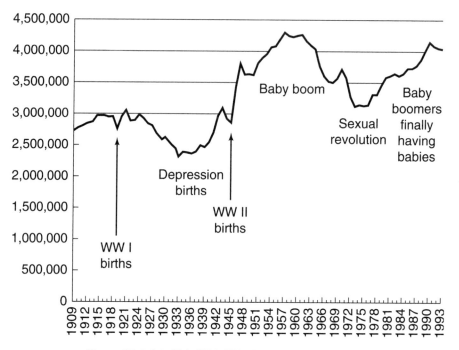

Figure 17–1. Actual births (1909–1993). (United Family, a Fortis company)

3. Death education for children. A death education service should be available to children through speakers, films in schools, and "tours" of a funeral home.
4. A knowledge of the dying process (see Chapter 4).
5. An understanding of the hospice movement.
6. An understanding of contemporary death and dying issues (e.g., Alzheimer's disease and AIDS).
7. A knowledge of current laws, or lack of, regarding "right-to-die" issues.

Bereavement

1. An understanding of the grieving process for adults and children.
2. An understanding of the different bereavement situations (death of a child, spouse, son, etc.).
3. An understanding of the factors affecting the grief process (sudden, premature, violent death).
4. A willingness to offer some type of bereavement aftercare follow-up for the families served (support group, counseling, seminars, literature, etc.).

Death Ceremony

1. Funeral service.
2. Memorial service.

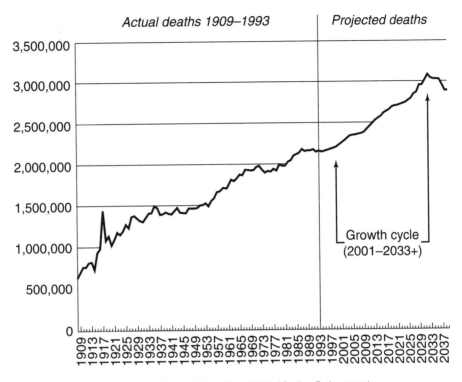

Figure 17–2. So . . . . what's our future? (United Family, a Fortis company)

3. Committal service.
4. Rituals—Whatever rituals are adopted, the important issue is that they be personally meaningful to the bereaved.
5. Memorial societies—These are cooperative, nonprofit consumer organizations, democratically run, that help members secure dignity, simplicity, and economy in funeral arrangements through advance planning. Although they are not run by funeral directors, their purpose needs to be clearly understood.

Certainly the role of the funeral director in the American funeral service is an emergent one. Yet it is not without great responsibility. The funeral director of the past may have been passive, with "little indication that intellectual challenges are welcome" (Kastenbaum and Goldsmith 1963, p. 212), but that is not the funeral director of the future. A complete understanding of the social and legal aspects of funeral practices, a compassion for people and their therapeutic rituals, a willingness to engage in continuing education, a creative mind that will invent new ways to meet the needs of the people he or she serves, and a professional, businesslike approach to the industry are just a few characteristics of the future funeral director in America.

SUMMARY

Although Jessica Mitford's attack on the funeral industry was made over thirty years ago, it still has an impact on the contemporary role of the funeral professional. The attack has prompted this author to substantiate the positive and necessary role of the funeral industry in America. First of all, Mitford seems to imply throughout her book, *The American Way of Death* (1963), that funeral directors place profit ahead of feelings. Many studies, including those of Glick, Weiss, and Parkes (1974) and Binger (1969), have demonstrated that, in addition to sustaining his or her personal livelihood, a responsible funeral director plays a valuable role in the psychosocial reestablishment of the griever.

Other criticisms by Mitford claim that funeral directors take advantage of people when they are vulnerable and do not understand the funeral needs of the communities they serve. On the contrary, funeral directors put forth a great deal of effort in meeting the personal needs of each family they serve. This opinion is supported by many other researchers. Mitford also criticized the funeral industry for not educating the consumer about its merchandise and available funeral options. However, in the last thirty years many changes have been made to help educate the general public about the funeral industry and its practices.

Alterations to funeral customs are largely due to social change. In addition to new social mores resulting from industrialization in this country, legislative rulings for funerary functions such as embalming have been added to the law. In recent years the funeral industry has worked toward assisting the bereaved in planning the funeral as well as providing services that can address their emotional needs. Funeral directors who offer assistance to the bereaved in developing meaningful rituals and working through the grief process are vital to the life force of their communities.

REFERENCES

Binger, C. M., A. R. Ablin, R. C. Feuerstein, J. H. Kushner, S. Roger, C. Mikkelsen. 1969. Childhood leukemia: Emotional impact on patient and family. *New England Journal of Medicine* 280:414–18.

Cassem, N. H. 1976. The first three steps beyond the grave. In *Acute grief and the funeral,* edited by V. R. Pine, A. Kutscher, D. Peretz, R. Slater, R. DeBelis, R. Volk, and D. Cherico. Springfield, Ill.: Charles C. Thomas.

Cook, J. A. 1981. Children's funerals and their effect on familiar grief adjustment. *National Reporter* 4:1–2.

———. 1983. A death in the family: Parental breavement in the first year. *Suicide and Life-threatening Behavior* 13:42–61.

Durkheim, E. 1954. *The elementary forms of religious life,* trans. J. Swaine. London: Allen and Unwin.

Fulton, R. 1965. The clergyman and the funeral director: A study in role conflict. *Social Forces* 39:317–23.

————. 1967. On the dying death. In *Explaining death to children*, edited by E. Grollman. Boston: Beacon Press.

————. 1976. The sacred and secular: Attitudes of the American public toward death, funerals, and funeral directors. In *Death and identity*, rev. ed., edited by R. Fulton. Bowie, Md.: Charles Press.

Glick, I. O., R. S. Weiss, and C. M. Parkes. 1974. *The first year of bereavement*. New York: Wiley.

Kastenbaum, R., and C. E. Goldsmith. 1963. The funeral director and the meaning of death. *American Funeral Director*, April–June: 5–7.

Lieberman, M. A., and L. D. Borman. 1982. Widows view the helpfulness of the funeral service. *National Reporter* 5:2–4.

Malinowski, B. 1954. Death and the reintegration of the group. In *Magic, science, and religion and other essays*, edited by B. Malinowski. New York: Doubleday.

Mandelbaum, D. 1959. Social uses of funeral rites. In *The meaning of death*, edited by H. Feifel. New York: McGraw-Hill.

Michigan funeral facts. 1993. Booklet published by Michigan Funeral Directors Association, P.O. Box 27158, Lansing, MI 48909.

Mitford, J. 1963. *The American way of death*. New York: Simon and Schuster.

Rando, T. 1984. *Grief, dying and death*. Champaign, Ill.: Research Press.

van Gennep, A. 1961. *The rites of passage*, trans. M. B. Vizedom and G. L. Caffee. Chicago: University of Chicago Press.

Volkart, E. H. (with collaboration of S. T. Michael). 1957. Bereavement and mental health. In *Explorations in social psychiatry*, edited by A. Leghton, J. Clausen, and R. Wilson. New York: Basic Books.

Section III

BEREAVEMENT AFTERCARE: ISSUES FOR THE CLIENT AND THE DEATH CARE PROFESSIONAL

18

A RATIONALE
FOR A MULTIDISCIPLINARY
SUPPORT SYSTEM

Cindy Skalsky

INTRODUCTION TO SECTION III

Most people in this country have access to a 911 phone number for emergencies, as well as opportunities to learn first aid and CPR. Yet how convenient or widely available are classes to deal with the grief and loss experienced by the roughly eight million (through death alone) newly bereaved members of our society each year? It seems as if we have professionals trained and equipped to deal with everything—marriage counselors, substance abuse, childhood development, financial advisers—except the one area that touches us all: death and dying. There appears to be no general agreement on whose job this is.

The concepts of aftercare and grief counseling are relatively new and have become specialized fields of attention only in the past fifteen to twenty years as understanding and recognition of "normal" grief processes have been studied and written about. This section will attempt to establish a framework for examining the broad range of aftercare delivery mechanisms and the roles of various professionals within those systems.

Specifically, these final chapters will address models of bereavement aftercare, present counseling techniques for helping the bereaved, discuss the unique, contemporary issues facing death care professionals in the area of aftercare, and recommend coping strategies to reduce stress and prevent burnout among those who regularly deal with grieving people. This first chapter of Section III serves as an overview to the remainder of the book, introducing concepts and constructs that are discussed in more detail later. In addition, it offers suggested actions that professionals may take who wish to improve the death education and bereavement aftercare in their communities.

NEED FOR AFTERCARE

Dictionary definitions of "aftercare" offer a medical model, explaining the term as the treatment of a convalescent patient, such as would be utilized following surgery. While at first glance this implies the existence of an abnormal or pathological condition, upon reflection there is a valid metaphor: something has been "cut out" of a griever's life, and the griever most certainly *does* require special handling. Where the metaphor stops, of course, would be in the suggestion that grief itself is abnormal or pathological.

In the death and dying profession, "aftercare" is defined as any postdeath or postfuneral program of survivor rehabilitation designed to help the individual through the grief process and successfully readjust to his or her environment. Although the term "rehabilitation" continues to imply pathology, its purest meaning involves restoring or learning new habits that promote a useful and healthful life. Indeed, as we will see, the best aftercare programs utilize the research that has occurred over the last few decades and approach the common problems bereaved people face with a systematic appreciation of the difficult emotional struggles they face.

Sociological Factors

The need for grief aftercare is peculiar to twentieth-century Western culture. In preindustrial societies, higher death rates meant that many people died at what we would consider relatively young ages, interrupting their role in society. Their deaths took place within the circle of the family and the community, and Blauner (1966) suggests that death was viewed as a social process with an immediate effect on society.

With industrialization, death rates were lowered, resulting in death occurring largely among elderly adults who have completed their societal role. Indeed, Rubin (1990) offers that the impact of those deaths do not affect the society as a whole and are only minor footnotes in the cycle of societal events.

But we now live in a postindustrial society, and Morgan (1995) attributes the need for aftercare to the technological advances that have changed our "normal" experiences. Longer life expectancies, higher degrees of mobility and resulting familial separations, plus the "removal" of death to institutions all mean that we have "unlearned" the concept of death as a natural part of the life cycle:

> Today, at least 75% of persons die in hospitals. The consequence of this is that dying is now seen by fewer people than it was previously. We do not have the mass deaths that once were viewed on streets, and we do not have persons dying at home. . . .
> . . . [W]e scarcely even see the aged. Few of us live within 500 miles of our place of birth. Consequently, we and our children do not see the aging process taking place. . . . [T]he elderly live in senior homes or retirement villages where they are seen only by other elderly or professionals. Consequently, death seems not to be a gradual process but a telephone call in the night. . . . As a result we have no role models either for our own dying process or for expressing grief at the time of another's death. (P. 37)

The absence of familiarity with—let alone a cohesive structure for—experiencing the grief process leaves untold numbers of people in our society "at loose ends" with their painful feelings. While much more assistance to the bereaved is available today than even ten years ago, the supply of aftercare is nowhere near sufficient to meet the "demand."

John W. James and Frank Cherry, founders of the Grief Recovery Institute, an internationally respected educational and outreach program based in Los Angeles, comment on this situation in the introduction to their *Grief Recovery Handbook* (1988):

> No matter how hard or how long we worked, no matter how many professionals we trained, no matter how many support groups were started, it didn't seem that we were doing enough. The number of people still in pain years after a loss is staggering. . . . Our purpose [in publishing the handbook] was, first, to help individuals recover from their grief, and then, ultimately to change the way each of us re-

sponds to those suffering from loss. We published five thousand copies of the book ourselves [thinking] that five thousand would last us a long time—within eight weeks we were out of books. (P. XII)

While the recognition of the need for aftercare is known to many mental health professionals, funeral industry leaders, medical personnel, caregivers, volunteers, and even enlightened employers, there exists no standard "blueprint" for the organization and operation of aftercare services or intervention strategies in our society. The efforts, advances, and roles of these (and other) helping individuals will be looked at later in this chapter.

Psychological Factors

As discussed earlier, numerous, variable factors determine the psychological context of each individual's unique grief experience. In a very real way, our knowledge of the grief process and its "influencers" has outstripped our ability to provide customized or even adequate aftercare. For example, is it advisable to form a support group that includes grievers who have lost close loved ones when the circumstances range from long illness to murder to a plane crash? What is the best way to meet the needs of grieving children? How do we help "disenfranchised" grievers—those whose feelings aren't recognized by society—with their unique problems? These bereaved may include friends, coworkers, AIDS survivors, a partner in an illicit love affair, or people who deeply feel the loss of a dear neighbor, mentor, aunt, or parent "surrogate." What of grievers who are mourning different types of losses—a longtime job, divorce, a pet, childbearing functions, a limb?

While there are themes and threads that run universally through the grief process, it is important that aftercare advocates, providers, and helpers be sensitive to the significant psychological variations that may be at work among grieving populations. It is not by accident that organizations with both educational and support functions have grown up around particular grief circumstances.

We are already aware of Compassionate Friends (an aftercare organization for parents who have lost a young child), Mothers Against Drunk Driving, and the Widowed Person's Service of the American Association of Retired Persons (AARP). By way of further examples, there are groups that specifically help parents whose babies died from sudden infant death syndrome (SIDS), as well as groups for survivors of violent death (including suicide). And in today's world, it is not surprising to learn that families of victims of natural disasters (hurricanes, fires, floods) or other forms of tragedy (such as terrorism) form self-help groups on their own to target and cope with the unique psychological impact such deaths leave in their wake. Collectively, these groups recognize intellectually and/or intuitively that they face special needs regarding the psychological factors of timeliness, preventability, fulfillment of the deceased's life, context of the death, and secondary losses. It is simply a fact that most communities are not presently equipped to serve even the range of contingencies mentioned here, and that, to a great extent, the bereaved themselves have perhaps been the most impressive pioneers in efforts to identify and meet their own needs.

PURPOSE OF AFTERCARE

This text has presented various models of grief characteristics, stages of grief, and tasks of grief work. Regardless of which models are preferred, the goal of any aftercare program is to facilitate the process through reassurance, education, permission to express thoughts and feelings, and social support within a nonjudgmental framework.

Before examining methods by which this goal can be achieved, it is important to first make the distinction between grief *counseling* and grief *therapy*. No one has clarified this issue better than Worden (1984), who summarized the differences in an article for the newsletter of the Association for Death Education and Counseling (ADEC):

> Grief counseling involves those interventions which help persons experiencing normal grief to deal with the tasks of mourning in order to complete these within a reasonable time frame. The focus is on recent loss, within the past year or so, and on normal grief . . . which is uncomplicated and which moves toward satisfactory completion.
>
> Grief therapy, on the other hand, has a different goal and focus. In grief therapy the goal is to help identify and resolve the conflicts of separation which *preclude* the completion of mourning tasks in persons whose grief is either absent, excessive, delayed, or prolonged. These aberrations of the grief process are what the Diagnostic Manual of the American Psychiatric Association categorizes as "complicated bereavement." (Pp. 1–2)

Worden (1984) determines that it is not so much who does the intervention or where it is done that is important, but the focus and goals of the treatment. What is also critical is that both counselors and therapists (whether volunteers or professionals) have grieved and resolved their own losses and are aware of their own competencies and limitations. Counselors and therapists need to have "the grace to refer a client who is grieving a loss with which [they] have difficulty dealing" (pp. 1–2).

Requirements of a Bereavement Program

Perhaps the "square-one" question should be answered first: Does intervention really help grievers?

In a study that followed 194 widows for thirteen months, Raphael (1977) conducted extensive initial interviews, assessing various psychological factors, and grouped the widows into two categories: those whose grief outcome was predicted to be "good," and those whose outcome was predicted to be "bad."

Those with favorable predictions received no counseling, and at the end of the study 80 percent indeed showed a good outcome. Of the widows predicted to have unfavorable grief outcomes, half were given regular counseling and half were not. At the end of thirteen months, those who received counseling were twice as likely to have achieved a "good" outcome as those who received no counseling.

As reported by Bowlby (1980):

> Widows in the counselled group showed a lower incidence of depression, anxiety, excessive alcohol intake and certain psychosomatic symptoms than did widows in the non-counselled group. The conclusion that counselling is in some degree effective is strongly supported by internal evidence derived from a detailed study . . . [in which] it was found that those who made best use of the counselling sessions had a significantly better outcome than those of the group who did not. (P. 198)

Because we have "unlearned" that death is a natural part of the life cycle, it becomes necessary to "unlearn" the responses to it we have been taught by our parents or by society. All the information now available clearly shows that burying feelings, keeping busy, expecting "time" by itself to create healing, or rushing to "replace" a loss will not promote authentic recovery from pain and permit a healthy foundation for life without the loved one.

Rando (1995) delineates seven steps to facilitate uncomplicated grief and mourning. They can serve as an excellent cornerstone for any *comprehensive* bereavement aftercare program:

1. Make contact and assess.
2. Maintain a therapeutic and realistic perspective.
3. Encourage expression of feelings and recollection of the deceased.
4. Help the mourner identify and work through secondary losses and unfinished business.
5. Support the mourner in coping with the mourning process.
6. Help the mourner accommodate to the loss.
7. Work with the mourner to reinvest in the new life.

In addition, an aftercare program must have the ability to identify complicated and/or pathological grief responses and offer appropriate treatment or referral to a professional competent in the area of abnormal grief responses. Comprehensive aftercare programs that meet all these requirements are rare in our society, but many programs exist that meet some or most of them.

The *Grief Recovery Handbook* (1988) developed by the Grief Recovery Institute (GRI) lays out five requirements for resolution of normal grief and guides readers through a program of activities and exercises that move them through the following "stages":

1. Gaining awareness that an incomplete emotional relationship exists
2. Accepting responsibility that in part you are the cause of its existence
3. Identifying recovery communications that you have not delivered

4. Taking actions to communicate them
5. Moving beyond loss through sharing with others

The GRI's recently developed companion workbook facilitates an individualized approach to grief recovery, presented in a commonsense, "plain-talk" style that dispels myths about death while offering comfort and practical advice to the user.

Although aftercare resources and services are "out there," often they are fragmented, inadequately publicized or coordinated, and may fall short of meeting the continuing needs of bereaved people as they work through the various stages of their grief. Furthermore, two factors affect the actual utilization of available assistance. First, the lack of general knowledge about the normalcy of grief and its symptoms may leave bereaved people feeling stigmatized and incapable of reaching out, and may inhibit loved ones from suggesting aftercare program participation; second, the bereaved may be too overwhelmed by or mired in grief to even recognize a need for these services. Until our societal attitudes and understanding of death and grief change on a widespread basis, it is incumbent upon those various professionals and "enlightened" caregivers to identify and reach out to bereaved people with information and encouragement to make use of appropriate aftercare opportunities.

Aftercare Opportunities

While the roles of various professionals and institutions in aftercare delivery will be covered more thoroughly in later chapters, it is logical here to give a brief description of the aftercare formats and media that are most available in communities today. These grief and bereavement "services" are not in any way mutually exclusive, and they may be offered by a variety of agencies—public, private, for-profit, not-for-profit, voluntary, or religion-based. Opportunity categories include

1. Print and video materials
2. Interpersonal activities
3. Individualized intervention

A wide range of helpful information is available to grieving people in the form of books, booklets, magazines, and videos. Published with "laymen" in mind, many current titles exist that discuss "good grief," living with loss, and warning signs that may indicate a need for professional assistance. Another category is books that take the form of a personal memoir or "diary" recounting the writer's specific, meaningful loss. These books may be extremely valuable to grievers who have suffered a similar or parallel loss.

Public libraries and bookstores are likely to offer at least a sampling of such books, and various denominational publishers may have a selection of titles that approach death and mourning from a particular spiritual point of view. These materials might be found in a church or synagogue library or a religious bookstore.

Thanatos is a quarterly journal that mixes a variety of articles (essays, educational pieces, poetry, recent research, book reviews) that address the emotional, psychological, and practical issues surrounding dying, death, and grief. In addition, there are publications aimed at people experiencing specific types of losses, for example, death of a spouse, parents suffering from stillbirths or neonatal deaths, and survivors of loved ones who died violently.

Educational filmmakers have also addressed the subjects of grief and bereavement with (typically) generic programs to help children and teenagers understand death and the grief process. Public libraries, school districts, and/or counseling organizations may have catalogs available for purchase or rental of these programs.

Interpersonal opportunities for aftercare might include workshops, lectures, grief support groups, telephone "hot lines," or even formal education in bereavement and its resolution. These platforms encompass a broad range of activities with varying formats and goals. A quick list of examples could include the following:

1. An afternoon or evening seminar on "Getting through the Holidays" following a death
2. Regular support group meetings for families and loved ones of AIDS-related deaths
3. A "drop-in" support group for the recently widowed, perhaps with an educational and social orientation
4. A "closed-end" (specified duration) series of professionally supervised meetings for teens who have lost a sibling or close friend
5. One-day seminars on "Understanding Loss" or "Coping with Grief"
6. A grief-facilitative class for adults using techniques of art and poetry therapy
7. A workshop on developing effective rituals to help heal grief
8. Employee assistance programs (EAP) on managing or working with bereaved employees
9. A concrete "coping skills" course for widowers with young children
10. A lecture on common legal and financial issues following a loved one's death
11. Crisis care teams or "task forces" of professionals and/or volunteers who assemble to help grievers in emergency situations
12. Supervised groups for young children to facilitate grief expression through "play" activities

Readers of this text should remember that any one, some, or all of these examples might be sponsored or "driven by" a funeral home, a hospital, a church, a community-based counseling organization, a hospice, a college or adult education program, or a freestanding bereavement center. Depending on the format and the audience, these activities may be conducted or led by a social worker, a psychologist, a member of the clergy, a medical professional, a bereavement educator, a trained volunteer, an academic expert, or "someone who's been there." There is almost no end to the creative, interpersonal opportunities that can be developed in communities when enlightened individuals and institutions come together to afford grieving people a place to meet, interact, talk, and learn from each other.

Individualized intervention can also take a number of forms, the most obvious of which is private sessions with an experienced psychologist or psychotherapist. Such attention is usually required in situations we have described as complicated bereavement, that is, the manifestion of excessive, delayed, prolonged, or absent grief. Not surprisingly, the "standards" by which these symptoms are defined are a source of constant discussion and debate among mental health (and related) professionals. Returning briefly to Rando's list of psychological factors influencing grief, we can speculate that other candidates for individualized intervention might include those who are experiencing additional stressors, such as concurrent or multiple loss.

As noted by Parkes (1972),

It should be emphasized . . . that care of the bereaved is a communal responsibility, and family members and others should not withdraw their support simply because a person has been referred to a psychiatrist. . . . [T]he powers of the psychiatrist are strictly limited and what [he or she] can do is not, in essence, different from what can be done by any sensitive empathic person. (P. 180)

There is also the personality factor to consider in individual intervention—the reality that some people are, by nature, "loners" and not comfortable in group settings. Some community bereavement programs, as well as churches and senior centers, offer what is known as "peer counseling." In general, these services provide one-on-one emotional support with a trained volunteer who has experienced a similar loss. The challenge, of course, is identifying individuals who might accept and benefit from such aftercare activity, since they are unlikely to seek or expect assistance with their grief. Outreach, then, becomes an especially important function of such aftercare operations.

Ancillary Resources

Very recently, a variety of services have appeared that afford dying people and bereaved people "nontraditional" opportunities to cope or find help with grief and its healing. GriefNet is a system on the Internet that lists resources and provides communications for professionals and bereaved persons dealing with dying, bereavement, and major loss in any way. It uses the systems known as gopher server and a web homepage, offering aftercare providers a bulletin board with listings of upcoming conferences, workshops, and seminars around the world as well as other useful Internet sites.

The Bereaved Persons Resource Center is GriefNet's giant "information house," with doors leading users to specific resources under a range of subjects including adoption loss, children's and adolescent resources, caregivers' resources, information on natural and human disasters, general bereavement resources, hospice information, chronic illness, widow and widower resources, among others.

Founder and editor Cendra Lynn of Ann Arbor, Michigan, reports that

GriefNet, launched in the spring of 1994, is accessed more than four thousand times a week from more than six hundred sites around the world.

DeathNet, the world's first website to specialize in end-of-life issues, was created by the Right to Die Society of Canada and the National Hemlock Society. It claims to offer the largest collection of right-to-die materials and services on the Internet.

Endeavors that may or may not prove popular with dying people and their loved ones are services to assist in creating "a remembrance archive"—a message or series of messages created by the dying person for grievers prior to death. Using video, audio, or print media, these messages, whether sentimental, philosophical, or personal, can be personalized and designated for delivery upon death, anniversaries, special occasions, or milestones in the survivors' lifes. Whether such activities, in general, promote comfort, support, closure, and healing is a matter for further study and debate.

ROLE OF DEATH CARE PROFESSIONALS

Depending on the circumstances of a death, families and loved ones may have contact with a variety of professionals whose attitudes, behavior, and interventions can influence the grief process. Typically, these professionals might nclude medical personnel, clergy, mental health professionals, hospice staff, and funeral service providers. Each group can offer unique assistance to grievers, in subtle or very direct ways.

Medical Personnel

The "problem" with physicians is that they are trained to regard death as an enemy to be conquered and the loss of a patient as failure. Physicians who regularly deal with terminal patients may, to protect their own emotional well-being, detach themselves from patients ("The transplant in Room 213 . . ."), or speak "about" them to family members as if they were not present. The effect is one of "killing" the patient socially before he or she has died. This can be extremely disturbing to both patients and their loved ones.

Nurses are more likely to be trained in the grief process and generally have more contact with patients and their families. Nurses can play an important part in allowing the terminally ill and family members to express their fears and concerns simply by listening and validating their feelings, and fully explaining what is being done for the patient. In the normal course of their duties, nurses may also become aware of situations within families that might benefit from contact with a hospital social worker or chaplain. Nurses should be familiar with hospital services in these areas and should feel empowered to make referrals.

It should be remembered that both doctors and nurses grieve when a patient does die, particularly if the relationship or the treatment has been a long one. It has been noted that a letter of condolence signed by the physician or attendance at the funeral can be of immense importance to the family, reassuring them that their loved received personal care and attention.

Clergy

While religious affiliations and spiritual beliefs will vary in both content and relative importance from one grieving person to another, the clergy play an important role in bereavement, as it is generally assumed they "understand" these matters better than the average person. As leaders or representatives of "helping" organizations who theoretically have both academic and practical experience with dying people and their families, members of the clergy are in a unique position to comfort, educate, follow up, and facilitate "good" grief, both in the funeral setting and afterward. As in all professions, however, there are differing levels of talent and skill, and it is physically (as well as practically) impossible for even the most well-meaning minister to give bereaved people the full complement of guidance they need.

Manning (1985) suggests:

> There is no set pattern for ministering to those in grief. Each minister must design his or her own method. The method must fit the personality of the minister and be suited to the time allotted. We are people with different gifts and different callings. Some of us will be more comfortable with this type of ministry than others. . . . This does not excuse us from dealing with people in grief, but it should relieve us of guilt and pressure. . . . Some ministers will need to concentrate on training others. Some will need to delegate the responsibility to staff members. Some will enjoy the work and find it to be a natural part of their lives. (P. 56)

He cautions that some clergy are prone to make the same mistakes as other would-be supporters, attempting to "explain" or intellectualize the death, rush the griever through his or her feelings, or even avoid the subject altogether.

Manning believes that, particularly where survivors are linked to a religious institution, clergy can facilitate a family's recognition of their mutual need to share their grief, to be honest with one another, and to help them arrive at a sense of significance of the deceased's life. In deaths where the clergy does not know the family well, he offers a more general role for the clergy to play during and after a funeral, which includes "being there," helping friends express their sympathies in comforting ways, and giving the grievers "permission" to feel their feelings. In Manning's opinion, the most important part of ministering to the bereaved is to listen to them. He refers to this as the "laying on of ears."

Mental Health Professionals

The role of mental health professionals in grief and bereavement work has been referred to throughout this text. Indeed, the majority of research resulting in what is known in this arena today has come from experts in the fields of psychology and psychiatry. In terms of aftercare, Chapter 19 in this section will address specific counseling techniques and facilitative interventions.

For our purposes here, let us simply note that mental health professionals are often the providers as well as the recipients of death education and training programs (discussed later in this chapter), and quickly review some of the common "forums" that afford mental health professionals and grievers the opportunity to make contact with each other:

1. Telephone "hot lines" offering comfort and/or advice
2. Hospital bereavement programs and/or social work departments
3. Hospice programs
4. Public school systems (counseling departments); colleges and universities (counseling centers)
5. Community bereavement programs (independent or through public agencies)
6. Private clinics or individual professional practices
7. Funeral service providers
8. Church or senior center support group programs
9. Primary physician and/or legal referrals
10. Voluntary "helping" organizations, such as the National SIDS Foundation and the American Red Cross

All death care professionals should be aware that not every mental health worker is knowledgeable or equipped to deal with issues of death and grief. Many have not been trained in this area and are uncomfortable when it is presented, often because they have not come to terms with and resolved losses in their own lives.

Returning to Worden (1984):

> If such losses are not adequately resolved in the counselor's life, they can be an impediment to a meaningful and helpful intervention. On the other hand the counselor who has experienced his own loss and adequately worked it through can be a superb resource to the person experiencing a recent loss of a similar kind. Again the key is knowing one's own limitations. (Pp. 1–2)

Hospice

It is necessary first to appreciate that hospice is not a place but a concept of caring that provides comfort and support both to people in the final stages of a terminal illness and to their families. Hospice services are often delivered in a patient's home, but they can also take place in hospitals, nursing homes, or residential facilities. Hospice care emphasizes the quality, not the length, of life, and generally takes a "team approach" involving medical personnel, clergy, social workers, volunteers, and counselors, among others.

There is validity to the opinion of some that the growing hospice movement is becoming the "warehouse" of bereavement information and aftercare sensitivity, since it includes involvement with families prior to deaths of many kinds. The National Hospice Organization is a nonprofit organization with more than fifteen hundred member hospice programs. It maintains an 800-number telephone HelpLine for information to members and the public. It would be unfair, however, to regard hospice professionals and programs as the ultimate source for delivering aftercare services, since their primary mission is to provide humane, patient-centered care and patient-centered decision making. As a model and resource, for the development of multidisciplinary approaches to aftercare, however, hospice is becoming an increasingly visible and valuable force in American society's ability to look at and deal with death.

Funeral Service Providers

In the contemporary funeral industry, aftercare is a word still searching for a definition. To some providers it may be a card to the bereaved family; to others it may be a series of timed mailings of helpful newsletters or commercially published booklets on coping with grief; to others it may be a program of support groups and/or public lectures on various aspects of loss; to others it may include follow-up phone calls to families and referrals to counselors or community resources.

As professionals who should be concerned with promoting a more comprehensive awareness of grief and loss, it is interesting that there is division within the funeral industry regarding its role in providing aftercare. One president of a mortuary science college recalls being told as a student not to become too close to families—to "just be available." The concern seemed to be in "overstepping boundaries" or "crossing a line" that belongs to therapists.

If funeral service is to be regarded as a social service, then it must offer society more than cars and caskets. Rosemary Hillman, of Grief Support Services in Des Moines, Iowa, has been quoted as saying, "Aftercare is not grief counseling. But funeral directors and cemetarians should make the bereaved aware of resources in their communities." She encourages death care facility professionals to know about, encourage, and direct survivors to information and support systems that are available after the funeral; she further believes they have a role in promoting general education in their communities on topics relating to death, dying, and funerals.

GriefNet's Cendra Lynn maintains the opinion that availability of aftercare services (whether provided directly or through referrals) not only is the wave of the future but will ultimately become "a competitive factor" among funeral service providers. In a recent interview a respected member and spokesperson of the National Funeral Directors Association "looks to the day" when funeral homes keep full-time social workers or psychologists and attorneys on staff to serve their clients' array of ongoing emotional and pragmatic needs.

ISSUES IN AFTERCARE

To a great degree, this entire chapter has raised many issues regarding aftercare:

- Whose job is it?
- What are its goals and purposes?
- What form does it take?

- How is it delivered?
- How do grievers find it, or how does "it" find them?

It should be clear by now that there are no hard-and-fast answers to these questions and that one very important key to building widespread, comprehensive aftercare programs is death education. We will use this term in a completely separate and distinct manner from the "education" of the bereaved that results from aftercare. Here, death education refers to any formalized curriculum or recognized institutional program designed to inform or train any "level" of student in the general or specific aspects of death, dying, or grief and its resolution.

Death Education

The availability of education in death-related issues in America is widely scattered. Bear in mind that this book may be utilized by college and university students in departments ranging from sociology to psychology to education to mortuary science. What's more, death-related issues may also be covered in certain courses offered by departments of anthropology, gerontology, religious/pastoral studies, and nursing. Naturally, each of these academic fields will address death and grief in the context of that particular discipline. It is perhaps only when one "graduates" into a chosen career or profession that further, cross-disciplinary opportunities for education and understanding of death and grief become available and important for ongoing competence and professional skill development.

Although we have already mentioned the Grief Recovery Institute (GRI) and the National Hospice Organization (NHO), it should be added that the GRI provides accredited programs in grief education at the university level for continuing education to interested licensed or nonlicensed professionals; it has also developed programs for dealing with loss that have been implemented in junior and senior high school throughout the United States and trained the schools' administrators, counselors, and/or teachers in their operation. It also provides speakers or delivers education, training, and/or consulting services to professional groups and associations such as nurses, alcohol and drug abuse counselors, highway patrolmen, fire department members, physicians, cemeterians, and even veterinarians.

The NHO holds conferences that, each year, target particular aspects or themes of hospice work, such as pastoral care, voluntarism, or psychosocial aspects of dying and grief, including multiculturalism and AIDS-specific hospice issues. These conferences, which attract experts and academics as well as hands-on professionals, are open to the public as well as to NHO members.

Additionally, death care education is fostered by the Hospice Foundation, a nonprofit organization that advocates the hospice concept of care by conducting programs of education and information for physicians and hospital staff, sponsoring research, serving as a philanthropic presence within the national hospice community, participating in public policy initiatives, and working for the inclusion of hospice principles in the American health care system. It has organized and sponsored several national teleconferences on grief and bereavement and has established a Pastoral Intern Program, which trains divinity students in principles of hospice.

No overview of death education would be complete without an introduction to the Association of Death Education and Counseling (ADEC), an international, multidisciplinary organization dedicated to improving the quality of death education and death-related counseling and caregiving. The ADEC was formed in 1976, and its members include, among others, educators, funeral directors, social workers, psychologists, nurses, nuns, rabbis, physicians, hospital volunteers, and hospice personnel.

Headquartered in Hartford, Connecticut, ADEC promotes the interchange of related theory and research among its members and provides support to them and all those studying and working in death-related fields. It aims to enhance the ability of professionals and laypeople to better meet the needs of those with whom they work in death education and grief counseling.

The ADEC takes an active role in educating the public on death-related issues and sponsors an annual conference with leading professionals and researchers. The organization also offers courses and workshops, and has established standards required for certification in death education and death counseling.

Death care professionals, or those whose jobs only occasionally bring them into contact with grieving populations, may have been exposed to commercially published death education and aftercare materials, curricula, and training programs. While it is not the purpose of this text to endorse or condemn any of these resources, given the current fragmentation of aftercare delivery, it is incumbent upon those attempting to provide quality programs and care to examine the credentials, philosophies, and references of organizations offering such materials or programs before committing their own (or their clients') time and money.

Fragmentation versus Coordination

The absence of clear areas of responsibility or frameworks for aftercare delivery can have different results in different communities: (1) Programs and opportunities are fragmented, perhaps serving only particular types of grievers; (2) programs and opportunities are scattered and/or inadequate; or (3) programs and opportunities are coordinated utilizing resources and skills from throughout the community to assist a wide variety of grievers facing a wide variety of loss. An example of the third possibility is the Centre for Living with Dying in Santa Clara, California. This facility, utilizing both professionals and volunteers, provides emotional support to individuals and families facing life-threatening illness or the trauma of having a loved one die. It also provides a broad-based educational program to the community on the subjects of grief and loss and how they impact the world around us.

Established in 1976, the Centre has developed specialized services to meet a wide range of needs. Senior citizens who have an ill spouse, have lost a loved one, or are experiencing loss of health or their home can receive group or one-on-one support. Grieving children and adolescents are served through peer support groups and one-on-one emotional support. Crisis intervention is available to schools that are experiencing death of a student or teacher, including needs assessment, classroom visits, faculty support, consultation on memorials or tributes, and follow-up support and referral.

The Centre also sponsors and coordinates groups for bereaved victims of violent crime, suicide survivors, a siblings grief group, widows and widowers, parents, people living with HIV, as well as their families and loved ones. It operates a corporate outreach program to address issues of loss and change in the workplace (whether through serious illness, death, or disaster), and it sponsors a Critical Incident Stress Debriefing team to deal with events that provoke unusually strong emotional reactions, such as those facing emergency workers in life-and-death situations. This type of coordinated, comprehensive care is unusual in the United States, but it shows what can be accomplished on a day-to-day basis when caring, committed people from a variety of disciplines pool their time and abilities.

At the national level, various organizations have developed emergency and disaster preparedness plans that take into account the grief and psychological consequences to both victims and workers when natural or man-made disasters of major proportions strike. Generally administered through state or local directors, coordinated response in times of intense crisis and stress might occur among groups such as the American Red Cross, the National Funeral Directors Association, the American Psychological Association, and the Salvation Army.

An important development in coordination of aftercare efforts involved the 1995 meeting between board members of the National Hospice Organization and the National Funeral Directors Association (NFDA). Although for years the NFDA has had representation on the NHO's Council of Hospice Professionals, this "first-time," three-day conclave for top-level discussion and identification of areas of mutual interest and cooperation is a promising signpost on the road toward multidisciplinary delivery of comprehensive aftercare.

It should be apparent by now that death care professionals do not—and cannot—work in a vacuum. The universal nature of loss and grief demands that professionals become familiar with all available local resources, identify areas of need and deficiency, and work together to create programs and delivery mechanisms that answer the requirements of their particular community.

SUMMARY

This chapter has defined aftercare as any program that provides help to bereaved people throughout the grief process. Noting the contributing sociological and psychological factors, the need for aftercare was discussed for both the "normally" bereaved and those grieving specific types of loss. We made the distinction between grief counseling and grief therapy, and offered several models of "goals" for aftercare efforts and programs. Various types of aftercare opportunities, formats, and media were presented to give readers some broad examples of program and activity possibilities, on both interpersonal and individual levels.

The unique roles of various death care professionals were reviewed, including medical personnel, clergy, mental health professionals, hospice workers, and funeral service providers. This led to exploration of two major issues in improving aftercare services: death education and fragmentation versus coordination.

REFERENCES

Andrus, P. 1994. Establishing community-based funeral home aftercare programs using the mourning after model. *Forum Newsletter* 20, no. 1:5–6.

Blauner, R. 1996. Death and social structure. *Psychiatry* 29:378–94.

Bowlby, J. 1980. *Attachment and Loss. Vol. 3, Loss.* New York: Basic Books.

Canine, J. D. 1993. Course syllabus. Wayne State University.

Centre for Living with Dying. 1995. *Information/outreach materials.* Santa Clara, Calif.:

Eisenberg, B., ed. 1994. *Living with grief: Personally and professionally. Teleconference Program Book.* Miami: Hospice Foundation.

Friedman, R., of The Grief Recovery Institute. 1995. Interview, August.

Gillen, G., of the National Hospice Organization. 1995. Interview, August.

James, J. W., and F. Cherry. 1988. *The grief recovery handbook.* New York: Harper and Row.

Janik, P. 1995. Divided light: A window into aftercare service. *Styx* 2, no. 1:12.

Lynn, C., of Rivendell Resources. 1995. Interview, August.

Manning, D. 1985. *Comforting those who grieve: A guide for helping others.* San Francisco: Harper and Row.

Morgan, J. D. 1995. Living our dying and our grieving. In *Dying: Facing the facts,* 3d ed., edited by H. Wass and R. A. Neimeyer. Washington, D.C.: Taylor and Francis.

Parkes, C. M. 1972. *Bereavement: Studies of grief in adult life.* New York: International Universities Press.

Pine, V., ed. 1974. *Responding to disaster.* Milwaukee, Wis.: Bulfin.

Rando, T. A. 1995. Grief and mourning. In *Dying: Facing the facts,* 3d ed., edited by H. Wass and R. A. Neimeyer. Washington, D.C.: Taylor and Francis.

Raphael, B. 1977. Preventive intervention with the recently bereaved. *Archives of General Psychiatry,* 34:1450–54.

Reynolds, J. J. 1995. Funeral home–based aftercare and liability: A question of quality. *Forum Newsletter* 21, no. 1:5–6.

Rubin, N. 1990. Social networks and mourning: A comparative approach. *Omega* 21, no. 2:113–27.

Skalsky, C. 1994. Grappling with grief. *LACMA Physician* 124, no. 11:23–5.

Wass, H., and R. A. Neimeyer. 1995. *Dying: Facing the facts,* 3d ed. Washington, D.C.: Taylor and Francis.

Worden, J. W. 1984. Grief counseling versus grief therapy. *Forum Newsletter* 7, no. 1:1–2.

19

COUNSELING TECHNIQUES FOR HELPING THE BEREAVED

Samuel L. Canine

Susan, Tom's widow, walks slowly into the funeral home. You notice her red, swollen eyes. Tears often accompany grief, but you cannot help questioning, "Is there something more?" Tom's death was unexpected. The heart attack that took his life at forty-seven did appear premature. Since Susan wants to talk, you listen. She explains, "Tom really was a good man even though we frequently fought. Could these heated arguments have shortened his life?" she asks in a shaky voice. Your eyes meet hers and you wonder, "What do I say? What should I not say? How can I help her in this grieving?"

What counseling techniques are appropriate in the grief context? This chapter seeks to answer this question, with special attention focused on those who help in funeral services. We will examine the nonverbal, listening, and verbal skills a funeral helper should exhibit when serving those suffering from grief.

NONVERBAL SKILLS

Nonverbal communication accounts for about two-thirds of our communication (Harrison 1965, p. 161). When we examine the emotional part of our relationships the proportion skyrockets to 93 percent (Mehrabian 1971, p. 77). In the grief context, recognition of nonverbal cues becomes essential in helping those who are grieving.

Nonverbal communication functions in four specific areas: (1) It can *strengthen* the words used. "I am so sorry for all I did wrong with . . ." may be accompanied by a tear-saturated voice. (2) It can *contradict* the verbal message. "I'm okay, I'm okay" said when the person is struggling for composure indicates she or he is not okay. (3) The nonverbal can *replace* any verbal communication. When you put your hand on a shoulder to steady a mourner or pick up a small child who doesn't understand, you may not be using words, but the message speaks volumes. (4) Nonverbal messages can *say more than* verbal ones. Posture, facial expression, and eye contact give you far more data about how the person feels than just the words spoken.

Ten areas surface when we consider nonverbal communication (Wolfelt 1990, pp. 51–57). Your awareness of these areas will enhance your relationship with those you serve.

Proxemics

Proxemics examines the use of space or distance between people. The more we desire a person, the closer we try to be to that person. Death creates distance, which the bereaved does not want. A loved one has died, and the separation makes any intimacy impossible. This creates frustration for those who once enjoyed an intimacy with the person who died.

In a time of crisis intimacy develops faster. Brothers or sisters who have not communicated may now want to be near to each other. Conversely, where strong dislike resides, distance will be present. A relative may attend the funeral but attempt to keep a distance from either family members or the deceased. An awareness of space usage will give you insights not obtainable by verbal means.

Facial Expression

Our face serves as the canvas where we paint our nonverbal messages. "We send more nonverbal messages with our faces than any other means, and the face usually reveals the highest accuracy of all nonverbal messages" (Gangel and Canine 1992, p. 88). At times we sense these messages without clear consciousness of where they originate. Our faces have a difficult time lying. They communicate our feelings in the vulnerable time of coping with death. A person may try to mask true grief feelings, but usually people see beyond the mask. The face shows the intensity of grief an individual experiences.

Paralanguage

Paralanguage examines the tonal areas of the verbal message. We constantly search for congruence between the tone and content of any message. As you relate to the bereaved, listen to how she speaks, not just to what she says. If a person says, "I will be all right," only to demonstrate he is anything but all right, we believe the nonverbal. We learn more about the relationship when we listen to the tone as well as the meaning of the messages we receive.

Eye Contact

Eye contact can tell us much about self-image. Guilt or inferiority sometimes surfaces because of a failure to connect with the eyes. The eyes serve as power brokers. In times of bereavement, power seems missing, and this can show up through the eyes. The deeply felt hurt accompanying death will frequently emerge from the eyes. The eyes of children require your special attention as they do not hide what the inner self feels.

Personal Attire

How we dress makes a constant statement about each of us. Our clothes, jewelry, and shoes send messages about who we are. While more casual attire seems increasingly popular, some still demonstrate their respect by wearing a suit and tie or best clothes to a funeral. What people do with clothing can reveal their station in life, their values, and their opinions of the funeral occasion. This may take the form of ostentation or abject poverty, but some message will be sent via this channel.

Hand Gestures

A person's hand gestures may serve as an indicator of anxiety during crisis. The grieving person can exaggerate or accelerate hand motions as he or she seeks to make sense of the situation. A person's background and culture should also influence your assessment of this nonverbal behavior. Some groups communicate more with the hands than others. As a general rule, you should watch for abnormal motion and confirm what you see with what you hear.

Body Position

Body position presents us with a subtle but powerful way to observe nonverbal messages. At times you can almost see the burden a person carries by the bend of the body. We include or exclude others by how we position the body. We best read nonverbal communication when we sit in an "L" position, which allows each person to pick up the body messages from the other. When we sit directly across from one another, we are in a competitive stance. A side-by-side arrangement distorts the accuracy of nonverbal messages. You will enhance your relationship possibilities if you arrange the environment for a ninety-degree or "L" sitting configuration.

Physical Environment

The physical environment and its control can either encourage or discourage maximum communication. Bright colors, flowers, good ventilation, good lighting, quality furniture—all help produce a better environment. Spacious surroundings foster better communication and help build a relationship atmosphere. An effective physical environment allows for intimacy or distance as the need dictates. A spirit of informality and warmth can be enhanced or hindered by the physical surroundings. An excellent question we might periodically ask is, "If I were walking into this room for the first time, how would it affect me?"

Posture

Our posture reveals the deeper feelings we have in any relationship. The hurt felt within surfaces through a person's body long before it does through speech. The numbing fatigue so often felt by the bereaved can appear as a weight on the shoulders that drags a person down. Ask yourself, "Does he seem overburdened in how he carries the body?" Do you notice a slowness of step and a slouch in the person you seek to serve?

Head Movement

A person's head movement reveals a more immediate relationship message. When the head moves up and down, we sense conscious agreement. If movement is from side to side, we immediately register it as negative feedback or disagreement. In grief, mixed messages can occur. A side-to-side motion may be used to attempt to deny reality. This usually will be accompanied by poor eye contact and facial expression that struggles to accept what has happened. At times, a person may transmit disconfirmation by turning away from you. A person may send the message "If I look away, you will not actually be present." Head movement or the lack of it continually communicates where we are in a given relationship.

LISTENING SKILLS

Barriers

Unfortunately, listening is something everyone can do and do poorly. At least eight obstacles block our effective listening. In the grief process, listening becomes more complicated because it is a time of personal and emotional crisis. Be attuned to these obstacles either in your experience or in the lives of those you seek to help.

Defensiveness

This often stems from preoccupation with our own self. A defensive person reaches a premature conclusion. Statements like "I know what you are going to say . . ." or "It has been our normal experience that . . ." can preface this behavior. We read into the other person's words our own expectations. Prejudices, or judgments before the facts are understood, characterize this defensive behavior. You may find yourself rehearsing specific responses. You mentally script out what you will say and what the other person will say. The problem arises when the real situation does not follow the planned one. Avoid trying to script ahead at the expense of listening. Certain words or phrases serve to ignite conflict in each of us. If a grieving relative resents the cost of the funeral, he or she may voice derogatory remarks about you. Watch out for emotionally laden words that may be triggers for defensive behavior.

Attitudes or Biases

A bias-free person probably does not exist. Even so, more prejudice resides in each of us than we are willing to admit. Consider a man arriving at your funeral home in an old beat-up dirty pickup to make funeral arrangements for his wife. He enters wearing bib overalls, which have obviously been worn more days than anyone else would dare. You look at his unshaven, unruly countenance and wonder who this man can be. Prejudice could easily enter the picture as you see a poverty-ridden man who could never afford a decent burial for his wife. But what if this same man was actually an eccentric multimillionaire? All of his outward signs and your own bias against him made you ready to reject him before you clearly grasped the facts. Your prejudice would initially hinder your ability to listen. Our prejudice influences early listening far more than we realize.

Personal Inner Struggles

When we are emotionally crippled by our own difficulties, we listen to others less effectively. Intrapersonal conflict can create a battleground within that reduces our listening skills. We can only give our energy to focus on one perspective at a time. If we are consumed by our own set of difficulties, we will not listen well to those we attempt to help. It is like standing so close to one tree that we cannot see other trees, not to mention the rest of the forest.

The more you inherently dislike an individual, the more difficult it will be to listen to him or her. Keep in mind that some individuals going through the grief process may be juggling so much guilt they cannot hear you clearly. This demands patience and simplicity in communication for those robbed of good listening skills by grief.

Interruption

This malady appears to be increasing in our society. You may find your mind moving much faster than the speaker's tongue. The grief-ridden individual often labors to express thoughts that normally would be easily uttered. Be careful about rushing in with your own words until you have heard the hurting person. Since our society seems dedicated to reducing all social graces, interrupting has become a way of life for many. We further compound the interruption problem by the fact that we listen about five to six times faster than we talk. This gives the listener time on his or her hands. Will we use it to pick up the nonverbal cues? Or will we cut off the speaker because we are ready to talk? Relationships are better built when we learn to not interrupt.

Overload

In this information age an overabundance of data plagues us in staggering proportions. In the mid-1980s the average individual processed about five hundred verbal messages a day. Just ten years later we find ourselves bombarded by over two thousand messages a day. We are not overloaded with data; we are drowning in it! Some solve this dilemma by tuning out or blocking the listening process. Filtering or blocking information greatly curtails what we actually process in listening.

Timing

We are increasingly aware of time's value. Many now view time as more valuable than money. Since time is fast becoming a scarce resource, many prize it highly. "I don't have time to listen to you . . ."; "I must run . . ."; "Can we talk about this later? . . ."—these are everyday experiences for nearly everyone. For you to give your time to listen to the grieving person may be your finest statement of relationship importance.

Physical Exhaustion

Since listening requires stronger concentration and effort, fatigue reduces our intake ability. When we experience loss of sleep, abnormal stress may sometimes be unavoidable. Even so, listening will suffer when these things are present. A lack of rest affects your entire personality. Fatigue distorts the thinking and the listening process, causing relationships to suffer. Fortunately, most physical exhaustion is only a temporary problem. Be alert to the short-term negative effect arising from the barrier of fatigue.

Filtered Listening

We often hear what we want to hear or what fits into our mind-set. If we have a positive predisposition, we will listen for the good. If we program our minds negatively, we listen for the bad. The more we reduce the extremes in filtering, the better we will listen. We need to hear things as they are without the superimposed filters that distort our listening and the reality around us.

Guidelines

The following seven guidelines should help improve our listening skills and help us to productively counsel those who are grieving.

Listen Actively

Little effort is required to speak, but we expend major energy when we listen. We depend on another person when we listen. We must lock into what that individual is saying, how they are saying it, why they are saying these words, and what they are not saying. Developing your skill in this area will take time. Don't be discouraged if progress is slow at the beginning. Listening is like any habit: repetition, review, recalling, memory, indexing—all must function well if maximum listening is to occur.

Listen with Empathy

Empathy puts the spotlight on the mourner (Wolfelt 1988, p. 160). This is more sensed than planned. If you genuinely care for hurting people, it will show. To empathize causes you to go into partnership with the grieving person. You assure him or her of your caring and compassion. Your actions will always reveal this better than your words. Do your eyes convey your concern? Familiarity may breed not contempt but rather monotony. As in any vocation, things can become routine. You must guard against a negative attitude that sends the message "This is just a job." Do you easily reach out to people in their distress and grief? Empathy relates to the measure of your reach as you seek to help those trying to cope with death.

Listen with Openness

We do this best when we reduce defensive behavior and filtered listening. Make every attempt to focus on the facts, not the inferences we so often make from the facts. To reduce our ever-present blind spots, the other person needs a sense of permission to give us criticism or negative feedback. If we are perceived as arrogant, this problem will continue until someone feels secure enough in the relationship to help us see how we are perceived.

At times, we hide our own lives too much. When we listen well, we share appropriate information with the listener. Each person going through the grief process longs to know if other humans have this problem. Usually, a discreet confession of your own humanity will generate more openness from the grieving party.

Listen with Awareness

Watch for agreement between what a person says and how he or she says it. Consistency is the goal of our awareness. We achieve greater accuracy when we listen with our eyes and ears. Work toward mastering more than just the content of someone's words. Why is she saying this? What is he not saying? Why is she saying these words with this intonation? What nonverbal cues agree or disagree with what he is saying? These type of questions will sharpen your awareness as you serve those who are hurting.

Resist External Distractions

Give the person your complete attention. This could mean physically repositioning yourself to more easily see the speaker. In some instances you will need to improve your ability to concentrate. Work on your ability to focus on what is said.

Hold Rebuttals

Normally, this will not be a problem, but someone will eventually test your ability to be gracious. It may be something said or done that undercuts your reputation or credibility. Exercise extreme care when someone hits your hot button. You can win a battle and lose a war with just your words. Usually unjust criticism reflects primarily on the sender, and time equalizes when we are patient.

Analyze Nonverbal Messages

Most emotional messages come via the nonverbal channel. In the grief process the mourner writes volumes. To what extent are tears appropriate? What proactive steps can be taken in managing grief? When is it time to stop or start physical movement during a funeral? Nonverbal messages normally answer these questions and others like them.

These guidelines, while not exhaustive, should assist the funeral helper in sharpening his or her listening skills. We best learn listening, like swimming, by doing it. Begin today to sharpen your ability to listen.

VERBAL SKILLS

Types of Questions

The following five major types of questions are helpful for the funeral helpers.

To Gain Facts

Here we focus on such details as family facts, occupational data, religious background, and type of funeral service.

To Reveal Facts or Feelings

Support as much as possible, set individuals at ease, assure your presence to help, and empathize with their grief (e.g., "What would you like in the way of music?").

To Clarify Facts or Feelings

Beware of ambiguity. Clarifying helps focus any discussion. Ask for more response in a loving and graceful way. When you clarify, you better determine areas of difference or agreement. Frequently, a clarifying question leads to more questions (e.g., "Would you prefer the family viewing on Friday night or Saturday morning?").

To Stimulate Thought

This serves to probe beneath the surface. You are requesting their opinions. This type of question often is open-ended. You may use a "why" question when attempting to stimulate thought. A question like this helps grievers see issues for themselves (e.g., "Why do you think he wanted the funeral in a church?").

To Summarize Discussion

You attempt to help the grievers see where they are in the discussion. It might be an internal summary. This question can serve as a prelude to their decision making (e.g., "We have talked about when the funeral should be, now who will you want to officiate in the funeral?").

Types of Comments

The following types of comments will assist you as seek to maximize the help you offer to each grieving person. Take care to focus on each individual as unique and to structure your comments from your heart as well as your head.

A Reflective Comment

Emotional diversity marks the work of a funeral helper. Everything from strong weeping to stoic coldness can occur. Therefore, you need to help a person reflect as to where he or she is and wants to be. When we cultivate this ability, we build more effective relationships between the funeral helper and the grieving person. Wolfelt (1990, p. 98) made five astute observations about the nature of feelings you will encounter:

- Feelings are neither good nor bad, they just are.
- Everyone has a right to his or her feelings.
- Feelings always make sense when considered in context.
- Feelings are not dangerous (actions can potentially be dangerous).
- Denying a feeling does not make it go away.

With these thoughts in mind, master the art of helping by using statements like "You seem especially quiet today and that's okay." "You are absolutely right; good memories stay with us forever."

A Challenging Comment

The appropriateness of this comment surfaces when barriers keep the mourner from a sense of well-being. Bathed in compassion, a loving, challenging comment may assist the grieving person. Great care should mark this type of comment. Usually the mourner exhibits dysfunctional behavior before we give this comment. The comment normally focuses on the future. You do not challenge the person's past or present grief but attempt to help him or her see that tomorrow will dawn and there will be a way to cope. Again, make this a positive comment about the person's ability to go forward with his or her life. For example, a statement such as "I suspect you will want to finish that course at the local college you are taking" can help the person refocus and see an ongoing life.

A Restatement Comment

You are not repeating the other person's words but restating the concept. The mourner might say, "I just don't think I can go on without her." You might reply, "I know you will miss her tremendously." Develop the skill of restatement. This is an ability to put the same concept in different words. A comment like this slows down the communication process and allows the grieving person to move at a slower rate. When feelings are keenly experienced, a slower rate of data processing becomes highly appropriate.

An Encouraging Comment

Look for something linked to the mourner that you can give a sincere compliment. Your words usually have either a building effect or a destructive effect. To establish a strong relationship, you want to use constructive words. Thanking the person for his or her cooperation during the funeral process may be one form of encouragement. A statement such as "In every area we have talked about you have provided us with just the right information, and I want to thank you for your splendid cooperation." Sincerity must mark your comments when you attempt to encourage the mourner.

An Assessment Comment

This statement tries to help the person evaluate an area calling for a decision. In times of grief, decision making becomes difficult or almost impossible. "I understand this is what you think would be best here" might be an assessment-related comment. You are giving the person feedback so she can affirm or disconfirm a decision she must make.

A Permission Comment

When the tears flow, a person will often apologize for them. Assure the individual that tears are normal in the grieving process (Wolfelt 1988, pp. 127–28). Sometimes a person needs to ventilate anger at life, at circumstances, or even at the deceased. This comment tells her it is okay to feel as she feels.

A Controlling Comment

At times emotions may run wild. The cathartic effect has passed and dysfunctional behavior prevails. A comment that takes charge can be appropriate. Wisdom should dictate the use of such statements. For example, a common "Let me help you . . ." and then taking the person's arm and assisting in whatever is needed can be appreciated. However, be careful never to rush appropriate grief expression.

SUMMARY

When you build a relationship with a bereaved person, you help that individual at one of life's critical moments. Since emotional expression marks this mourning time, the awareness of and response to nonverbal messages enhance the relationship-building process. Sharpening listening skills gives you tools to enhance your counseling ability. Your skill in asking questions and making comments renders help in one of life's most difficult times. Always remember that the bereaved person will remember who you were long after he or she has forgotten what you said and did.

REFERENCES

Burley-Allen, Madelyn, 1995. *Listening: The forgotten skill*. New York: Wiley.

Falcon, Chuck. 1995. *Happiness and personal problems: Psychology made easy*. Lafayette, La.: Sensible Psychology Press.

Flatt, Bill. 1987. *Growing through grief: Comfort and counseling*. Nashville, Tenn: Gospel Advocate Company.

Gangel, Kenneth O., and Samuel L. Canine. 1992. *Communication and conflict management in churches and Christian organizations.* Nashville, Tenn.: Broadman Press.

Harrison, Randall P. 1965. Nonverbal communication: Exploration into time, space, action, and object. In *Dimensions in communication,* edited by James H. Campbell and Hal W. Hepler. Belmont, Calif.: Wadsworth.

Jones, Mary. 1994. *Love after death.* Bristol, Pa.: Taylor and Francis.

Margolis, Otto S. 1981. *Acute grief: Counseling the bereaved.* Westport, Ct.: Columbia University Press.

———. 1985. *Loss, grief and bereavement: A guide for counseling.* Greenwood.

Mehrabian, Albert. 1971. *Silent messages.* Belmont, Calif.: Wadsworth.

Oates, Wayne E. 1976. *Pastoral care and counseling in grief and separation.* Minneapolis, Mn.: Augsburg Fortress.

Redmond, Lula, M. 1989. *Surviving when someone you love was murdered.* Clearwater, Fl.: Psychological Consultation and Education Service.

Wiersbe, Warren W., and David W. Wiersbe. 1985. *Comforting the bereaved.* Chicago: Moody Press.

Wolfelt, Alan D. 1988. *Death and grief: A guide for clergy.* Muncie, Ind.: Accelerated Development.

———. 1990. *Interpersonal skills training: A handbook for funeral home staffs.* Bristol, Pa.: Accelerated Development.

Worden, William J. 1991. *Grief counseling and grief therapy.* New York, N.Y.: Springer.

20

MODELS OF BEREAVEMENT AFTERCARE

Polly K. Nielsen

THE NEED FOR BEREAVEMENT AFTERCARE

This chapter describes the various kinds of support—known as "aftercare"—available to the bereaved as they move through the grieving process after the death of a loved one. Aftercare can take different forms, including bereavement programs sponsored by funeral homes, state-regulated hospice bereavement programs, support groups, and self-help groups. The chapter also discusses contemporary issues that have given rise to newer bereavement programs, such as support groups for survivors of suicide or for those bereaved by acquired immune deficiency syndrome (AIDS) or by sudden infant death syndrome (SIDS). Finally, specific programs from various geographic locations are discussed.

Making the transition—from a world with the deceased in it, regardless of what that means or how it manifested, to a world without the deceased—is the ultimate goal of mourning. The overall transition can be viewed as a series of smaller transitions—from wife to widow, from parent of four to parent of three, from best friend to just being by oneself. Because we are human, we often resist making these painful, yet necessary, transitions. The bereaved may stall at a particular stage of mourning, unwilling or unable to move through grief's basic tasks. Everyone who experiences bereavement requires comfort and consolation. Most often—and ideally—comfort and consolation come from strongly sympathetic and supportive family members and friends who are willing to be available for weeks and months after the death has occurred.

Raphael (1983) has written, "The pain and suffering of grief has been known to human society for a long, long time. Just as it has been suggested that this distress may have evolutionary significance for the human group, it might also be hypothesized that the comfort and consolation human beings offer to each other are powerful reinforcers of the bonds so essential for family and community life. Much of the meaning of bereavement takes place in the warmth of family life and friendship" (p. 352). Traditional means for facilitating grief include family, church, funeral rituals, and social customs. Unfortunately, not every family is warm, loving, and supportive. Some are too fractured by dysfunction; others may be widely scattered by geography. And the bereaved's extrafamilial support network may be less than ideal as well, unable to provide the level of support the bereaved requires, or unaware of the importance of ongoing support once the immediate shock has worn off and funerary rites are over. Often friends return to the routines of their lives before the death, unmindful of the long and difficult road ahead for the bereaved.

Societal norms once provided clear, well-defined, and accepted "rules" regarding bereavement such as dress, demeanor, and duration. These norms have changed, weakening and even erasing those rules and often leaving the bereaved feeling (and in fact being) quite alone within weeks or even days after the death. American society encourages the quick fix, exhorting those who suffer a loss to "put it behind you and get on with your life." Such attitudes discount the bereaved's very real grief, and can contribute to a sense of isolation.

There can also be difficulty resolving grief when the bereaved chooses to participate in few, if any, of the rites and/or rituals commonly associated with death. Some bereaved have the deceased cremated and have no religious funeral or any kind of memorial service by which to mark the occasion and facilitate the process of accepting the loss. The absence of any sort of funerary service may also result in the bereaved's receiving limited social support from those who would otherwise have been present. Absence of any sort of rite of detachment can leave family members and friends sufficiently uncertain regarding the bereaved's situation that they do little, if anything, by way of offering support to the bereaved.

The importance of ongoing support in bereavement should not be minimized. The nature and strength of the bereaved's social support network has already been identified as a key factor in predicting bereavement outcome. The stronger and more supportive the network, the better the outcome. Individuals who have what they perceive as nonsupportive or nonexistent social support networks are most likely to have poorer bereavement outcomes (Raphael 1983, p. 372).

According to Rando (1984), "What the griever needs most is acceptance and nonjudgmental listening, which will facilitate the expression of emotions and the necessary review of the relationship with the lost loved one. He will then require assistance in integrating the past with the new present that exists" (p. 79). This view is supported by Jacobs et al. (1994), who wrote "widows report that active coping, social supports, and social involvement were most effective for them for coping with bereavement" (p. 557).

BEREAVEMENT AFTERCARE PROGRAMS

The absence of ideal support configurations has given rise to the development of other resources for bereavement aftercare. These resources can be used in concert with the bereaved's support network, or they may constitute the only support the bereaved has available in resolving the grief. The goal of grief counseling, writes Worden (1982), is "helping people facilitate uncomplicated, or normal, grief to a healthy completion of the tasks of grieving within a reasonable time frame" (p. 35).

Parkes (1987) identified three major categories of bereavement aftercare: (1) professional, (2) self-help and/or support groups, and (3) hospice (a combination of professional and trained volunteers). "The care offered usually ranges from individual counseling in the bereaved person's home, to group meetings, which may be 'social groups,' or 'therapy groups.' The latter are usually led by a professional" (Parkes 1987, p. 259).

According to Raphael (1983), "Professional and professionally supported services and self-help services are capable of reducing the risk of postbereavement morbidity. . . . The goals for . . . effective programs are: the encouragement of grief and the promotion of mourning. Not only may the bereaved person be comforted and consoled, but he may, sensitively and appropriately, be assisted in the resolution of his loss" (p. 372).

Writes Worden (1982) regarding the overall goals of grief counseling:

> The overall goal of grief counseling is to help the survivor complete any unfinished business with the deceased and to be able to say a final good-bye. Specific goals correspond to the basic tasks of grieving.

1. To increase the reality of the loss;
2. To help the counselee deal with both expressed and latent grief;
3. To help the counselee overcome various impediments to readjustment after the loss;
4. To encourage the counselee to make a healthy emotional withdrawal from the deceased and to feel comfortable reinvesting that emotion in another relationship. (P. 36)

Worden's aftercare model is similar to Parkes's, but is more detailed:

1. Professional services by trained doctors, nurses, psychologists, or social workers who can support a person who has sustained a significant loss (individual or group setting)
2. Volunteers selected and trained by professionals (i.e., Widow-to-Widow program)
3. Self-help groups (i.e., Compassionate Friends)

It is useful at this point to distinguish between "support groups" and "self-help groups," as they are often considered synonymous. While their goals may be the same—the effective, healthy resolution of grief—their processes are in fact quite different. Support groups are generally run by a combination of professionals (i.e., doctors or social workers) and volunteers who are trained by those professionals. Support groups "have predetermined outcomes and a strong separation between helpers and helpees" (Klass 1985, p. 354).

Self-help groups, on the other hand, are made up of members

who share a common condition, situation, heritage, symptom or experience. They are largely self-governing and self-regulating, emphasizing peer solidarity rather than hierarchical governance. As such, they prefer controls built upon consensus rather than coercion. . . . They advocate self-reliance and require equally intense commitment and responsibility to other members, actual or potential. They often provide an identifiable code of precepts, beliefs and practices that include rules for conducting group meetings, entrance requirements for new members and techniques for dealing with "backsliders. . . ." They generally offer a face-to-face, or phone-to-phone fellowship network usually available and accessible without charge. Groups tend to be self-supporting, occur mostly outside the aegis of institutions or agencies, and thrive largely on donations from members and friends. (Klass 1985, p. 354)

Professional Services

Professional services are generally those provided by a psychiatrist, psychologist, licensed professional counselor, or social worker who is specially trained in working with the bereaved. Typically, professional services entail a one-on-one relationship between the professional and the bereaved. Sessions may take place in the bereaved's home or at the professional's office. Session length and duration vary based on the bereaved's need, as evaluated by the professional (and likely agreed to by the bereaved). Professional services can be quite costly, depending upon individual practitioners' fee schedules.

The goal of professional grief counseling is to facilitate the accomplishment of the basic tasks of grief within a reasonable, albeit indeterminate, time frame.

Self-Help and Support Groups

Self-help groups tend to be programs of attraction. That is, members join out of a perceived need or desire to share their experience with others who have gone down the same path before them. One example of a bereavement self-help group is the Compassionate Friends, an organization founded in England in 1969 for parents who have experienced the death of a child. According to Klass (1985), "A central tenet of the TCF process is that only those who have lost a child can understand" (p. 355).

The process of joining a self-help group is the same as that followed by parents who decide to join TCF. There are three steps: (1) deciding to attend a meeting; (2) deciding to affiliate (forming bonds with other members); and (3) deciding to help others (Klass 1985, pp. 356–67). As the healing progresses, members gradually move from a "taking" mode typical of newcomers to a "giving" mode, in which they have gained the knowledge, experience, strength, and hope required to begin to help others.

Support groups are typically run by professionals with the help of specially trained volunteers. There are support groups for a variety of bereaved individuals. One is a group called Widow-to-Widow, in which widows support each other during the mourning process. "In adult support groups there is typically a common problem or concern among the members and an emphasis on peer help. These groups can be viewed as surrogate systems of help to be used by people for whom such systems are inadequate or absent. Support groups differ from traditional psychotherapy or counseling groups because they do not aim to ameliorate intrapsychic or interpersonal difficulties, even though this may occur as a result of participating in the group" (Zambelli, Grace, DeRosa 1992, p. 484).

But adults are not the only ones who can benefit from support group participation. Recently, increasing awareness has led to the formation of support groups for bereaved children. "The goals of most children's support groups is to help children cope with the death of a parent. Typically, the groups are short-term and utilize the following techniques: art making, game play, therapeutic stories, role play, and discussion" (Zambelli, Grace, DeRosa 1992, p. 484).

The overall goals of child bereavement groups vary somewhat from those for adults because children often have widely differing views on death from those held by adults. Schilling et al. (1992, p. 406) identified three goals for child bereavement support groups:

1. Normalize the loss process.
2. Provide peer support.
3. Create a safe, nonthreatening environment in which to express fears, fantasies, and ambivalent feelings about death. (P. 406)

Hospice Programs

Hospices are commonly and mistakenly believed to be organizations that focus only on caring for dying patients and supporting their families prior to the time of death. While this is true, hospice guidelines generally include recommendations for counseling and support of the bereaved. According to Worden (1982), "Comprehensive care includes work with the bereaved family. Most hospice programs use some combination of professionals and volunteers to do the counseling" (p. 37). In fact, the National Hospice Organization's own standards state, "Family needs continue after the death of one of their members" (Rando 1984, p. 293).

Hospices are regulated by federal and state standards that are designed to ensure a baseline quality of care for the terminally ill and their families. Federal standards, which fall under the auspices of the Health Care Financing Administration (HCFA) of the Department of Health and Human Services, mandate the following:

> Counseling services must be available to both the individual and the family. Counseling includes bereavement counseling, provided after the patient's death as well as dietary, spiritual and any other counseling services for the individual and family provided when the individual is enrolled in the hospice.
>
> (a) Standard: Bereavement counseling. There must be an organized program for the provision of bereavement services under the supervision of a qualified professional. The plan of care for these services should reflect family needs, as well as a clear delineation of services to be provided and the frequency of service delivery (up to one year following the death of the patient). (42 CFR Ch. IV, 10–1–90 edition)

One model of a comprehensive bereavement aftercare program is that of the Michigan Hospice Organization, which has a five-pronged approach to aftercare. This program reflects the standards outlined previously and includes the following, as described in the organization's manual:

1. A bereavement correspondence program, consisting of regular monthly mailings (for a maximum of fourteen months). Each mailing contains information on grief and another selected topic, such as insomnia, journaling, children and death, depression, anger, and readjustments. In addition, mailings provide information about other bereavement services that are available.
2. A grief recovery program, a five-week support program.
3. A support group "to promote and encompass healthy grief through better understanding and information of the grief process and to allow the bereaved to move through their grief in a mutually supportive environment."
4. A getting through the holidays seminar, which is held before Thanksgiving and consists of information and exercises, including a guided meditation,

designed to help the bereaved during the Thanksgiving–Christmas–New Year's holiday season.

5. Memorial services, scheduled periodically for the bereaved and for hospice staff members.

The Michigan model stresses that bereavement services begin prior to death and are available twenty-four hours per day, 365 days per year. Introductory letters explain the services that are available. At the time of death, a bereavement counselor sends a note to the bereaved. Two weeks after the death, the counselor contacts the bereaved again. Four to six weeks after the death, the counselor schedules a home visit for a bereavement assessment. If the bereaved declines a visit, the counselor sends a packet of information about available services and support, information about natural responses to grief, inspirational materials, such as poems, and a service evaluation questionnaire (information courtesy of Michigan Hospice Organization, 900 3rd Street, Suite 101C, Muskegon, MI 49440; 616-722-2257).

MODELS OF BEREAVEMENT AFTERCARE

Hospital-Based Support Programs

Henry Ford Medical Center

The Henry Ford Medical Center (HFMC), in Dearborn, Michigan, provides a bereavement support group, which is facilitated by a social worker and a priest with a degree in sociology or psychology. The stated purpose of the support group is "to provide an opportunity to share experiences and concerns with others who are grieving, following the loss of a loved one. It is normal to feel uncertain or to deny one's emotions. Let us help you gain support during this time." The HFMC bereavement support group meets every third Tuesday, during the early evening, making the time convenient for most people. HFMC also provides listings of other local area bereavement support groups and listings of area grief counselors, all with contact information.

Supplementary information includes a pamphlet entitled "Grief after Suicide" (a publication of the Mental Health Association in Waukesha County, Inc., Waukesha, Wisconsin); a handout explaining normal grief reactions, complete with recommendations for further information; and copies of articles relating to the value of tears and recommendations for telling children about death.

The bereavement support group at HFMC Fairlane is sponsored by the Henry Ford Hospice. The flyer provides contact information for those seeking details about the program (information courtesy of Henry Ford Medical Center, Health Education Center, Dearborn, Michigan).

Mercy Medical Center

In their mission statement, Mercy Medical Center makes this pledge to the bereaved: "We are committed to helping people accept death as a part of life; to receive support and comfort during their experience with death; and to grow in the understanding of loss and grief."

Mercy Pastoral Care provides bereavement classes, "offering information, support and education for adults who are grieving the loss of a loved one." A separate program is available for bereaved children. Mercy's adult program has four key components:

1. A bereavement information and support group—Offers professional support; is a "safe," confidential place to share thoughts and feelings; is free of charge; and meets bimonthly.
2. Bereavement library—Books and other reading materials on bereavement may be borrowed by program participants or others for up to two weeks.
3. Bereavement education series—Offers a five-week program providing organized education program about grief issues; is free of charge; and is presented quarterly.
4. Pastoral counseling—By appointment for individuals and/or families.

Mercy's children's program brochure has two purposes. First, it provides the parent or caregiver with a basic education regarding ways in which children experience death. The brochure outlines the factors that influence the child's reaction, such as age, personality, and relationship to the deceased, and provides basic principles for helping children deal with their bereavement. Second, the brochure provides information about the bereavement support group for children and adolescents, aged three to eighteen. The group meets every other week and requires preregistration (information courtesy of Mercy Medical Center, Roseburg, Oregon).

Funeral Home Grief Aftercare Programs

Aftercare service provided by funeral homes is a relatively new concept, and while not all funeral homes support the idea, increasing numbers do. According to Louis L. Lawson, "One of the simplest things a funeral home can do is to establish itself as a referral service for community members. One of the few places people can and do talk about death is in the funeral home. So it seems natural for someone in the funeral home to have done the legwork and provide a list of support groups to give their families" ("Emerging Trends in Aftercare," by Louis L. Lawson. Originally published in AFDToday Magazine. Reprint courtesy of ACCORD, Inc.).

"Post funeral programs range from simply making referrals to a therapist or a local self-help group, to providing written material and/or a newsletter, to establishing a full bereavement follow-up program. They can be performed by the funeral director, a paraprofessional, or a mental health professional. They can be extensive or minimal" ("Post Funeral Care Programs Help Clients, Funeral Homes," by Margaret H. Gerner, MSW. Reprint courtesy of ACCORD, Inc.).

ACCORD

Writes ACCORD president Sherry L. Gibson about her organization, "At AC-CORD we have a philosophy that aftercare is a continuum of care. . . . AC-

CORD's main focus is teaching funeral directors how to develop follow-up and grief-counseling services." ("Aftercare/Preneed Represent a Continuum of Care," by Sherry L. Gibson. Courtesy of ACCORD, Inc.) ACCORD provides extensive written materials to its client funeral homes, including booklets, pamphlets, and newsletters. It also provides the following types of materials directly as well as indirectly (through the funeral home) to bereaved families:

Booklets. ACCORD publishes an untitled, fourteen-page booklet that contains three main sections: What Will I Be Feeling?, How Can I Cope?, and Where Can I Find Support? The booklet provides, in a question-and-answer format, the definition and explanation of grief, some practical questions, and an emphasis on a wide range of feelings that the bereaved experience, while stressing the need for the bereaved to "experience your feelings." The booklet discusses rest, nutrition, exercise, and journaling as important coping strategies.

Newsletters. Newsletters come under two titles. One, "In Accord," comes directly from ACCORD via funeral directors, while the others bear the logo of the individual funeral home. Each newsletter generally contains three articles (the first is typically authored by ACCORD's founder, Dr. Sandra Graves), perhaps a question-and-answer page, and some practical, everyday hints in a column lightheartedly entitled "How to Boil Water."

Pamphlets. ACCORD has pamphlets specific to various losses, including widowhood; loss of a parent, grandparent, sibling, baby, son or daughter, or "someone special"; or loss of a loved one who died from AIDS, suicide, and death by trauma. There are also pamphlets geared to bereavement by age group, such as "How to Help Children Cope with Death" and "Teen Grief" (information courtesy of ACCORD, Inc., 1930 Bishop Lane, Suite 947, Louisville, KY 40218-1937).

Maximum Living Bereavement Services

Maximum Living Consultants, Inc., in Birmingham, Michigan, under the direction of Dr. John D. Canine, provides funeral homes with two levels of aftercare service. According to Dr. Canine, the goal of both levels is identical: "To improve the quality of life by examining the facts and psychological theories associated with the bereavement process and then, relate these facts and theories concerning death, dying, and bereavement to an individual's personal feelings, values, and priorities." Funeral homes can choose aftercare service that provides information about bereavement (general information on grief, a list of counselors, and a list of support groups) that is sent directly to the bereaved, as well as follow-up survey services regarding customer participation and quality of service. If the funeral home wishes to provide more comprehensive aftercare services, it can choose services that include greater personal contact with the bereaved, including one-on-one counseling, designated house calls, and organized monthly support groups.

The Maximum Living program uses two books, written by Canine, as core resources. *The Challenge of Living* (1983) walks the reader through a basic education about death, including societal attitudes that help us avoid confronting our own deaths. Canine (1983) believes that death awareness is central to living a healthy life:

> The whole point of death awareness is to make a person so aware of his own death that a "new" individual emerges, an individual who sees life from a more meaningful perspective. Because this person's sense of value has changed or deepened, his new view of life makes him "creative beyond any expectations," and he experiences a fuller existence.
>
> Death acceptance is the key to coping effectively with your emotions about death. To fear death is to keep it locked in the closet. To accept death is to bring it into the open thus removing your fear. It is the purpose of death awareness to unlock the doors of communication allowing people to share with each other their thoughts and feelings about death.
>
> Death awareness helps you deal with these emotions through learning and sharing in an unthreatening environment. This is where the healing process begins, then you are on your way to effectively coping with your personal loss. (Pp. 21–22)

Canine then takes the bereaved through what can be expected emotionally, and ways in which the bereaved can help him- or herself heal over time.

Canine's *I Can, I Will* (1990) is a support group guide, written for support group leaders as well as the bereaved. Central to this handbook is Canine's list of "Seven Steps to Assist Those Who Are Grieving." Those steps are

1. Actualize the crisis.
2. Help identify and express feelings.
3. Assist in living without the deceased and ease emotional withdrawal.
4. Alert yourself to time.
5. Interpret normal behaviors.
6. Allow for individual differences.
7. Give continued support. (Pp. 39–43)

Canine's program emphasizes the universality of the grieving process while acknowledging the unique nature and aspects of each mourner's experience. The handbook contains exercises to be performed by individuals or support group members that will assist them in tracking and evaluating their personal grieving process. The culmination is a short questionnaire—entitled "How Do I Know I Am Better?"—in which the bereaved can document the progress or the completion of the grieving process (information courtesy of Maximum Living Consultants, Inc., 640 N. Woodward Avenue, Birmingham, MI 48009).

Models from Hospices and Other Groups

Hospice Services of Santa Barbara

Hospice Services of Santa Barbara, California, provides an extensive package of written materials, designed for hospice volunteers and support group participants, that gives information about the grieving process and the support group process.

Materials include the following:

1. "Grief Work Is Love Work" contains quotations about personal views of grief and asks two questions "For Reflection" based on those quotes.
2. "Participating in a Support Group" summarizes the group's purpose and goals, and explains the overall format ("nonconfronting, small group"). It is followed by a list of guidelines that stress listening, sharing experiences, not seeking/giving advice, respecting group member confidentiality, and non-judgmental respect for and acceptance of others' experiences and opinions.
3. "Typical Responses during Grief" (reprinted from Hospice of Schenectady) lists expected/normal reactions to grief, including physical sensations, thoughts, psychological, spiritual, behaviors, and feelings.
4. "The Tasks of Mourning" lists five tasks, similar but not identical to those posed by Worden and Rando: accepting the reality of the loss; experiencing and expressing feelings; beginning to put our lives back in order; placing the loss in a wider context of meaning; and reaching out to others. Below the list of tasks are four questions for group members, for example, which tasks seem hardest, and where do members feel progress is being made?
5. "Reminders for the Journey" is a list that stresses self-awareness and self-acceptance: the importance of experiencing our own feelings; the need to accept whatever it is we are feeling; the importance of expressing what we are feeling; the need to go at our own pace; and the need to be aware of movement and shifts within our lives. (Information provided courtesy of Hospice Services of Santa Barbara, 22 East Canon Perdido, Santa Barbara, CA 93101.)

Grief Education Institute

The Grief Education Institute (GEI), in Denver, Colorado, is a nonprofit corporation, formed "for the purpose of promoting the successful resolution of grief resulting from death." GEI provides six services, including the grief line (a telephone hot line); educational experiences for the public; support groups (for adolescents and adults, led by a facilitator, which meet for ten weeks); facilitator training (for support group leaders); a lending library and *The Journal* (a quarterly newsletter); and a leadership manual for leading support groups (a manual that describes in detail all of the issues covered in facilitator training) (information courtesy of the Grief Education Institute, 4596 Iliff Avenue, Denver, CO 80222).

This has provided a small sampling of the myriad bereavement programs available nationwide; most hospitals and communities, as well as an increasing number of funeral homes, offer bereavement aftercare programs.

ARE AFTERCARE PROGRAMS EFFECTIVE?

Some skepticism about the effectiveness of bereavement aftercare programs still exists; academics disagree on whether or not bereavement outcomes are significantly affected by post-death intervention because few empirical studies have been conducted. My own experience and that of others involved in aftercare, however, has been that aftercare programs are most valuable to the bereaved, particularly when there are unusual circumstances surrounding the death of the loved one that could result in prolonged or unresolved grief.

It is widely believed that bereavement aftercare can assist the bereaved in making an ultimately healthy adjustment to the loss of a loved one. Longman's (1993) study on hospice aftercare program effectiveness concluded: "That the hospice bereavement programs were perceived as beneficial to the participants was evident in their comments and attendance at the programs. Perhaps the contribution to nursing is the knowledge that such programs are available and can assist interested individuals in their bereavement" (Longman 1993, p. 173).

Schilling et al. (1992) voice tentative support for the benefits of bereavement groups for children, writing, "Clinical observations . . . suggest that early intervention can facilitate mourning and promote better adjustment to environmental changes following the death. . . . [I]ntervention studies across many other risk domains have demonstrated that children learn to cope with stress and challenges by watching, listening to, and interacting with their peers" p. 407).

More recently, Schneiderman et al. (1994) concluded that

> there is little sound evidence either in favour of or against bereavement programs. It is entirely likely that social class, pre-morbid family functioning, social supports, the age of the dead family member and of the survivors as well as the nature of the death (sudden, expected, suicide, etc.) have as much to do with individual and family functioning during the bereavement period as any intervention we might provide. . . . [I]t is entirely possible that bereavement programs may work for some families under certain conditions. (Pp. 216–17)

Effectiveness of bereavement aftercare programs is typically judged, to some extent, on their widespread use, and the fact that their attendance is continuously high. Practitioners believe that if participants were not deriving some benefit from the programs they would stop attending. More research, which quantifies program results rather than merely providing descriptions of programs and participants, is needed.

SUMMARY

This chapter has looked at the various bereavement aftercare programs that are available in most communities today. It also discussed the reasons why aftercare programs have come into being and have endured, such as the fragmentation of the family, the lack of social support, and the absence of clear social norms to guide the bereaved through the grieving process. Hospitals, funeral homes, social service agencies, and private practitioners have filled the void once occupied by family and friends. Professional counseling services, support and/or self-help groups, and hospice organizations all are available to provide bereavement aftercare. Some services are costly; many are free of charge to participants.

This chapter briefly looked at a variety of aftercare programs from across the United States, demonstrating the principles of most, if not all, programs were similar in nature, with the emphasis on helping the bereaved move through the tasks of grief to a healthy conclusion of the mourning process. Some organizations provide literature only, while others provide literature and services, such as one-on-one counseling or participation in a facilitator-led support group. Finally, the chapter briefly examined the effectiveness of bereavement aftercare programs.

REFERENCES

Canine, John D. 1983. *The challenge of living*. Birmingham, Mich.: Maximum Living Consultants, Inc.

———. 1990. *I Can, I Will*. Birmingham, Mich.: Ball Publishers.

Couldrick, Ann. 1992. Optimizing the bereavement outcome: Reading the road ahead. *Social Science Medicine* 35, no. 12:1521–23.

Fauri, David P., and Dana R. Grimes. 1994. Bereavement services for families and peers of deceased residents of psychiatric institutions. *Social Work* 39, no. 2:185–90.

Jacobs, S., S. Kasl, C. Schaefer, and A. Ostfeld. 1994. Conscious and unconscious coping with loss. *Psychosomatic Medicine* 56:557–63.

Klass, Dennis. 1985. Bereaved parents and the compassionate friends: Affiliation and healing. *Omega* 15, no. 4:353–73.

Levy, Leon H., Karen S. Martinkowski, and Joyce F. Derby. 1994. Differences in patterns of adaptation in conjugal bereavement: Their sources and potential significance. *Omega* 29, no. 1:71–87.

Longman, Alice J. 1993. Effectiveness of a hospice community bereavement program. *Omega* 27, no. 2:165–75.

Parkes, Colin Murray. 1987. Models of bereavement care. *Death Studies* 11:257–61.

Rando, Therese A. 1984. *Grief, dying and death: Clinical interventions for caregivers*. Champaign, Ill.: Research Press.

Raphael, Beverly. 1983. *The anatomy of bereavement*. New York: Basic Books.

Schilling, Robert F., Nina Koh, Robert Abramovitz, and Louisa Gilbert. 1992. Bereavement groups for inner city children. *Research on Social Work Practice* 2, no. 3:405–19.

Schneiderman, Gerald, Patricia Winders, Susan Tallett, and William Feldman. 1994. Do child and/or parent bereavement programs work? *Canadian Journal of Psychiatry* 39:215–17.

Wheeler, Inese. 1994. The role of meaning and purpose in life in bereaved parents associated with a self-help group: Compassionate Friends. *Omega* 28, no. 4:261–71.

Worden, J. William. 1982. *Grief counseling and grief therapy*. New York: Springer.

Zambelli, Grace C., and Arnold P. DeRosa. 1992. Bereavement support groups for school-age children: Theory, intervention, and case example. *American Journal of Orthopsychiatry* 62, no. 4:484–93.

21

CONTEMPORARY ISSUES INFLUENCING BEREAVEMENT AFTERCARE

Polly K. Nielsen

CHAPTER OUTLINE

....

When we speak of "modern" death, what we are actually talking about is the late-twentieth-century *reaction* to and means of coping with death in all its aspects. Some ways of dying are more socially "acceptable" than others. While we view a disease like acquired immune deficiency syndrome (AIDS) as terrifying and unique, it should be remembered that many other cultures in many other times have experienced diseases far more devastating than AIDS. One example is the bubonic plague, nicknamed "Black Death," which killed between one-quarter and one-third of the entire population of Europe in a two-year period, from 1348 to 1350, striking particularly hard in congested cities and towns.

Other deadly killers have stalked humans before and since, including smallpox, diphtheria, and malaria. Modern-day scourges such as the epidemic of inner-city murder are also not new. Throughout history, particularly in western Europe, war and murder were frequent causes of death; 80 percent of all newborns in medieval Europe died prior to their fifth birthday. For many centuries, life was hard and short.

As a result, it is incorrect to view certain kinds of deaths in the 1990s as "new." Rather, these "new" causes of death, such as AIDS, Alzheimer's, murder, have been known since time out of mind, albeit sometimes in different guises. What is new is the way in which people in late-twentieth-century America live (family configuration), where they live (extended families living long distances from one another), and the blurring and subsequent dissolution of many societal norms and traditions surrounding death and mourning. Each factor has contributed to an overall lessening of social support for those grieving the death of a loved one.

Late-twentieth-century America is a nation in which fully 50 percent of all marriages end in divorce; once-stable families disintegrate with frightening regularity. The mores that once kept couples together, and families intact, no longer exist. Shattered families can, and often do, become blended families, but the bottom line is that the primary family structure, in many cases, has broken down, taking with it the traditional sources of support in times of bereavement.

Another facet of the problem is geography. Many families—intact and otherwise—are physically located great distances from other family members. In the event of a death in the family, the members all converge for funeral home visiting hours, the wake, and the funeral, but often are en route to their respective homes in a matter of days, leaving those who are most deeply affected by the death to manage alone. The hundreds or even thousands of miles dilute, if not destroy, much-needed ongoing support for the bereaved.

At this moment in history, Western cultures appear to have forgotten or abandoned the time-honored notion that the prescribed period of mourning is at minimum one year. Denying death at every opportunity, we now see the immediate mourning period—defined as the time from the death through the funeral, and perhaps a month or two afterward—as ample for completing the basic tasks of mourning. As such, social support is withdrawn from the bereaved at a time when it may be most needed. The clarion call to "get on with your life" denies and discounts the need to complete the grieving process in a nonspecific time frame.

These societal pressures are exacerbated when combined with "nonstandard" means of death. Some deaths, such as those from AIDS, suicide, elective abortion, sudden infant death syndrome (SIDS), or murder, fall sufficiently outside the mainstream that they inspire anxiety in all of us, and often fall into the category Worden identified as "unspeakable." As a result, beyond the immediate time of death and funerary ritual completion, these deaths are often ignored because of the extreme discomfort they generate in those surrounding the bereaved. Discomfort appears to produce a sort of social paralysis, one in which people who would ordinarily be supportive of the bereaved decline to take on their support roles and instead fade into the background. Not knowing what to say or do, they say and do nothing.

It should be understood that no matter what the cause of death, the bereaved must do their grief work and move through the basic tasks of grief if they are to successfully heal. No death cause is more "significant" or more worthy of grief than any other. No bereaved person can be said to be more bereaved than another; the mother who loses a son to AIDS hurts no more or no less than the mother whose son is killed in a car wreck. The common denominator in "nonstandard" death causes, which distinguishes these mourners from others, is the sense of isolation they feel because of other peoples' reactions to the mode of death.

This chapter explores six types of "nonstandard" deaths: AIDS, SIDS, Alzheimer's, suicide, murder, and miscarriage and/or abortion. It discusses the issues that complicate the grieving process, and suggests ways in which the bereaved can be helped with their grief work.

ACQUIRED IMMUNE DEFICIENCY SYNDROME

Family and Friends' Grief Issues

Family and friends of people killed by AIDS are burdened by three factors, in addition to the pain of their loss. First, many AIDS victims' survivors often feel shame because AIDS is often (but by no means always) a sexually transmitted disease. AIDS is particularly frightening because it is highly communicable and always fatal. Because the earliest victims of the ongoing AIDS epidemic were homosexual males, there has been widespread condemnation of AIDS victims for certain behaviors that are seen by some as perverted and self-destructive.

In addition to ordinary citizens who are frightened by the specter of a fatal disease for which there is no cure, some politicians and even some religious leaders have called for the identification and quarantine of those who are HIV-positive and those suffering from full-blown AIDS. It has even been suggested that funding for further AIDS research should be abandoned because one way of contracting AIDS is via homosexual contact. The media have been rife with reports of emergency medical technicians, doctors, and other health care providers refusing to assist or treat AIDS patients. Many AIDS victims are abandoned by their own families when the cause of their illness is revealed. And the stigma associated with AIDS remains so great that even obituary notices frequently list fictitious, more socially acceptable causes of death such as cancer or pneumonia rather than AIDS.

It is into this environment that the bereaved are thrown after losing a loved one to AIDS. The second factor facing them is social isolation. That the bereaved experience a sense of isolation under these circumstances is unsurprising. Traditional sources of support are often missing, particularly when families deny that AIDS was the cause of death.

Gregory and Longman (1992) detail the experiences of several women who lost sons to AIDS. One woman, named Anne, was forbidden by her employer from telling her coworkers that her son was dying of AIDS. Still more cruelly, the employer asked Anne's fellow employees not to attend the funeral, for fear of creating panic among the employees should they find out the real cause of death. "Anne experienced discrimination and stigmatization in the workplace. As a result, her public discourse on the death of her son was silenced. Also denied were opportunities for sharing her suffering with her friends and co-workers. . . . Restrained in sharing her suffering, Anne became a speaker for an AIDS project. . . . This activity helped Anne work through her suffering" (pp. 339–40).

Such experiences are common. Social condemnation contributes to social isolation, which results in the mourning process being stymied. With little or no social support in their grief, the bereaved walk a long, lonely road toward healing.

Their road is further complicated by a third factor—the fear of becoming infected themselves. This fear is not limited to sexual partners of AIDS victims but includes caregiving family members as well. Such fear can cause the bereaved to distance themselves from the person who is dying, which can produce enormous guilt in the bereaved once death comes. Thus, the grief process is complicated even further.

Societal Attitudes toward AIDS

AIDS, despite heroic efforts to educate the public to the contrary, remains a socially unacceptable way to die. Hand in hand with fear go disgust and disapproval—directed at those who contracted HIV and AIDS through homosexual activities or intravenous drug use. Some sliver of societal compassion remains for those perceived as contracting AIDS "innocently," such as babies infected in utero, people infected by blood transfusions with tainted blood, and perhaps those who became infected through heterosexual sexual contact.

Aftercare Issues for the Bereaved

Social stigmatization results in shame, isolation, and concomitant withdrawal or absence of social support precisely when it is most needed—during the death and subsequent grieving for a loved one who died from AIDS. As mentioned earlier, while the grief of the person bereaved by AIDS is no greater or less than the grief of anyone else who has lost a loved one, the circumstances and cause of death are different and, in the eyes of some, less worthy of grief than other losses from other causes.

It has been well documented in the literature that perhaps the single most critical component in producing an uncomplicated bereavement outcome is the presence of strong, continuing social support. When that support is limited or nonexistent, what resources are available to those bereaved by AIDS that will facilitate the healing process? Two come to mind.

As documented by Gregory and Longman (1992) in their study on mothers whose sons died of AIDS, active participation in AIDS awareness and prevention activities helped mothers to heal. One resource was the creation by one mother of an AIDS quilt panel that she designed to depict the progress of her son's life. These mothers, in their search for meaning in the midst of their grief, crafted highly individual solutions and helped themselves to heal by breaking out of the shame, silence, and isolation imposed by a society frightened by AIDS. In so doing, they memorialized their sons by helping stem the epidemic's spread.

The second avenue the bereaved can choose is less public and less vocal, but it can be valuable in the grieving process—becoming a member of an AIDS bereavement support group. Membership in any support group immediately bestows upon participants the valuable gift of comembership; no longer need they be isolated. Membership bestows the knowledge that participants are not alone in their situation or their grief.

A support group can provide a safe place in which to express or explore feelings, share experiences, and ultimately assist others. Amelio (1993) writes of one AIDS bereavement support group, which was open to anyone bereaved by AIDS:

> By encouraging parents, wives, gay and straight lovers, adult children, and siblings to talk about their grief with one another, the concept of AIDS as a 'gay disease' has dissipated and the isolation experienced by so many of the members in their lives outside of the group is diminished. . . . The group has been an outlet for all members to express their fears, mourn their losses, and share their rage. Through mutual support and non-evaluative listening these issues can seem less overwhelming and isolating. (Pp. 48–51)

SUDDEN INFANT DEATH SYNDROME

Family and Friends' Grief Issues

"Sudden Infant Death Syndrome (SIDS) is the sudden unexpected death of a previously healthy infant that remains unexplained after investigation. SIDS is the leading cause of death in the United States among infants one week to one year of age. The suddenness and absence of definitive cause make a SIDS loss one of the most severe crises that can occur in a family" (Carroll and Shaefer 1994, p. 273).

SIDS strikes suddenly, without warning, and because it remains poorly understood, the family in which a baby has died of SIDS has special grief issues with which it must deal. In particular is parental guilt for not having adequately cared for the baby. This guilt can be exacerbated by a lack of support from family and friends. According to May and Breme (1983), "Because the etiology of SIDS remains unknown, relatives and persons outside the family may state or imply that the parents were neglectful or even abusive to the child, thereby isolating the family in their grief" (p. 65). Further, they assert that SIDS deaths precipitate family crises of gigantic proportions: "Because of the sudden and unexpected nature of SIDS and the unknown etiology of the child's death, families almost universally experience a feeling of ultimate responsibility which represents the primary way in which SIDS deaths differ from other losses. This responsibility is occasionally projected onto another (i.e., physician or sibling), but is typically personalized in the form of guilt" (p. 61).

Another issue with SIDS, frequently overlooked, is the impact that the baby's death has on its siblings. Not only do siblings grieve the loss of the dead baby, often experiencing unwarranted guilt about the death themselves, but they must also deal with their parents' grief over the loss. Further, SIDS siblings experience more anger than might be anticipated. Anger is a normal response to the loss of a loved one. With SIDS, however, sibling anger can be part of the overall family grief dynamic. Hutton and Bradley (1994) report that "anger may occur with two foci: as directed at the parents for allowing the death to happen, or for being over-protective after the death; or as directed at the dead baby for causing the grief, or for terminating the eagerly-awaited 'big sister' or 'big brother' role" (p. 725).

Legal ramifications in the aftermath of an SIDS death can be profound, as law enforcement agencies may be called in by medical service providers to investigate when the cause of death is uncertain. Dealing with the police in the aftermath of a baby's death from SIDS can make an already difficult situation—one filled with the shock and numbness associated with sudden, unexpected deaths—more stressful for the families of the SIDS victims.

Aftercare Issues for the Bereaved

SIDS deaths often leave a grieving family to wonder exactly what happened to the dead baby, and why. May and Breme (1983) write that

> Early crisis intervention including an explanation of the nature of SIDS to parents and the performance of an autopsy can help to prevent subsequent emotional problems in the family. . . . [A] diagnosis of SIDS should be made as soon as possible where the gross autopsy reveals no other cause for death. To learn from

the physician, nurse, pathologist or other emergency room personnel that the infant's death was not their fault can prevent the establishment of erroneously based patterns of guilt and blame, and can provide enormous relief to families. (P. 65)

In the event that the information has not already been provided, another important factor in aftercare is stressing that the death could not have been prevented. The funeral home director and/or clergy are uniquely positioned to provide SIDS information to surviving family members, as well as to note the presence or potential for complicated grief reactions and make the appropriate referrals (May and·Breme 1982, p. 71).

May and Breme (1983) suggest that professionals working with SIDS families exercise caution when the couple expresses a desire to quickly have another child in an apparent effort to "replace" the dead baby. As it is impossible to replace a dead child, and being such a "replacement" baby may be damaging to the subsequent child, "the decision to have subsequent children should be made in a rational fashion after the emotional resolution of grief has been accomplished" (p. 67).

According to Carroll and Shaefer (1994), support groups, which require grieving parents to reach for help outside the family unit, were attended by less than 50 percent of the couples they studied. "The use of seeking help outside the family remained the least used of all the coping patterns for participants. . . . communication and spousal support were the predominant coping methods" (p. 280). Considering these findings, those involved in aftercare with an SIDS family would do well to advise and if possible facilitate maximum open communication and sharing of feelings, not only of the parents but also of surviving siblings.

ALZHEIMER'S

Family and Friends' Grief Issues

Alzheimer's is a disease of the brain that produces progressive dementia and, ultimately, death. Because Alzheimer's kills its victims slowly, often over many years, families (generally adult children or spouses) are frequently cast in caregiving roles for extended periods of time. Depression is common among Alzheimer's caregivers, as is increasing isolation from sources of social support as the disease progresses and demands on the caregiver increase.

While it might be assumed that once death occurs caregivers experience, along with their grief, a sense of relief that the caregiving responsibilities are finally over, this is not necessarily the case. Bodnar and Kiecolt-Glaser (1994) report on three studies which indicate that "feelings of guilt also increased, reflecting continued caregiver distress postloss. . . . One key mechanism related to continued vulnerability appears to be the persistence of thoughts or recollections about the stressful experience" (pp. 372–73). Further, they found that while the caregiver presumptively has more time for social contacts and social activities after the death has occurred and caregiving duties have ended, social contacts in fact decreased. One cause may be growing older, but another may be that "the multiple sacrifices made during caregiving (job, finances, social activities, gratifying activities, etc.) may be difficult to redress when caregiving ends and may effectively accelerate diminution of some facets of their social networks" (p. 378).

Aftercare Issues for the Bereaved

As with anyone else grieving the loss of a loved one, the Alzheimer's caregiver's grief work can be significantly helped by the presence of strong, ongoing social support during bereavement. Continued rumination about the caregiving experience is associated with continued caregiver distress and depression. In such situations, social contacts are likely to assist in dispelling such distress. One way in which Alzheimer's caregivers may differ from others grieving a loss is that they are likely to be people who are in either their middle years (as in the case of adult child caregivers) or their later years (surviving spouse). Everyone who has experienced a loss needs social support in the form of someone who will listen to them as they relate their experiences. Particularly with respect to elderly Alzheimer's survivors, social isolation may be exacerbated by a lack of mobility, either physical (due to illness or disability) or in transportation (due to an inability to drive or own a car, or perhaps to drive after dark, etc.). In such circumstances those who would provide social support—family, friends, clergy, funeral home director—may need to travel to or facilitate transportation for the bereaved in order for the bereaved to have access to that and other forms of support throughout the grieving process.

SUICIDE

Family and Friends' Grief Issues

People whose loved ones die by taking their own lives are known as "survivors of suicide." Such individuals are left with the by now familiar tasks of grief experienced by anyone who loses a loved one. But survivors of suicide have other, extremely complex issues to resolve as part of their grief work.

Wagner and Calhoun (1991–92) report: "Studies examining societal responses to survivors of suicide list potential negative behaviors that survivors are likely to encounter: blame, rejection, lack of understanding, inability of others to understand the survivor's sadness, continued and stylized behavior, negative attitudes about the deceased, and pressure to stop grieving" (pp. 61–62). It may be that no other cause of death produces such a large gap between the bereaved and those from whom they would like to receive support.

Although the survivor may experience a strong need for support, the support system's ability to fulfill this need adequately may be adversely affected by the suicide. In addition to the more negative social perception, the social context is further confused by the lack of prescriptive social rules to guide the behavior of potential comforters, creating awkwardness and social discomfort: it is easier to avoid the bereaved than to make social mistakes. (P. 62)

Wagner and Calhoun further report that participants, who were survivors of suicide, reported feelings of anger, abandonment, hurt, loneliness, depression and hopelessness. Most also reported feeling guilty and having a strong need to know why the suicide occurred in order to make sense of the death.

Allen et al. (1994), in a study on the effect of the cause of death on responses to the bereaved, found that "survivors of suicide are perceived to be different from individuals grieving deaths from other causes. The individual bereaved by a suicidal death was viewed as more psychologically disturbed, more ashamed, and more able to prevent the death than were survivors of accidental or natural deaths" (p. 44).

This negative and judgmental view can create or contribute to the isolation felt by the bereaved. Wagner and Calhoun (1991–92) found that of the twelve survivors of suicide studied, eleven reported experiencing "negative" support (inadequate, inappropriate, hurtful). Those who would provide support under different circumstances often withdraw, thereby providing little support, or negative support, because of their own feelings about suicide, and their uncertainty about and discomfort in dealing with someone bereaved by suicide.

In the main, Western society condemns suicide, except in extreme cases, such as physician-assisted suicide of a chronically or terminally ill person. Social support networks in an effort to make sense of a suicide search—often angrily—for someone to blame. When a person chooses to die, survivors cast about for explanations, rationalizations, and people, circumstances, or organizations to hold accountable. Recently a young Episcopalian priest aptly pegged suicide as "a very terrible weapon," which deeply wounds survivors (personal communication).

Aftercare Issues for the Bereaved

In Wagner and Calhoun's (1991–92) study, all survivors of suicide indicate that they felt they had received "helpful support" from others, but "seven [of the twelve] survivors sought 'outside' help, expressing the feeling that suicide requires a special type of support. . . . it was support from other suicide survivors that gave these survivors what they wanted most" (p. 66). More than one survivor stated that only those who have experienced surviving the suicide of a loved one could truly understand, empathize, and give the support they required. There is a strong belief that the needs of suicide survivors are significantly different from those of people bereaved in other ways, and thus that only other suicide survivors can understand them.

Again, it is a postbereavement support group that likely will provide the supplementary social support suicide survivors require. Like the AIDS bereavement support group mentioned earlier, a suicide support group can provide the kind of safe, nonjudgmental environment suicide survivors need for working through their feelings of grief, guilt, and anger. It appears that, to a greater degree than other bereaved individuals, suicide survivors have a need to make sense of why their loved one chose to end his or her life, in order to fully heal and move forward.

Those who would give support to suicide survivors are advised by Wagner and Calhoun's study to provide lots of attentive listening, so that survivors can verbalize their thoughts and feelings, and in so doing move toward a successful bereavement outcome.

HOMICIDE

Family and Friends' Grief Issues

A glance at the headlines of any major city newspaper, or a few minutes spent listening to local or network newscasts on any given day, confirms the worst fears of many citizens—that Americans are killing each other in increasingly large numbers. Causes often cited include, but are by no means limited to, illegal drug trafficking, domestic violence, and gang activities. While murder is hardly limited to any one segment of society—witness the 1994 murders of Nicole Brown Simpson and Ronald Goldman, as well as the 1994 drowning murders of young Michael and Alex Smith by their mother, Susan Smith—murder is a major cause of death for young African-American males in urban areas. In many cases, children are killing other children.

Bereavement following the murder of a loved one, according to Parkes (1993, p. 49) is "surely . . . one of the most traumatic types of loss experienced," and he lists seven factors in murder that can contribute to the development of problems in the bereavement process. They are

1. Sudden, unexpected deaths
2. Untimely deaths
3. Witnessing of horrific circumstances
4. Threat to the life of the survivor or other loss of personal security
5. Guilt at having survived
6. Intense anger or ambivalence
7. Deaths by human agency, particularly when compensation is involved

Among the typical reactions of people bereaved by murder are numbness, rage against the person who committed the murder, guilt for not having protected the victim or in cases where the killer was a relative, and fear, particularly when the killer has not yet been apprehended. According to Parkes (1993),

> People who have suffered major bereavements commonly lose the sense of invulnerability that enables most of us to move about the world without undue anxiety. It is hardly surprising that some of those bereaved by murder experienced chronic fear, shut themselves up at home, avoided people and places associated with the loss, and were unable to go to work.

Many of the symptoms reported by bereaved people in the wake of murder or manslaughter can be seen as those of a post–traumatic stress disorder (PTSD). . . . [T]hus, haunting memories, sometimes associated with nightmares of the murder and leading to fear and hyperalertness were common. Reminders of the murder (e.g., by the press) would evoke severe distress, and often led to avoidant behaviour. (P. 51)

Burman and Allen-Meares (1994) also report that reactions among children who witness the murder of one parent by the other parent resemble the symptoms of post–traumatic stress disorder:

The symptoms manifested by a violent catastrophe of this magnitude have been likened to those of posttraumatic stress disorder. These symptoms include recurrent intrusive thoughts, images and sounds of the incident; nightmares; feelings of emotional detachment coupled with anxious attachment; a wish to avoid all feelings and reminders of the incident; a chronic fear of recurrence; and poor concentration and performance. (P. 28)

Children, in addition to losing both parents (one to death, the other to the penal system), must also cope with the uncertainty about their futures that such a murder inevitably produces. Where and with whom will they live? Will they have to change schools? Will they be together, or will they be separated? Their grieving process is further complicated by the presence of conflicting loyalties—to the dead parent as well as to the parent who committed the murder.

Aftercare Issues for the Bereaved

Bereavement from murder, considering the issues listed above, is unlike any other bereavement; the circumstances of the death set into motion a daisy chain of events from which it is difficult to extricate oneself. According to Parkes (1993), the overwhelming nature of bereavement by murder affects the grieving process in several ways:

(a) By inducing post-traumatic stress—a kind of emotional shock which generates anxiety, depressive avoidance, and vivid mental imagery; (b) by evoking intense rage towards the offender and all associated with him at a time when there may be little opportunity to vent that rage effectively; (c) by undermining trust in others, including the family, the police, the legal system, and God; (d) by evoking guilt at having survived and at failing to protect the deceased. . . . The bereaved people in this clinic saw themselves as in a rut from which they could not escape. (Pp. 52–53)

It seems likely, considering the nature of bereavement following murder, that professional help may be necessary if the grief process is to proceed normally. The goals of such professional help should include the following components: reassurance; recovery of a sense of control over one's life; find out what happened; strong support from family members; creation of memorials (Parkes, 1993, p. 52). In addition, self-help groups, such as Parents of Murdered Children, can give the bereaved a place to share their grief and rage among others who have experienced similarly traumatic losses. It also provides the opportunity, ultimately, to assist others as they work their way through their grief.

Aftercare Issues for Children

Children traumatized by the murder of a loved one experience emotions similar to those of adults—feelings of rage, depression, and guilt are common—but do not have the same abilities to articulate those feelings. The aftercare techniques that work for adults are generally not suitable for helping young children, which necessitates development of age-appropriate and developmentally appropriate therapies.

Burman and Allen-Meares (1994) report on two young boys who witnessed their father murder their mother, and describe the activities that helped the boys to resolve their grief and confront the other issues the murder created. Regarding these two particular children, they write: "Early and ongoing environmental supports were shown to mitigate some of the profound effects of these traumas. Intergenerational family strengths and values (embodied in the aunt who often acted as surrogate parent, as well as positive church and school influences) were the foundation of the rehabilitative process" (p. 30).

Any person who has experienced the loss of a loved one, needs to be able to talk about the experience and the feelings it produced. According to Burman and Allen-Meares (1994), this is especially true for children:

> Therapy with the children centered around . . . through symbolic play, fantasy, art, and storytelling. . . . [T]hrough the use of storytelling, clay, hand puppets, and photographs, representations of the past were relived. Painful feelings were expressed through the puppets. . . . Photographs of their mother abetted the grieving process by displaying happier images and memories, detracting from their last horror-filled moments with her.
>
> [T]hrough months of reexperiencing and confronting the past, they moved toward the future. . . . [B]y sharing, validating, reflecting, and reframing events and responses in a supportive environment, the process of coping more realistically and adaptively was developed. (Pp. 31–32)

Support groups for children bereaved by murder also can be useful, particularly in light of the fact that children traumatized by violence often grow up to be adults who use violence themselves. About the two boys in their study, Burman and Allen-Meares (1994) write: "Children's groups, using role plays, behavior rehearsals, and direct communication and feedback, dealt with anger and conflict resolution; feelings about specific traumatic events; and the improvement of self-esteem, communication, and social skills. The children realized that others experienced similar traumas, thus lessening the isolation and stigma involved with parental murder" (p. 32).

MISCARRIAGE OR ABORTION

Family and Friends Grief Issues

Only in recent years has there been any significant level of awareness regarding bereavement following a miscarriage (or spontaneous abortion) or an elective abortion. Previously, it was believed that, particularly in the case of a miscarriage occurring in the earliest weeks of pregnancy, the parents either did not grieve or had no real need or reason to grieve, since the pregnancy was so short. Today, however, there is growing awareness of the very real grieving that parents, and particularly mothers, experience when a wanted pregnancy ends in miscarriage.

Grief issues with respect to miscarriage appear to center around the degree to which the developing baby was perceived as "real" by its parents, particularly its mother. The more real the baby, the greater the sense of loss when the pregnancy terminates. For parents to whom the baby is not yet real, there may be little or no grief.

In the case of elective abortion of a wanted baby because of a fetal abnormality, the grief issues become increasingly complex. Not only is the baby dead, but, according to Kolker and Burke (1993), "unlike other perinatal losses, in this case the parents must take active steps to bring about the death of their baby; they 'play God.' Experience indicates that the parents' response to abortion after CVS [choironic villus sampling, a first trimester genetic test] is similar to that of abortion after amniocentesis. The critical factor is wantedness, not gestational age" (p. 520).

In addition to experiencing grief over their choice to terminate a wanted pregnancy and thereby bringing about the death of the developing fetus, parents commonly experience guilt, as described by Kolker and Burke (1993): "Regardless of how strongly they believe their decision was right, the bereaved parents worry about being criticised for 'killing' their baby. They may avoid telling acquaintances, co-workers, or relatives who might tell them they should not have had the abortion or, in the case of parents who are known carriers of serious genetic abnormalities such as Duchenne's muscular dystrophy, that they should not have gotten pregnant" (p. 521).

Unlike other kinds of deaths, our culture generally bypasses any rituals involving babies who die in utero or shortly after being born. In these cases the babies are neither named nor baptized, much less given funerals. This absence of ritual can complicate parental grieving for the dead baby; there is no baby to hold, and no baby to name, but the fact of the baby is grieved nonetheless. "Parents who did not have a chance during the abortion to see and hold the baby and who have neither memories nor mementos such as a photograph, may find it more difficult to let go" (Kolker and Burke 1993, p. 522). There is, however, a growing awareness of the need for rituals that acknowledge the loss and assist with grieving and closure, and such awareness has spawned a response from the funeral home industry. For example, the Detroit-area R. G. and G. R. Harris Funeral Homes provide free funerals for the parents of such babies.

As a result of this absence of closure and letting-go activities, recovery can take years. "Paradoxically, a factor that facilitates healing is parental bonding with the baby, the perception that the loss is one of a real son or of a real daughter rather than of a vaguely acknowledged fetus" (Kolker and Burke 1993, p. 522).

Aftercare Issues for the Bereaved

It appears that one of the keys to a successful grief recovery after the abortion of a wanted but abnormal fetus is the acceptance of the dead baby as real. A major part of bereavement aftercare in such circumstances is preparing the parents for unanticipated emotions and reactions to the abortion *before the termination*. Kolker and Burke (1993) offer guidance to aftercare givers and those who would support the grieving parents:

> We wish to emphasize merely that genetic counselors, medical staff, and members of the bereaved couple's informal networks need to be more aware of the repercussions of this experience so they can offer the couple more support. Couples undergoing prenatal diagnosis deserve more complete information about the consequences of the alternative procedures so they can make truly informed decisions. Women having an abortion must be given candid information about the abortion process and encouraged to bond with the baby before they let go. Finally, in the aftermath of the termination, the couple must be treated by society as the bereaved parents they are and allowed to mourn the death of their baby. (P. 524)

This view is supported by Iles and Gath (1993) in their study of women who terminated their pregnancies because of fetal abnormality:

> Grief counseling can play a part in the management of these women. Before the termination, the women and their families can be advised about the likely emotional reaction to the termination. After the termination, they can be provided with support. Sensitive and informed enquiry should be used to encourage the women to describe their symptoms. The women also need to be advised that they may experience a worsening or recurrence of their symptoms both at the expected date of the baby's birth and at the anniversary of the termination. (P. 413)

SUMMARY

Those who are bereaved for any reason are in particular need of support from their traditional social network because, as mentioned in earlier chapters, the most important component in a successful, uncomplicated bereavement outcome is strong, ongoing social support. This kind of support is often precisely what is lacking in "nontraditional" deaths. The social support network, through disapproval and/or discomfort, is unavailable to provide necessary help. The subsequent feelings of isolation can prolong and complicate the bereaved's grief work process.

With the exception of those bereaved by SIDS, who preferred not to seek help outside their immediate family, subjects in the studies discussed found solace and a sense of belonging by participating in specialized bereavement support groups. People in each category—AIDS, suicide, and murder—reported feeling less isolated when they became support group members. They were comforted by the fact that they were no longer alone in their experience or in their grief.

AIDS survivors found outlets for their grief by participating in AIDS aware-ness projects and in creating a panel for the national AIDS quilt. Both activities were a type of memorial to the deceased. Similar memorial creation was seen to be useful for those bereaved by murder.

Survivors of suicide appear to have the strongest need for outside support, particularly from others who have also lost a loved one to suicide. The experience of having a loved one take his or her own life is sufficiently traumatic and unique that survivors report that only other survivors can understand their feelings.

The parents of babies being aborted due to fetal abnormalities are in a singu-larly unique bereavement situation. Not only do they know the death will occur, they take deliberate action to have the death take place; they make the decision to terminate the pregnancy. In this situation, counseling prior to the abortion can mitigate the bereavement process by alerting the parents to the kind of emotions they may experience after the termination.

REFERENCES

Allen, Breon G., Lawrence S. Calhoun, Arnie Cann, and Richard G. Tedeschi. 1993–94. The effect of cause of death on responses to the bereaved: Suicide compared to accident and natural causes. *Omega* 28, no. 1:39–47.

Amelio, Robert C. 1993. An AIDS bereavement support group: One model of intervention in a time of crisis. *Social Work with Groups* 16, nos. 1/2:43–54.

Bodnar, Joy C., and Janice K. Kiecolt-Glaser. 1994. Caregiver depression after bereavement: Chronic stress isn't over when it's over. *Psychology and Aging* 9, no. 3:372–80.

Burman, Sondra, and Paula Allen-Meares. 1994. Neglected victims of murder: Children's witness to parental homicide. *Social Work* 39, no. 1:28–35.

Carroll, Ruth, and Sarah Shaefer. 1994. Similarities and differences in spouses coping with SIDS. *Omega* 28, no. 4:273–84.

Gregory, David, and Alice Longman. 1992. Mothers' suffering: Sons who died of AIDS. *Qualitative Health Research* 2, no. 3:334–57.

Hutton, Claire J., and Benjamin Sylvester Bradley. 1994. Effects of sudden infant death on bereaved siblings: A comparative study. *Journal of Child Psychology and Psychiatry,* 35, no. 4:723–32.

Iles, Susan, and Dennis Gath. 1993. Psychiatric outcome of termination of pregnancy for foetal abnormality. *Psychological Medicine* 23:407–13.

Kolker, Aliza, and B. Meredith Burke. 1993. Grieving the wanted child: Ramifications of abortion after prenatal diagnosis of abnormality. *Health Care for Women International* 14, no. 6:513–26.

May, Harold, and Frederick J. Breme. 1983. SIDS family adjustment scale: A method of assessing family adjustment to sudden infant death syndrome. *Omega* 13, no. 1:59–73.

Parkes, Colin Murray. 1993. Psychiatric problems following bereavement by murder or manslaughter. *British Journal of Psychiatry* 162:49–54.

Wagner, Katharine G., and Lawrence G. Calhoun. 1991–92. Perceptions of social support by suicide survivors and their social networks. *Omega* 24, no. 1:61–73.

22

ISSUES FOR THE DEATH CARE PROFESSIONAL

John D. Canine

We know that the separation of the aged, the ill, and the dying in our society creates problems for loved ones in processing their grief. But it is not widely recognized that those professionals and volunteers to whom the care and ministry of dying people fall need to grieve as well. This population might include doctors, nurses, hospice workers, counselors, funeral directors, emergency workers, clergy, social workers—anyone whose job entails working with individuals and families facing death.

The investment death care professionals make is one of emotion as well as time and skill. It requires regularly confronting their own mortality, and when bonds are formed between caregiver and client, the death will provoke a grief response that must be acknowledged and processed.

This chapter will discuss the factors that place death care professionals at risk for stress and burnout, offer a model for recognizing burnout stages, and address techniques that can be adopted on an individual as well as an organizational basis to manage and prevent this debilitation of caregivers and reduction of their performance on the job.

RISKS FOR DEATH CARE PROFESSIONALS

Stress takes a toll on people—physically, mentally, emotionally and spiritually—and when stressors are assigned "value," as on the Social Readjustment Rating Scale, death is rated as the highest stressor of all. People whose jobs bring them into contact with pain, chronic illness, death, disaster, and dying are particularly susceptible to the phenomenon known as burnout.

Canine (1994) states, "Burnout is rooted in an individual's desire for meaningfulness. We want our lives to be significant. And each of us determines what that meaning is—and isn't—that allows us to feel fulfilled . . . in harmony with ourselves." When we are thwarted, either by external or internal circumstances, from realizing our meaningful, "ideal" selves, we no longer feel good and may begin to experience bouts of anxiety, depression, guilt, and disillusionment. The consequences of burnout may include loss of health and well-being as well as a decline in professional performance.

Definitions of Burnout

There are several excellent definitions of burnout, alternately characterizing it as a syndrome, a condition, a loss, and a state:

1. A debilitating psychological condition brought about by unrelieved work stress, which results in depleted energy reserves, lowered resistance to illness, increased dissatisfaction and pessimism, increased absenteeism and inefficiency at work (*The Work Stress Connection: How to Cope with Job Burnout*, by Robert Veninga and James Spradley).
2. A progressive loss of idealism, energy, and purpose experienced by people in the helping professions as a result of the conditions of their work (*Burnout*, by Jerry Edelwich with Archie Brodsky).
3. A state of physical, emotional, and mental exhaustion caused by long-term involvement in situations that are emotionally demanding (*Career Burnout "Causes and Cures,"* by Ayala Pines and Elliot Aronson).

Indeed, a variety of research studies have demonstrated higher-than-average stress levels among funeral directors, palliative care unit nurses, and emergency workers with experience in incidents of critical stress. The potential for burnout increases as stress—for this discussion, death—occurs in serial or consecutive fashion with little or no time to grieve one loss before the next one happens. Dr. Ronald Barrett, a psychologist at Loyola Marymount University who gives seminars to health care workers treating and attending persons with AIDS, has coined the term "bereavement burnout"—a situation that develops when there is such an accumulation of unresolved, compounded grief that an individual may simply grow numb.

Regardless of how we choose to think about burnout, or what form it might take in each of us, burnout tends to be progressive—indicating that there are steps and activities we can undertake to prevent the serious damage it can inflict on our ability to be compassionate to ourselves and others.

Expectations of Caregivers

Rando (1984) offers some thoughts on death care professionals' vulnerability to burnout that are distinct from the external issues inherent in such work:

> Many caregivers enter their respective professions because they are "rescuers" who want to save people from distress. Being a rescuer may set a caregiver up for the unrealistic goal of rescuing the dying patient, when there needs to be acceptance of the inevitability of death and of the fact that it ultimately vanquishes us all. In some cases caregivers will pay lip service to the goal of palliation, but continue to be task-oriented, searching for a cure. It is important for both patients and caregivers that the rescue fantasy be relinquished. Otherwise patients lose the emotional support they need from caregivers, and caregivers continually frustrate themselves by trying to accomplish tasks that can't be done. (P. 433)

Barrett (1993) suggests that professional caregivers often begin their careers with naive enthusiasm, which may include the expectation of making a difference, a dent in the problems facing their clientele. While a new social worker, for example, may indeed offer significant comfort or facilitate communication between dying people and their families, she may soon become overwhelmed by the sheer volume and urgency of need she confronts on a daily basis.

It is not unusual for visiting nurses or home hospice workers to become deeply emotionally invested in the families they serve; when a death occurs, the isolated nature of their work often leaves them bereft of opportunities to interact with colleagues and process feelings. In addition, these individuals are constantly adjusting to diverse settings as they move from patient to patient, creating even more stress.

Organizational Hazards

Also contributing to burnout potential are the factors of systemic design and organizational procedures under which many death care professionals work. Rando (1984) observes: "Since the care of the terminally ill is different than traditional medical care, there are often unclear expectations for those who are working with the dying. [This] lack of clarity . . . makes caregivers more open to stress because they are unable to ascertain the criteria against which they will be assessed" (p. 437). Further, mechanisms to reduce stress, manage threat of burnout, and process grief are frequently all too absent from an organization's perhaps already overtaxed resources. A lowering of morale, a sense of being "alone" with one's feelings, reduction in job satisfaction, and negative interpersonal dynamics may result.

While some hospitals and hospice groups offer regular "debriefing" and even ritualized opportunities for staff members to deal with specific deaths, many do not. Communication channels between and among levels of caregivers may be informal, logistically problematic, or even discouraged. And since caregivers often believe they are supposed to be "strong" and not ask for help themselves, when an institution does not foster opportunities to share information and/or feelings, it is easy for professionals to become caught in a repeated cycle of attachment and loss, attachment and loss, attachment and loss—until emotional *disinvestment* seems to be the only option to survive on the job. At this point, all their resources are devoted to simply coping.

EXAMINING STRESS AND BURNOUT

The serious threat burnout poses for a decrease in physical, social and professional effectiveness requires an awareness of both its symptoms and its stages. Among the symptoms of burnout that have been identified are exhaustion, despair, powerlessness, apathy, alienation, depression, loss of self-esteem, irritability, loss of energy, cynicism, poor concentration, nightmares, loss of creativity, and negative attitudes. These can be reflected in behavioral changes that not only affect coworkers and quality of client care but may seriously affect an individual's personal relationships.

Stages of Burnout

The stages of burnout (see Figure 22–1) are marked by five progressive "points" that have accompanying mental, emotional, and physical ramifications.

The first stage is characterized by the initial stimulation of a new job and the enthusiasm and desire to succeed and prove oneself. This is the positive, if perhaps unrealistic, time when a death care worker feels ready, willing, and able to "do it all."

The second stage is reached when stress has started to build and fatigue and job disappointment set in. The professional may come to believe (correctly or incorrectly) that the organization, agency, or society of which he or she is a part doesn't share the same level of commitment to the work and its urgency. This is particularly the case with health and human services personnel serving the AIDS community, who can become further burdened with stress by the homophobia, ignorance, and social stigmas they may encounter as part of their work. An interesting footnote is that there are support groups for HIV-negative caregivers, due to

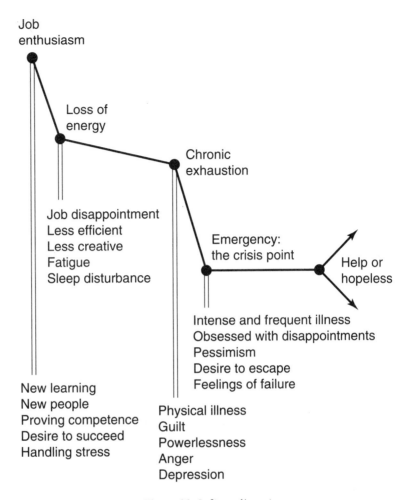

Figure 22–1. Stages of burnout.

the belief of some factions within the HIV-positive community that those without the virus cannot really understand or be effective with those who are so afflicted.

Chronic exhaustion, the third stage of burnout, brings a higher intensity of emotion and possible physical symptoms. Anger, depression, proneness to accidents, and conscious or unconscious guilt may come into play. The individual may become less communicative and begin to withdraw socially. Use of addictive coping mechanisms such as caffeine, alcohol, nicotine, or other drugs may increase substantially during this stage.

The fourth stage is that of emergency, or the crisis point. If no intervention has taken place, the death care professional is at risk for opportunistic illness and is likely to demonstrate aversive behavior on the job, such as coming in late, leaving early, taking longer breaks, becoming angry when demands are made, and treating clients impersonally. Simultaneously, the professional is experiencing feelings of failure and pessimism, and may obsess over his or her disappointments and loss of values that were held so brightly in the first stage.

The fifth stage is the crossroads between help or hopelessness. It should be a goal of every death care professional and their managers to prevent a "stage five" situation from happening. A relevant sidelight to a study of funeral directors suffering symptoms of critical incident stress revealed that those in the group reporting increased symptomatology (those thirty to thirty-nine years of age) were also most likely to "drop out" of the funeral business.

Although no direct cause-and-effect relationship can be drawn from the data, it should suggest to institutions and employers that if vulnerable groups can be identified, there should be programs or mechanisms or techniques in place to help them before burnout claims more sorely needed death care professionals.

A Professional Model for Caring for the Dying

It has been noted that the increased "kinship" between terminally ill patients and their network of caregivers results in death care professionals becoming "surrogate grievers." This notion may soon be disabused as it becomes more widely recognized that caregivers' grief is neither a substitute nor a replacement for a faraway family's grief but an authentic response to loss—particularly if the person was in some way special or memorable in the professional's life.

Reynolds (1993) observed:

> The number of mortalities the average care hospital experiences is staggering when one considers the major service areas of neonatology, cardiology, oncology, AIDS, and "med/surg." To become intimately involved with patient/families during the crisis of an acute episode and then to precipitously end our helping efforts at the time of death is a travesty and breech of the individual and institutional helping contract. . . . We need to explore the development of comprehensive bereavement support and outreach programs within the context of the acute care hospital. (P. 10)

And it must be comprehensive enough to extend to the caregiving staff.

Fortunately, there is a model that follows the adaptation process that health care professionals must go through in order to work with patients who are facing death. In 1977 Harper developed the Schematic Growth and Development Scale in Coping with Professional Anxieties in Terminal Illness. This "charting" of normative stages reflects the understanding and conflict-resolution ability caregivers must develop so they can care humanely for dying people, build their capacity to help, and enjoy freedom from the incapacitating effects of burnout. Readers should appreciate that this scale is not a guideline for burnout prevention but instead presents issues and objectives that prevention programs may wish to take into consideration.

The maturing of the professional who copes with stress in caring for the dying is likely to encompass the following stages:

1. Intellectualization: knowledge and anxiety—Caregivers are uncomfortable with death and manage anxiety by focusing on professional knowledge and factual issues of policies and procedures. Conversations with the patient are not personal.
2. Emotional survival: trauma—The caregiver feels death on an emotional level and grieves his or her own mortality. This is accompanied by pity for patients whose death is unavoidable, guilt at their own health, and trauma at the reality of death.
3. Depression: pain, mourning, grieving—This is the "grow or go" stage where caregivers must accept the fact that death does exist and is painful. Mastery of self is a challenge; if the reality of death is not accepted, workers may leave the field.
4. Emotional arrival: moderation, mitigation, and accommodation—No longer preoccupied with their own death or incapacitated by depression, caregivers' emotional responses are appropriate. They are sensitive enough to grieve and resilient enough to recover.
5. Deep compassion: self-realization, self-awareness, and self-actualization—Caregivers are able to relate compassionately to the dying patient, in full acceptance of the impending death. Behavior and performance are enhanced by the dignity and self-respect they afford themselves, enabling them to give dignity and respect to the dying patient.

Although a model for managing burnout will be presented shortly, the ability to "work through" Harper's five stages implies that caregivers are noting and managing their stress along the way. Barrett (1993) suggests some "prescriptions" that death care professionals might wish to practice to keep their stress levels within reasonable bounds:

1. Be reality-oriented: accept the "givens" of a system.
2. Develop reinforcement alternatives; look for different ways to "validate" your success.
3. Use time management techniques.
4. Conduct routine attitude tests or assessments.
5. Seek information that might make the job easier.
6. Establish and maintain support systems.
7. Take time out.
8. Monitor diet and physical fitness.
9. Learn to delegate.
10. Nurture and cultivate spirituality.

MANAGING BURNOUT

In a very real way, managing burnout is parallel to leading a well-balanced, harmonious life. The difficulty for death care professionals, of course, is that their emotional, physical, and mental resources are often stretched beyond "normal" limits due to the trauma, pain and suffering, serial losses, and compounded grief they deal with on a regular basis.

A Holistic Approach

Canine's model illustrating management of burnout (see Figure 22–2) identifies five major arenas of life that death care professionals must attend to in order to minimize their potential or likelihood for burnout. The model is intentionally circular, as it is meant to resemble a wheel, since "a wheel goes somewhere." As Canine told an audience at the 1994 conference of the National Funeral Directors Association, "If one area of the wheel is flat, the wheel doesn't go anywhere. We must care for the whole person. At the center you see a diamond shape. A

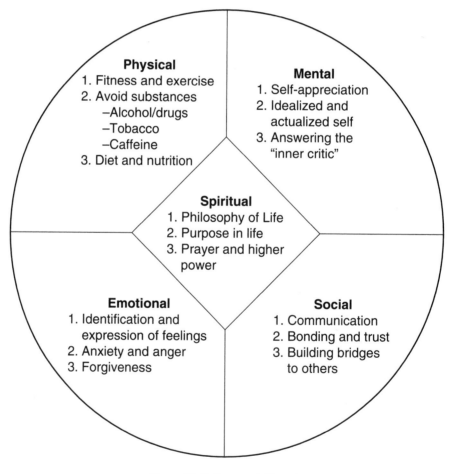

Figure 22–2. Management of burnout.

diamond is a gem. This is the spiritual center from which you design your destiny."

The significance of this "core" does not require religious affiliation. What is referred to here is the unique world perspective, or philosophy of life, that filters each experience an individual has and how he or she responds to it. For example, a person riding a crowded bus who believes someone is carelessly poking him with an umbrella may turn to discover a blind person fumbling with his white cane. Anger turns to acceptance, for he is now filtering his experience through a philosophy that values understanding and compassion for the blind.

Death care professionals need to be cognizant and aware of their spiritual filter, their purpose in life, and how to best exercise their spiritual muscles—whether through prayer, meditation, journal writing, communing with nature, self-examination and reflection, or practicing the tenets of a particular religious faith.

One outer "section" of the wheel involves the mind: What is the mental state of the person at risk of losing balance and tumbling into burnout? Does the nurse appreciate herself and her abilities? Is the minister at war with himself over a real or imagined flaw in his character? Are the funeral director's behavior and attitude congruent ("in sync") with his values and beliefs? Is the doctor forever putting herself down?

This mental arena for burnout management relates to self-image, self-esteem, and self-criticism. In order to feel good and maintain harmony within, it is necessary to appreciate and honor one's talents and accomplishments (large and small), keep one's "actual" self as close as possible to one's "ideal" self (living as much as possible according to one's personal moral and/or ethical code), and not being afraid to answer our inner critic when it has something to say. This could mean reaffirming how worthwhile we are when we're feeling "down," or it may require listening carefully to what the inner critic is telling us we need to change by modifying our behavior, taking a sharper look at our idealized self, or both.

Another arc on the holistic wheel is the caregiver's emotional life. This addresses the good feelings that result when emotions are identified and expressed. Canine (1994) observes, "We learn so much when we communicate. The identification and expression of feelings has the potential to remove conflict in our thinking—to remove cognitive distortion."

He eschews the "strong, silent" macho stereotype that American men are taught to emulate, and recommends that emotions (particularly negative ones) not be allowed to "free-float" where they may land on scapegoats or innocent victims. Emotions should be identified, expressed, and locked onto the appropriate object. For example, if a funeral director is genuinely disturbed when burying a child, his emotional well-being is better served by sharing the truth of his feelings with a colleague than by going home and kicking the cat.

The goal is to grow better, not bitter.

Two very strong emotions that plague caregivers (and others) are anxiety and anger. In burnout management, it is important for individuals to recognize that these feelings are generally triggered by a lack of understanding or a lack of control. When faced with anxiety and/or anger, it is crucial to ask yourself (and possibly check in with others) what it is you don't understand or what it is you can't control that may be creating these uncomfortable emotions.

The final component of the holistic wheel's emotional quadrant is the need in life to embrace forgiveness. Canine believes it is impossible to live a meaningful life without forgiveness, so if burnout is rooted in the desire for meaningfulness, every caregiver should remain aware of Joan Borysenko's (1987) definition of forgiveness: "Accepting the core of every human being as the same as yourself, and giving them the gift of not judging them" (pp. 41–42).

A third area on the burnout management wheel is the physical condition of the at-risk professional. It is common sense that no one embark on a regimen of exercise without first consulting a physician. But once achieved, physical well-being can be maintained with approximately twenty minutes of exercise four times a week. The particular form of activity is not as important as the heart rate at which the workout is performed. An accepted formula is to start with the number 225, from which one subtracts one's age and then calculates 75 percent of the remainder figure. This is the maximum heart rate that should be targeted for the exercise period.

Concurrent with regular exercise, people wishing to avoid burnout should avoid alcohol, drugs, tobacco, and caffeine, and should monitor a careful level of fat and sodium intake in their diet. Overall nutrition should incorporate recommended percentages of protein, carbohydrates, vitamins, minerals, and fibers.

The fourth quadrant on a wheel of life that's "going somewhere" is the social arena. This includes the primary relationships—personal and professional—as well as the casual ones in a caregiver's life. Those who find fulfillment in communicating with others, and who maintain satisfying hobbies and/or social activities are unlikely to experience burnout.

The ability to communicate and to respond to others' needs in a dependable fashion creates bonds and trust. Reaching out to others socially throughout life affords an opportunity to build sustaining bridges with others that are rewarding and meaningful.

Meaning and Mourning

Death care professionals play a special role in our society. Their willingness to assist in what are often the most difficult moments in people's lives places unusual demands on their energies and can be depleting and draining, particularly when many deaths are experienced in a short period of time.

Barrett (1993) warns that people in these fields often neglect their own need to get emotionally "caught up" and that unresolved grief becomes "excess baggage" that may lead to mental health complications, physical distress, and problems with interpersonal relationships. "Life moves so quickly," he says, "we don't have an opportunity to remember the significance of a person, or their specialness.

We need to ask: What happened here? How do I feel about this? What does this mean to me? How am I challenged by this?"

When losses aren't acknowledged, the accummulated grief can wear us down, burn us out, literally make us sick. Death care professionals must develop a regular coping system and mourning mechanism to put each death into context.

Barrett (1993) believes that individuals, as well as institutions dealing with death, must develop mechanisms or rituals to grieve their losses. These can take a variety of forms and may include some type of tribute to the dead person. One method might be to simply write down the person's name and concentrate on that person. Who was she? What was special about him that you will miss? What was her impact on your life or his gift to you? If you could convey a message to him, what would it be? How would you bring closure to the relationship? What gesture might you make? Is forgiveness, of yourself or the other person, needed so that you can go on from here?

He suggests that we take a moment to grieve every day.

Delayed and unresolved grief will not stay swept under the rug indefinitely, and those most at risk for burnout are those who "care too much." The answer is not to "pull back" and become emotionally unavailable to support your clients but instead to recognize and accept that caring and hurting go hand in hand.

SUMMARY

Issues for death care professionals addressed in this chapter involve the dangers of stress and burnout and the need for organizational and individual mechanisms for coping, communicating, and grieving. The progressive stages of burnout were examined, along with a professional model that caregivers who wish to mature may consider in "charting" their own emotional progress.

A holistic approach to managing burnout was presented, taking into account the full spiritual, mental, emotional, physical, and social requirements for a harmonious, well-balanced life. The relationship between meaning and mourning, and its importance in burnout prevention was offered as a concept death care professionals must integrate into their lives.

REFERENCES

Barrett, R. 1993. Burnout management 201: Is there life after burnout. Speech before National Skills Building Conference. Recorded by Advanced Technological Productions USA, Inc., Mineola, N.Y.

Borysenko, J. 1987. *Minding the body, mending the mind*. Reading, Mass.: Addison-Wesley.

Canine, J. 1994. Battling burnout: How to work out of a slump. Speech before National Funeral Directors Association. Recorded by Mobiltape Co., Inc., Valencia, Calif.

Edelwich, J., and A. Brodsky. 1980. *Burnout: Stages of disillusionment in the helping professions*. New York: Human Services Press.

Fulton, R. 1979. Anticipatory grief, stress and the surrogate griever. In *Cancer, stress and death,* edited by J. Tache, H. Selye, and S. Day. New York: Plenum.

Harper, B. C. 1977. *Death: The coping mechanisms of the health professional.* Greenville, S.C.: Southeastern University Press.

Kroshus, J., D. Swarthout, and S. Tibetts. 1993. Critical incident stress among funeral directors: Dramatic impact, dramatic outcome." *Forum Newsletter* 19, no. 5:8–9.

Rando, T. 1984. *Grief, dying and death.* Champaign, Ill.: Research Press.

Reynolds, J. 1993. Bereavement and the acute care hospital: The forgotten family." *Forum Newsletter* 19, no. 3:10.

Veninga, R., and J. Spradley. 1981. *The work stress connection: How to cope with job burnout.* Boston: Little, Brown.

Worden, J. W. 1982. *Grief counseling and grief therapy.* New York: Springer.

INDEX